The
BAJA
HIGHWAY

a geology and biology field guide
for the Baja Traveler

by   John Minch and Thomas Leslie

Illustrated by Edwin Minch

John Minch and Associates, Inc.

27126 Paseo Espada, Suite 1601
San Juan Capistrano, CA 92675
(714) 496-3080, Fax (714) 496-3650

Acknowledgements

There are numerous people who contributed to the spirit of this book, both directly and indirectly. We wish to thank all of them for their measure of support. Particular thanks go to the help and support given by our wives, Carol Minch and Jeanine Leslie who put up with the endless hours of work on the manuscript and with the numerous trips into the heart of baja to compile and check on the information in the logs.

Angela Carlucci, Mary Amelotte, and Debbie Thompson typed most of the numerous revisions of the manuscript. Edwin Minch drew and drafted most of the illustrations. Jim Ashby and John's compadre Jorge Ledesma, Profesor de Geologica, Universidad Autonoma de Baja California en Ensenada, provided assistance and extensive critical technical review adding important information on the geology of the Baja Highway.

Our special thanks also goes to Edwin Allison and Gordon Gastil who provided the spark of interest in Baja which led to a lifelong love affair with the peninsula.

For copies of this field guidebook write to:

The BAJA HIGHWAY
John Minch and Associates, Inc.
27126 Paseo Espada, Suite 1601
San Juan Capistrano, CA 92675
Phone (714) 496-3080, Fax (714) 496-3650

First printing 1991
Printed in the United States of America

ISBN: 0-9631090-0-6

HOW TO USE THIS BOOK

The logs in this book are keyed to the kilometer markings on the Baja Highway. These markings have remained relatively constant for the last ten years and should change little. The log segments correspond with the consecutive numbering system between major points. The kilometer markings, in each segment, increase in Baja California Norte from the border to Guerrero Negro and decrease to La Paz and Cabo San Lucas in Baja California, Sur. It is possible to pickup the book at any kilometer marking and read about the biology and geology along the highway. At this Printing the Laguna Chapala to San Felipe stretch is largely unpaved with poor and changing kilometer markings. As a result this particular log is only generally accurate and descriptions may be off slightly.

For the most direct route to the south, get into the third lane from the center of the road as you drive under a large gray arch (a pedestrian overpass) and continue across a bridge over the Tijuana river. Do not change lanes until you are heading north down the Tijuana River. Shortly after you cross the river, you will come to a division in the road. The left two lanes will take you into the central district of the city of Tijuana. Unless you want to shop, DO NOT TAKE THESE LANES! Stay in the lane to Ensenada! At the split you will be in the far left lane of the right three lanes. If you stayed in the third lane, as directed above, you will continue around an approximately 270 degree circle under several bridges and head northwestward along Highway 1D, paralleling the Tijuana river. This road then bends to the left and parallels the International Border (the "Tortilla Curtain" as it is sometimes called) on your right (north).

BAJA HIGHWAY LOG SEGMENTS

Each of These Highway Segments are Featured in This Book

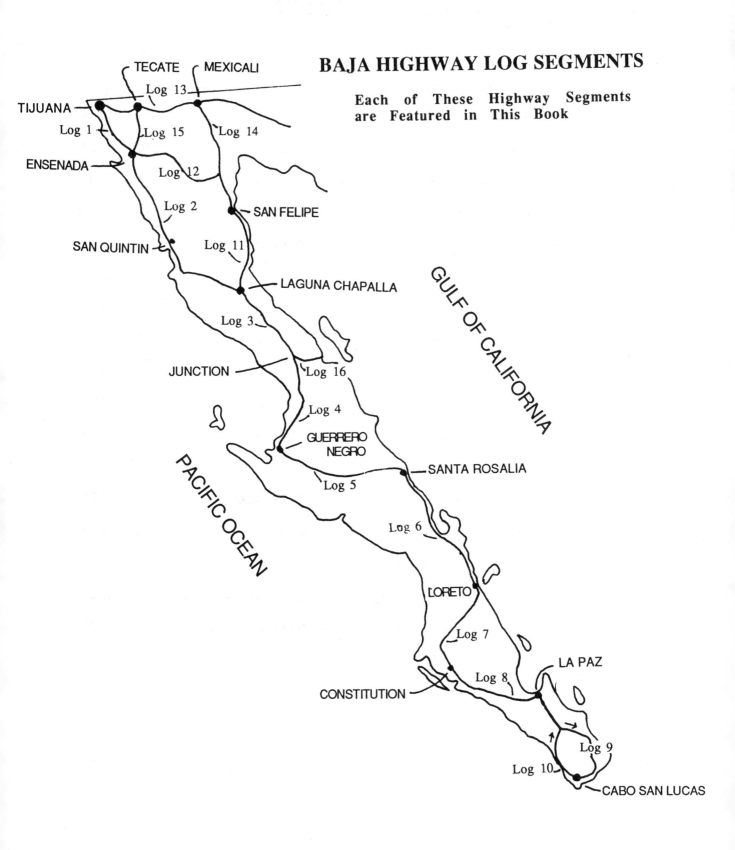

TABLE OF CONTENTS

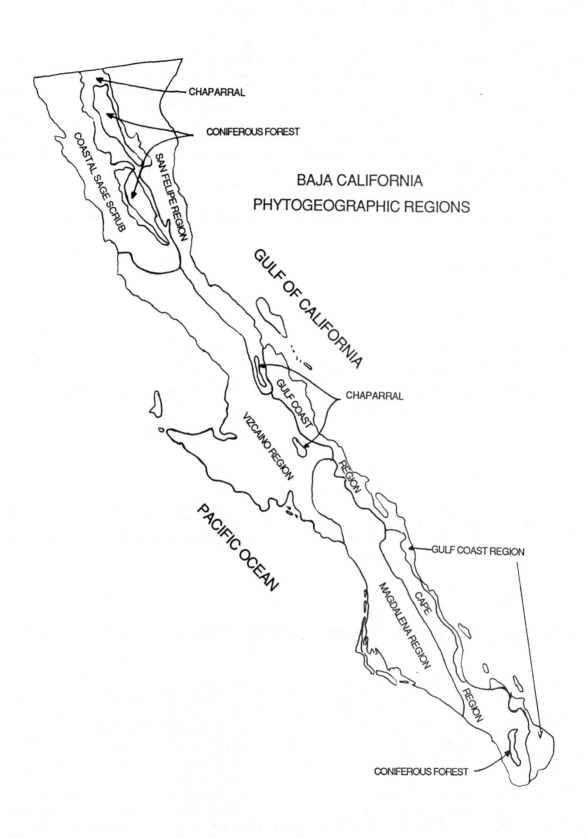

CHAPARRAL

CONIFEROUS FOREST

COASTAL SAGE SCRUB

SAN FELIPE REGION

BAJA CALIFORNIA

PHYTOGEOGRAPHIC REGIONS

GULF OF CALIFORNIA

GULF COAST

CHAPARRAL

VIZCAINO REGION

REGION

PACIFIC OCEAN

GULF COAST REGION

MAGDALENA REGION

CAPE

REGION

CONIFEROUS FOREST

Summary of the Biology Of the Baja Highway

Many travelers driving southward along the Baja Highway say they only see a monotonous barren desert seemingly devoid of life. However, with only a minimal amount of reading, careful observation and a few illustrations and explanations this desert will be seen as a regularly changing, starkly beautiful desert diorama, teeming with numerous varied and often unique plant species. A few preplanned or spontaneous stops and short nature walks, if only for a short distance, to either side of the highway will reveal an interesting variety of plant and wildlife species. Many of these species are lightly colored to survive the heat of the dry desert or camouflaged to protect them from predators and are therefore not readily visible to drivers and passengers as they travel through the peninsula. The unique vegetation of this arid peninsula is well adapted for survival in a harsh environment.

Stop, stretch, take a short walk and the wonders and variety of the life along the highway will surprise you.

The two most obvious forms of life to the casual observer are the plant and bird life to either side of the highway.

BOTANICAL WORK ON THE PENINSULA

Much work has been done on the higher vascular plant species of Baja. Plant collecting was conducted in Baja as early as 1841 by the early naturalist I. G. Voznesenskii. In this century several excellent botanical collections, botanical accounts, and published references have become available which detail the floristics of the vascular plants of Baja for interested travelers, students, naturalists, and serious botanists. Those references which are particularly noteworthy and useful are by Standley (1920-26), Shreve and Wiggins (1964), Felger and Lowe (1976), Axelrod (1979), Wiggins (1980) and Copyle, 1990.

Virtually all of Baja California is classified as a desert, but distinct regional differences known as **Phytogeographical Regions** (*See* map on opposite page) exist and are characterized and recognized by specific plant (or groups of plant) indicator species. A traveler following this guide southward will be able to anticipate, observe and understand the changes in plant life along the Baja Highway. A detailed explanation of each Phytogeographical Regions is given as the highway enters a new region.

BIRDING IN BAJA

One of the things regularly impressing and/or puzzling travelers is the apparent lack of animal life along the Baja Highway.

Hot, dry desert conditions exist throughout most of Baja and as a result animals are rarely seen during the daytime since they are evading these arid conditions by hiding in protective foliage, caves, and subterranean burrows. Birds are the exception and are commonly seen during the day along the Baja Highway. A traveler taking a walk into the different plant communities adjacent to the highway will be rewarded with views of a great variety of birds. Although there are some areas that are inhabited by more species than others, some Baja travelers think birding is wonderful throughout the entire peninsula. The birds of Baja generally exhibit regional habitat preferences and so we find, as with plants, that specific species of birds tend to be found in specific geographical locations. So from north to south the variety of birds seen along the highway is great and changes locally with the season, geography, latitude, temperature, and weather. Binoculars, lightweight trousers, and boots are essentials for

1

birdwalks in Baja's thorn scrub areas. A little preparation, involving looking at pictures of birds commonly seen in Mexico will help identify the birds commonly seen on or closely adjacent to the Baja Highway.

The birds of Baja's arid deserts are poorly known, species lists are incomplete, and very few studies concerning the ecology and densities of breeding pairs per acre have been conducted and reported. In the more arid, desert regions of Baja there are fewer birds per acre than in the more luxurious California region and those commonly seen are generally drab colored for camouflage and thermoregulation. Most of the species seen along the highway, with the exception of a few endemics, are also seen in Alta California and the Sonoran Desert of the American Southwest. Most of Baja's plants lose their leaves during the drier parts of the year and consequently birds have little cover to hide behind so they are more visible to birdwatchers. Four species in particular distinguish the avifauna of the peninsula deserts. They are Scrub Jay, California Quail, Xanthus' Hummingbird, and Gray Thrasher. The last two are both endemics of the southern two-thirds of the peninsula and are found in both the desert areas and the Cape Region.

Since most of the birds commonly seen along the Baja Highway are also commonly seen throughout both of the Americas, it is difficult to typify the various regions of Baja on the basis of its avifauna. However, an attempt has been made in this guide to list those species most commonly seen along the Baja Highway as the traveler passes through the six phytogeographic regions of the peninsula. Some of Baja's bird species are cosmopolitan over the entire peninsula and so are listed in more than one phytogeographic region. Seven cosmopolitan bird species occurring from the International Border to the Cape and along both coasts and on the Gulf islands are Costa's Hummingbird, Gila Woodpecker, California Quail, Raven, House Finch, Ladder-backed Woodpecker, and Wrens.

The following information is intended as a brief outline presenting in a general fashion the birds commonly seen along the highway in each phytogeographic region, along Baja's shoreline, on gulf islands, and Baja's raptors and migratory birds.

Californian Phytogeographic Region:
The bird species of the Pacific coast of Northern Baja are the same as those found in the Californian Region of Alta California. The dominant species of the California Region are the California Thrasher, Anna's Hummingbird, Black-chinned Hummingbird, Red-shafted Flicker, and Nuttal's Woodpecker. (See Km 35.5 in the Tijuana to Ensenada log.)

Sonoran Central Desert Phytogeographic Region, including its four subareas (Magdalena Plain, Vizcaino Desert, San Felipe Desert, and Central Gulf Coast Desert):

Cape Region:
The most commonly encountered species of the Cape Region avifauna (estimated to be 250 species) are the Yellow-billed Cuckoo, Bell's Vireo, varied Bunting, common Ground Dove, and Blue-gray Gnatcatcher. Many of the more commonly encountered Cape species are also found in the Sonoran Desert of the American Southwest.

Baja's Shoreline And Gulf Island Birds:
The most common shore birds are the American Oystercatcher, Osprey, Gulls, Terns, Pelicans, Egrets, Magnificent Frigate-birds, Blue and Brown-footed Boobies, and the Great Blue Heron. These species are often seen on both the Pacific and Gulf coasts of the peninsula and on virtually every Gulf island. Although there are several peninsular endemics, there are no endemic birds on the islands in the Gulf of California. There are other species of shore birds but they are more patchily distributed in mangrove-fringed beaches and coves on the larger southern islands and along the southern peninsular Gulf coast.

Raptors:
The raptors enjoy a wide and cosmopolitan distribution throughout the peninsula because they lack a particular habitat preference and are capable of traveling over long distances. The species of raptors most widely distributed in Baja include Red-tailed Hawks, Turkey Vultures, American Kestrels, and the Peregrine Falcon. Most of these predatory or scavenging birds are year round residents of the entire peninsula.

Migratory Birds:
Baja lies on the Pacific Flyway, the pathway of many bird species that breed in the summer in western North America and winter in Baja or further south. As a consequence, a large number of birds are seasonally seen in Baja.

NOTE: At the beginning of each phytogeographic region a list of the commonly encountered birds of that phytogeographic region is listed. At specific points along the Baja Highway, where a particular species of bird has been commonly seen, a brief natural history discussion will be presented for that bird, along with a line sketch of the bird illustrating distinctive identifying characteristics. The birds Mexican name is included if known.

BAJA CALIFORNIA GEOLOGIC TIME SCALE

ERAS	PERIODS	EPOCHS	EVENTS IN CALIFORNIA
Cenozoic	Quaternary	Recent or Holocene	Continued faulting & uplift
		Pleistocene	principal uplift and tilting of Ranges
	Tertiary	Pliocene	mouth of Gulf of California opens
		Miocene	widespread volcanism-central Gulf opens
		Oligocene	first movements on lateral faults
		Eocene	Auriferous rivers flow across ranges
65my		Paleocene	shallow coastal seas-tropical weathering
Mesozoic	Cretaceous		Subduction Zone, Formation of Batholith,
	Jurassic		Cretaceous Geosyncline, and Coast Ranges
230my	Triassic		Melange
Paleozoic	Permian		Volcanism
	Pennsylvanian		shallow seas over much of
	Mississippian		Baja California
	Devonian		
	Silurian		
	Ordovician		Oldest rocks in Baja ?
600my	Cambrian		
Precambrian			

Summary of Baja Geologic History

Paleozoic - The Quiet Time

The Pre-Mesozoic history of Baja California is obscure and very fragmental. We know that the later North American and Pacific Plates were part of a larger plate which was moving eastward closing the Proto-Atlantic Ocean on its way to a collision with Europe and Africa. The west coast was in the middle of a plate (*see* Figure 1) much like the present eastern coast of North America. Metamorphosed Lower Paleozoic carbonates and shales and sandstones occur in at least one place while Upper Paleozoic rocks have been identified in a number of isolated and scattered areas. Some of the metamorphic gneisses and schists such as the Julian Schist are most likely of Paleozoic age.

FIGURE 1 - PALEOZOIC ACCRETIONARY WEDGE ON STABLE EDGE OF CONTINENT

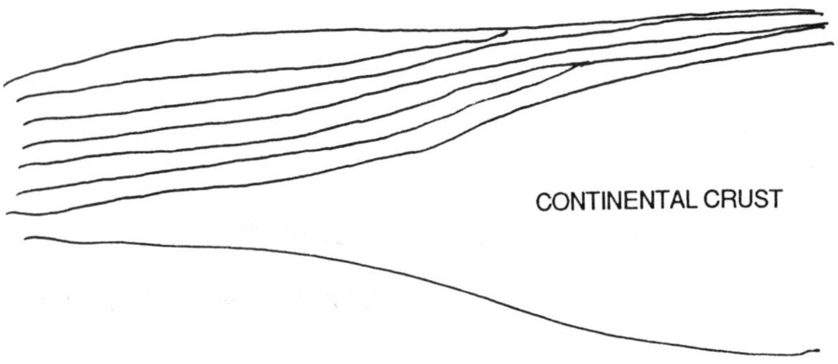

CONTINENTAL CRUST

Mesozoic - The Big Squeeze

At the beginning of the Mesozoic the motions changed. As the Atlantic opened, North America began to move westward pushing against the Pacific part of the plate causing subduction and the formation of an Island Arc. Parts of Baja may have been brought from other areas as small land masses on the East Pacific Plate. However, the majority of the intrusive igneous and metavolcanic rocks in Baja were formed in this subduction zone (*see* Figure 2).

As the Pacific plate was pushed under the continent, the friction caused melting and the formation of magmas. Continual pushing raised these magmas closer to the surface. Some of them cooled at depth to form the granitic rocks of the Peninsular Ranges Batholith with its accompanying metamorphic rocks. Some of the magma spewed out on the surface and formed volcanic islands and volcanics derived sedimentary basins. Continual subduction and burial of these rocks caused low grade metamorphism and formed the Alisitos Formation and other metavolcanic rocks. As the mountain mass was raising, erosion carried much of the debris westward into the trench basin forming large Mesozoic sedimentary basins offshore. The subduction continued for a hundred million years resulting in the formation of more plutonic rocks after the earlier plutonic rocks were uplifted to the surface and the eroded sediments deposited offshore in a geosynclinal basin and on top of the earlier granitic rocks (*see* Figure 3). The fringes of this basin are exposed as the Rosario Formation along the coastline in northern Baja and as a 30,000+ foot thick geosynclinal basin under the majority of southern Baja. The overriding of the East Pacific Rise by the North American plate resulted in the end of the subduction in places.

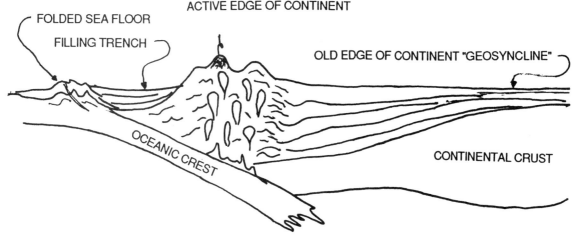

FIGURE 2 - EARLY STAGES OF SUBDUCTION ZONE

ACTIVE EDGE OF CONTINENT

FOLDED SEA FLOOR

FILLING TRENCH

OLD EDGE OF CONTINENT "GEOSYNCLINE"

OCEANIC CREST

CONTINENTAL CRUST

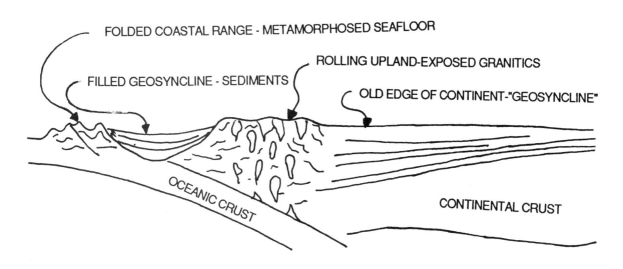

FOLDED COASTAL RANGE - METAMORPHOSED SEAFLOOR

ROLLING UPLAND-EXPOSED GRANITICS

FILLED GEOSYNCLINE - SEDIMENTS

OLD EDGE OF CONTINENT-"GEOSYNCLINE"

OCEANIC CRUST

CONTINENTAL CRUST

FIGURE 3 - FINAL STAGES OF SUBDUCTION ZONE

Cenozoic - The Big Split and Ripoff

In the Early Cenozoic, the peninsula was again a relatively quiet place. The Peninsular Sierras were worn down and a gently rolling erosion surface was developed on the exposed batholithic rocks. This surface stretched to the east well into Arizona and Sonora. Major rivers, bearing gravel, flowed across the area from central Arizona to the Pacific.

The North American Plate overrode the East Pacific Rise and began the great rip-off. Coastal California and Baja California began to slide northward along strike slip faults like the legendary San Andreas Fault System in California and the San Miguel Fault, Agua Blanca Fault, Vizcaino Fault, Magdalena Bay Fault and others in Baja California (*see* Figure 4).

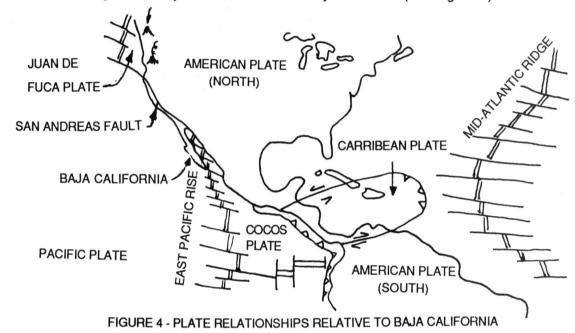

FIGURE 4 - PLATE RELATIONSHIPS RELATIVE TO BAJA CALIFORNIA

The middle Cenozoic opening of the rift, later to become the Gulf of California, took tens of millions of years. Great sheets of lava and pyroclastic rocks with accompanying volcani-clastic sediments were spread over large areas of the peninsula during the Miocene and Pliocene and shallow Miocene seas spread across low areas of the southern part of the peninsula to fill tectonic basins opening in the Proto-Gulf area. The present shape and form of Baja California was developed in the last 5-10 million years as the continent finally yielded to the stretching and opened the areas of the Gulf finally opening the mouth about 5 million years ago. The splitting of the continent tilted the peninsula westward forming the asymmetric tilted fault blocks of the main ranges of the Sierra Juarez, Sierra San Pedro Martir, Sierra la Giganta and uplifting other ranges such as the Sierra la Asamblea and Sierra la Victoria (*see* Figure 5).

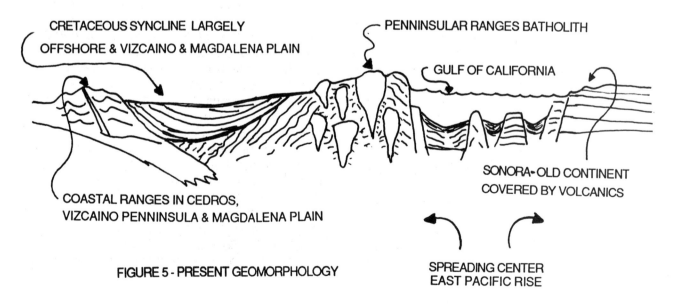

FIGURE 5 - PRESENT GEOMORPHOLOGY

6

Log 1 - Tijuana to Ensenada [110 kms = 68 miles]

The Baja Highway climbs west out of the Tijuana River Valley through steep roadcuts in the terraces developed on the conglomerates and sandstones of the ancestral Tijuana River delta. It then turns south on the slopes between the high mesas and the low terrace of the Playas de Tijuana to follow the rugged basalt sea cliffs along the elevated Pliocene shoreline with steep rugged canyons, then drops onto a narrow, late Pleistocene terrace cut into the basalt cliffs and finally out into an area of gently rolling basalt and tuff hills. The Baja Highway skirts Rosarito Beach on the Pleistocene terrace with views of volcanic capped Mesa Redondo and Cerro Coronel and the rolling volcanic hills, then continues past Punta Descanso where the rolling hills are largely underlain by the marine sediments of the Rosario Formation.

By Descanso the Baja Highway is alternately following the narrow late Pleistocene terrace or climbing onto the numerous slump blocks of volcanic rock from the high Miocene basalt capped mesas which form the back drop for the seacliffs. The Baja Highway crosses the steep sided canyon of the Guadalupe River and travels along a wide segment of the Pleistocene terrace at La Salina before climbing back onto the mesas and slump blocks with the high mesas of resistant basalt overlying the soft marine sediments. At San Miguel the Baja Highway again follows the Pleistocene terrace past steep hills of marine sediments and then metavolcanic rocks to Ensenada.

Kilometers:

0   International Border: As you cross the international border, you will briefly pass through Mexican customs. Generally, no American citizen is required to stop here before leaving the U.S.
The highway passes under an arch and makes a sweeping 270° bend to the left to follow the Tijuana River northward toward the border (*See* the Introduction for complete directions).

2   The highway bends to the left and parallels the International Border (the "Tortilla Curtain" as it is sometimes called) on the right (north).

FLOOD CONTROL ON THE TIJUANA RIVER: The dissipater system of flood control on the Tijuana River can be seen to the northeast. Flooding has been a continuing threat in the Tijuana River valley (Pryde, 1977). About 73% of the 1,731 square miles of drainage basin is in Mexico. The river flows across the International Border 9.4 Kilometers to its mouth at the Tijuana estuary in Imperial Beach, California. Although about 72% of the basin is controlled by reservoirs, even moderate rainfalls have caused serious flooding in the lower reaches of the river. In 1966 a joint flood control project was approved by both governments. Construction began on the Mexican side in 1972, and by 1976 the first phase of the project was completed. This consists of a concrete channel 80 meters wide and extending 4 Kilometers to the southwest from the border.
It was feared that a similar concrete channel on the U.S. side of the border would cause major environmental damage to the fragile and endangered habitat of the Tijuana estuary, so the portion in the U.S. has been constructed as a dissipater system. (The system includes flood plain zoning throughout most of the valley; levees for the low-lying areas along the Mexican border and Interstate Highway 5, a 1.1 Kilometer low energy dissipater structure at the border to slow down and spread out major run-offs entering the U.S. from Mexico, and a low flow channel with a desilting basin to handle minor floods.) A land use plan was also adopted which provides for an enlarged state park in the west end of the valley

and for agriculture in most of the east end.

In the latter months of 1984 serious flooding and overflowing of the Tijuana sewage system forced closures of many of the beaches in southern San Diego County. The dissipater system seemed to function as planned, but the sewage input was not considered in the original plan. The Mexican and U.S. governments have reached a tentative agreement to construct a sewage treatment plant to remedy this problem and prevent its recurrence.

4   The highway begins to climb steeply into the hills to the west, leaving the flat Tijuana River Valley behind. As the highway ascends it passes through a series of road cuts which expose gravels and sandstones which represent a fluvial part of the Pliocene age San Diego Formation. These delta sands and gravels were deposited into the San Diego embayment by the ancestral Tijuana River during the Pliocene and Pleistocene. Notice the steep almost vertical slopes of the road cut to the left (south). The delta material of this road cut is stable enough to resist gravity and stands in almost vertical slopes.

6.3   Turn right to stay on Highway 1D at the junction of the bypass segment and the business segment of Highway 1D from town. The Tijuana River and the International Border are still on the right (north).

Highway 1D was completed across this canyon in 1964. At one time the small culverts under the highway were the only passageways for flood waters.

> **AN UNEXPECTED DAM:** During the winter of 1965-66 an unexpectedly violent storm occurred and torrential rain produced a raging river in the usually dry canyon bottom. The waters of the swollen raging river were loaded with mud and debris that quickly clogged the small drainage culverts which pass to the north under the highway. As a result the highway fill acted as a dam, and 2/3 of the canyon to the south of the Highway was filled. The "lake" threatened to flood the adjacent Imperial Beach and Rheem field area in the U.S.A. Several weeks were anxiously spent pumping water out of the "lake" until workers were able to free the clogged culverts.

9   Highway 1D curves southward towards Ensenada. A turnoff here heads westward from the highway and is the only access to the "Bullring by the Sea" and the housing development of Playas (beaches) de Tijuana. The Playas de Tijuana are developed on a 55,000 year old Pleistocene terrace equivalent to the low Nestor Terrace in the San Diego area.

> **SEA CLIFFS, WAVE CUT BENCHES, MARINE TERRACES, AND BEACHES -- LANDFORMS OF MARINE EROSION:** As waves pound against shorelines, their impact (6,000 lbs./sq.in.) erodes uplifted **sea cliffs** back until a **wave-cut bench** or platform develops at its base. As erosion continues, the wave-cut bench widens until its width absorbs most of the wave energy and a **beach** forms along the now low-energy shoreline. The sea cliff diminishes as weathering and landsliding erodes it down to the same level as the **terrace**. In regions of coastal uplift in Baja wave-cut benches raised above sea level and are called **marine terraces**. Generally, the highway will traverse these marine terraces whenever it is near the Pacific coastline. Several marine terraces will be discussed as the road heads southward.

Log 1 - Tijuana to Ensenada

UPLIFTED WAVE CUT PLATFORM COVERED BY SEDIMENT

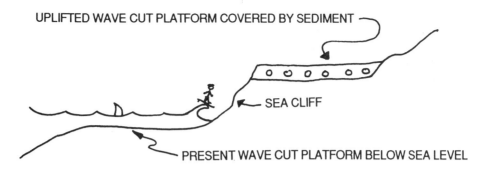

SEA CLIFF

PRESENT WAVE CUT PLATFORM BELOW SEA LEVEL

There is a good view to the west of the Islas Coronados. The toll road (Highway 1D) skirts around the eastern border of the Playas de Tijuana area and continues southward to Ensenada through marine conglomerates and sandstones of Pliocene and Pleistocene age which represent the edge of the ancient Tijuana Delta. Deltas form when a stream carrying lots of suspended sediments enters standing water, where its velocity is checked, and the suspended sediments drop out which forms a fan-shaped or triangular delta similar to the Greek letter "delta".

Along the beach in the region of the Playas de Tijuana there has been serious sea cliff erosion in the soft terrace sediments which resulted in the disappearance of several city blocks from the coastline. Eventually this coastline erosion may destroy more of the housing development presently located there.

10   There are three "Casetas de Cobro" (hut of the fees) toll gates between Tijuana and Ensenada. The fee at each tollgate fluctuates, and is usually the highest on week-ends when greater numbers of travelers utilize the roads. The fees can be paid in either Mexican or U.S. currency.

12   If you need help anywhere along the highway on the way to Ensenada, there are 29 solar-powered phones, located on 7 meter high light-blue poles, and marked by large, highly visible blue and white rectangular signs bearing the internationally recognized distress letters "S.O.S." These emergency phones are located about every two or three Kilometers on alternate sides of the toll highway. No coins are needed for these emergency phones.
As the highway heads southward to the Cape region, a number of vegetational changes are obvious. Changes in regional and local vegetational associations will be discussed as they are encountered.

THE CHANGING OF THE FLORA ALONG THE HIGHWAY: As the highway proceeds to the south from the International Border, to Santa Rosalia, a gradual change in the vegetation is very noticeable. The **Californian Phytogeographic Region** dominates Baja Norte. In this area there are three vegetational areas which consist of the **Coniferous Forest** area, the **Pinon Juniper Woodland** area, and the **Chaparral** area. Each area is typically characterized and recognized by its association of dominant plant species known as indicator species. Each of these three areas and their dominant species will be discussed in detail as they are encountered along the highway.

WHAT ARE INDICATOR SPECIES: Plant ecologists believe every plant is a product of the conditions under which it grows and is a measure of its environment. Certain plant species may be restricted exclusively to a single soil type or may occur in only a certain climatic regime and are referred to as indicator species. For example in Baja Creosote Bush grows only in arid deserts, Smoke Trees grow only in washes where they receive water and their seeds can be scarified, and Pickleweed grows best in alkaline soils. The presence of certain

9

Log 1 - Tijuana to Ensenada

indicator species tells a great deal about the general ecological characteristics of an area, and plant communities are often named for the indicator species.

12.5 The hills to the left (east) reveal exposures of fossiliferous Pliocene-Pleistocene sandstones and conglomerates of the San Diego Formation.

13 The first exposures of the sediments of the Middle Miocene Rosarito Beach Formation are located near the southern end of the Playas de Tijuana. They were first defined by Minch (1967) as a series of basalts (a red-brown to black fine-grained igneous rock), tuffs (a fine-grained fragmental rock largely of volcanic ash), and tuffaceous sediments (fluvial erosional deposits of tuffs) of Middle Miocene age (14.5 m.y.) which are exposed between Tijuana and Rosarito.
Many efforts have been made to utilize the scarce resources of Baja as effectively as possible. For example, the maize (corn), beans, and other table vegetables growing on the steep hillsides along the left side of the highway are being watered with sewage effluent which provides water and fertilizer for these crops.

14 The hills to the left (east) are largely composed of the basalts and tuffs of the Rosarito Beach Formation of Miocene age with a very thin veneer of sandstones and conglomerates of the San Diego Formation of Pliocene-Pleistocene age. The San Diego Formation was deposited in a near-shore environment. The Pliocene shoreline above the highway is a few hundred feet further inland and a few hundred feet higher than the present day shoreline. The shoreline has moved further westward as this area was uplifted.

14.8 A stop at this kilometer mark will afford the opportunity to observe the geology and biology of this region.
The large gray building in the canyon to the left (east) of the highway is the Tijuana recycling and cogeneration plant called TITISA.
At the La Jolla turnoff the strata (rock layers) exposed in the roadcut are composed of volcanic tuffs (ash) overlain by basalts. These tuffs and basalts are part of the Costa Azul Member of the Rosarito Beach Formation. A prominent bake zone of reddish tuff is exposed in the outcrop to the left of the guard station. It formed as the normally white tuffaceous material was baked at extremely hot (2000° F). Molten basalts flowed over them during the Middle Miocene. The La Jolla turnoff provides an opportunity to observe the lithologies and relations between two members of the Middle Miocene Rosarito Beach Formation and the Upper Pliocene San Diego Formation.

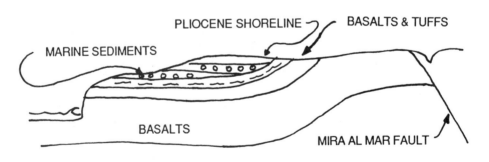

FRANCISCAN-TYPE DETRITUS: The base of the section is located about .5 kilometers up the arroyo to the east around the southeast side of the ridge. Exposed there is the lowest member of the Rosarito Beach Formation -- the Mira al Mar Member. This member is exposed in the core of the monocline and is composed of a light-gray, medium to coarse-grained, arkosic, sandy matrix breccia. These breccias contain fragments of Franciscan-type detritus such as glaucophane schist and other schists (medium to coarse-grained foliated rock with visible mineral grains), serpentine, sausuritized gabbro, bedded chert (a dense, hard, siliceous rock), quartzites, and minor amounts of acidic, volcanic and plutonic rocks (Minch, 1967). In another canyon an oolitic limestone (lithographic limestone with oolites -- spheroidal or ellipsoidal particles formed by chemical precipitation in shallow, wave-agitated waters), and tuffaceous sandstone are exposed in this section. This indicate a relatively quiet deposition between the lobes of this submarine mudflow fan complex.

This member has been interpreted to represent a series of mudflow deposits originating from a western landmass (basement uplift) which were deposited on a narrow shelf against and onto the slope of the landmass area to the east. Ocean currents and wave action reworked the mudflows which produced sandy matrix breccias next to the lobes and sandstones and shales more distant to the lobes. This area was periodically swept by strong currents with periods of quiescence between the offshore volcanic highlands and the Baja California mainland. This unit is exposed along this arroyo and in canyons along the Los Buenos Fault in the Tijuana-Rosarito coastal area (Minch, *et al.*, 1984). This member is correlated with the Los Indios Member exposed to the south in the La Mision area.

A short walk along the dirt road and to the left leads to a fossil locality in the near shore Pliocene San Diego Formation which overlies the basalts and tuffs of the Coastal Azul Member at this site. (Ask permission at the guard station before entering the area if a guard is present.)

The fossils occurring at this site (and in another notable locality in the hills east of Km 15.2) are found in poorly-sorted yellow-brown conglomeratic sandstone beds resting directly on the weathered surface of the eastward-sloping Miocene basalts.

Do not collect Baja's fossil materials since they are all needed to illuminate Baja's past. It is against Mexican federal laws to collect any of the peninsula's resources!

THE CHAPARRAL is the first vegetational community encountered after crossing the border. The chaparral area is a continuation of the vegetational communities of the southern portion of California. The name of this plant community is derived from the Spanish word Chaparra which means evergreen Oak. This community is composed of dwarfed woody trees and shrubs covering the hills and lower mountain slopes of the Pacific coast of Southern California and the western slopes of Baja California from the International Border to Valle Santo Tomas to the south.

There are two distinct kinds of chaparral in the Californian phytogeographic region of northern Baja. Both types of chaparral are important in flood control and in the prevention of soil erosion of the watersheds of Northwestern Baja.

The **COASTAL SAGE SCRUB** of Baja is located at lower elevations along the Pacific coast. The flora of this type of chaparral is short (.3 to 2 meters tall) and less dense than the true chaparral discussed below. The annual precipitation of the coastal sage scrub is 25 to 50 centimeters and coastal fog keeps the summers cooler than in true chaparral. The dominant plant indicator species of the Coastal Sage Scrub are: California Sagebrush, Purple Sage, Black Sage, Lemonade Sumac (the only tall plant), Yarrow, and several species of wild Buckwheat.

Located inland from the Pacific coast the **TRUE CHAPARRAL** is found at slightly higher elevations on the hills and western slopes of the two mountain ranges of northern Baja (below 1,000 meters) southward to Valle Santo Tomas. True chaparral is made of stiff-branched small-leafed densely growing, woody trees and shrubs. The trees and shrubs are somewhat taller than those of the Coastal Sage Scrub Chaparral (1 to 3.5 meters). Plants of the True Chaparral are adapted to long hot summers and receive approximately 35-60 centimeters of precipitation annually. The True Chaparral is recognized by the following indicator species: Chamise, Toyon, Buckthorns, Scrub Oak, Mountain Mahogany, Yucca, Ceanothus, and Manzanita.

While traveling to the south, notice that fires frequently destroy the visible vegetation of the chaparral. The vigorous plants of the chaparral sprout again -- arising from the ashes like the Phoenix bird -- from seeds or underground root crowns that easily survive the intense heat of the fires.
Several common chaparral species were used by Indians in both of the Californias. An acidic tea was made by soaking the fruit and seeds of the Lemonade Sumac (*Rhus*) in water. Leaves of the Wild Buckwheat Brush (*Eriogonum*) was used variously as a decoction for headaches and stomach pains A tea from the flowers of wild Buckwheat was used as an eye wash, and Buckwheat stems were boiled for a tea to treat bladder problems.

15.2   A richly fossiliferous San Diego Formation locality on the north side of this canyon immediately east of the highway yielded an invertebrate fauna of 36 species from lensing gray sandstone beds that are located about 6 feet above the contact with Miocene volcanic rocks.

A MARINE PLIOCENE SHORELINE AND FOSSILS: The rich fossil fauna of the two localities (Kms 14.8 and 15.2) is dominated by shells and shell fragments of the following extinct molluscs: *Pecten healeyi, Acanthina emersoni, Anadara trilineata* and *Chalmys parmeleei*. These extinct fossil species are characteristic of Pliocene strata found on both sides of the International Border.
Because of studies comparing the environmental living conditions of both the extinct and extant (living) species of mollusks in this region, scientists feel that the paleo-environment where the above mentioned extinct mollusks lived, was one in which the ocean temperatures were cooler than those presently encountered in the San Diego-Tijuana region. Such studies comparing past and present environments are extremely important to geologists and biologists, as they seek to reconstruct the past history of the earth and predict its future.
The fossil fauna found at the two localities can be divided into two cool water components. The first is a **littoral** and **inner sublittoral epifauna** which lives on an exposed coastal rocky or shelly-substrate. This component is represented by the following indicator genera: *Acanthina, Calliostoma, Balanophillia, Penitella, Tegula,* and *Thais.*
The second component consists primarily of the following **sublittoral** indicator genera: *Acila, Dentallium, Dosinia, Laevicardium, Nuculana, Panope, Protothaca, Siliqua, Spisula, Terebra,* and *Tresus.* The known environmental requirements of these genera suggest a sublittoral, semi-protected silt or sand substrate environment. The mollusc *Calyptraea mammilaris,* a warm water organism, indicates that a warm infaunal element also existed as a subcomponent of this generally cool water environmental element.
Also present at this locality is a substantial vertebrate fauna which consists of the large teeth of *Carcharadon megalodon,* the huge extinct cousin to the modern

Log 1 - Tijuana to Ensenada

Great White Shark (*Carcharadon carcharias*). The presence of this species at this locality is the first published record (Ashby and Minch, 1984) in the late Pliocene. *Carcharadon sulcidens*, another Great White Shark, is also present here, as it is in many Pliocene rocks throughout Baja and Alta California. This species has been synonymized (Espinosa, 1983) with the modern Great White Shark.

Other vertebrates present at this locality include whale and dolphin remains, a Mako shark (*Isurus planus*), a bay shark (*Carcharias sp.*), and a bay ray (*Myliobatis sp.*). *See* Ashby and Minch (1984) and Rowland (1972) for more detailed discussions of the paleontology at this locality.

15.5 The roadcut on the left (east) exposes a series of prominent cross-bedded Pliocene sandstones. These overlie Miocene basalts of the Rosarito Beach Formation. A whole rock K/Ar radiometric date on this basalt gave an experimental age of 14.3 ± 1.2 million years. This date is probably close to the true age although the moderate degree of alteration of the sample poses some uncertainty. In general, it seems reasonably close to the widespread 15 m.y. ages for basaltic vulcanism on the Continental Borderland and these rocks are probably representatives of a volcanic province which was active in mid-Tertiary time and extended as far westward as the continental slope (Patton Escarpment) north to the Transverse Ranges and eastward to the Gulf Of California (Hawkins, 1970)

BEDDING (STRATIFICATION) AND CROSS-BEDDING: Stratification is a sedimentary rock structure also commonly referred to as layering or bedding and is the most distinctive feature of sedimentary rocks. In general, each bedding plane marks the termination of one period of deposition and the beginning of another. The layers (strata) seen in sedimentary rock are formed when a sediment is laid down. They are later revealed by exposure due to weathering and erosion. Bedding is usually horizontal, but cross-bedding occurs at some angle when wind or water deposits a sediment on a slope. The cross-bedding at this site resulted from shifts in the ocean currents along a rugged coastline.

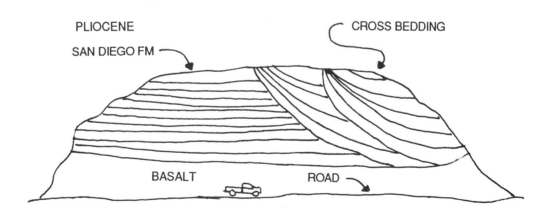

16.1 From the Punta Bandera turnoff the highway follows a narrow strip of the Late Pleistocene Nestor Terrace all the way to Rosarito. From this point good exposures of the Miocene fluvial sediments are also visible on the middle rock of the north island and the south island of Islas Coronados.

A short walk north along the beach at this turnoff reaches excellent classical exposures

13

of airfall lapilli tuffs and basalts in the Costa Azul member of the Rosarito Beach Formation.

19.0   The highway crosses Canon San Antonio de Los Buenos. The Tijuana sewer outfall now utilizes this canyon as an access to the ocean. Three Kilometers up this canyon the Mira al Mar Member of the Rosarito Beach Formation contains Franciscan detritus (*See* Km 14.8) and Miocene fossils. Fossils from this well-developed Pleistocene terrace consist of shallow water marine invertebrates mixed with aboriginal (early man) and land mammal remains.

In this region the Nestor Terrace was very heavily occupied by several Indian cultures. Evidence of prior habitation is found in numerous areas along the terrace in the form of "kitchen or trash middens".

> **INDIAN KITCHEN OR TRASH MIDDENS:** On the north side of Canon San Antonio de Los Buenos an extensive Indian trash midden is exposed in the cliff just above the highway. The upper dark soil layer represents remains of aboriginal occupation of the terrace. For many years native Indians lived along the Pacific coastline. They did not have permanent villages, but lived together in small family camps which they moved when the area was "fished and clammed out" or became infested with fleas (pulgas). In this way the camps moved up and down the coast and over the years an almost continuous layer of midden (trash heap) material was deposited. Some anthropologists believe it is possible that Indians may have occupied this particular area as early as a thousand years ago. Excavations done at midden sites like these are very valuable to archaeologists and anthropologists; they provide many man-made artifacts, burials, and organic remains (plant and animal).
>
> Do not disturb the midden or remove anything from Baja. It is **ILLEGAL**! (*See* Km 171 of San Quintin log for a more detailed, extensive discussion of the prehistory of early man in Baja.)

22.0   This Late Pleistocene Nestor Terrace area near San Antonio Shores has also experienced severe sea cliff erosion during the last decade.

> **PLEISTOCENE LAND MAMMALS:** Excavations on the Nestor terrace at San Antonio shores have yielded the remains of a possible new species of mastodon -- *Stegamastodon sp.* -- a relatively recent relative of the modern horse (*Equus caballus*) and other mammal bone fossils. These fossils represent a land fauna which occupied this low coastal terrace following its late Pleistocene emergence.

22.5   The roadcuts for the next 11 Kilometers expose basalts and tuffaceous rocks of the Rosarito Beach Formation. The reddish tuffs near the top of this section were baked by the overlying basalts during the Miocene (*See* Km 14.8).

23   The gently rolling hills to the left (east) of the highway are developed on the basalts of the Rosarito Beach Formation which weathers to a very rich fertile clay soil. The lighter colored sediments in this area are sandier tuffaceous beds which do not weather into good soil on the slopes in this area. To the south near La Mision almost the reverse occurs. The Los Indios member of the Rosarito Beach Formation, which is largely clayey tuffaceous sediments, is the one most farmed. There the clayey tuffs form good soil on the flat areas and the basalts form very rocky areas. Geologists are aided in the mapping of the distribution of tuffs in the La Mision area by noting where the native Mexicans have farmed the land. They have found that there is almost a 100% correlation between the farming and the locations of the good soils produced by the clayey tuffs.

Log 1 - Tijuana to Ensenada

24.5   This is the turnoff to Rancho del Mar.

25   As the highway makes a slight bend observe the rugged shoreline. The surf along this stretch of the coast is often quite spectacular due to the rougher topography which makes the waves crash on the shore which produces a loud "boom"!
        Tankers delivering fuel to the Rosarito Power Plant are often seen moored just offshore.

27   The Rosarito Power Plant to the right burns fossil fuels to supply much of the electricity for northwestern Baja California.

27.3   As the highway descends from an upper level to a lower terrace level of the Pleistocene Nestor Terrace, it crosses the active Agua Caliente Fault which offsets the terrace in this area. This fault was given this name because it runs through the Caliente Race Track and is responsible for the Agua Caliente Hot Springs at the race track. The Agua Caliente Hot Springs is one of a number of hot springs located along faults in Baja California (*See* Km 176 of the Tijuana log). This fault also runs through the area of the Rosarito Power Plant and tank farm.

27.7   Excavations in a road metal quarry to the north of the highway have yielded a diverse and abundant Late Pleistocene assemblage of marine invertebrates. White sandstones high on the cut at the northeastern end of the quarry near the crest of the hill into which the quarry is excavated yielded 55 species of invertebrates at two localities. No southern faunal forms have been recognized. A conglomerate on the floor of the southeast face yielded only 7 species and includes the extinct mollusc *Crepidula princeps*.

29.4   The Rosarito turnoff is a business loop through the small town of Rosarito that eventually returns to the Cuota (toll-road) near Km 35. A number of good motels and shops (including restaurants, pharmacies, bakeries, and other conveniences) are located in Rosarito. Shopping here is sometimes more affordable than shopping in Tijuana or Ensenada.

29.8   The Tijuana "Libre" (toll-free) road joins the toll-highway. The highway continues south on the Late Pleistocene terrace cut on the Miocene volcanic sequence.
        East of the highway, is the prominent steep-sided flat-topped Mesa Redonda. The prominent peak to the right of Mesa Redonda is called Cerro Colonel. Both hills are capped by Miocene basalts and are underlain by Eocene and Upper Cretaceous strata. Mesa Redonda was formed as the sedimentary rocks of the Eocene and Cretaceous periods were eroded by through-flowing streams which dissected the landscape. This left the flat-topped uplands (mesas) standing above more readily erodible areas.

33.6   Just south of town at the turnoff into Rosarito is the long-standing Renee's Rosarito Beach Motel for which the Rosarito Beach Formation was named.

34.5   The loop road from Rosarito returns to the Cuota (toll) Highway at the same place where the Tijuana Libre road leaves the highway. It parallels this segment of the highway from here to the south to La Mision. You can follow either segment. The free road provides more access to local beaches, etc. However, it is somewhat slower. This road log (guide) follows the toll (Cuota) road

35.5   Caseta (Tollgate)
        If time permits, stop at a turnoff or along the coast and observe the bird life (avifauna) of the Californian coastal region.

Log 1 - Tijuana to Ensenada

THE CALIFORNIAN REGION AVIFAUNA: The bird species of the Pacific coast of Northern Baja are the same as those found in the Californian Phytogeographic Region of Southern California.

In Baja the Californian Region extends from Tijuana to Valle Santo Tomas. The following species are typically seen along the northern peninsular Pacific shoreline and in the chaparral and oak-woodland plant communities of the Californian phytogeographic region:

BIRD COMMON NAME	MOST LIKELY LOCATION
American Kestrel	Telephone wires and fence posts
American White Pelican	Gliding along the shore
Anna's Hummingbird	In the chaparral-feeding on red or yellow tubular flowers
Black-chinned Hummingbird	In the chaparral-feeding on red or yellow tubular flowers
Cactus Wren	On cacti
California Brown Pelican	Gliding along the shore
California Quail	On the ground
California Thrasher	On the ground
Greater Roadrunner	Crossing the highway
Killdeer	On the edges of marshes, shorelines, and salt flats
Loggerhead Shrike	Telephone wires and fence posts
Nuttal's Woodpecker	In the chaparral and oak woodlands
Pyrrhuloxia	In the chaparral and oak woodlands
Red Shafted Flicker	In the chaparral and oak woodlands
Red-Tailed Hawk	Tops of telephone poles and fence posts
Scrub Jay	In chapparal and oak-woodlands
Starling	Flocking on telephone wires,trees, grain fields, and in orchards
Turkey Vultures	Soaring in the skies or feeding, on carrion, on the highway
Western Meadowlark	Fence posts and fence wires

NOTE: At specific points along the *Baja Highway* where a particularly common species of bird has been frequently seen, a brief natural history discussion will be presented for that bird along with a line sketch of it, a discussion of distinctive identifying characteristics, and the bird's Mexican name, if known.

36 South of the toll station, the highway follows another Pleistocene terrace developed on the Rosarito Beach and Rosario Formations which is locally interrupted by landsliding where weak sediments underlie the capping basalts.

39 There is a prominent hill to the left of the highway with what looks like vertical columns or posts. They are the result of a geological phenomenon known as columnar jointing.

COLUMNAR JOINTING: The vertical columns are called columnar jointing and are a result of shrinkage due to cooling of the volcanic rock. This hill is the neck (volcanic plug) of a volcano younger in age than the Rosarito Beach Formation. (It was not a source for the volcanics of the Rosarito Beach Formation). It is one of a number of volcanic plugs that dot the International Border area from Tijuana to the east for tens of kilometers into the back country.

16

Log 1 - Tijuana to Ensenada

VOLCANIC PLUGS are cylindrical masses of rock which seal the vents and conduits of volcanoes. These vents become exposed as the more erodible surrounding rock of the original basalt cone is removed.

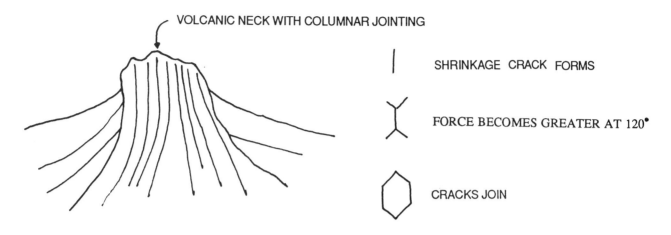

VOLCANIC NECK WITH COLUMNAR JOINTING

| SHRINKAGE CRACK FORMS

FORCE BECOMES GREATER AT 120°

CRACKS JOIN

42   The volcanic outcrops of the Miocene Rosarito Beach Formation have been largely replaced by marine sedimentary outcrops of the Cretaceous Rosario Formation. The Pleistocene terrace was once more extensively developed along the highway. As a result of the softer sediments underneath, the terrace has been undermined and reduced to remnants (mass wasting) with intervening areas weathered into rounded hills and gullies.

> **Late Pleistocene marine terrace deposits** rest on Miocene volcanics here and elsewhere along the local coastline. On the west side of Punta Descanso just north of the point about 2 meters of fossiliferous material is exposed adjacent to the cut terrace surface along about 40 meters of sea cliff. The lower one meter of that deposit is an unconsolidated pebble conglomerate in a sand matrix. The upper one meter is unconsolidated rubble with a matrix of alluvium and comminuted shells. Together these two rock layers have yielded about 150 invertebrate species. They are chiefly molluscs, including the southern *Chione picta* (living from Bahia Magdalena southward) and the northern *Velutina laevigata* (living northward from Cayucos, California).

44.5   An Indian midden is exposed in the upper few feet of the roadcuts on both sides of the road for the next 0.5 km. If left undisturbed these middens will provide valuable information about the history of man in Baja as future archaeological studies are conducted.
Remember it is illegal to collect or disturb these materials!

45   Here the basalts of the Rosarito Beach Formation overlay the Rosario Formation and are well exposed in some of the natural cliffs east of the highway.

46   The brick-making operations east (left) of the highway utilize the clays of the Rosario Formation. The old method of making firing kilns is used. The bricks are hand formed in wooden molds and sun dried. They are stacked in the shape of a loosely filled hollow "room"; the "room" is plastered with mud, filled with firewood, and lit. The fire hardens the bricks.

46.5   For the next four kilometers there are good views to the east of Cerro Colonel. The small basalt mass offshore is known as Moro (snout) Rock because of its resemblance to a nose.

48   For the next kilometer there are good exposures of the Rosario Formation in roadcuts along both sides of the highway.

The telephone poles and wires in this region are usually good places to look for American Kestrels.

The **AMERICAN KESTREL** (*Falco sparverius*) is the smallest and most vocal among Baja's birds of prey and is the most commonly seen falcon of the open country in Baja. It hunts from poles, wires, or trees and is frequently seen hovering in the air before it stoops to capture some ground-dwelling insects or small rodents.

49   This is the turnoff to the beachfront communities of Cantiles and Puerto Nuevo. When the highway was originally built, there were a number of extra turnoffs. The turnoffs were eliminated because early travelers found that they could quickly bypass the toll stations by using these turnouts. They have been reopened.

51   Lobster dinners are available at the restaurants in Puerto Nuevo and are very popular with the tourists. Puerto Nuevo is reached by the turnoff at Km 49.

52.2   The highway crosses Valle El Morro. The bridge over the highway provides an unpaved access to the valley from the old road. A rock quarry located in this valley is easily reached by an average high-clearance four-wheel-drive vehicle.

At the quarry located in Valle El Morro a **buttress unconformity** of the Rosario Formation against a metavolcanic hill of the Alisitos Formation is very apparent. It was formed as the deep water mudstones of the Rosario Formation were deposited against a submarine hill composed of the resistant metavolcanic rocks of the Alisitos Formation.

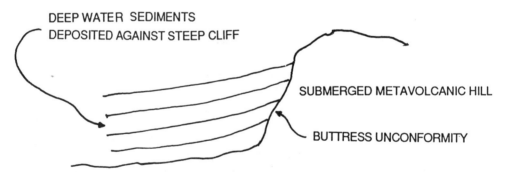

DEEP WATER SEDIMENTS DEPOSITED AGAINST STEEP CLIFF

SUBMERGED METAVOLCANIC HILL

BUTTRESS UNCONFORMITY

Watch for California Quail (*Callipepla californicus*) on the drive into this valley.

CALIFORNIA QUAIL: They are members of the pheasant subfamily and are small plump bodied intricately colored birds which live in the coastal and foothill chaparral, live-oak canyons, deserts, and palm oasis throughout Baja. These gregarious birds are commonly seen along the *Baja Highway*. They travel and feed in large coveys or sit on trees or fence posts. Their most identifiable field characteristics are their bobbing black top-knot feathers and scaled chests. Depending on the location of the accent the voice of these shy skittish birds seems to say "*come* right here" or "where *are* you?".

If you are a game bird hunter, Northern Baja provides an opportunity for excellent sport. Wingshooters are particularly interested in the large populations of quail and doves. Be sure you have a Mexican hunting license.

53.0   At the Canta Mar turnoff there is no toll to leave the Cuota (toll) highway; however, there is a toll to return.

54   The Medanos coastal dune field formed as a result of ocean sands blown on shore by strong winds coming from the open sea. The dunes are stabilized (they don't migrate) by the roots of the vegetation which grows on them. Sometimes the dunes can be "blown out" by wind, exceptionally high waves, or torrential rains. If this occurs, they start to move and are no longer stabilized. Biologists often study plant succession in such dune areas as these. When the dunes are "blown out", biologists study a secondary type of plant succession known as "old dune succession" as vegetation returns to stabilize the dunes.

55.5   Beyond the next roadcut is the first view of the high mesas of the La Mision Member of the Rosarito Beach Formation. For the next 40 Kilometers between here and San Miguel (just north of Ensenada) the highway will skirt these mesas and pass between them and the Pacific Ocean.

56   The small white church on the hill north of Arroyo Descanso is on the former site of Mision Descanso. It was established in 1814 as the northernmost Dominican mission and was the next to the last mission established in Baja California.

58.6   Cuenca Lechera is one of the reopened turnoffs. This name probably refers to the nearby dairy. It provides access to Medio Camino and the "Libre" or free road. You cannot return to the toll road south.

59.4   The Medio Camino (Half Way House) is a favorite stop for tourists. It is located approximately halfway between Tijuana and Ensenada.

> The Half Way House is built on tuffs and basalts of the **Rosarito Beach Formation**. The mesas visible to the east of the highway are capped by the Rosarito Beach Formation overlying the Cretaceous Rosario Formation. The gently-dipping tuffs of the **Punta Mesquite Member** of the Rosarito Beach Formation outcrop in the sea cliffs for a short distance north and south of this point. The lithic tuffaceous sandstones beneath the Half Way House are slightly different in composition from the tuffs to the north. They are coarser and contain interbeds of silts and shales. They have been highly dissected by faults. A walk along the beach to the north of the Half Way House reveals beautiful exposures of this tuff.
>
> Textbook quality examples of sedimentary structures that can be examined include: channel cross-bedding, hummocky cross-stratification, channel cross-stratification, load structures, rip-up clasts, and bioturbation (*Omphiomorpha*) of various kinds.
>
> This area is interpreted as proximal to the offshore volcanic highlands during the Miocene. Deposition of these sediments was above storm wave base (Hummocky cross-stratification) and well-oxygenated (bioturbation). The sedimentary structures all exhibit an eastward transport direction. This area defines the oldest exposures recognized to date of the Rosarito Beach Formation.

Log 1 - Tijuana to Ensenada

Preliminary findings indicate that these tuff exposures represent a portion of the western margin of the basin during the Middle Miocene.

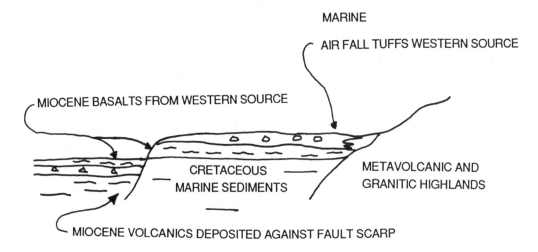

MARINE

AIR FALL TUFFS WESTERN SOURCE

MIOCENE BASALTS FROM WESTERN SOURCE

CRETACEOUS MARINE SEDIMENTS

METAVOLCANIC AND GRANITIC HIGHLANDS

MIOCENE VOLCANICS DEPOSITED AGAINST FAULT SCARP

60   Tuffs are exposed in the northbound lanes (east side of the highway). The local coastal dunes are stabilized with Brittle-Bush and atraplex.

61   In late spring (May-June) notice the gray-white "dots" of vegetation growing on the hillsides to the left of the highway. These long flowering stalks are called Siempreviva or Live-Forevers (*Dudleya pulverulenta*).

LIVE-FOREVERS are perennial, herbaceous succulents which commonly grow in the poorer rocky soils in the Coastal Sage Scrub and foothill chaparral communities of the beaches and coastal bluffs from the International Border south to El Rosario and eastward into the San Felipe Desert. Other species grow southward throughout the peninsula.

62   To the north is a panoramic view of the coastline with Punta Descanso in the distance. The tuffs of the Rosarito Beach Formation are exposed in the near sea cliff. On a clear day the southern island of Islas Coronado is visible offshore.
Look for the pelicans which are commonly seen skimming close to the shallow waters just offshore.

white

brown

The **American White Pelican** (*Pelicanus erythrorhynchos*) and the **California Brown Pelican** (*P. occidentalis*) are the large aquatic fish- eating birds seen along both coasts and on many of the gulf islands in Baja where they nest in large colonies. They are commonly seen flying in long straight lines (brown pelican) or "V" shaped formations (white pelicans) only centimeters above the surface of the water. Feeding is accomplished by diving into the sea from as high as 50 meters (brown pelican) or by bill-scooping as they wade or swim in shallow coastal or lake waters (white pelicans). The slow deliberate flight of the brown pelican, low over the water with sudden plunges for fish, makes its identity unmistakable. The brown pelican is the semi-tame pelican commonly seen begging for food on fishing piers around the docks at Guerrero Negro and Puerto Escondido. Mexicans know the large Brown Pelicans as Pelacano Gris or El Alcatraz.

Log 1 - Tijuana to Ensenada

62.3 Slump blocks are common along the highway for the next 3 Kilometers. The closed depressions are unaltered by drainage. Many of the slumps project into the sea like brown gnarled fingers.

> **COASTLINE SLUMP BLOCK FAILURES:** South of this area the toll highway crosses Quaternary or modern aged landslides for approximately 40 kilometers of rugged coastline ranging up to 500 feet above sea level. Most of the seacliffs are underlain by a thick sequence of flat to gently southwest-dipping upper Cretaceous mudstones, sandstones and conglomerates of the Rosario Formation. These softer and more easily erodible sedimentary layers are capped by resistant Miocene basalts of the Rosarito Beach Formation. Marine erosion and slumping has formed high cliffs in the thick sequence of soft Cretaceous sedimentary rocks. This has resulted in the undermining and mass-wasting of the resistant Miocene basalt caps. Failures along the coastline of this region (slumps and landslides) are influenced by the thickness of the resistant volcanic units, the lithology of the underlying sediments, the north-south jointing and faulting, the angle and attitude of the bedding planes, and groundwater. The dominant cause of the failures is the inherent weakness of the underlying mudstones and over steepening caused by the marine erosion. Most of the slides are rotational slumps; however, some sliding may be due to block glide where dips are favorable. The toe of the slide block is commonly uplifted offshore. Even during calm seas muddy water may be found at the toe of a slide. This indicates recent movement.

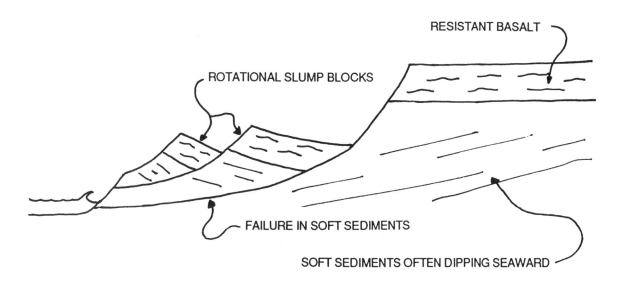

64 To the right is Plaza del Mar with a replica of a Mayan Pyramid. It is built in the middle of a massive landslide bowl. This area exhibits a low hilly (hummocky) topography and indicates that many landslides have occurred here. At various times in the distant past the whole coastline has slid downward and westward. Locally, prominent terraces have developed in the La Mision and older members of the Rosarito Beach Formation which attests to the relative stability and antiquity of some of these landslides. Many of them occurred in excess of 50,000 years ago.

66 The La Fonda turnoff is the last turnoff for traffic between the toll road and the free road. The toll road is the shorter route to Ensenada. La Fonda is a popular tourist area situated on a basalt seacliff on the very narrow coastal Pleistocene terrace.

67.5 A good view of the older development of La Mision reveals a fine flat beach and a scenic rocky headland. At one time this was the only developed area along the highway between Tijuana and Ensenada. The roadcuts in this area expose the basalts of the La Mision Member of the Rosarito Beach Formation.

69.2 The highway crosses the estuary of the Guadalupe River which originates in the high Sierra Juarez near Laguna Hansen. Deep wells in this valley provide much of the water supply for the city of Tijuana. The surge tower of the pipeline can be seen on the hill north of the estuary.

Estuarine Environments exist where the ocean tides meet the outflow of a river current. The water of this environment may be alternately fresh or brackish.

Where the Guadalupe River meets the ocean, an estuarine environment has resulted in the development of a wet land known as a marsh. Marsh and aquatic plants are the mainstay of one of the most important wildlife groups in this area -- waterfowl. In addition, plants of this environment are of great value to shorebirds, to some small game mammals, and to songbirds such as the Red-winged Blackbird, Sparrow, and Marsh Wren. The marsh is rich in both plant and animal species. The characteristic plants of this environment are members of the rush family. Spiny Rushes (*Juncus acutus*) (*See* diagram below) are tufted grasslike herbs commonly found growing in moist places like the Guadalupe Estuarine Marsh. The durable stems of this herb were used by early man in the construction of baskets. This is a good place to stop and view some of the common dominant plants and animals of this estuarine environment.

The most common plant of this estuary is the Spiny Rush (*Juncus acutus*). Other prominent plants of this marsh are Yerba Mansa, Salt Grass, Alkali Heath, Heliotrope, Sea Lavender, Salt Cedar, Glasswort, Pickleweed, Sea Purslane, and Sea Blite.

The animals most often seen here are birds such as the Killdeer, Red-winged Blackbird, Egret, and Heron. The following discussions will help you identify these four common birds.

The **Killdeer** (*Charadrius vociferous*), a member of the Plover Family, is widespread throughout the entire peninsula. This commonly seen bird, with its plaintive lonely cry of *kee-kil-de-dee*, is often seen and/or heard in agricultural fields, short grassy areas, and along the borders of salt marshes and the shorelines of both of Baja's coasts. The most distinctive identifying characteristics of the Killdeer are its double black-banded white neck and the "broken-wing routine" it regularly performs when nests or young are threatened.

Their open depression-like nests are usually built on gravelly soils. Because of its plaintive lonely cry, early Spaniards named this bird El Perdido, which means "the lonely one."

Red

The **Red-Winged Black Bird** (*Agelaius phoeniceus*) is a resident of fresh water cultivated marshes, fields, and moist grasslands in northern Baja. The males are easily recognizable by their red shoulder epaulettes. The epaulettes are used to defend their territory from other male Red-Wings. They are most often seen aggregating together in large noisy flocks.

Log 1 - Tijuana to Ensenada

The **Great (Common) Egret** (*Casmerodius albus*) resides throughout the lowlands of Baja near fresh and salt water streams, marshes, and estuarine environments. This is one of the larger wading birds in Baja -- larger than any other heron except the Great Blue Heron (*See* below). The Great Egret has white plumage, a yellow bill, and shiny black legs and feet. Like the Great Blue Heron, the Great Egret is a slow moving patient hunter of shallow water fish.

The **Great Blue Heron** is often seen in the marshes or on the beaches, or even in the dry fields of Baja. The tall, lean solitary figure of the Great Blue Heron (*Ardea herodias*) can be seen standing motionless in a pool of water or advancing slowly one step at a time, lifting each foot stealthily from the shallows without a ripple. Herons may stand as still as a statue for over half an hour while waiting for prey. With a lightning-quick forward lunge of their long neck and bill the heron captures its prey. The Great Blue Heron prefers fish but will also eat birds, small mammals, insects, snakes, frogs, and crustaceans.

Whether it is on land or in the air, a Great Blue is easily recognized by the long snake-like neck held in an "S" shaped curve, the slow wing strokes, long legs, and nearly 2 meter wing span. In Baja look for the stately, solitary Great Blue Heron on piers, docks, boats in harbors, rocks along the coast, sandbars, tombolos, or in estuaries, coves, marshes, cultivated fields, and the riparian woodland in the bottoms of desert river canyons.

69.5   An excellent turnoff alongside the highway provides easy access to a wide and flat beach. Beaches form along low-energy shorelines as sands are deposited on the slopes of the shoreline.

70   The basalt forming the roadcuts here and on which the coastal homes in the area are built is older than the basalt which forms the mesa top to the east (left) of Highway 1D. This basalt was deposited against the Cretaceous seacliff and filled much of the area. This resulted in the flooding of the basalts over the sea cliff and onto the Cretaceous terrace. The overlying tuffs were stripped from much of the coastal area which left a flat surface along the coast for several kilometers. The Late Pleistocene Terrace (50,000 years old) has developed on top of this and shows the antiquity and stability of some of the coastline between Tijuana and Ensenada. Further south the coastline is highly unstable and is actively moving downward and seaward. This is demonstrated by the numerous repairs that are continually being made in the undulating "bumpy" highway.

A-SLIPPING AND A-SLIDING: Because much of the coastline is slumping into the Pacific along this stretch of the highway, the pavement from here to San Miguel undulates considerably. There are many repair spots. Between Salsipuedes and San Miguel (further south along the toll road) active sliding caused by marine erosional undermining requires continuous highway maintenance to compensate for the seaward movements of large slide blocks. Portions of the highway have been down-dropped several meters. New pavement (asphalt) marks the lateral edge of several slide blocks, and fresh scarps several meters high in natural ground mark the up-slope boundary of active sliding. Preventative and corrective road work in progress includes unloading (removing a portion) of the head of the slide, draining groundwater in and beneath the slide, and rechanneling surface drainage to prevent further infiltration of water into

23

the slide mass. One might wonder why the engineers located the highway here. The only alternative route would be an inland one which would require expensive extensive engineering work to traverse the steep rugged hills and valleys to the east. However, slumping to the east is just as bad, and a road there would not be able to avoid the landslides. Thus, it would seem that the engineers made the best decision -- it is better to build a cheaper coastal highway and repair it when it moves than to build a more expensive inland route that would also require repairs.

72   On the right is Baja Ensenada RV Trailer Park. Note the elevation of the park in relation to the super-tidal area to the left of the highway. It is likely that during some future particularly violent Pacific storm, this park will be inundated by high tides.
The Nopales cacti growing along the highway on the left were planted by local residents and are cultivated and harvested for use as food. Look carefully as the highway heads south, Nopales are being cultivated all the way to Cabo San Lucas -- "Lands End" (*See* Km 10 of the Mexicali log for more details).

73   The tidal flat (salt marsh) of La Salina just south of the turnoff is also a super-tidal area. Frequently the mouths of many of Baja's coastal river valleys are semi-sealed by a sand bar, stretches of beach, or dunes that separate the open sea front from the tide fronts to the rear (landward). This provides the tidal flat with occasional access to the sea.
At one time this tidal flat must have been very popular with the Indians, as fairly extensive Indian kitchen midden (trash) materials extend to the eastward from the highway for about a kilometer on both sides of the marsh. The highway turnoff cuts through and exposes a small portion of this vast midden. A very large (12 cm.) perfectly worked spear point of black metavolcanic material was discovered in the triangle of ground formed by the two roads which enter and exit the highway. (Refer to Km 17 of the San Quintin log for the history of man in Baja.)

TIDAL (MARSH OR MUD) FLAT ENVIRONMENTS: In general Baja's tidal flats occur between mean high tide and mean low tide levels, are vegetated by unicellular and larger forms of algae, and are bordered on their inland edge by intertidal Pickleweed and other halophytes (salt loving plants). Intertidal Pickleweed begins its best growth at the average high tide line.
Tidal flats are the home or favored resting place for many living organisms adapted to life in this extremely harsh saline environment. Organisms that inhabit tidal flats face severe changes in daily environments. They are alternately immersed by high tides or exposed by low tides. not to mention spring, neap, storm, and wind-driven tides. Part of the tidal flat will always be underwater in sloughs and channels, and part will be above the high water mark. Because of these changing conditions, variations in soil salinity are to be expected.
In the flattest lowest portion of the mud flats the salt concentrations may exceed 6% which prevents the growth of all plants except marine algae. Nearer the shallows and edges of the flats, salinity both decreases and fluctuates with fresh water runoff and rain. Temperature ranges are broad which necessitates other adaptations for surviving temperature fluctuations of as much as $50^{\circ}F$ in one day.
Closer to the shore, away from the shallows and on the banks bordering the tidal flat, halophytic (salt loving) plant roots capture silt, mud, and sand substrates. Some of the halophytes which can be seen growing around La Salina marsh are listed below. They are divided into two communities based on their relationship

to the tidal flat (salt marsh). The **dune and strand line flora** which is predominated by halophytic Sand Verbena, Sand Bur, Beach Evening Primrose, Beach Fig, Door Brush, and Ice Plant; and the **saltmarsh flora** predominated by halophytic Yerba Mansa, Salt Grass, Alkali Heath, Heliotrope, Spiny Rush, Sea Lavender, Salt Cedar, Glasswort, Pickleweed, Sea Purslane, and Sea Blite.

Further inland as the land slopes up to the surrounding hills covered by indicator species of true chaparral, the more salt-tolerant plants are replaced by those which are less tolerant. Although they are not very obvious, animals thrive in mud and tidal flats. Due to increased nutrient flows tidal flats are very fertile and are more prosperous than many other natural communities . Tidal flats (salt marshes) are busy places especially for birds, such as Pintails, Mallards, Coots, Gulls, Terns, curlews, Willets, Dowitchers, Yellow Legs, and Whimbrels open mollusc shells and search for worms and shrimp in the squishy tidal flats.

76   The highway passes through a roadcut in the tuffs and tuffaceous sandstones of the Rosarito Beach Formation. The tuffaceous strata of the Rosarito Beach Formation has yielded a Middle Miocene marine fossil fauna which includes: *Chione temblorensis*, *Anadara topangansis*, *Turritella ocoyana*, and numerous marine vertebrates. These strata have also yielded a camelid which has been tentatively identified as *Oxydactylus* cf. *longpipes*. This combination of marine and nonmarine species in the same locality suggests a marine-nonmarine tie-in between the Middle Miocene Hemingfordian North American land mammal age and the West Coast Temblor marine molluscan stage (Minch *et al.*, 1970).

77.8 The private coastal resort of Baja Mar at Jatay offers a golf course, villas for rent, and a restaurant. The golf course has been described by many players as being "very challenging" because the fairways are "islands" in a "sea" of Cactus, Agave, and Coastal Sage Scrub. It has been said that errant players are just as likely to find their ball impaled on a cactus as resting on the fairway.

78   Just south of Jatay the hills to the left of the highway seem to be quite straight (linear in relation to the coast) and have a concave upward slope. This concave upward slope is the headwall of a very large rotational slump block. The land that this portion of the highway is on has slumped down and rotated. All along the highway in this area there are numerous concavities which are indicative of the rotation of numerous such smaller slump blocks.

84   The turnoff to El Mirador occurs on a dangerous curve. Exit carefully! The edge of a 300 meter escarpment at El Mirador provides an excellent view of several coastal features which are visible in this area and include a view of Islas de Todos Santos.

      ISLAS DE TODOS SANTOS: The two islands of Islas de Todos Santos are composed of middle Cretaceous metavolcanic rocks of the Alisitos Formation overlain by basalts (La Mision Member) and sediments (Los Indios Member?) of the Rosarito Beach Formation. Also present on the islands is a well-developed, Late Pleistocene marine terrace. Legend says that the Islas de Todos Santos were the inspiration for Robert Lewis Stevenson's "Treasure Island".
      These islands are a common destination for short weekend get-aways for people with American sports boats and yachts. The beaches are excellent for clamming. Watch out for the "no-see-ums" (small, black biting flies).

      NO-SEE-UMS: Diptera (flies) is the fourth largest insect order. Dipteran mouthparts, which display the widest range of any insect order, range from piercing-sucking to sponging-lapping. Nearly all adult flies feed on liquids especially plant juices and **blood**. Some of the **blood-suckers** are important human and animal pests. Flies are divided into three sub-orders, but only one (sand flies) concerns the Baja traveler.

Sand flies (*Phlebotomus*) of the sub-order Psychodidae would hardly be noticed except for a painful bite the females inflict in order to suck blood. Sand fly adults occur near water while their larvae live in moist soil. Bring a good insect repellant for use in the rainy season and follow the Mexican custom of wearing long pants and shirt-sleeves to avoid the irritating but relatively harmless bites of the female sand fly.

IRONWOOD AND INDIANS: Ironwood (*Olneya tesota*) is found growing on bajadas (low elevation foothills) and in Wash Woodlands below 600 meters throughout the entire peninsula and the west coast of mainland Mexico. Due to its great density this wood is very heavy and extremely durable. The Seri Indians of mainland Mexico's west coast at Bahia Keno in Sonora have carved this wood into spear shafts, arrow points, and agricultural implements. Since the 1950's the Serri (originally inhabitants of Isla Tiburon in the Gulf) and enterprising Mexicans have carved beautiful enduring black-red wood sculptures in a variety of animal shapes sometimes sold at this turnoff..

The panoramic view of the coast to the south shows the mudstones, sandstones, and conglomerates of the upper Cretaceous Rosario Formation overlain by the basalts of the Rosarito Beach Formation. Numerous slumps are evident along the coast. Some have dropped capping volcanics to sea level where they now form resistant shore promontories. The spine of Punta Banda, which encloses the south side of Bahia Ensenada is often visible in the distance. It is a fault block bounded on the northeast and southwest sides by two branches of the Agua Blanca Fault. Islas de Todos Santos are the offshore Islands.

85   If you missed the turnoff to El Mirador at Km 84, this turnout has a view similar to that at El Mirador. This spot provides a good place to look at the flat terraces below the highway on the Pacific side. Each terrace is a rotational slump block. The viewpoint produced by the rotational movement of a slump block is directly above one of these terraces.

86   There are several small olive groves on the west side of the highway. The Russian Olive (*Olea europaea*) is a hardy drought resistant tree. Originally a native of Europe and western Asia, this tree was brought to the west as a food crop. It has some importance as a food source to wildlife, since its fleshy silvery-yellowish fruit clings to the plant throughout most of the winter.

A careful inspection of this olive grove may reveal several species of birds. One of the most commonly seen birds is the mourning dove which is a favorite of wing shooters from California.

 **Mourning Doves**: (*Zenaida macroura*), members of the pigeon family, are small slim birds with long sharply-tapered tails. They are commonly seen in northern Baja in fruit orchards or gleaning seeds among the stubble of cultivated grain fields in the late summer or fall. They are frequently seen in cattle grazing ranges on dry uplands and in many of the villages and desert areas of Baja. Except for an occasional American Kestral, Doves are the

largest birds that commonly perch on telephone wires where their long sharply-pointed tails make them easily identifiable. This dove is extensively hunted by wingshooters for its small but delicious breast muscle. As you reach the southern part of the peninsula, watch for a close relative of the Mourning Dove -- the White-Winged Dove.

87.5 Salsipuedes: In Spanish this word aptly means "Get out if you can". Early sailors sheltered in the cove below but found it difficult to climb the steep sea cliffs. A road to the right leads to a small rancho and tourist fish camp.
Watch for Brown Pelicans which soar along on sea cliff thermals between here and Ensenada.

89 It is worth stopping at the south end of this high bridge to view the stone-on-stone construction. At the top of the piers the spans are sitting on blocks about 3 0 centimeters square and 12 centimeters wide. Some of these blocks appear to be slightly tilted possibly due to movement caused by slumping. Good exposures of the mudstones of the Rosario Formation can be seen outcroping in the roadcuts south of the bridge.
As you look at the waters just off the beach, you may notice dark, caramel colored masses of vegetation floating near the seas surface, this is an algae known as Giant Kelp.

GIANT KELP: is the common name for the Marine Algae *Macrocystis pyrifera*. It forms great kelp beds in the deep waters near the shore. This algae often washes on shore in this area, and forms unsightly odoriferous masses of rotting vegetation which attract numerous flies. Giant Kelp beds provide an important habit of many marine organisms.

91 From here to Km 94 there are exposures of the massive sandstone and conglomerate lenses of the Rosario Formation. One of these submarine-fan systems is best seen east of the highway at Km 92. At this stop the sediments record an upward transition from the slope (outer-mid fan) to the inner fan deposits. Here the section rests on a dark shale of the Rosario Formation (Middle Mudstone Member) that is overlain by a diamictite unit 12 meters thick. This is overlain by 7 meters of inversely graded imbricated conglomerate which represents slump and channelized debris flows. Above the conglomerates are 37 meters of submarine turbidite flows composed of sandstone and mudstone which fill a small submarine canyon. The overall thinning and fining upward nature of this sequence indicates an inner-fan channel of a submarine fan.

CRETACEOUS ROCKS NEAR ENSENADA: Sediments deposited in this area during the Late Cretaceous are derived from the uplifted Peninsular Ranges Batholith. These sediments developed as a clastic wedge, which is thicker to the west, and consists of fluvial and alluvial sediments to the east and deep marine facies to the west. During Turonian time, fluvial and alluvial sediments were deposited as fans; these deposits are known as the Redondo Formation. The overlying sediments comprise the Rosario Formation which are Campanian-Maastrichtian in age (Late Cretaceous), and the contact with the underlying Redondo Formation is unconformable. In Campanian time sea level rose and deposited a transgressive sequence (beach to offshore deposits are represented). The shoreline was defined by steep bedrock cliffs with encrusting molluscan assemblages such as the rudistid-molluscan bivalve assemblage at Rincon de la Ballena (See Km 14 on the Punta Banda road). At the same time storm sedimentary deposits (hummocky cross-stratification) are recorded in the same area. The sea level rose with the deposition of a thick shale (mudstone) unit described by Kilmer (1963) in the type area until Late Campanian time. The sea level fell in Early Maastrichian and formed huge deltaic sequences. This regression dumped large amounts of sediment on the steep narrow shelf and caused gravity-flow deposits which developed numerous submarine fan systems.

94.5   In the cove directly below a Mexican battleship tender was run aground at full speed during the night of Cinco de Mayo, 1967. The crew had mistaken the point at El Mirador for the one further south at Ensenada. It has been completely broken and washed away by the surf. Only one small metal beam was sticking above the surface of the water to mark the spot. Remember the seven destroyers that were run ashore by the U.S. Navy at Point Arguello. Both Mexican and American vessels have had trouble navigating this rugged coastline.
The highway median contains beautiful red Geraniums (*Pelargoniom sp.*) which grow between large Nopales Cactus and Oleander.

95.2   This is the site of a major landslide which once disrupted travel along the highway for a number of months. During that time the old road was used as a bypass. Workers have worked to stabilize the landslide by de-watering and repaved the highway, and it has proved to be relatively stable since then.

96   The topography along both sides of the highway from here to Km 98 is very rugged with many irregular small hills. Each hill represents an individual landslide area on the main point of Punta San Miguel. The entire coastline in this area is actively sliding into the sea due to the undermining of the point by the ocean.

98   The first view of the small fishing village of El Sauzal and the site of another massive highway failure which occurred in 1978 are visible. The slope failure on the hills to the left resulted in the loss of a number of residential homes which once overlooked the ocean. Look carefully to the left (east) to see the remnants of some of these homes. The wall of one of these homes still protrudes precariously over the edge of the cliff. Each one of these homes was built on its own landslide block "terrace". When the blocks failed (moved down toward the highway), the homes were destroyed.

> **LANDSLIDE SURFACES** offer attractive building sites to the unsuspecting developer because they are often flat with unobstructed views. The low density development on some of the stabilized blocks has not immediately created unstable ground. However, more development on presently stable landslides may create disastrous effects as shown by continuing problems in the San Miguel area. When structures are built on landslides, there is an increase in the ground water due to residential watering and waste disposal. This additional water infiltrates into the landslide; it acts to weaken, load, and lubricate the slide mass so that it becomes unstable and slides. The demand for beach-front property is rapidly increasing, and more of these stabilized blocks are becoming developed. More landslides, property loss, and possibly casualties are inevitable.

98.5   This is the last Caseta de Cobro as the *Baja Highway* heads southward.

99.2   At the junction of the Tijuana Libre Highway and Highway 1D there is a final view to the rear, of the remnants of the houses destroyed by the 1978 landslides and the neighboring houses on more landslides.
The village of San Miguel is visible to the right of the highway.

100   The highway between here and Ensenada follows the Late Pleistocene Terrace which it has been intermittently following since leaving Tijuana.

Log 1 - Tijuana to Ensenada

101   The hills to the left of the highway for the next several kilometers are composed of upper Cretaceous marine sandstones which were deposited along an exposed rocky shoreline. The large house on the left behind the Russian Olive grove belongs to General Abelardo Rodriguez (*See* Km 101.6).

101.3   The turnoff to the right leads 114 Kilometers to Tecate on Mexico Highway 3.

101.6   The fish canning industry supports the village of El Sauzal. A new harbor has been built here to shelter the fishing fleet. This is one of the enterprises of the late General Abelardo Rodriguez, a former Governor of Baja California and briefly the President of Mexico until the election of Lazaro Cardenas in 1933 (he replaced Ortiz Rubio in 1932 after Jefe Maximo Pluttarco Elias Calles forced Rubio to resign). His Ensenada home is on the low hill east of the highway at Km 101 and is beyond the Russian Olive orchards (*Olea europaea*) which were planted to supply olive oil for the canning of the fish.

105   A road metal quarry is located on the hillside east of the highway. The basement rocks which form the Late Cretaceous coastline are exposed in the ravines immediately in back of the quarry and along the highway to the south.

106.5   The Universidad Autonoma de Baja California with its Escuela Superior de Ciencas Marinas is located to the right of the highway on Punta Moro. This very prestigious marine biology school obtained legal rights to the property where the school is built after the students squatted on it which forced the governor of Baja to give it to them. The Centro de Investigacion Cientifica y Educacion Superior de Ensenada (CICESE) is the series of buildings and domes on the hills to the left of the highway. Both of these schools enjoy a good reputation in Mexico and the United States.

107   This is the intersection of the alternate route to Ensenada (by Calle 10a) and the coastal route to Ensenada. Geologically the coastal route is more interesting to follow. It provides beautiful views of Punta Banda and Islas de Todos Santos as you drive the last mile along the coast into Ensenada.

109.7   This roadcut exposes prebatholithic massive andesitic breccia. The prebatholithic rocks in this area are metamorphosed volcanic flows, pyroclastic rocks and sedimentary rocks of volcanic derivation. The most common rock types were basic to intermediate tuffs and breccias, basaltic and andesitic flows, and volcanic graywackes. The age of the rocks in the Ensenada area is still in doubt. Similar rocks range in age from Late Jurassic to the north in San Diego County to Early Cretaceous south of Ensenada. Here they are quarrying the rocks to use to enlarge the harbor. During the quarry operation some of the cliff rocks collapsed onto the highway, so a detour was built around it.

109.8   **ENSENADA** has been a natural port for a long time and blossomed into a major port during the west coast shipping strike in 1974. The strike was a boom to this city and resulted in the enlargement of the harbor. With this enlargement came more business even after the end of the strike. The availability of large blocks of Metavolcanic rock in Chapultepec hill has made the task of building the Mulle (pier) and enlarging the port easier and cheaper than importing rock from a more distant quarry. Recent hightides and large waves have demonstrated that the rocks may not be large enough to hold after occasional violent storms which lash the area. Work on the mulle is continuing. Notice the "Topes" (speed bumps) signs. These speed bumps are especially large as the highway enters the city of Ensenada.

110   This is the intersection of Ave. Gastelum and Calle Primera in Central Ensenada. Follow

Log 1 - Tijuana to Ensenada

Mexico Highway 1D (Blvd. Grae L Cardenas) southward along the Malecon on the right. The main tourist shopping district, the destination of many American tourists, is one block to the east. There are a large number of good restaurants and hotels in Ensenada. (The authors like the recently enlarged colonial style Mision Santa Isabel on Av. Lopez Mateos y Castillo).
A trailer park is conveniently located on the right at the end of the Malecon.

> **LAS TRES CABEZAS:** The monument on the Malecon (Blvd Grae L Cardenas) commemorates three famous figures of Mexican history: **Benito Juarez,** a great president of Mexico and a full-blooded Indian; **Miguel Hidalgo,** the priest who nailed El Grito to the church door which declared Mexican independence from Spain; and **Venustiano Carranza**, the writer of the Mexican Constitution.

At the south end of the Malecon (Blvd Gral, L Cardenas) the highway jogs several blocks to the left on Ave. Gral. Agustin Sangines passing a large hospital and social services center. Then it turns right on Avenida Reforma (Highway 1) which is the main highway to the south.

At the corner of Agustin Sargines and Avenida Reforma there is a Pemex station to the left and a very large supermarket on the right with a pharmacy and a panaderia.

Log 2 - Ensenada to San Quintin [196 kms = 122 miles]

The Baja Highway travels south on the Pleistocene terrace bordered by metavolcanic hills to the left with views ahead of the metavolcanic spine of Punta Banda and the Agua Blanca Fault Zone. It then drops into the alluviated fertile Maneadero Valley and climbs back onto the terrace before turning inland up a valley through the metavolcanics to generally follow along the trace of the Agua Blanca Fault Zone to crest a small pass where it crosses the Agua Blanca Fault Zone, and drops into and follows Santo Tomas Valley which is developed in the metavolcanics along the Santo Tomas and Agua Blanca fault zones. Santo Tomas and the grade south of town are in the Santo Tomas Fault Zone.

The Baja Highway then follows a series of Oak woodland valleys through more metavolcanic ridges with alluvial valleys and tonalite outcrops to enter the rolling mixed granitic hills and gentle alluviated valley areas of the San Vicente Plain. Beyond the San Vicente Plain the Baja Highway descends a grade and turns seaward through metavolcanic hills to Colonet on the northern edge of the San Quintin Plain.

At Colonet the Baja Highway turns south to parallel the ocean and follows the Plio-Pleistocene marine terrace developed on marine sediments of the Rosario Formation and the Pliocene Cantil Costero Formation. The high hills to the east are part of the metavolcanic Alisitos Formation. They formed the shoreline during the development of the Plio-Pleistocene terrace. The Baja Highway will alternately climb onto the terrace and drop into alluviated valleys. South of Vicente Guerrero the Baja Highway drops onto the lower late Pleistocene terrace with views of Laguna Figueroa, San Quintin Bay and the basalt cones of the San Quintin Volcanic Field. Near San Quintin the higher marine sedimentary terrace forms a series of mesas backed by the high metavolcanic hills.

This log and the kilometer measurements start at the shopping center at the intersection of Calle Gral. (General) Agustin Sangenes and Ave Reforma - Highway 1.
Head to the south along Ave Reforma.

6 The highway heads south parallel to the coast on the wide, well developed 10 meter Late Pleistocene terrace. In front and to the right are views of the spine of Punta Banda and of the active coastal dune front which is partially stabilized by vegetation characteristic of the chaparral region of the Californian Phytogeographic area.

> The **metavolcanic hills** to the left consist of a well preserved section of pyroclastic rhyolite and dacite in a large syncline which plunges to the west. The stratigraphic section exposed here consists of 2,400 meters of lithic and crystal dacite tuffs, breccias, welded tuffs; welded lithic tuff, and andesite; tuffaceous andesite breccia and sandstone, and tuffaceous andesite breccia. A quartz diorite pluton limits the structure and stratigraphy on the north near the Cementos California plant, while a granodiorite pluton terminates the section on the south near the small village of Maneadero. No fossils have been found in this section, but its lithologic characteristics indicate that they are probable representatives of the Late Jurassic and early Cretaceous volcanic episode(s) which have been dated to the south of the Agua Blanca fault.

11 This is the 2 da Zona Militar.

12 The Ensenadas 2 da Zona military airport is for both military and commercial flights. Commercial flights can be obtained here on cargo planes which service canneries in remote parts of the Vizcaino Peninsula.

Log 2 - Ensenada to San Quintin

Just beyond the airport there is a good view to the right of Isla Todos Santos, the point of Punta Banda, and Bahia Ensenada.

13   The side road to the right leads to Estero Beach Resort on Playa Esteros a good place to get away for a short weekend trip.

16   The highway leaves the Terrace and descends through Pleistocene dune sands into the fertile Valle de Maneadero. Commercial produce crops are grown in this fairly flat valley, and several plants for the commercial processing of chiles are located here as well (*See* Km 55.5 of the San Quintin log for a discussion of Chiles).

As the highway crosses the Valle de Maneadero there is a view of the hills of Punta Banda. The Agua Blanca fault line, the terraces, the offset streams and the vegetation lineaments show where ground waters have risen to the surface along the faults of this area. The highway approaches the Agua Blanca fault line and will follow it up the valley to the left.

18.5   The side road to the left leads to San Carlos hot springs and resort (20 Km.) situated on a fault zone in the metavolcanics of the coastal range.

 **Hot Springs:** A hot springs is at least 10° warmer than the mean air temperature. Hot springs do not normally require abnormal heat sources. The earth's temperature increases about 1° Fahrenheit per 100 feet of depth. Subsurface ground waters are heated to the temperature of the surrounding rock so the 10° warmer water need only come from 1000 feet below the surface. Faults provide an avenue for the rapid rise of hot ground water to the surface which results in hot springs. Most of the hot springs in the western United States are along faults. Some such as Yellowstone and Lassen are near volcanic centers and are due to magma near the surface.

22   This is the turnoff to Punta Banda and La Bufadora (20 kilometers). The main highway veers left to leave the valley and climbs onto the coastal terrace.

> **SIDE TRIP TO LA BUFADORA AND PUNTA BANDA:** Maneadero - The side road turns right towards the coast and makes a number of right angle bends to avoid crossing cultivated fields. Olives and other agricultural crops, particularly table vegetables like corn, squash, and green peppers which are sold in the U.S., are grown in this region. Olives are harvested, sold, and consumed locally and shipped to mainland Mexico where they are used for oil, eating, and exportation. As the road approaches the hills, the trace of the Agua Blanca Fault Zone is obvious at the break between the slope of the steep hills and the gentler fans.
>
> 7   The buildings and trees on the right (west) side of the road are part of the La Grulla Gun Club. The north edge of the slough beyond the club is a scarp and sag pond of the Agua Blanca Fault. The road crosses this scarp about 1/2 km to the southeast, and many more subdued fault features can be seen along the base of Punta Banda Ridge ahead.
>
> 7.5   As the highway curves, notice the rushes (*Junco sp.*) growing in on the left side of the road. Numerous resident Red Winged Blackbirds are seen building nests here in the spring (*See* Km 69.2 of the Tijuana log).

8   Castor Bean, Junco (rush), Typha, composites, and Giant Reed are found in roadside ditches. Tamarix and olive trees form wind breaks. The area is coastal swamp - "estero" or salt marsh. Other distinctive plants in the area include Giant Reed (Arundo donax of the Toyon grass family), California Pepper Tree, Indian Tree Tobacco (a disturbed soil indicator), Laurel Sumac, Rabbit Brush, and Datura.

9   The sand spit separating the estero from Bahia Ensenada can be seen ahead to the right. Numerous hot springs along the recent break of the Agua Blanca Fault lie at the edge of the estero a few hundred feet to the right (north) of the road. The westernmost hot spring is on the main beach and faces the ocean near Km 11 almost opposite the northernmost house. The springs are noted on Baja maps as Agua Caliente (hot water). It is possible to dig in the sand here at low tide and encounter hot water (*See* Km 18.5).

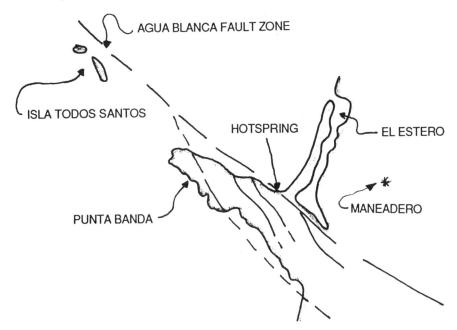

10   Typical coastal scrub chaparral Chamise and Rabbit Brush with agave and mission cactus vegetation grow on the hills. Residents have home crops of cactus for nopales.

10.6   This is the turnoff to Punta Estero and the Baja Beach and Tennis Club. The Pleistocene terrace materials are exposed in the roadcut. The side road turns to the right toward the sand spit, Punta Estero. This is a diked area of the lagoon. Pickleweed, Alanofria, and other halophytes grow in the sands of the estero.
Ephedra along with sparse low atraplex and tumbleweed grow on the hills. The dunes are stabilized with Wild Buckwheat, Beavertail Cactus, Ice Plant, and many annual sunflowers. Only halophytes grow in this region. California Pepper Trees are planted around residences as ornamentals. Datilillo is planted around residences and gate houses which gives more of a tropical flavor to the environment. Annual grasses take advantage of the highway edges.
The avifauna of the mudflat near the mainland in the upper part of the estero consists of Dowagers, Godwit, Cattle Egrets, Western Gulls,

California Gulls, and Turkey Vultures. The birds dig for invertebrates, clams, etc. in the mudflats.

11   The road leaves the estero and goes toward Punta Banda.
The vegetation consists of the opportunistic Indian Tree Tobacco, Mango, trees and other ornamentals along the edge of the mudflat. The vegetation on the hills is typical of the chaparral flora and consists of Cheese Bush, Toyon, Wild Buckwheats, Black Mustards, Locoweed, Tamarisk, and Mission Cactus, Lombardi Poplars planted for windbreaks, Cattails, and Castor Beans.
Some of the roadcuts are in faulted and deformed intrusive dacite porphyry. This rock is part of a large metavolcanic mass that is the backbone of Punta Banda. For the next three kilometers the road traverses Pleistocene and upper Cretaceous rocks that have been faulted against and/or deposited on the metavolcanic older rocks along the north side of the point.

12   Toyon rounded trees Myoporum California Pepper Tree by clusters of houses.

12.5   The tourist village of La Jolla.

13.2   To the left rear is a view of the trace of the Agua Blanca Fault. The fault passes through the notch in the skyline and follows the base of the slope.

13.6   The small community on the right is El Rincon; it is a small fishing village with several tourist camps.

14.2   Cretaceous age rocks were first recognized and described in Baja California at this location. The road into the gully past the houses on the right leads to a small quay on the beach. The Cretaceous rocks are exposed in the sea cliffs along the beach near the quay and in road cuts for the next two kilometers.

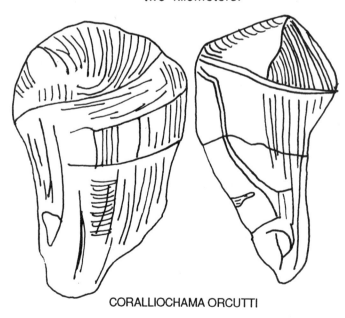

CORALLIOCHAMA ORCUTTI

Coralliochama orcutti: C.A. White (1885) described *Coralliochama* (aberrant clams) bearing rocks on Bahia Todos Santos. This genus is one of the most characteristic elements in the late Cretaceous near-shore faunas of Northwestern Baja California. Abundant accumulations of specimens, some with shells attached and partially abraded, can be seen in these sea cliffs along the north side of Punta Banda near the village of El Rincon. The upper Cretaceous beds at this locality are more highly deformed than at any other localities known in this region. This is probably due to their proximity to the Agua Blanca Fault which lies just offshore.

16.5   Rocks of the gray-green Alisitos Formation are exposed along the road.
The ground at this turn out is covered with Ice Plant
(*Mesembryanthemum sp.*) a leaf succulent naturalized from south Africa.
Ice Plant is commonly seen on sea cliffs, dunes, beaches, and sandy soils
as far south as central Baja.

17.8   The road crests a grade and briefly passes along the spine of Punta Banda.
The Parry Buckeye grows in arroyos and on hillsides.

18   The village of La Bufadora can be seen below the road to the left. Several
Pleistocene marine terraces are obvious along this segment of the point.
The vegetation on the terrace, which consists of Toyon, Wild Buckwheat,
Sumac, Chamise, Agave, Jojoba, Broom Baccharis, and Indian Tree
Tobacco, is growing alongside the road in the disturbed soils at the
pavement's edge.

20   This area of Punta Banda is composed of massive highly jointed
metamorphosed andesite porphyry. The blowhole is developed along a
large metamorphic joint.
The contact between the andesite and the rounded boulder conglomerates in
the Pleistocene terrace is exposed along the road.

21   **La Bufadora:** Trailer parks, campsites, cafes, and numerous small
curio shops are located on Punta Banda. These commercial establishments
have developed to serve the visitors who come to view the activities of the
world's largest blowhole.

> **THE LA BUFADORA BLOWHOLE** is reputed to be the largest
> blowhole in the world. Waves approaching the shore of Bahia Papalote
> trap air in a rocky cave on the northern shore of the bay and block the
> cave mouth. As the wave crest moves into the cave, it compresses the
> cave air until the release of pressure along cracks in the roof of the
> cave forces a plume of water skyward. The steepness of the wave front
> and the amount of water blocking the cave entrance determine the
> strength and height of each plume of water. If there are not many
> swells, the blowhole may not put on much of a show.
> Another attraction can be experienced by divers just offshore in the
> form of hot springs that have developed along the Agua Blanca Fault.
> Some divers have hard boiled eggs in the hot waters which rise out of
> the spring (*See* Km 18.5 of the Ensenada log).

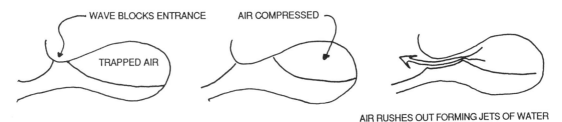

WAVE BLOCKS ENTRANCE   AIR COMPRESSED

TRAPPED AIR

AIR RUSHES OUT FORMING JETS OF WATER

Log 2 - Ensenada to San Quintin

From La Bufadora you return to the main highway at Km 22. You may turn right and continue to the south or return to Ensenada.

MANEADERO:

23   An immigration station is located at Maneadero, but it is not always open. Proof of U.S. citizenship may be required. Often only a certified copy of a birth certificate is acceptable, and a single-entry tourist visa must be filled out and stamped by immigration officials on duty. The process is simplified if you have already filled out the slip which may be obtained where you bought insurance or at the American Automobile Association. Be prepared for bureaucratic delays. The immigration "officers" often insist on rigid adherence to rules and routines. Be patient!

24   A coastal Pleistocene terrace is visible to the left above Maneadero.
There is a panoramic view to the north of the Miocene basalt mesas, Islas de Todos Santos, Bahia de Todos Santos, the point of Punta Banda, and the long spine of hills which comes down from Punta Banda along the Agua Blanca Fault Zone.
Notice the long straight nature of this spine, the flats along the spine, and the lines of vegetation. Near the middle of the spine and close to the highest point, there are a series of houses on a flat terrace. These houses sit directly on the Agua Blanca Fault Zone. Note the alluvial fans coming down from the fault zone. On either side of the houses there are offset streams which indicate right lateral movement. To the left is a notch in the hills through which the highway will eventually cross into the valley occupied by the Agua Blanca Fault Zone.

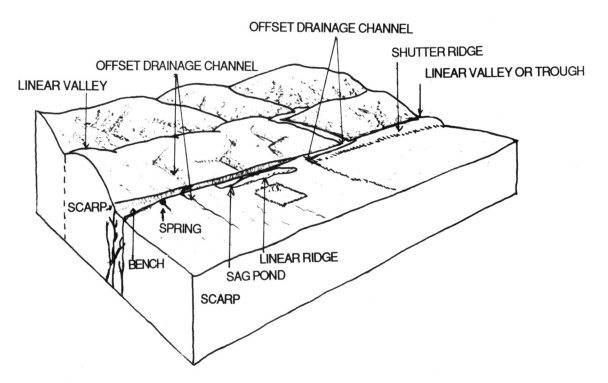

Fault zone topography. Typical landforms found along recently active strike-slip faults.
From: R.D. Borcherdt, ed. "Studies for Seismic Zonation of the San Francisco Bay Region. "U.S. Geological Survey Professional Paper 941-A:1975.

24   A brick making operation is located to the left of the highway. Bricks are manufactured from the adobe soils developed on the metavolcanic rocks of this region. For many kilometers the highway will follow canyons in the metavolcanic rocks of the Alisitos Formation.

> **Age of the metavolcanic strata:** There are numerous Cretaceous fossil dates along the peninsula south of the Agua Blanca Fault Zone and one Jurassic age date in Arroyo San Jose (Minch, 1969). North of the Agua Blanca Fault Zone there are no lower-upper Cretaceous fossils in the metavolcanic strata. The next fossiliferous rocks are in the San Diego area; they contain uppermost Jurassic fossils (Fife et. al., 1967). Between the Agua Blanca Fault Zone and San Diego County, there are no fossil or radiometric dates on the metavolcanic strata.

33   As the highway follows Canon las Animas, it more or less parallels the Agua Blanca Fault Zone which is located to the right. On the ridge above the highway are examples of shutter ridges, benches, vegetation lineaments, and offset streams which typically characterize a major fault zone.

39   Black-shouldered Kites (*Elanus caeruleus*) are commonly seen flying, hovering, and hunting along this stretch of highway.

Black-shouldered Kites are large falcon-shaped gray birds with notched white single black-barred tails. They may be seen flying, soaring, or hovering along the *Baja Highway* as they hunt small reptiles, rodents, and large insects.

40   The Agua Blanca Fault Zone runs diagonally across the field of view from the right rear to left forward and the middle part of the hills.

41   Camping at Urapan is available in the grove of scrub and live oak on the left.
The metavolcanic rocks outcroping here are intruded by a variety of granitic bodies and dikes.

45.3   The highway provides spectacular views of Valle Santo Tomas.
Between the sharp curve to the right at the top of the grade and a hairpin curve to the left (at Km. 46.1), numerous shears and crushed rock provide evidence of the Agua Blanca Fault Zone that crosses the highway near the top of the grade.

47.8   The graded road to the right leads to La Bocana and Punta China (26 kilometers) where the upper Cretaceous Alisitos Formation was first defined by Santillan and Barrera, 1930 for the rocks near Rancho Alisitos.

This graded road is the newer higher road that has been cut into the side of the hills to avoid the frequently flooded and washed out older roads of the valley bottom. A cement quarry on Punta China has been developed in the limestones of the Alisitos Formation.
There is a beautiful developed camping spot 5 kilometers down this road in the old Oaks and Sycamores at the old Mision Santo Tomas.

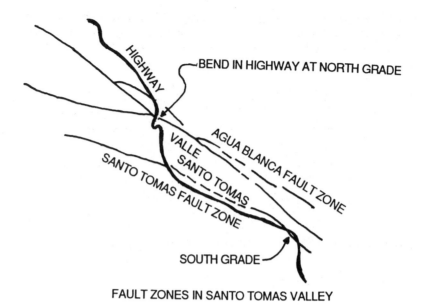

FAULT ZONES IN SANTO TOMAS VALLEY

50.5 The highway crosses the broad faultline valley of Valle Santo Tomas. The large river bed of the meandering Rio Santo Tomas usually contains only a small perennial stream except during periods of heavy precipitation when it may become a large raging river. The waters of this river probably originate as a series of freshwater springs from subsurface ground which rise upward through the crushed rock produced by movement along the Agua Blanca Fault Zone. A Riparian Woodland borders Rio Santo Tomas.

This small water source once supported the small Dominican Mision Santo Tomas and was the reason for the mission's location here. An expedition of Portola and Father Serra named this valley "Canada de San Francisco Solana". In June, 1794, Father Loriente founded a second mission, the Mission of Santo Tomas de Aquino, after abandoning the first mission which was located 5 kilometers further downstream closer to the Pacific Ocean. The ruins of the second mission are behind a house near Highway 1D. Take the new road or the dirt road on the north edge of town to find the first mission .
This old road down the valley eventually reaches Punta China and La Bocana over a rougher but more scenic route.

> **WHAT IS A RIPARIAN WOODLAND?:** Vegetational communities which grow along streams and other drainage ways are referred to as Riparian Woodlands. Since the climatic regime over much of Baja is an arid one, the local occurrence of permanent standing or running water has a dramatic influence on the composition and quantity of vegetation. Localities with permanent standing or running water are generally bordered by large deciduous trees, shrubs, and herbs which only grow on the banks of such water courses. Where river valleys are broad, the Riparian Woodland is correspondingly broad; at higher elevations where the water courses are narrow and the stream banks are steep, Riparian Woodlands may form a very narrow strip which is only a few meters wide.

51 **SANTO TOMAS:** The small village of Santo Tomas is located in the green fertile Valle Santo Tomas. This old agricultural community, which stretches all the way to the sea, dates back to mission times. It was the original site for the famous Santo Tomas Winery. However, the winery was eventually moved to Ensenada and today olives are the main crop of Santo Tomas. Today, the small village consists of a few clustered houses adjacent to the highway.

Log 2 - Ensenada to San Quintin

To the north and south of the valley the steep hills are densely covered by chaparral.
The El Palomar Pemex (Nova only), restaurant and store are worth a short visit. The restaurant is directly in the Santo Tomas Fault Zone. This fault forms the south side of the valley and the Agua Blanca Fault Zone forms the north.

> **Looking at Baja's faults:** Sit on the white rocks at the outside edge of the shaded parking area across from the gas tanks and look at the hills on the north side of the valley. On your left side to the north, the Agua Blanca Fault passes through the same low pass as the highway. The trace is marked by a series of benches about 1/3 of the way up the hills from the valley floor. These benches descend to the valley bottom at the major stream arroyo which is almost directly across the valley. They give way to a valley which parallels the main valley. To the right the fault follows the notch between the two low yellow-brown hills which are parallel to the axis of the valley, and behind the far right ridge finally passing out of view up the valley to the far right.

52   To the left (east) of Valle Santo Tomas are the Sierra El Encino Solo Mountains.

56   The single-story white house across the valley at the base of the hills on the left marks the site of a spring which is located on the main trace of the Agua Blanca Fault Zone.

57   Numerous small fans which mark a trace of the Santo Tomas Fault have developed at the base of the hills to the right. Due to relatively recent uplift along the faultline streams are cutting into the small fans.

60.1 The highway climbs the grade where roadcuts exhibit numerous sheer and crushed rock zones typical of the trace of a major fault zone. The turn-off to the left provides a good valley view.

61   The turnoff near this kilometer marking provides a good view of the Agua Blanca Fault Zone which extends through the valley to the north. There is a line of bushes and very small trees which cut across one of the points just above and to the right of the white ranch house on the opposite side of the valley. This vegetation line is replaced by the low notch to the west where the crushed rock of the fault zone was easily weathered.
The northern end of the Agua Blanca branches near here. The branches form the north and south sides of Punta Banda. Between these two branches a resistant sliver of metavolcanic rocks of the Alisitos Formation forms the spine and point of Punta Banda.
The streams and valleys in this area exhibit several Riparian Woodland species of Oaks, Willows, and California Sycamores, while the hillsides contain the typical chaparral vegetation represented by species of Brittle-Bush, Laurel Sumac, Broom Baccharis, Chamise, Wild Buckwheat, and Dodder or "Witches Hair" which grows densely in this area.

63   At the crest of the highway, there is a well-graded side road to the left which leads to a microwave tower on Cerro el Zacaton. This road crosses the Agua Blanca Fault Zone.
The mountains to the left of this winding highway are the Sierra Peralta.

68   The area to the left is Valle San Jacinto. The side road to the right is one of several which lead to Punta Cabras and Punta San Jose (to the northwest) and Erendira (to the southwest). Both of these areas have beautiful sea cliffs and pocket beaches.

> **SEA CLIFFS AND POCKET BEACHES:** There are many beautiful coves and sandy pocket beaches of Pleistocene terrace material which overly the Rosario Formation which is located in this area. They resemble the beautiful beaches at

39

La Jolla, California. Generally the sea cliffs in this area are formed on the Cretaceous Rosario or Alisitos formations. The pocket beaches form when the sea cliff is capped by softer marine terrace deposits. The fractures in the harder cliffs are enlarged by the waves. This leaves an amphitheater and a pocket beach, which usually consists of coarse sand and gravel.

69   Stop near this kilometer sign and look to the left rear. A series of light-colored exposures run along a bench in the middle of the skyline ridge. These exposures are the crushed rocks which mark the trace of the Agua Blanca Fault Zone.

73.3 The metamorphosed volcanic and sedimentary rocks of the Alisitos Formation are especially well exposed in the roadcuts along this arroyo. Some of the small holes in the rock are the impressions of the shells of gastropods which have been leached from the rock.

75.5 The resistant ridge, which crosses the highway at this bend near La Angastura, is formed by a series of light-gray limestones within the Alisitos Formation. These limestones are quarried at Punta China by a commercial concern - Cementos California. The limestones, which are low in magnesium and aluminum, outcrop in a belt which extends southeast from Punta China. The large reserves and their proximity to deep-water shipping facilities make it an important source of limestone for cement along the Pacific coast of Mexico.

78.5 A paved road marked "Erendira" leads south 6.6 kilometers down Canon Guadalupe and Canon San Isidro to Arroyo San Vicente, and then turns to the west to the small coastal agricultural community of Erendira and Bocana Erendira. The Rio San Vicente, which originates to the northeast in Canon Agua Caliente, runs through Canon San Isidro.
      Surf fishing from the rocky or sandy beaches along this section of the coast is especially good during the fall or winter, as large schools of yellowtail, white seabass, and barracuda move into Bocana Erendira. Commercial fishing for rock cod and diving for sea urchins, abalone, and seaweed is common in this region.
      About 100 meters down the paved road toward Erendira a dirt road to the right leads to the northwest over the Alisitos metavolcanics to the ocean at Punta Cabras and to the south end of Punta San Jose. This road eventually connects with the road which leads to Enrendira.

80.5 The highway crests over a ridge with a panoramic view of the San Vicente plain. This plain is extensively dry farmed for wheat and barley. Grapes, olives, and chiles are also grown here which makes San Vicente one of Baja's important agricultural communities. Table vegetables which are consumed locally and exported to the U.S.A. are grown here.
      Near San Vicente the metavolcanic rocks of the Alisitos Formation change to tonalite. Much of the San Vicente plain is underlain by tonalite and mixed metamorphic and plutonic rocks.
      Mision San Vicente Ferrer is located on the right before the bridge. Check the telephone wires along the highway for a small falcon, the American Kestrel (*Falco sparverius*).

89   The village of San Vicente originated in 1780 as a Dominican mission site, but it fell into obscurity until the 1940's. Rejuvenation of the community was the direct result of agricultural development in the area.
      Services at San Vicente include two Pemex stations (Nova only), stores, two bakeries, a hotel, and auto parts stores.

93 For the next kilometer the low linear mounds of light-colored boulders form good examples of the weathered remnants of resistant granitic dikes which have filled shrinkage cracks near the top of the batholith. The surrounding country rock (tonalite) is less resistant and more easily weathered and eroded. This leaves the ridges of dike rock.

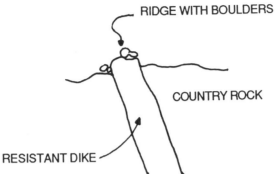

102 This flat plain is called Llano Colorado (red plain) because of the weathered red Alisitos volcanics. The skyline view to the east is the metavolcanic foothills.
Valle Llano Colorado supports some of the most extensive grape vineyards and olive orchards in Baja.

A DRUPE: Nearly 40 species of evergreen trees and shrubs of the olive family (*F. Oleaceae*) are grown world-wide for their edible drupes - the fleshy single seeded fruits of the olive (*Olea europaea*) plant. Baja has many olive orchards. The olives are cured and consumed or sold locally and exported.

A BERRY: Some members of the grape family (*F. Vitaceae*) are edible and are good thirst-quenchers. Numerous wild and cultivated species of the genus *Vitus* occur in both Alta and Baja California. Some grape species have been cultivated since they were first introduced into Baja in 1732. Botanically, the grape is a berry, a many seeded fleshy fruit, that has been used to make wine, grape juice, jelly, and preserves, and is also eaten whole. Wild species of native non-cultivated grapes occur in Riparian and Oak Woodland habitats throughout the peninsula.

107.5 The highway crosses an arroyo with dense Saltbush plants of the genus *Atriplex*.

Saltbush is a halophyte which has modifications which enable it to grow in very salty dry soils. Research by one of the authors of this guide (Tom Leslie) has shown that the seeds of the Saltbush contain chemical growth inhibitors which dissolve when exposed to sufficient amounts of water, which could be provided during a good rainfall. These inhibitors ensure that the seeds will only germinate when sufficient quantities of water are available to allow the germinating seedling to complete its life cycle.
Saltbush can grow in soils with a high salt content. The salt is absorbed into the plant through its roots. The leaves can be used as a flavoring for foods, and the parched ground seeds make a tasty coarse meal or fine flour.

109 Notice the granitic dikes along the grade.

115 The highway descends through granodiorite and gabbro outcrops into Arroyo Seco where the highway turns toward the sea to follow the arroyo. Metavolcanic rocks of the Alisitos Formation are exposed along the upper Arroyo Seco.

This point was the end of the paved highway for many years. Until the completion of Highway 1 the sign read **"AL FIN DEL PAVMIENTO"** (to the end of the pavement). The roadbed was prepared all the way to San Quintin but was not paved. "World class" potholes were encountered on this graded segment. Most of the traffic made new "roads" alongside the graded segment in an attempt to avoid the potholes and ruts.

116.5 This is Ejido Alfredo Bonfil.

WHAT IS AN EJIDO?: The term "ejido" (ay-hee'-dough) refers to agricultural land held in common by the members of the "ejido", which cannot be sold. The concept of an "ejido" dates back to the end of the 19th century. It was of great importance during the Revolution of 1910-1918 to secure land for the peasants who had none. It became a political reality in 1970 when President Lazaro Cardenas distributed 45 million acres to "ejidos". To form an "ejido" a group of farmers petition the government for land that is currently not in use. Under certain conditions the government grants them the land, helps with the purchase of equipment, brings in irrigation, and provides seeds, etc., through government supported loans drawn on the Banco Rural. The debt to the government is repaid from crop proceeds. Some of the crops will be bought by a government food distribution corporation called "CONASUPO" which has first right of refusal on the "ejido's" crops and guarantees a fair price; the remainder of the produce can be sold on the open market. Look for "CONASUPO" stores as you pass through Baja's villages, towns, and cities. Some "ejidos" are more prosperous than others. This is often due to the skills and knowledge of their "comisario," the man elected by majority vote as the leader of the "ejido". (He may also serve as judge and justice in the absence of civil authority.)

118.5 This side road leads to the southeast to the village of San Telmo and also goes to the east into the high San Pedro Martir Mountains. However, the best road into San Pedro Martir is at Km 140.9.

THE TWO SIERRAS OF NORTHERN BAJA: In northern Baja California two major granitic mountain ranges dominate the view to the east. They are the Sierra Juarez and the Sierra San Pedro Martir. Only the Sierra San Pedro Martir is apparent to the *Baja Highway* traveler. These ranges extend 200 kilometers to the south from the International Border. Both ranges average 1,500-2,800 meters or more in elevation. Their western slopes are covered with coniferous forests which receive 50 centimeters of precipitation per year on the average. The dominant species of the coniferous canopy are Jeffrey Pine, Incense Cedar, Sugar Pine, Lodgepole Pine, and Colter Pine. At lower elevations Quaking Aspen and Canyon Oak frequently occur. The understory of the forest consists of shade-tolerant annuals, grasses and widely spaced shrubs.
At elevations below 1,000 meters the western slopes of these two ranges are clothed by true chaparral and coastal sage scrub. The drier eastern slopes of these ranges are sparsely covered with vegetation which is characteristic of Desierto San Felipe, a southern extension of the Colorado Desert of the United States. (The vegetation of Desierto San Felipe will be discussed in the section of the guide from the International Border at Mexicali to San Felipe, Km 108).
At the southern end of the Sierra San Pedro Martir the flora is in transition between the chaparral vegetational area of the Californian phytogeographic region and the desert flora of the southern Sonoran Central Desert phytogeographic region. As a result, the southern slopes are covered with a

mixture of northern chaparral species and the desert vegetation of Desierto El Vizcaino. This region of overlapping floras is called an *ecotone* and extends approximately 160 kilometers from Valle Santo Tomas, to as far south as El Rosario.

WHAT IS AN ECOTONE?: On the Pacific west coast of the Californias the chaparral shrub community ends in the area of Valle Santo Tomas. The 160 kilometers from Valle Santo Tomas to El Rosario represents an ecotone. This ecotone is an area of transition separating the northern chaparral community from the southern Central Desert Region. This zone contains mixed chaparral and desert flora which grade into one another at the respective ends.

123.5 There is a bakery in the brown house on the right. They usually bake for the evening meal, so the selection in the early morning is often limited. The "beehive" oven (horno) is visible from the back of the building.

124 The hill to the left is Cerro Colorado.

126 This Gas Station and restaurant was once run by Wilmont Bradley, a Baja pioneer who died of cancer. He built the medical clinic on the hill. For many years this clinic was the local center for the Flying Samaritans. A group of doctors still fly into Mexico on weekends to set up clinics here which provide medical care that is often otherwise unavailable.
The gravity-fed glass gas pump seen here is still in use. In the old days you were lucky to even find a gas pump.

126.4 The highway crosses Arroyo Seco. The side road to the right just before the bend in the highway leads to Johnson Ranch and San Antonio del Mar which is located on a beautiful sandy beach.

126.6 The highway passes through the village of Punta Colonet.

128 Look to the right rear for a view of Punta Colonet. This point was named after an English sea captain who for some unknown reason ran his ship aground on this treacherous coast. The survivors walked all the way to Ensenada.

130 The highway dips into a small steep gorge whose rocky cliffs are formed by the weathering of the Alisitos Formation.

131.5 The low range of hills in the distance, to the west of the highway, are stabilized coastal dunes.

CAUTION: Be careful of cattle which feed along the pavement edges on this stretch of the highway and sometimes wander onto the road. Be careful of Mexican drivers especially if you drive at night. They may use only their parking lights or may drive without any lights at all!

132 The red clay soils in this area are derived from the iron-rich Alisitos Formation.
Llanos de San Quintin is extensively dry farmed. It produces several commercially important crops since irrigation is becoming more common. San Quintin serves as the market center for the agricultural products of this region. Many of California's winter vegetables, especially early and late tomatoes and strawberries, are grown on this plain. Because the growing season is slightly earlier and slightly later than the United States, produce can command high prices.

TOMATO (*Lycopersicon sp.*) is native to South America and is widely cultivated in Baja for its edible, fleshy, usually red fruit. The name "tomato" is a variant of the earlier Spanish word "tomate" which originated from the Nahuatl Indian tribe word "tomatl". Tomatoes are one of the principal commercial fruits of a large family (Solanaceae) of New World Plants which includes, potatoes, peppers, egg plants, and tobacco.

133   The highway begins to follow a flat 30 meter terrace which is often called Llanos de San Quintin. From here all the way to San Quintin the highway follows this marine terrace. To the left are the foothills of the Alisitos Formation. The shoreline of the ocean during the Cretaceous, when the terrace rocks were deposited, and during the late Pleistocene, when this terrace was cut, is roughly equivalent to the edge of the terrace and the low foothills to the left.

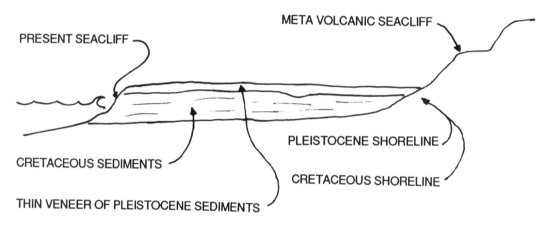

140.9 The road to the left leads to the small village of San Telmo (10 Km), the Meling Ranch (50 Km), Mike's Sky Rancho, the pine groves of San Pedro Martir National Park, and the new National Observatory (87 Km). Gas is not available along this route.

Plutonic rocks of the Peninsular Ranges: Reconnaissance mapping in the Peninsular Ranges has resulted in the identification of 387 plutons over 1 km in diameter which cover 28,000 square miles. These plutons are smaller on the western edge of the range; the axial portions of the range are occupied by a relatively small number of much larger bodies. Most of the plutons are circular in outline and many show concentric structures. Granite and gabbro form the smallest plutons, while most of the largest plutons are composed of tonalite. These plutons yield isotopic age dates of 95 to 119 million years before present (MYBP) K/Ar dates of 75 to 85 MYBP. in the western edge and 60's on the eastern edge yield cooling dates or ages of metamorphism (Gastil *et.al.*, 1972).
The rocks on the road to the Meling Ranch and the high San Pedro Martir exhibit a cross section of the pre-batholithic and batholithic rocks of the Peninsular Ranges. The road begins in the metavolcanic and metasedimentary of the Alisitos formation. This area is stratigraphically the lowest strata in the type area of the Alisitos Formation. A few kilometers up the road there are the strata which contain Albian fossils (Allison, 1974). Nearer the ranch these rocks are progressively more metamorphosed until they become schists and gneisses. At the ranch a pluton of granite rocks is exposed. As the road climbs to the observatory, it enters an area of extensive granitic rocks.

Log 2 - Ensenada to San Quintin

The transitional ecotonal vegetation of this region consists of a mixture of the following chaparral, coastal scrub and desert plant species: Candelabra Cactus, Wild Buckwheat, Burrobrush, Burr Sage, Agave, Jumping Cholla, Brittle-Bush, Beavertail Cactus, annual composites, and introduced Russian Thistle. The small flower stalks of the thistle (*Cirsium sp.*) can be eaten, since they are wild artichokes.

141.3 A road metal quarry has been developed in the Alisitos Formations on the left.

149.5 Mesa de San Jacinto is the flat-topped feature to the left (southwest).

151.5 As the highway climbs through more upper Cretaceous Rosario Formation outcrops, notice the road metal quarries on the right. Pliocene fossils have been collected from the Pliocene Cantil Costero Formation in the second and third quarry at Km 155.5.
This area is an uplifted fault block called a "horst". Erosion of the uplifted area causes the exposure of the sediments.

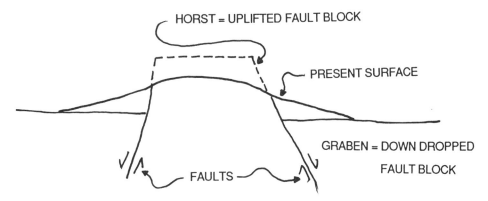

153 Some of the hummocky topography on the horst is probably due to stabilized coastal dunes. These dunes are much more obvious on the next rise to the south.

154.3 Pliocene fossil localities are located in the road metal quarries.

156 The highway begins a descent and passes first through metavolcanic outcrops and then through Pliocene outcrops on the southern side of the horst.

157 Camalu is a very small settlement which is located along the highway. Its services include a Pemex station (Nova only), a bus station, phone, medical clinic, auto parts store, restaurant, and other stores. You may be stopped by the Cruz Rojo (Red Cross) as you drive in this area. You can refuse to contribute.

165 Some of the roadcuts in this area are composed of dunal sands. The rolling hills in this area are a stabilized coastal dune field that is extensively plowed and planted with various agricultural crops. This could lead to the destruction of the fragile dune environment and to the development of "dust bowl" conditions if the plowing and planting is not done properly and at the correct time.

> **DUNE STABILIZATION:** The stabilized dune systems of Baja provide a delicate environment that is home to numerous plants and animals. Farmers take advantage of the retained moisture to plow the dunes and grow crops. However, plowing eliminates the vegetation that stabilized the sand, and winds may blow away the dune. Dry farming and the environment provided by stabilized dunes for the support of plants and animals may be eliminated. For these reasons care

Log 2 - Ensenada to San Quintin

should be taken in developing stabilized dunes for agricultural purposes. It has been noted that there is an increased amount of sand which blows across the road. This is due to the disruption of dune stabilization caused by careless farming practices.

169   This turnoff leads east 4 kilometers to the ruins of Mision Santo Domingo. This mission has been abandoned since 1885.

169.8   The highway crosses Arroyo Santa Domingo. This bridge was washed out in early 1978. It was rebuilt and a second one was added to accommodate future flood waters.
The hills to the left of the highway are composed of metavolcanic and metasedimentary strata of the Alisitos Formation.

170.2   Stores, restaurants, a hospital, a gas station, banks, a "panaderia" (bakery), and a propane storage area can be found in the small town of Vicente Guerrero.

176   From the crest of this hill there is an excellent view of the San Quintin volcanic field and of the surf which breaks on the beach. The most northern volcanic cinder cone is Isla San Martin, a small island located several kilometers offshore.

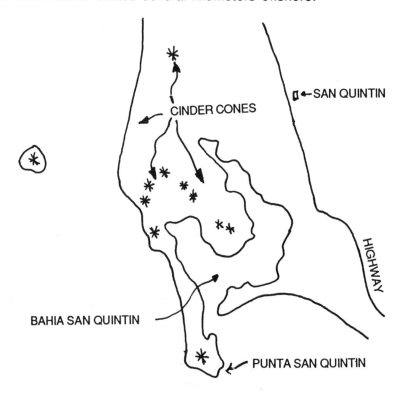

San Quintin Volcanic Field: Approximately ten small cones of the San Quintin volcanic field are visible from the highway. To the left of the main group of cones is the low silhouette of Isla San Martin, another volcanic cone visible 4 kilometers offshore. Woodford (1928) was the first to describe the San Quintin volcanic field in great detail. This field is a series of olivine basalt cinder cones and flows of Pleistocene to Recent age. Locally, marine terraces are developed on the lava flows. This indicates that the eruptions predate the falling sea level and the 125,000 year old Sagamonian Terrace.

Log 2 - Ensenada to San Quintin

As the highway descends to traverse Llanos de San Quintin, the shallow Laguna Figueroa is visible behind the dunes along the coast of Bahia San Ramon. This area has been exploited for salt since mission times.

178   Empaque ABC is located here.
The San Quintin plain is extensively dry farmed and irrigated from groundwater wells. The over usage of the groundwater near the bay has resulted in salt water intrusion; the salty groundwater under the bay pushes inland (intrudes) and displaces the fresh water which is withdrawn. This area is extensively used by seed companies. It also produces many early season tomatoes, strawberries, and other commercially important table vegetables which are exported to Alta California, U.S.A.

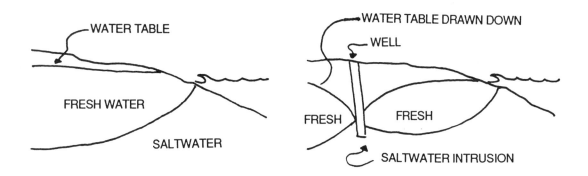

183.1 The authors were involved in an automobile accident near the store. All of our premiums on Mexican auto insurance were returned when we slid into a Mexican truck which made an illegal left turn. Be sure you have Mexican Insurance!

187   Along this segment of the road the hills to the left consist of the Cretaceous Rosario Formation

189.5 At **San Quintin** a Pemex station (Extra) and stores with adequate supplies, a good auto parts store, mechanics, hotels and banks, and an Ice House (on the left of the highway) are available.

191   The bridge at this kilometer marks the south end of Ciudad San Quintin.
The hill to the right is Volcan Media Luna (half-moon) and is one of the basaltic cinder cones of the San Quintin Volcanic Field.

193   Lazaro Cardenas is the site of a large military base. There is a phone in Lazaro Cardenas across from the military base; there are stores and a gas station here.

193.8 This turnoff leads west to the Old Mill (Molino Viejo) and Ernesto's Motel on Bahia San Quintin.

> **Old Mill (Molino Viejo)** About 1885 an American company tried to settle the area. They built a flour mill and pier, and tried dry farming the area for wheat. Today modern drip methods and deep wells are providing a thriving agricultural industry.

196   The kilometer markers along the side of the road at Km. 196 change to 0.

Log 3 - San Quintin to Bahia de Los Angeles Turnoff
[285 kms = 177 miles]

San Quintin to El Rosario - *South of San Quintin the Baja Highway skirts a dune area and follows the low terrace along the base of the high mesa of Cretaceous marine overlain by Pliocene marine sediments. The high mesas become much wider in this area following a relatively straight Cretaceous shoreline. The steep metavolcanic hills are out of view to the east.*

At Consuelo the Baja Highway leaves the coastal terrace and climbs up a valley through Cretaceous hills to the high mesa surface with the metavolcanic hills in the far distance to the east.

The Baja Highway briefly crosses the mesa before descending a steep canyon through the Rosario Formation to El Rosario Valley and El Rosario.

El Rosario to Catavina - *This stretch of the Baja Highway travels almost directly east. From El Rosario the Baja Highway turns inland up the Rio Rosario on a river terrace, crosses the river, and turns inland through rolling hills of Cretaceous marine sediments. The Baja Highway climbs up on the rolling mesas with distant views of the resistant Paleocene mesas to the south and the high granitic San Pedro Martir to the north. The Baja Highway crosses the Cretaceous shoreline into the rolling metavolcanic foothills and descends a grade into a series of gentle valleys developed in the steep hills of metavolcanic and granitic rocks. The Baja Highway then follows a broad strike valley with steep ridges of metavolcanic rocks on both sides of the valley.*

After El Progresso and a low pass in the metavolcanics the Baja Highway begins to traverse the San Agustin Plain on lakebed sediments. The steep metavolcanic hills to the left formed the shoreline of the lake. The Baja Highway follows a flat to rolling surface developed on fluvial conglomerates with higher hills of granitic and metavolcanic rocks to the south. To the north is the extensive flat area of the San Agustin Plain which is broken by isolated low metavolcanic hills in the western part and volcanic mesas in the eastern part.

After passing between several volcanic mesas the Baja Highway enters the rolling hills of a picturesque bouldery tonalite area, finally descending through Arroyo Catavina to Catavina.

Catavina to L. A. Bay Turnoff - *The Baja Highway crosses a palm studded arroyo to Rancho Santa Ynez then turns south through a rolling area of bouldery tonalite. Along the route the volcanic mesas become more numerous until, at Jaraguay, the Baja Highway climbs to cross an extensive undulating basalt plateau dotted with cinder cones. The bouldery hill of Pedregoso rises through this plateau. The Baja Highway then skirts the edge of the plateau in mixed granitic and metamorphic rocks and drops into the flat alluvial valley and lakebed of Laguna Chapala with dunes at the south edge of the lakebed.*

After a brief climb into a low pass in the steep tonalite hills the Baja Highway crosses the Peninsular Divide with views of a wide rolling valley of the spectacular rugged Sierra de la Asamblea.

The Baja Highway drops into the alluviated valley through tonalite and then Miocene fluvial sediments to the granodiorite hill of Cerrito Blanco.

After again passing over a very gentle Penninsular Divide, in alluvium, the Baja Highway begins to descend the Arroyo Leon drainage through the Miocene fluvial sediments to the junction with the highway to Los Angeles Bay.

0 The kilometer markers along the side of the road at Km. 196 change to 0.

2 Look and listen closely for Western Meadowlarks (*Sturnella neglecta*) on the fences along the highway.

The **Western Meadowlark** belongs to the same family as blackbirds and orioles (F. Emberizidae) which breed in summer in the northeastern part of Baja and winter throughout the entire peninsula where they are commonly seen and heard in fields and on fences. Physically, the Western Meadowlark is a heavy-bodied medium-sized bird. The most distinctive identifying field characteristic is a black "V" on its bright yellow breast. This bird cannot be confused with any other bird in Baja because of this breast marking. The voice of the Western Meadowlark is a rich loud and bubbling whistled song that suddenly interrupts the silence of Baja's desert landscape. The Mexicans know this bird as "Sabanero".

3.9 This turnoff is the best road to take to the Old Mill (Molino Viejo).

5 The highway takes a wide swing to the left to cross the arroyo over a high new bridge near the hills. The hills to the left which form the low bluffs, are part of the Rosario Formation and are overlain locally by the Pliocene Cantil Costero Formation. The San Quintin volcanic field is visible to the right (*See* Km 20.5).

> **WASHOUTS:** In the past the main road went straight ahead through the wash at this location. After repeated washouts most of the traffic followed an easier route which crossed the wash at the base of the hills near Consuelo. When the highway was finally paved in the early 1970's, it once again went directly across the wash. It was washed out numerous times and was finally permanently located nearer the hills.

8 The highway approaches the base of the Rosario sea cliffs where it roughly parallels an ancient shoreline. The highway is built just above what would have been the old shoreline when the Llanos de San Quintin was cut as a marine terrace.

> **CHANGING SHORELINES:** South of Colonet the Cretaceous and Pleistocene shorelines correspond. The metavolcanic hills at the edge of the terrace formed both the Cretaceous and Pleistocene shorelines. South of San Quintin the edge of the low terrace represents only the Pleistocene shoreline. The Cretaceous shoreline has undergone a greater amount of uplift and is on the level of the upper terrace. A climb onto this terrace will yield a view to the east of the Cretaceous shoreline which is fringed by the same metavolcanic hills that are seen to the north.

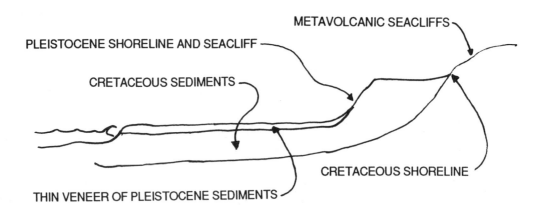

PLEISTOCENE SHORELINE AND SEACLIFF

METAVOLCANIC SEACLIFFS

CRETACEOUS SEDIMENTS

CRETACEOUS SHORELINE

THIN VENEER OF PLEISTOCENE SEDIMENTS

8.5   The highway crosses a large arroyo by a high well-built bridge. This used to be the small town of Consuelo. There was a restaurant here, and it was the end of the bus line before the transpeninsular highway was paved.

        If you want to see the outcrops of the Rosario Formation close to the highway, park on the left just before the bridge and walk into the road metal quarry about 100 meters from the highway. There are well exposed red beds and mudstones of the Rosario Formation at this location.

10   The Tamarisk-lined side road to the right leads to Hotel La Pinta and Cielito Lindo Motel and RV Park. Juanita, who runs the Cielito Lindo Motel, is one of the best hostesses that the authors have found in Baja. Some say that they have never had a better meal than her rock crab claw plate. For many years this hotel was the site of an American movie colony retreat which was owned by a cinematographer. Among the more notable frequent guests were Jimmy Stewart, Henry Fonda, and John Wayne who actually paneled one of the rooms.

        TAMARISK TREES (SALT CEDAR): The side road which leads to Hotel La Pinta crosses a by-passed segment of the old road. It travels down a very picturesque lane which is arched by two parallel wind rows of old Tamarisk trees which were planted to form fast-growing wind breaks for the agricultural areas of this region. A ride down this road at night is a little eerie. Tamarisk Trees (*Tamarix pentendra*) were introduced into North America in the early 1800's for use as decorative plants and the formation of fast-growing windbreaks. This plant spreads rapidly; a single plant may produce 600,000 seeds per year. Its leaves secrete salt -- an adaptation to reduce the tree's salt content which allows it to live in saline soils. Surface soils under the tree accumulate salt which inhibits the germination and establishment of non-salt-tolerant natives. The large quantities of duff (litter) produced by the Tamarisk encourages fire. They can resprout from their own roots following a fire, while many native species cannot. All these factors aid in the spread of the Tamarisk and reduce the numbers and influence of native species.

        Soils inhabited by Tamarisk soon become arid, since each tree transpires hundreds of gallons of water daily from the soil. This further reduces the numbers of native species.

        BEACH DUNES: At Cielito Lindo the beach dunes are migrating to the south along the surface of the beach. They are approximately 4-6 feet high and continually migrate which exposes material that was covered earlier. During high tides the dunes are often wave-leveled; this forms a gently rolling surface. As the beach dries, the sand again forms migrating dunes.

WARM SANDY BEACHES AND HIGH TIDES: The warm sandy beaches along Bahia Santa Maria and Cielito Lindo RV Park are some of the finest in Baja. They are very wide and flat and are covered with sand dollars and Pismo clam shells.
At low tide the live sand dollars form interesting and unusual patterns as they move their small spines to burrow into the sand. Good clamming is available here -- as evidenced by the large numbers of opened clam shells which litter the beach.
There are several places where you can cross the dunes and drive on the beach for kilometers. This area is very close to sea level and is a supra tidal area which is inundated by sea water during high tides and storms.
Hotel La Pinta used to have a swimming pool and a sea wall with a downstairs bar and restaurant. High tides and tropical storms in 1976 put three feet of water into the lower story of the hotel and filled the pool. The sea wall is gone and the dunes are encroaching upon the area. However, the hotel is still open even though its lower floors are often flooded during storms.
The brackish water marsh which surrounds the Hotel La Pinta has expanded greatly in the last 10 years. At one time a private duck hunting/gun club flourished in this area. Coots, Cormorants, California Gulls, Western Gulls, ducks, and several species of Grebes are commonly seen in or near the marsh.
The marsh vegetation consists of salt-tolerant halophytic plants such as Sand Verbena and the many branched, jointed stemmed, succulent Pickleweed (*Salicornia pacifica*). This salty plant is edible in salads and can be boiled and used as a pickling mix.

17   The hills of the Pleistocene shoreline converge with the road as the low terrace narrows and disappears under a dune field.

18.5   The highway passes Rancho Las Parritas on the right and climbs onto the Socorro Sand Dunes. These dunes originated from the sand which was blown from the beaches near Cielito Lindo and Bahia San Quintin. When the migrating dunes reach the curve in the coastline on the east, they are blown inland.

20.5   At the crest of the first small hill there is a sweeping view to the rear of the San Quintin volcanic field and the flat Llanos de San Quintin with its extensive fields of agricultural crops.

THE HIGHWAY EDGE EFFECT: Along the roadside in the soils which were disturbed during the construction of the highway, there are several species of mesic opportunistic plant species. The most obvious are large yellow sunflowers, Jojoba, gray *Atriplex*, Burro Weed and several species of small herbaceous annuals. These opportunists are not seen growing far from the highway.
In the desert regions of Baja the dominant vegetation consists of plant species adapted to long hot dry summers. Dry adapted desert species which require little water are known as xeric plants. (The word xerox means dry and has been used commercially to refer to dry copies produced by Xerox machines as opposed to the wet copies produced by older mimeograph equipment). In a region as rigorous as the Californian and Central Desert Regions of Baja, microclimates become particularly important. Any fortuitous or fortunate circumstance which provide habitats a little less xeric, where moisture remains somewhat longer than in

more open environments, favors the growth of opportunistic vegetation. Highway pavement edges are classic examples. Concentrations of taller greener and more mesic plants flourish along the pavement edges because additional moisture needed to support more mesic species which are not adapted to the dry desert, is available along the edge of the highway.

21 The plants commonly seen on the stabilized sand dunes are *Ephedra*, annual grasses, composites, Bursage, Burro Weed, Jojoba, Ice Plant, and several species of cacti. The dune vegetation visible here is usually less than one meter tall and is fairly dense.

In the old days crossing the dunes was very torturous and treacherous. Shifting sands across the road made it very difficult for a 2-wheel drive vehicle. Loads of cobblestones were brought into the area in an attempt to improve these conditions. However, this resulted in a jolting and jarring drive over the cobblestoned road. Accidentally driving off the cobbles onto the smooth sand meant getting stuck.

The view across the dune field shows rows of stabilized longitudinal dunes with unstabilized dunes closer to the beach and the San Quintin volcanic field to the rear in the distance.

SAND DUNES IN BAJA: THEIR FORMATION, MOVEMENT, STABILIZATION, AND DISTURBANCE: In the deserts of Baja wind often heaps sand particles into mounds and ridges called "dunas" (dunes). They move slowly in the direction of the wind. In Baja dunes are found wherever there are sand grains and where the wind direction is fairly constant. All dunes result from local interruptions in the general wind-flow patterns. When the prevailing wind is obstructed by rocks and plants, it is forced to drop its load of sand grains. A dune or series of dunes build. Once they are formed dunes migrate with the prevailing wind. Sand is transported from windward to leeward where it gathers at the dune foot and constantly encroaches on new territory. However, not all dunes travel. Where winds seasonally reverse or are multidirectional, they tend to remain stationary. Vegetation often helps to stabilize smaller dunes, particularly those that have developed around an embedded plant.

Although a sand dune looks like an inhospitable dry environment, it supports a great many trees such as Mesquite, Tamarisk, and Catclaw Acacia; bushes such as Four-winged Saltbush, Creosote Bush, Desert Buckwheat, Golden Bush, and Mormon Tea; and grasses such as Ricegrass and Big Galleta. A number of annuals carpet the dunes during rainy parts of the year. Some of the most commonly seen annuals on dunes in Baja are the Sand Verbena, Evening Primose, and many species of composites. These trees, bushes, grasses and seasonal annuals enable the dunes to remain where they are by stabilizing the sand with their branches and roots. Although dunes may look dry, they are not. Almost all precipitation that falls on the dunes soaks in and very little runs off. Though the surface dries quickly which gives the impression that the interior is moistureless, water remains in the lower levels of the dunes long after the regions surrounding the dunes are dry. This provides moisture for lush plant growth.

The dune vegetation provides shelter, food, and protection for numerous animals which include insects, centipedes, scorpions, birds, lizards, rodents, rabbits, gophers, and ground squirrels. The stabilized dune systems of Baja provide a delicate environment that is home to numerous plants and animals. Mexican farmers often plow the dunes to take advantage of the retained moisture to grow crops. This disturbs and often destroys a highly productive habitat.

Log 3 - San Quintin to L.A. Bay Turnoff

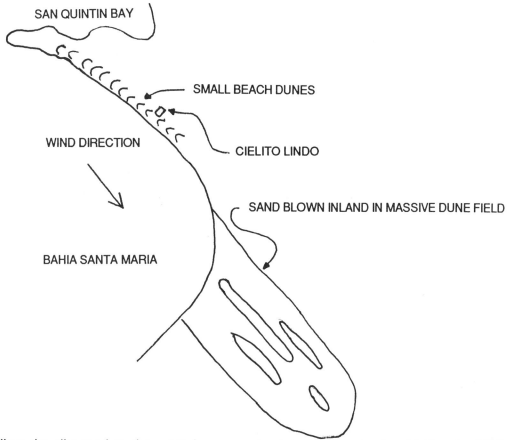

23.5 Follow the dirt road to the west for approximately 1 kilometer to old Rancho El Socorro and to Pacific beaches with dry campsites and pit toilets.

24 This little used side road leads toward the east, up Arroyo el Socorro, and into a very remote part of the high country of South San Pedro Martir, and to Rancho Nuevo and beyond. There are numerous abandoned mines and small ranchos in this area.
The highway continues to the south over a Pleistocene marine terrace cut into the Cretaceous Rosario Formation. The Cretaceous shoreline is now several kilometers inland. It will be crossed again near Km 80 south of El Rosario. The hills to the left consist of Rosario Formation mudstones in the lower part and are overlain by Paleocene Sepultura Formation.

> **THIS AREA LOOKS BURNED-OUT!:** Due to the dry harsh nature of the caliche soil (*See* Km 152.5 about Caliche) the vegetation along this stretch of the highway looks as though it has been burned. However, there are quite a few different kinds of plants growing here. Purple Bush is the dominant plant cover of the flats. There are a few interspersed specimens of Desert Thorn, Velvet Cactus and Bursage. Tamarisk is the dark-green plant of the wash bottoms, and patches of red-colored Ice plant and young Brittle-Bush grow in the disturbed soils at the pavement's edge.

29 The small hill to the right on the sea cliff is an old stabilized dune which was reactivated by the erosive action of the sea as the vegetation was removed. This process is still in progress. Other dunes such as this can be seen at kilometers 36.5 and 41. The sea is cutting into the base of the sand dune which demonstrates that there has been regression of the sea cliff since the formation of the dune.
There are a number of roads in this area that lead to the sea cliffs a few hundred meters to the west. The beaches here are quite gravelly, but some of them provide good camping.

35   This good road leads down the arroyo to the beach.
Dead *Agave* flowering stalks protrude above the low vegetation like wispy ghosts on the surrounding hills.

40   The Cantil Costero Formation was named for the exposures of marine Pliocene rocks which cap the mesas to the left of the highway. Distinct wave-cut terraces seen in this area were cut by the sea over a period of time. The highest terrace is developed on the Cantil Costero Formation (Late Pliocene). The Pliocene shoreline occupied nearly the same position as the present shoreline but has been tectonically uplifted approximately 100 meters since it was formed. The cutting of the marine terrace into the Cantil Costero Formation during the Pleistocene has exposed the old shoreline. The lower terrace, where the highway is constructed, corresponds with the Sagamonian high sea level stage approximately 125,000 years ago. The large gray blocks on the slope to the left are fossiliferous conglomeratic limestone from the Cantil Costero Formation. In many places slightly above the limestone are fossils which include specimens of the large barnacle *Balinas tintinabulum*, which may be 15 centimeters tall. A commercial operation has removed most of these barnacles to be sold in shell shops.
Along the seashore a pair of stabilized dunes have been cut by the sea. The southernmost dune is still partially stabilized.

41.5   The highway turns inland at El Consuelo, and follows the bottom of a deep arroyo. It climbs Canada San Quintin through the subdued hills of the Rosario Formation to the top of the mesa.
This side road leads down Arroyo Los Troncos to the coast. It continues to the south to some very nice, although rocky, secluded beaches; the last view of the Pacific Ocean for several hundred kilometers can be seen here.
The vegetation becomes more dense. The plant species commonly seen along the highway are Burrobrush, Pitaya Agria, Agave, Garambullo, Beavertail cactus, Brittle Bush Nipple cactus, *Ephedra*, Velvet Cactus, Hedgehog Cactus, and occasionally Candelabra, Ice Plant, Maguay, Cliff Spurge, Lichen, and Milkweed. Locoweed (*Astragalus sp.*) is the plant which grows abundantly along the pavement's edge.

LOCOWEED: Many species of locoweed grow in the Californian phytogeographic region of Baja Norte. They are distinguishable by the length of floral parts and the size of the wooly seed pods. *Astragalus*, members of the pea family (F. Leguminosae), exhibit a variety of colored flower spikes (purple, pale yellow, and white) and occur in many different types of plant communities. Their leaves are alternately arranged along the narrow stems and are unequally pinnately compound (the leaf veins give the leaf a feather-like appearance).
Astragalus is commonly known as locoweed because it contains an accumulative toxin, selenium, that is poisonous to practically all livestock. They repeatedly eat the toxin and go "loco" prior to dying from selenium poisoning. Although it is poisonous to cattle, early Baja Indians chewed the shoots to cure soar throats, used locoweed poltices to reduce swelling, and boiled roots which produced a decoction which was used to wash granulated eyelids and ease the pain of toothaches. "*Astragalus*" comes from Greek and means ankle-bone, an early name for leguminous plants. Thus, the plants name may have referred to their low prostrate growth habit which placed them at ankle height.

4 5   Although the vegetation of this area looks "burned-out", it is becoming denser and taller.

4 9   The highway climbs a grade toward the top of a mesa through mudstone exposures of the Rosario Formation.
       Baja's old dirt road is in the canyon below.

5 0   At the top of Mesa las Cuevas the vista to the northeast consists of mesas which are composed of Paleocene rocks which overly the Rosario Formation.

5 2   The highway descends a grade into Canada el Rosario and passes through the sandstones, mudstones, and conglomerates of the Rosario Group.

> **Rosario Group:** Kilmer (1963, 1965) mapped and named four formations of Late Cretaceous age: the Rosario Formation for the upper marine part, the El Gallo Formation for the underlying nonmarine unit, the Punta Baja for a lower marine unit and the La Bocana Roja Formation for a basal nonmarine unit. All four formations were part of Beal's original single Rosario Formation. The total thickness of the Rosario Formation near El Rosario is 2900 meters.
>
> "[Fossil] collecting in the vicinity of El Rosario [has been] a continuing project since 1965...". Morris (1974) has described vertebrata fossils from the El Gallo Formation and says, "the fauna is small due to difficulties in collecting, scarcity of specimens, and the almost unique sedimentary environmental framework. Dinosaurian archosaurs related to *Lambeosaurus* of the Canadian Rocky Mountain foothills and Alberta plain are the most common herbivores. Some were 17 meters long and were more aquatic than terrestrial. A large carnivorous dinosaur has been recognized by isolated teeth as well as cranial material. It was morphologically near *Gorgosaurus* [The large tyrannosaur *Albertosaurus S.F. tyrannosaurinae* is more widely recognized by its synonym *Gorgosaurus*. (Benton, 1984 and Paul, 1988)].
>
> **THE "TERRIBLE LIZARDS" DINOSAURS**: Dinosaurs evolved from reptilian ancestors sometime in the Anisian stage of the early Triassic period about 235 million years ago and suddenly became extinct at the end of the Mesozoic during the Maastrichian stage of the late Cretaceous 65 million years ago. The earliest dinosaurs were not really lizards at all but were members of a group of early crocodile-like thecodonts which are known as archosaurs. Eventually dinosaurs populated all of the large land masses except Antarctica.
>
> Paleontologists have delineated two orders of dinosaurs -- the Saurischia (lizard hipped) and the Ornithischia (bird hipped). It has been determined that if a strictly phylogenetic classification were used, it would be correct to say that modern birds are descended from the Saurischians and are living dinosaurs.
>
> In 1822 the first fragmentary dinosaur fossils were found in England by the wife of Gideon Mantell, an English medical doctor and avid fossil collector. He named the dinosaur that his wife found *Iguanodon*. The discovery was first briefly described in an 1822 publication followed by a formal scientific publication of the discovery in 1825. The very first dinosaur fossil discovered in North America was a hadrosaur (duck-bill) tooth found in Montana in 1854 in the Judith River Formation by paleontologist Ferdinand Hayden. The very first complete dinosaur skeleton, which was also a duck-bill, was found in Haddon Field, New Jersey, in 1858 by William Parker Foulke. Until this time most dinosaur fossils which had been found were bone and tooth fragments and most were found in Europe. Today, however, the American West presents the richest and most varied collection of dinosaur fossils anywhere in the world. The United States has become the center for the study of dinosaurs, and today most of the

field research and the interpretation of the bones takes place in The United States and is conducted primarily by American Paleontologists.

Near El Rosario, Baja California, several dinosaur bones and tooth fragments have been found and assigned to the Family Hadrosauridae. Paleontologists attempt to re-create the history of past life from fossils. Some of the most exciting and challenging material they work with is related to the fossilized traces of dinosaurs.

Fossil materials collected in Baja have contributed significantly to the increase of knowledge about the history of the geology, climate, and biology of the peninsula. Additional studies are needed to help clarify Baja's past.

Do not collect Baja's fossil materials, since they are needed to illuminate Baja's past. It is against Mexican federal laws to collect the peninsula's resources!

MAMMALS: Although Cretaceous mammalian fossils are exceedingly rare, they have been found in Baja. Specimens consist of isolated teeth but several jaws have been collected and are related to forms found in Cretaceous deposits which outcrop along the eastern side of the Rocky Mountains.

REPTILES: A crocodilian which is close in ancestry to the lineage which leads to modern alligators has been uncovered.

BIRDS: A very significant avian fossil has been collected. This specimen represents the only terrestrial bird recovered from Mesozoic strata other than the famous *Archaeopteryx* from the Solenhofen Limestone of Germany. Preliminary study indicates that it will serve as a phylogenetic link between the Jurassic *Archaeopteryx* and modern terrestrial aves."

54.5 The canyon on your left at approximately 8 o'clock contains exposures of the Rosario Formation. In the right fork of this canyon fossils of Mesozoic *Ammonites* have been found high on the slopes and ridges on the right side of the canyon.

The first Datilillo "living fences" are seen here.

LIVING FENCES: The fence posts along this section of the highway and in many other parts of Baja are made of the cut branches and trunks of several cactus species, primarily those of the genus *Pachycereus*--the Cardon, the Galloping Cactus or Pitaya Agria (*Machaerocereus*) and a member of the Lily family, such as; the Datilillo, (*Yucca valida*).

After the plants were cut and placed in the ground for fence posts, they rerooted and continued to grow. It is possible to asexually reproduce many plant species by placing cuttings of their stems or branches in moist soil. The cuttings develop adventitious roots and become whole new plants. Numerous desert plants in Baja reproduce in this fashion. For example several species of Baja's Cholla cactus have pads which readily fall from the main plant, develop adventitious roots, and become new plants. These plants are said to have propagated by vegetative asexual reproduction. Other species which reproduce in this manner include Cardon, Yucca, and Datilillo. The phenomenon of vegetative reproduction allows desert plants to avoid the costly water and energy-consuming processes of sexual reproduction and permits the spread of plant species even when its too dry for seed production and the establishment of new plants by seed germination.

Log 3 - San Quintin to L.A. Bay Turnoff

55.5 El Rosario is a small fishing and agricultural community which has a few small stores, cafes, and two gas stations. In the past prior to the completion of the paved highway in 1974 this small farming community was considered the last outpost of civilization before the trip into the remote "interior" of the peninsula. It was the last town until Rosarita, which was two hard days of travel down the unpaved old road. The road to the right at the corner leads to the ocean. It forks and crosses the arroyo to the old mission ruins and ends at Punta Baja. The climate is slightly drier than that of Ensenada since it receives only half the annual precipitation.
The shade trees around the residential houses are commonly introduced non-native species of Tamarisk, California Pepper Tree, Italian Cypress, and Olive Trees.

56 The highway follows Arroyo El Rosario which is located on a recent river terrace, to Kilometer 61. Rocks of the Rosario Formation are exposed in the hills on both sides of the arroyo. Across the Arroyo to the south there is a series of flat "benches". These recent benches are called river terraces and were formed by the downward cutting action of Rio del Rosario. The land in this area is gradually rising relative to sea level. This enables the streams to cut deeper into their beds which leaves behind parts of their former channel. The terrace which the highway crosses is one of these abandoned river terraces.

AS LAND IS BEING UPLIFTED THE RIVER CUTS

DOWNWARD AS IT CROSSES ITS FLOOD PLAIN.

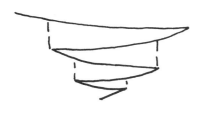

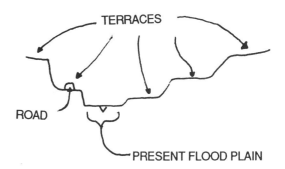

UPLIFT CAUSES IT TO ABANDON PARTS

OF THE FLOOD PLAIN AS TERRACES.

To the east of El Rosario along the left side of the highway farmers often cover the hills with chili peppers and allow them to dry in the sun before marketing them.

"CHILIES PEQUENOS" = SPICY, HOT CHILI PEPPERS!: Capsicum (chili) peppers, members of the potato family (F. Solanaceae), are commonly used as a spice to flavor foods in Baja, on the mainland Mexico, and in many other parts of both the New and Old World. The capsicums are perennial woody plants which are cultivated in vegetable gardens throughout Baja. There is a wide range of varieties.
The diet of tropical countries has always contained monotonous staples such as starchy grains and roots. It is not surprising that the use of spices became very important. Peppers are New World natives that originated and grew wild in Central Mexico and South America. They have been eaten for at least 7,000 years and have probably been cultivated for almost as long. Capsicum peppers are known in the New World from prehistoric burial sites in Peru, and they were widely cultivated in the New World before the arrival of Columbus in the 1490's. They were brought to Baja by the first settlers of the Loreto region as spices for their fairly bland starchy diet of maize, beans, and squash.

Spices are derived from edible plant parts that are not consumed as much for their food value as for their aromatic flavor-producing qualities. They are valued world-wide for three reasons: 1) they save the diet from becoming monotonous, 2) they disguise the unpleasant flavor of spoiling unrefrigerated foods, and 3) they increase the rate of perspiration and help to cool the body -- important in semi-tropical and tropical regions such as Baja. Spices may aid in the digestive processes, act as preservatives for foods and dead bodies (Egyptian papyri, biblical Songs, and Psalms record their use in embalming and mummification of the dead), and act as deodorants. Their strong pleasant odors are used to mask the unpleasant odors of the human body. Animals also use the deodorant properties of spices; Baja's wood rats take the leaves and branches of highly aromatic spice plants such as black and white sages into their burrows to hide their scent from predatory snakes.

The use and cultivation of spice plants goes back to the beginning of recorded history. In China and in the ancient civilizations of Egypt, Greece, and Rome spices were so highly valued that they were used for money. Dried berries of the true pepper (*Piper nigrum*) were used to pay taxes and rents in medieval England. Some of the exploration of the world was for the purpose of finding spices; Columbus was looking for a shorter route to the spices of India when he discovered the Americas. The exorbitant cost of Magellan's voyage around the world (1519-1522) was paid for by the cloves and other spices that his one surviving ship brought back to Europe.

The flavor and aroma of spices are due to essential oils. These oils are organic substances of varied composition which tend to have relatively small molecules. This makes them volatile (readily vaporizable at low temperatures). These oils belong to a group of hydrocarbons known as terpenes. The terpene of capsicum peppers is a volatile phenolic compound called capsaicin ($C_{18}H_{23}NO_3$), a substance so powerfully affecting human taste buds that even a dilution of 1:1,000,000 is detectable. The greatest concentration of capsaicin is found in the pepper's placenta, the tissue which joins the seeds of the capsicum pepper to the fruit wall. Seeds of capsaicin peppers also have a lot of capsaicin. The fruit wall (ovary) has the least capsaicin. Because its presence or absence is due to variation in a single gene some peppers lack capsaicin. Many people who are not used to eating spicy peppers such as those encountered in Baja remove the seeds and placenta before eating or using capsicum peppers as a spice. This produces a milder "cooler" flavor.

Capsicum peppers are eaten alone or used to flavor many dishes in Baja. They vary in size from large bell peppers, which are not peppery at all, to small extremely hot ("picante") red chili peppers known as "chilies pequenos". "Chilies pequenos" (*Capsicum annuum*) is the potent tiny red pepper which is commonly encountered in Baja. There are four closely related species involved in the production of economically useful peppers worldwide, and bell peppers and chili peppers may both be produced by the same species (*Capsicum annuum* or *C. frutescens*). In addition to their use as spices, capsicum peppers are rich sources of vitamin C and have laxative properties which are partially responsible for the diarrhea many Baja travelers experience after eating foods highly spiced with chili peppers.

58   South of El Rosario the vegetation changes dramatically with the appearance of the first endemic Cirios (*Idra Columnaris*).

> **PENINSULAR ENDEMISM:** Plant ecologists have studied peninsulas such as Baja for many years. They have found that these places often have endemic (indigenous or native) plants and animals which are confined naturally to the peninsula and are not found anywhere else in the world. Due to the semi-isolation Baja California has experienced in past geological times, endemism is common. As a result many spiders, plants, and reptiles are peculiar to the Baja Peninsula. Endemism is especially evident among the cacti. Over 110 species cactus have been reported in Baja; 80 of these are found in no other parts of the world. Other notable Baja endemics which are commonly seen include the Cardon cactus and the Elephant Tree. This endemism contributes to the picturesque uniqueness of Baja's vegetation.

60   The "greener" vegetation which grows along the pavement's edge consists of Indian Tree Tobacco, Broom Baccharis, and several species of desert annuals.

> **WHAT ARE DESERT ANNUALS?** After rainy periods, whose times and amounts vary from desert to desert, the landscape is covered briefly by colorful "blooms" of annual ephemeral desert wildflowers. Their showy variously colored flowers (primarily white and yellow) stand out vividly against the earth tones of Baja's desertscape. Wildflower blooms are most often seen in the early spring in northern Baja and in the summer in the southern part of the peninsula. Annuals cannot withstand drought and may lie dormant for decades until the right conditions occur for growth. Then the desert "blooms" with colorful floral displays. It is the function of the seeds to be the source for the next generation. These plants, which are so characteristic of the desert, evade the harshest desert conditions of Baja.

62   A high bridge crosses Arroyo El Rosario.
The dirt road up the north side of Arroyo Rosario leads to the small Rancho Provenir. The majority of the hills along Arroyo Rosario consist of the mudstones and sandstones of the Rosario Formation. For the next 20 kilometers the highway climbs through subdued exposures of the Rosario Formation.

> **ANOTHER WASHOUT:** The hurricane of 1967 did extensive damage to the El Rosario area. In early 1979 before the bridge was built, the paved highway was completely washed out, and some travelers waited for as long as four days to cross. Vehicles either forded or were towed across the wash by a caterpillar tractor. Hopefully, the new high bridge will not wash out.

63   The purple globose "shells" (tests) and spines which have been dumped along the highway on the left (east) are the remains of Sea Urchins (*Strongylocentrotus francisconus*) which were collected by urchin fisherman along the Pacific Coast near El Rosario. The gonads (ovaries and testes) of the urchin are considered a delicacy. The gonads may be eaten locally or exported to the orient. Similar piles of shells may also be seen along the shoreline of Alta California's Channel Islands, such as Catalina Island.

EL CASTILLO: An interesting castle-like formation complete with battlements which has been dubbed "El Castillo" can be seen upstream to the left as the highway crosses the bridge. Movement on a fault parallel to the arroyo has resulted in the veneering of the canyon side with resistant flat-lying conglomerates that form the castle. The yellow brown band high on the hills is the boundary between the Cretaceous and Paleocene rocks in this area.

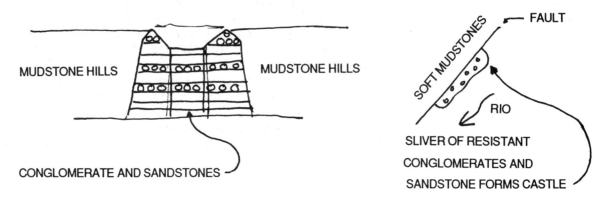

68   The roadcuts located on either side of this kilometer provide a good opportunity to stop to inspect excellent exposures of the mudstones of the Rosario Formation. Kilometer 68.3 has a good turn-out for safe parking.

69   The sandstones and mudstones of the Rosario Formation are exposed in the roadcuts along this grade. The highway ascends a canyon and passes the first occurrences of specimens of Cirios (*Idra columnaris*) on the left.

BAJA'S WIERD CIRIOS: The cirio trees of Baja are claimed by some as one of the many endemics of the peninsula. However, a small colony of cirios are also found on the mainland of Mexico south of La Libertad. It is one of the most distinctive and interesting plant species in Baja. This tall candle-like plant derives its name "cirio" from the Spanish word for wax taper (candle). It has also been called a "boojum" because of its similarity to the fanciful creature described in Lewis Carroll's "The Hunting of the Snark". Cirios have tall trunks which taper to a point approximately 20 meters above the ground in the largest specimens. However, due to the arid conditions of the peninsula, specimens rarely reach their maximum height. The whole plant looks somewhat like an upside-down carrot, with whip or root-like limbs which curve up and down in a grotesque fashion.

A story of doubtful authenticity has been told by some "Baja Travelers" in an attempt to explain the strange shapes of the whip-like grotesquely curving limbs. This desert is very dry, so dry that when there is a fog, there is more moisture in the air than in the ground. In order to survive the Cirio trees turn upside-down so that their "roots" are in the air in order to reach the "fog water". Since the fog layer is thin, the "roots" quickly grow above the fog and bend toward the ground to get back into the moisture-laden fog. But alas! They grow toward the earth and grow below the fog. Once again they turn upward away from the ground. This repeated upward and downward growth of the root-like branches in an effort to utilize the "fog water" (Agua de

Neblina) "explains" the strange shapes of the whip-like grotesquely curving limbs of the Cirio.

Because of its strange appearance, the cirio has often been called the most unusual plant of Baja. Cirios are related to the Ocotillo but have white instead of red flowers. During the dry seasons the small leaves of the Cirio fall, and the trunk is dormant and protected from desiccation by a thick waxy epidermis. When it rains, new leaves form from protected lateral buds. The cirio prefers to grow on the west-facing slopes of hillsides and alluvial plains from south of Rio Del Rosario across the peninsula through the volcanic fields and into the Central Gulf Coast Desert. Cirios are also found along the road to Bahia de Los Angeles.

They are of little value to man, since they have no edible fruits and do not provide building materials or firewood.

The Cirio is a dominant member of the flora of the Sonoran Central Desert phytogeographic region (Vizcaino Desert area) (*See* Km 74.5).

71   A "grove" of cirios is growing on the hills to the left of the highway.
       The same Parry Buckeye, (*Aesculus parryi*) which are seen on the road to La Bufadora near Ensenada are growing on the northern slopes along this stretch of the highway.

71.5   Good exposures of conglomerates of the Rosario Formation are visible.

74.5   The highway crosses a large arroyo.
       STOP HERE- There is a small turnout on the grade which provides a good view of the varieties of vegetation which are characteristic of the Desierto el Vizcaino Region.

THE SONORAN CENTRAL DESERT PHYTOGEOGRAPHIC AREA: The chaparral flora of the Californian phytogeographic region declines near Valle Santo Tomas. In the intervening 160 kilometers between Valle Santo Tomas and El Rosario a transitional (ecotonal) flora which consists of a mixture of chaparral and desert species predominates. Extending to the south from El Rosario east to the Gulf and to the south to La Paz is the drier Sonoran Central Desert Region. In contrast to the 25 to 50 centemeters of annual precipitation received by the more northerly Californian phytogeographic region, almost no rain falls in the Central Desert Region for two or more years. A region is considered a desert if it receives less than 20-25 centimeters of precipitation per year. This region is truly a desert and is characterized by low humidity, widely fluctuating high ambient air temperatures, high surface and soil temperature, low organic content of the soil, strong winds, high mineral salts content, erosion by wind and water, poor drainage, and scarcity of water.

As the highway proceeds to the south through the Sonoran Central Desert Region, it passes through four subregions which are recognized and characterized by plant species

These four subregions are the San Felipe Desert, the Central Gulf Coast Desert, the Vizcaino Desert, and the Magdalena Plains Desert. The San Felipe Desert and the Central Gulf Coast Desert will be discussed in detail in the section of this guide from the U.S./Mexico border town of Mexicali to Bahia de Los Angeles and south from Bahia de Los Angeles to the Cape Region.

The highway between the Pacific coastal towns of El Rosario and Santa Rosalia on the Gulf coast passes through both the heart of the Desierto el Vizcaino and a small portion of the northernmost extension of the Magdalena Plains Deserts (*See*

Log 3 - San Quintin to L.A. Bay Turnoff

Kms 73 and 40.6 of the Guerrero Negro to Santa Rosalia log).

The extremely dry **Desierto el Vizcaino** covers the vast plain in west-central Baja California and extends from El Rosario to the south approximately 505 kilometers to the region of the date palm oasis town of San Ignacio. The floral dominants of the Vizcaino Desert Region are Cardon, Cirio, Century plants, Maguay, Datilillo, Agave, Yucca, Burbrush, and Ball Moss.

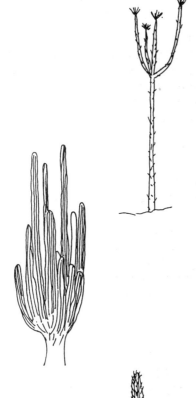

VEGETATION OF THE DESIERTO EL VIZCAINO VISIBLE FROM TURNOFF AT KM 74.5

The **Cirio** or Boojum is the tallest plant of the visible flora. It looks like the tap root of a plant that has been turned upside down. *See* the discussion at Km. 69 to review the details about this strange plant.

El Cardon is a cactus which resembles the Saguaro cactus of the Sonora Desert of mainland Mexico and the deserts of the southwestern U.S.A. The Cardon (*Pachycereus sp.*) is a true Baja endemic. It is usually found on rocky hillsides, in deserts, and on level plains from El Rosario to the tip of the peninsula and is the most widely spread of the peninsula's larger vascular plants. Since the cactus lacks leaves, photosynthesis takes place in the modified epidermal cells (chlorenchyma) of the trunk. The trunk is a true cladophyll (a stem acting like a leaf).
Nests of predatory hawks and Osprey are often seen in the upper branches of this giant columnar cactus. Hawks, buzzards, and ravens use the Cardon as hunting, resting, or sleeping perches.
Extensive stands of Cardon are called *cardonals*. An excellent place to view an extensive dense cardonal with exceptionally tall specimens of Cardon is at the southern end of Bahia Concepcion south of Santa Rosalia along the *Baja Highway*.

Pitaya Agria is a dark green-gray stemmed cactus which grows in dense thickets from Ensenada to the Cape Region. The spines are reddish-gray with darker tips. The fleshy red fruit is edible, and because of its high Vitamin-C content, it was eaten by early Spanish sailors to cure scurvy.

"Old Man" Cactus or Garambullo is an erect colonial cactus "tree" which grows to 4 meters tall and usually branches near the base. The tips of the star-shaped stems are densely covered with many long gray coarse hair-like spines which give the cactus a whiskered "old man", look. The fleshy red fruit is edible but is not nearly as good as the fruit of Pitaya Agria. It is commonly seen from the highway south of Rio Del Rosario to the Cape Region.

Organ Pipe Cactus is a many branched erect cactus without a main trunk. It might be confused with the cardon; however, the Organ Pipe Cactus, which branches nearer the ground, lacks the main trunk characteristic of the Cardon. It looks like a set of organ pipes. The fleshy watermelon flavored red fruits were used by Indians as a food source in the late summer and fall. Like the Pitaya Agria and "Old Man" Cactus, the fruits are also a good source of Vitamin-C.

Agave or century plants are members of the Amaryllis family. In Baja four species of the genus *Agave* are commonly referred to as Agave or century plants. It takes determination and a brief comparative study to tell the three species apart. About 20 species of them are known to occur in Baja, but few of them are well known botanically.

The various species of *Agave* have a long history of usefulness in Mexico.
In the Yucatan Peninsula of mainland Mexico cultivated species of *Agave*, also known as "green gold", were once extensively cultivated for the fiber henequen (sisal). Botanically the *Agave* fibers are long sclerenchyma, modified parenchyma fibers, like the "strings" in a stalk of celery. Until the end of WW II the Yucatan Peninsula supplied much of the world's henequen (sisal) fibers and which were used in the production of ropes, rugs, twine, and wall hangings.
In Baja and other parts of North America native Indians utilized the *Agave* for food. They roasted and ate the immature flowering stalks and basal crowns, and the seeds were ground into a meal. The fermented products from the plant are still used to produce the alcoholic beverages of Tequila (distilled in Jalisco, Mexico), Pulque (brewed throughout much of Central Mexico), and Mezcal (distilled in Oaxaca, Mexico).
Careful observation of specimens which grow along the highway will show evidence of the continued harvesting of the *Agave* by Baja's inhabitants and travelers.

Ball Moss or Gallitos, a member of the pineapple family (F. Bromeliaceae), is an herbaceous epiphyte that commonly grows on other plants but does not damage it or derive nutrition from it. In this region it is a commonly seen commensalistic epiphytic plant which grows on Cirios, cacti, shrubs and even telephone wires (*See* Km 16.5 of Bahia L.A. log). Some Baja travelers mistakenly identify Gallitos (little chickens) as birds nests. The ball moss is placed by plant taxonomists in the genus *Tillandsia*. Species of *Tillandsia* are commonly sold as decorative plants at florist shops and "swap meets" in Alta California. Ball Moss is desiminated from plant to plant by wind-borne sticky seeds or by birds' feet or bills.

63

Ramalina is a lichen. Lichens are a partnership formed by a combination of two plants which grow in such close companionship that their separate tissues can only be determined under a microscope. This partnership consists of microscopic photosynthetic green algal cells which live inside the cells of a non-photosynthetic fungus (mushroom). The relationship formed is known to botanists as a mutulistic symbiosis. A lichen is an algae and a fungus that have "taken a liken to each other"; both plants benefit. The fungus provides water and protection for the algal cells. In return it utilizes the sugars, which are produced by the photosynthetic algae, for its source of energy. When times are difficult, the fungus will digest the algae. Instead of being "eaten out of house and home", the algae is eaten by its home!

In this area of Baja lichens grow epiphytically on Cirios or encrust boulders. Different species of lichen are visible as vivid red, blue, silver-gray, and even black splashes of color.

7 6   Mesa la Sepultura is the flat feature which is straight ahead. This mesa is the type area for the Sepultura Formation, which was named by Santillan and Barrera in 1930. Sepultura means "tomb".
The highway continues to pass through the Rosario Formation which extends far inland (northeast).

77.3   This side route leads across Mesa San Carlos into Arroyo San Fernando to Abelardo Rodriguez (31 kilometers) and San Vicente. It ends on the coast at the base of Mesa San Carlos at Puerto San Carlos (60 Kilometers). It is a long dead-end route, but the solitude, shell collecting, clam digging, and surfing may make the trip worthwhile.

7 9   The highway curves to the northeast and drops through prominent exposures of conglomerate into the main wash of Canada El Aguajito near the old Rancho of El Aguajito. As the highway drops into the wash, Cardons, Rabbit brush, Burbush, Burrow Weed, and Wash Woodland-type vegetation predominate the landscape. On the left, just after crossing the wash, is another good place to view the typical Vizcaino Desert flora represented by Cardon, Cirio, Pitaya Agria, Ocotillo, Garambullo, Agave, Organ Pipes, Cheese Bush, Burro Bush, Broom Baccharis, Mesquite, and epiphytic ball moss which grows on the Cirios.
If you take a walk through the vegetation, you may see and hear the flitting red-capped Gila Woodpecker (*Melanerpes uropygialis*).

Red

The **Gila Woodpecker** is a medium-sized red-capped woodpecker often seen perching or flitting around among willows and cottonwoods in riparian habitats and in low desert cardonals and stands of mesquite in Baja. This is the only desert woodpecker with a plain gray-brown belly, head, and neck and white wing patches which show during flight. They frequently makes nests in Cardon cacti and cottonwoods throughout the peninsula. Gilas feed primarily on insects and the fruits of mistletoe and cacti.

The old road along the wash crosses the highway at this point. It follows along the bottom of Canada El Aguajito.

Conglomerates which contain lenticular sandstones of the Rosario Formation are exposed in many places in this wash.

80.2 The contact between the Rosario and the Alisitos Formations is two thirds of the way up the grade beyond the wash.

82.2 At the top of the grade is a spectacular view. A series of concordant summits of the mesa tops can be seen to the northwest down the canyon toward the beach at El Rosario. To the north and east is the granitic spine of Sierra San Pedro Martir. Picacho del Diablo, 10,126 feet elevation, is the highest peak in Baja California. To its right is Pico Matomi, a Miocene volcanic core of andesite porphyry. The range to the east is the Sierra San Miguel. To the south is Mesa la Sepultura.

83.9 The road to the right leads to El Aguajito. Note: At one time the actual distance in kilometers painted on the road was actually one less than the number of kilometers shown on the sign.

Due to run-off, exposure, and winds, life on this ridgeline is extremely harsh. The vegetational "cover" is sparsely represented by coastal chaparral species such as Cirio, Cardon, and Agave -- all true xerophytes.

> **WHAT IS A XEROPHYTE?:** Xerophytes are plants. In Baja xerophytes include succulents, such as various cacti or members of other families which have fleshy stems and leaves which enable them to store water for a long time. They frequently have shallow root systems and are able to utilize the soil moisture from light rainfall, heavy dew, or fog. Such plants take advantage of the little precipitation which falls in the four desert areas of Baja by storing precipitation, dew, and/or fog (neblina) in their pith and cortex parenchyma tissues for months or even years. Many succulents such as cacti have leafless and ribbed stems, two more adaptations for survival in desert environments. Leaflessness reduces the surface area through which water is lost by transpiration. The ribbed stem allows the stems to swell like an accordion and store water when it becomes available.

84 The old road led up the arroyo and to the right. The zig-zagging switchbacks of the old road, which climbs the grade up the ridge, are rapidly disappearing due to erosion. This was the first real grade along the old unpaved road. It marked the end of the cobblestone roads in the washes and the beginning of the rough and sharp metavolcanic section of the road. It was sometimes referred to as "Hot Water" (agua heat-o) grade.

Along this ridge to the right are beautiful views of Mesa la Sepultura. Mesa la Sepultura and Mesa San Carlos are composed of the Cretaceous marine Rosario Formation in the lower parts and are overlain by the Paleocene-Eocene marine Sepultura Formation (Santillan & Barrera, 1930). The Sepultura Formation consists of conglomerates which grade into mudstones with conglomerate channels to the west. This Cenozoic section extends inland 30 kilometers. It becomes thinner and more coarsely clastic and nonmarine with sandstone, conglomerate and scattered thin shale partings which pinch against an irregular buried topography.

85.3 The metavolcanics of the Alisitos Formation are well exposed on the right side of the highway.

To the right (east) at 2 o'clock are the white buildings and scar of the abandoned La Turquesa turquois mine.

> **LA TURQUESA:** Turquoise, a light-blue to blue-green triclinic phosphate mineral, is formed as a secondary deposit which fills cracks and shears in the metavolcanic rocks of the Alisitos Formation. Turquoise, which is the birthstone for December, usually occurs in cracks and as reniform masses with a botryoidal (the form of a bunch of grapes) surface in the zone of alteration of aluminum-rich igneous rocks.
> The La Turquesa mine became a series of "gopher (go for) holes" as the miners followed the illusive mineral. They mined only what was absolutely necessary. Several other abandoned mines are located in the area.

In this area there is usually a distinct contrast between the rounded reddish-brown hills of the Alisitos and the badlands of the Rosario mudstones and conglomerates.

86   Exposures of the reddish soils of the Alisitos Formation can be seen along the sides of the highway.

86.4   There is a rather spectacular little gorge in the Alisitos Formation to the right.
There is an obvious change in the vegetation from the mudstones and conglomerates of the Rosario Formation to the reddish-brown soils of the Alisitos Formation. This change is due to differences in soil chemistries, soil moisture, soil salinity, and other soil edaphic factors.
The obvious vegetational cover consists of Teddy Bear Cholla, Barrel Cactus, Cirio, and variously colored crustose lichens which look like paint that has been "splattered" randomly on the rocks. Each color is a different rock.
The highway climbs through the reddish-brown beds of the Alisitos Formation which is well exposed here.

88.5   At the top of the grade the rocks are a very light gray. There is a spectacular view of the coastal plain, Mesa San Carlos to the south, the closer Mesa la Sepultura, and to the west the hills of the Rosario Formation stretching off to the north.
The highway descends the new Aguajito grade through adamellite and the metavolcanic rocks of the Alisitos Formation.

88.6   The side road is the turnoff which leads to the abandoned turquois mine, La Turquesa.

89.6   As the highway crosses a small arroyo, a few feet of the old road is visible to the right.

90   To the south is the obviously bedded Alisitos Formation which dips slightly to the south. Excellent exposures of the Alisitos Formation, which is composed of rhyolite, ignimbrite, basalt and andesite, outcrop in this area.
Lemonadeberry (*Rhus sp.*) is the large darker green plant which grows alongside the highway. Indians prepared a tasty lemonade-like drink by soaking the bright red berries of this large shrub in water. Because the berries contain a large amount of malic acid, they act as a diuretic (increasing the flow of urine).

91   The zig-zag pattern of the old road can be seen to the right.
Fierro Blanco in his book *The Journey of the Flame* writes of the last moments of Señor Don Juan Obrigón, The Flame, Who died alone at the great Cardon, near El Rosario, with his face turned to the south. Could this be the "great Cardon"?
The Cirio on the right contains a raptor nest which has been used year after year -- probably by the Red-Tailed Hawks which are commonly seen in this area.

92   The old road crossed a flat valley on a Tertiary conglomerate which may have been an ancient river channel. This conglomerate may be correlative with the Lusardi

conglomerate of Cretaceous age which was formed when the area was first elevated and eroded due to the pushing of the Pacific plate under Baja California.

For the next several kilometers excellent exposures of the Alisitos Formation rocks outcrop on the down grade of the highway into Rancho Arenoso.

95   As the highway drops into a little narrow deep valley (gorge), notice the view to the north toward Sierra San Miguel (in the near distance) and Sierra San Pedro Martir with its flat summits (in the far distance).

One of the roads to Cerro Blanco passes to the left down this arroyo. There are several abandoned mines including a copper mine in the area.

Abundant Beavertail Cactus, Agave, Barrel Cactus, Pitaya Agria, Broom Baccharis, Toyon, sparse Cardons, and tall Cirios which are covered by the lichen *Ramalina*, comprise the vegetational cover of this portion of Desierto el Vizcaino.

97   The highway crosses a prominently jointed adamellite (looks like a dike). The old unpaved road also crossed this very rough area.

99   The small unseen Rancho Los Martires is located off the highway to the left.

101   This kilometer marks the beginning of a very large cardonal and Cirio forest. The vegetation of the area is typical of Desierto el Vizcaino flora and is dominated by Desert thorn, *Mimosa sp* (a cat-claw relative), Mesquite, Desert Mallow (along the pavements edge), Cirio, Datilillo, Garambullo, Beavertail, Jumping Cholla, Barrel Cactus, Tamarisk (in washes), Yucca, Cardon, and Palo Estribo.

The highway passes Rancho Arenoso, one of the numerous, old-time cattle ranchos of the peninsula. The old road led right to the front door of the ranch house where earlier Baja travelers stopped for cold refrescos and a respite from the rough bone-jarring road.

106   Slightly past this kilometer sign, approximately two o'clock to the right (west), there are a couple of low hills. The large four-branched Cardon visible on top of the higher hill makes a very scenic photograph in the right light. In the late spring these attractive Cardon produce numerous beautiful flowers and globose fruits.

Along the highway there are several large interesting barrel cactus which are known to biologists as the "compass plants" of Baja.

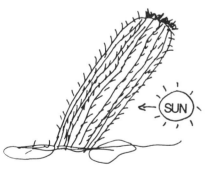

BAJA'S "COMPASS PLANTS": Because of their tendency to grow toward the intense light of the southwest (to reduce the harmful effects of the sun during the hottest times of the year), they are sometimes called the "compass plant".

In an emergency the Barrel Cactus (*Echinocactus sp.*) will yield approximately a pint of alkaline juice from its pithy cortical parenchyma (water storage tissues of the stem). However, drinking the alkaline juice for too long a period will induce diarrhea

The tops of the cactus are surrounded by reddish-thorns. In the late spring they have a ring of beautiful waxy yellow flowers.

108   The highway roughly follows a strike valley (Strike=horizontal compass bearing of the edge of the beds) in the metavolcanics of the Alisitos Formation. In the hills ahead and to the right two interesting erosional curves in the dipping limestone beds are visible.

112   The highway enters a strike valley in the Alisitos Formation with beds which dip toward the east at approximately 45 degrees.

Prominent ridges which contain limestone are exposed on both the right and left sides of the highway. The highway roughly parallels the strike of the Alisitos Formation for several kilometers. Look to the left at the long strike ridges (45 degree dip) across the valley in the near distance. This is reminiscent of the plateau area of northern Arizona and southern Utah, except the age of the rocks and the vegetational cover differ.

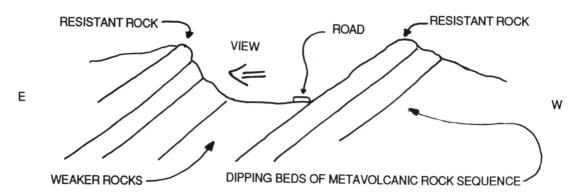

Metavolcanic rocks: Large areas of Metavolcanic rocks without fossil or radiometric dates are exposed throughout much of the Pacific slope of northern Baja California. South of the Agua Blanca Fault, the volcanic sequence includes a variety of sedimentary strata. Limestone, calcareous siltstone and mudstone are interbedded with volcanic sandstone, volcanic conglomerate, tuff and volcanic breccia, and represent a wide variety of depositional environments. Deposits range from deep to shallow marine and nonmarine, from coarse sedimentary breccia to clean limestone, and from basalt to rhyolite. Andesite and andesite breccia are the predominant volcanic rocks. The entire sequence is thought to be thousands to tens of thousands of meters thick. It varies widely in stratigraphic components from area to area. No two measured stratigraphic sections are alike. Additional mapping and stratigraphic work will be required before subunits can be recognized and correlated (Gastil *et al.*,1972).

113   Yuccas begin to be more apparent.

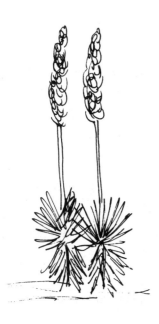

YUCCAS are 2'-18' high shrubs of the lilly family with thickly clustered, sharply pointed leaves and a large flowering stalk which supports terminal panicles of whitish flowers. The flowers are pollinated by tiny night flying Pronuba moths. Neither the Yucca nor the moth can propagate its species without the aid of the other. The moth larve feed exclusively upon the Yucca seeds and the Yucca flowers are only pollinated by the moth. Eliminate one of the symbiotic mutualists and the other will die.
Both man and cattle make use of parts of the Yucca. The stalks are rich in sugar; the saponins stored in the roots are used as a substitute for soap. (Do you remember Yucca-Do-Shampoo?) Saponins are plant glucosides that form a soapy colloidal solution when mixed and agitated with water. Saponins are used in detergents, synthetic sex hormones, foaming agents, and emulsifiers. The flowers are edible by man and cattle. The green cucumber-like fruits can be eaten raw, roasted, or dried for future use. The long sclerenchyma leaf fibers were used in making baskets, sandals, and mats.

114 This kilometer sign marks the turnoff to Mision San Fernando de Velicata (5.8 kilometers) down the arroyo west of El Progresso. It was founded in 1769 by Father Junipero Serra as he traveled north to Alta California. It is the only mission in Baja California established by the Franciscans. It has deteriorated into a series of low walls and mounds since its abandonment in 1818.

115.2 The highway crosses Arroyo Los Torotes slightly north of El Progresso.

116.5 This is the new Rancho El Progresso.

119 The highway ascends to the top of a small grade and passes through the metavolcanics of the Alisitos Formation. The old Rancho Santa Cecilia, which is marked by the windmill, is visible to the right of the highway.
The old road went to the right, around the hill, and up the wash while the paved highway goes to the left, over the rise, and cuts across the hill which avoids the destruction by flood waters that run seasonally through the wash.

120 The view to the north (left) is Valle El Ronoso. The view to the south is the flat plain of Llanos de San Agustin.

> **A Pleistocene lake bed:** The light-colored brownish-tan (buff) sandstone, siltstone and limestone which occupies the bottom of Valle Santa Cecilia were part of one of a series of Pleistocene lake beds that occurred in this part of the peninsula. Various freshwater vertebrate fossils that include fresh water turtles have been recovered from the sediments of the lake. The possibility for finding more vertebrate remains is fairly great in this area. The sediments of this "fossil" Pleistocene lake are fine-grained, and this part of the highway was very dusty when dry.

122 The highway traverses the very flat upper surface of the sediments on what was the actual lake bottom. On the north side of the highway the shoreline of the lake is visible at the base of the low hills where it was in contact with the metavolcanics of the Alisitos Formation. In the distance, on the south side of the highway are low rolling hills that are part of the major sedimentary unit of the fluvial part of the Paleocene-Eocene Sepultura Formation. This relationship continues for several kilometers along the highway.
The vegetation cover of the flat old lake bottom sediments is primarily Creosote Bush (*Larea tridentata*).

CREOSOTE BUSH is a very common resinous desert shrub of the southwestern U.S.A. and Baja. Unlike many other desert plants, it is green the year around. The waxy coating on its leaves reduces water loss by transpiration and allows the shrub to withstand long periods of extreme drought. The strong-smelling resinous leaves resemble the odor of the coal tar distillate-creosote. Notice that very few plants grow under the Creosote Bush. The roots of this shrub produce a toxic substance that inhibits the growth of other plants. After heavy or frequent rains, when it is leached from the soil, it permits the growth of desert annuals. As the soil dries, the inhibitor accumulates and poisons the outsiders. This phenomenon is known as allelopathy, and it helps to eliminate the competition for water in a dry desert environment. Creosote Bush was considered a cure-all by Baja's early Indians, and early Spaniards used a decoction of this shrub to treat sick cattle and saddle-galled horses. In more recent times a leaf extract has been used to delay or prevent butter, oils, and fats from turning rancid. Creosote Bush leaf extract is not widely used, because the compound is now synthetically manufactured.

115 The flat plains of this region are part of an exhumed erosion surface.

What Is An Exhumed Erosion Surface? This area is in the middle of the peninsula with a wide open area that consists of flat plains fringed by "not-too-steep looking" hills. The hills of Llanos de San Agustin were base-leveled; that is, they were eroded to a relatively flat surface by streams during the Early Tertiary period. The remnants of the deposits from one of these streams can be seen as gravels on the road to Santa Catarina. This base-leveled surface was covered by Miocene fluvatile sediments, basalts, and rhyolites which stretched across the peninsula. The area was uplifted sometime during the last 10 m.y. It was dissected by erosional processes and exumed, and left lava-capped mesas scattered over the area as erosional remnants. Later impounded drainage filled the low places with lakebed sediments which are now being dissected by present streams.

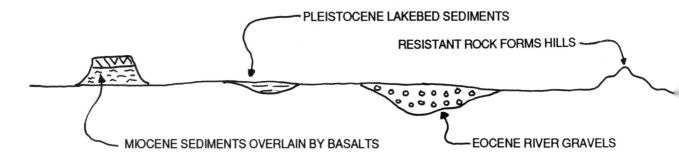

STYLIZED SECTION OF LLANOS DE SAN AGUSTINE

The vegetational cover is very sparse and is represented by only a few small specimens of Cirio, Cholla, Ocotillo, *Agave*, Creosote Bush, Yucca (resembles the Joshua Tree), and Mesquite.

In the wash against the base of the Alisitos hills the flora is dominated by large bright green stands of *Mimosa sp.*, which clearly delineates the course of the wash which is visible from Kms 122 to 135.

124.5 At Los Cuates the highway crosses a wash. The old road followed this wash to the east. It is a rough sandy ride at best!

126.1 The buildings along side the highway are part of the new Rancho Penjamo. This turnoff leads to the old Rancho Penjamo which is the series of buildings at on the left 10 o'clock. Several more of the old ranchos dot the old road on the left. The paved highway is approximately two kilometers south of the old road at this point. It follows the flat surface of the Pleistocene fluvial lake beds discussed at Km 120.

127.8 The side road to the left leads southwest to Santa Catarina and Puerto Catarina on the coast. The road follows the coast for many kilometers to the south and finally rejoins the highway near El Tomatal (Km 68.5 of the Bahia L.A. to Guerrero Negro log). It is a fairly rough, but quite picturesque, side road. It is only recommended for 4-wheel drive vehicles and group travel. We spent three weeks and four days camped on this road near Arroyo San Jose. Only two parties passed us during that time.

128   The turnoff to the left leads to Rancho Guyaquil.

129   This is a good vantage point for viewing Llanos de San Agustin. The flat Llanos de San Agustin are mantled by a blanket of fluvatile sedimentary rocks which were extensively covered by Miocene rhyolite flows. The little flat mesas and buttes that seem to stride the highway are part of these rhyolitic flows, but they have been removed by erosional processes.

131.5 This side road to the left (east) leads to the ranchos of El Aguila, San Agustin, Resolana, and San Luis and rejoins the highway near Rancho San Pablo. The highway is to the right (west) of the old road (in the wash by the hills) and cuts through the volcanic hills, via a pass, before it heads straight across the bouldery granitic terrain toward Catavina.

135   The flat reddish-colored mesa ahead is Mesa Redonda; it is capped by resistant volcanics of Miocene age. Most of the flat hills in this area are mesas which are capped by these same resistant volcanics.
Another large raptor nest is visible in the large Cirio on the right side of the road at the base of Mesa Redonda.

136.2 The side road to the left leads through Valle Santa Teresa to Rancho Santa Teresa. The high peak behind the rancho is Cerro Santa Teresa.

137.3 The first Elephant Trees which are visible from the highway are growing on the slope to the right (west). These unique trees will be discussed in detail at Km 9 of the Bahia L.A. Turn-off to Guerrero Negro log.

138   At the crest of this low pass there are good exposures of gneisses and schists in the roadcut.

140.5 The turnoff to the left leads to the new Rancho San Agustin. The newer buildings which are seen on the left are part of the highway department maintenance system.

141.1 The windmill of the rancho of old San Agustin is visible about 1 kilometer to the left (east) down the arroyo. It has a very deep well with very good water; it was the "best" water available in the past. This well was drilled to supply water to the abandoned onyx mines which are located at El Marmol.

141.5 The side road to the right leads to San Pablo.

142   As the highway crests over a rise at the top of the hill there is another good view of the flat plain of Llanos de San Agustin and the extensive flat-topped Miocene volcanic mesas which are located on either side of the highway.

143.5 The new Rancho Tres Enriques is located along the highway to the left. The old Rancho is over the hill approximately one kilometer to the left (east) on the old road.

144   This is the turnoff to the abandoned El Marmol Onyx Quarry (15 km) at El Marmol (marble). The road to the mine is well graded and passable with most passenger vehicles.

EL MARMOL is the location of hot springs and a Travertine (onyx) deposit which was mined between 1900 and 1958 by the Southwest Onyx and Marble Company. Travertine is usually formed as a precipitate in a hot spring. Hot mineralized solutions from the El Volcan hot springs rise to the surface along a fault line, flow out on the surface, and evaporate as they cool. Travertine is deposited in layers. There is a large amount of unmined travertine at the abandoned mine. The old onyx school house is still standing, and an interesting graveyard is located nearby.

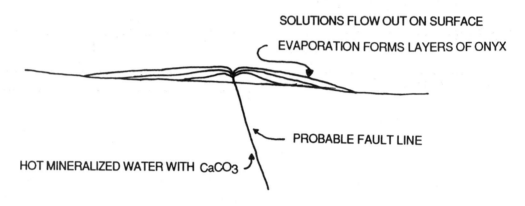

SOLUTIONS FLOW OUT ON SURFACE

EVAPORATION FORMS LAYERS OF ONYX

PROBABLE FAULT LINE

HOT MINERALIZED WATER WITH $CaCO_3$

EL MARMOL ONYX DEPOSIT

144.3 The small Rancho Sonora is located along the highway to the right. Notice the living Datilillo fences and leaning barrel cacti growing in this region.

145 The highway continues over Llanos de San Agustin. To the north (left rear) 40 kilometers in the distance are the two high peaks of the Sierra San Pedro Martir: the granitic pluton of Picacho del Diablo, 10,126 feet, the highest peak in Baja California, and Pico Matomi, a Miocene volcanic core of andesite porphyry, to its right. To the far right (west) are the irregular hills of the metavolcanic Alisitos Formation.
The predominant vegetational cover consists of stands of Ocotillo.

147 For years there has been a Red-Tail Hawk nest in the large Cardon just to the right of the highway. Careful observation of other large plants along the *Baja Highway* may reveal other nesting sites of some species of Baja's predatory birds (*See* Km 128 of the L.A. Bay turnoff to Guerrero Negro log concerning Ospreys).

PREDATORY BIRDS OF BAJA: Over 270 species of birds of prey hunt in the daylight around the world. Over 140 species of owls are the world's nocturnal predators. In Baja there are 16 species of daylight and 4 species of nocturnal predators.
Predatory birds exhibit numerous anatomical and behavioral adaptations which enable them to lead a predatory lifestyle. For example, birds of prey generally have long curved tallons for seizing their victims and strongly hooked beaks for tearing them apart. They are masters of soaring and swooping (diving). Baja's Peregrine Falcon (*Falco peregrinas*) may reach 175 mph as it dives for its prey. In certain hawks the eyes are larger and more acute than those of humans; like man's, they are binocular instead of being set on the side of the head as in most non-predatory birds. The most commonly seen predators along the *Baja Highway* are Red-Tail Hawk, Red-shouldered Hawks, Northern Harriers (Marsh Hawks),

Ospreys, and Turkey Vulture (Buzzards). Each will be discussed at kilometer marks where they have been commonly seen.

148   The prominent flat-topped mesa to the right (west) is Mesa las Palmillas; it is covered with beautiful stands of Elephant Trees and the weird Cirios. This is a good point to make a rest/photo stop and view these two interesting trees.

149   An interesting "lone Cardon" is located on the point of the flat-topped mesa nearest the highway. It looks as though it is keeping watch over passing travelers. In the right light it makes a great photograph.

152.5 As the highway passes through this roadcut, a well-developed Caliche layer can be seen. The mission padres used Caliche layers for lime to make mortar for the missions.

SOIL HORIZONS

Baja's pedocal soils generally have the following structures:

O-horizon-   Layer of fresh leaf drop and partially decomposed organic material.

A-horizon-   Decaying organic materials mixed with mineral material. This is a rather nutrient-void horizon because water which is pulled down by gravity carries most of the organically derived nutrients from the A-horizon and deposits them in the B-horizon below.

B-horizon-   In Baja an impervious calcium carbonate caliche (hardpan) layer develops which water cannot percolate. Caliches commonly form under Baja's desert grass, brush, and cactus.

C-horizon-   Weathered rock fragments close to the bedrock. Unweathered bedrock.

CALICHE (Hardpan) refers to gravel, sand, or desert debris cemented by porous calcium carbonate. In North America there are three major types of soils: laterites, pedalfers, and pedocals. Baja's soils are primarily pedocals. Pedocals form as calcium carbonate is deposited in the soil profile, particularly in the "B" horizon. This process occurs in areas where the temperature is high, the rainfall scant, and the upper level of the soil is hot and dry most of the time (Baja!). Under these conditions water evaporates before it can percolate into the soil and remove the calcium carbonate. The calcium carbonate remains in deposits near the surface of the soil in the B horizon as Caliche, a thin layer of whitish accumulation made up largely of molecular calcium (lime) carbonate. Caliche is a Spanish word which means lime. Because of the scant rainfall in Baja, the processes of chemical weathering occur very slowly, and clay is produced less rapidly than in wetter environments. As a result, pedocals have lower percentages of clay than some other soil types. The climate of Baja produces red and gray nutrient-poor desert soils, and the vegetation which grows on them is mainly grass, brush, and cactus. The plants that do grow in pedocals often show the effects of poor soil. The plants may start out fairly well, but as soon as their roots reach the caliche (hardpan) layer, their growth is severely hampered. In Baja, plants are often stunted in size, show evidence of die-back, commonly appear burned, are widely spaced to reduce competition for water, and are infested by such parasites as Mistletoe, "Witches Hairs" and Ball Moss. (*See* Km 16.5 Bahia de L.A. log "Parasites and Epiphytes".)

153.5 Some of the first granitic, bouldery outcrops of the La Virgenes region begin under the volcanic-capped mesas, visible to the right of the highway. This region, known as Las Virgenes, is full of large, spectacularly picturesque, granitic rock formations and many varieties of cactus and other desert vegetation. This region is also known as the Catavina Boulder Field or Gardens.

 Spheroidal weathering can easily be explained. This area receives little rainfall; weathering proceeds slowly on the surface of the rocks. Since there are three surfaces at corners and two at edges, the rocks tend to weather into spheres. The weak running water carries the finer particles away which leaves the rounded boulders.

154 Notice the large numbers of Barrel Cactus (Baja's Compass Plant) which are all slanted toward the southwest in an effort to reduce the harmful effect of prolonged exposure to the southwestern suns searing rays during the hottest months of the summer.

155 The view to the rear consists of several volcanic-capped mesas which are about the same elevation and are underlain by fluvatile sedimentary rocks.
At this kilometer mark there are granitic rocks with a knobby appearance that are exposed under volcanics. The knobby granitics are part of the Peninsular Range Batholith.
The vegetation in this area is stunted due to the extreme aridity of the Vizcaino Desert. The vegetational dominants are Brittle Bush and a few scattered specimens of short Cirios, Ocotillo, Datilillo, several species of annual composites, an occasional Creosote Bush, *Ephedra*, Burro Weed, *Agave*, Garambullo, Barrel Cactus, and Jojoba (goat nut).

157 The vista opens to the south to reveal numerous lava-capped mesas with cinder cones on top and the picturesque bouldery outcrops of the La Virgenes area which are well exposed.

161 This is the location of the new Shrine Rancho La Virgen.

162 Some Baja travelers have named the small, conical, breast-shaped hills on the right (west) Mammary Hill.

162.5 This side road goes to La Bocana and Rancho San Jose (95 Km). Follow Arroyo La Bocana to the southwest for views of prehistoric painted Indian rock art (pictographs). A small display at the Pariador gives some information about the "Zona Arqueologica" in this region. Rock art can also be seen in Arroyo El Palmarito (Km 170). Adopt the motto of naturalists everywhere: "take only pictures and don't even leave foot prints" so that others may continue to enjoy looking at the evidence of past inhabitants.
There is also an excellent view of the bouldery granitic tonalite terrain with basalt-capped flat hills of the Las Virgenes region. The high peaks to the right (west) are part of the Alisitos Formation.
The vegetation is typical of the Vizcaino Desert flora and consists primarily of Cirio, Cardon, Elephant Trees, Garambullo, Cholla, Creosote Bush, Barrel Cactus, annual composites, Teddy Bear Cholla, Pitaya Dulce, Pitaya Agria, and scattered Acacia and Datilillo. Smoke Trees and Mesquite are restricted to the washes; they look like puffs of smoke from a campfire. Smoke Trees are common plants of **Wash Woodlands**.

SCARIFIED SEEDS AND SANDY WASHES: Smoke trees are well represented in the washes of this part of the peninsula. Like the Palo Verde tree, they grow primarily in areas that are periodically visited by flash floods. The hard outer coating of the seeds of these two trees must be scratched (scarified) by the action of water and sand before they will germinate. This is an adaptation to the extremely arid Vizcaino Desert. It ensures that the seeds will only germinate when a sufficient amount of water is available for germination and growth of the seedling into a plant which is capable of reproducing more seeds.

ARROYOS are deep gullies cut by intermittent streams and flash floods. Baja's arroyos, which are normally dry, are infrequently filled with water after it has rained for a few days. At these times there are flash floods which fill the arroyos from wall to wall with violently moving, sand-laden waters. The washes may run for one to several days depending on the amount and duration of the preceding rains. Just a few days after these flash floods, the arroyos will again be as dry as if they had never conducted a single drop of water.

165   Around the next curve the vista again opens with dark basalt which covers the high hills in the background. Pinkish granites with spheroidal weathering are apparent in the foreground.
       This vegetational cover of this area is predominated by Elephant Trees, numerous large specimens of Cirio, Palo Adan, Cardon, Creosote Bush, Garambullo, *Mammalaria,* Jojoba, and Burro Weed. The orange "hair-like" plant which grows parasitically on the Elephant Trees is Dodder ("Witches Hair").
       The opportunistic Brittle-Bush is taking advantage of the Highway Edge Effect.

166   Some particularly picturesque rock formations and flora are found along this stretch of the highway.
       Good camping is available anywhere along the highway in this area especially along part of the old road which winds close to the right (west) of the highway.

170   The highway begins a descent into Arroyo Catavina (Arroyo El Palmarito). To the left (east) flat-lying volcanics cap the erosion surface of the granitics.
       The white building in the distance to the southeast across the Arroyo La Bocana is Pariador La Pinta de Catavina.
       Take some time in this area to explore and take pictures. In this region dawn, dusk, and afternoons are particularly picturesque and photographic times of the day.

171   Along the left side of the highway and a short distance up Arroyo Catavina a large lush stand of native palms are growing; they include specimens of fan palms (*Washingtonian falifera,* and *W. robusta*), and blue fan palm (*Erythea brandegeei*). The presence of palms in the desert always indicates the presence of perennial springs.
       Pools in or water down Arroyo Catavina can be seen most of the year. Downstream to the west on the "nose" of a large granitic mass, large, smooth, water-polished boulders are visible 20 feet above the water. At some time there must have been at least 15-20 feet of water in this arroyo to have polished the tops of these enormous boulders.
       Archaeological evidence indicates large numbers of prehistoric native Indians once occupied the area and made use of the perennial springs located in this region. In boulder areas west and north of Pariador Catavina, stone chips and broken arrowheads can be seen littering the surface of the ground for several kilometers. Inquire at La Pinta Hotel or at Rancho Santa Ines for a description of how to get to the prehistoric rock paintings (pictographs) located to the southwest in Arroyo La Bocana. These pictographs are known locally as "Cueva de las Pinturas Rupestres Gigantas" (*See* Km 162.5).

       THE HISTORY OF MAN IN BAJA: The early history of man in Baja is not well known. The authors of this guide have found and explored, but not disturbed, many archaeological sites over the past 25 years, but little scientific work has been performed by anyone anywhere on the peninsula. Some work has been done on the Gulf islands, but as one author wrote, even the islands remain "...largely an archaeological terra incognita." All that is known for certain is that man has long inhabited the peninsula as evidenced by the numerous painted caves, petroglyphs, pottery shards, spear points, scrapers, manos and matates, debitage, carved bone, stone circles, rock cairns, lithic knives, shell middens, fragments of Yucca and Palm sandals, baskets, ceremonial effigies, bird points, and living structures.

Using stratigraphic and Carbon-14 data, some scientists calculate that the appearance of man in the Americas occurred between 10,000 and 35,000 B.C. Evidence indicates that man was in mainland Mexico about 11,000 years ago. It has been estimated that man first appeared on the Baja peninsula and some of the Gulf islands about 8,000 years ago. The only Indians currently living in Baja as a tribe are located at Catarina east of Ensenada. Extensive excavations and mapping of human habitation of the peninsula remains to be done to illuminate the history of human occupancy of Baja. The few investigations of human occupancy that have been done are either site reports or studies of artifact collections. The exact origins of the prehistoric Indians of the North American continent is unknown. One of the most popular theories of the origin of the American Indian states that millenia ago man came from Asia across the Bering Strait of Alaska either by way of the Diomedes Islands (whose formation served as a ladder) or the Aleutian Islands. It is thought that the various races of Indians arrived at different times and in several different migratory surges.

NATIVE PALMS OF BAJA: Native palms were very important to Baja's native Indians. They ate both the thin fleshy portion we normally eat and the large seed and usually ground them together. During times of famine they also boiled and ate the moist pithy center of the tree.

Palm fronds made numerous useful products such as sandal-like footwear, baskets, ceremonial effigies (dolls) of the dead, and house and roofing materials. There is evidence that the Indians also burnt the trees periodically to kill insects and mites and to improve the date yield or the next harvest. Palm berries are also eaten by birds and other animals. Orioles use the fibers from the leaf for nesting material.

Other vegetational dominants of the area are large Dodder-covered Elephant Trees, Barrel Cactus, branched Cardons, and stunted sparse Cirios.

171.5 The highway passes through a low saddle and "Rio Catavina" flows to the right (southwest) in Arroyo La Bocana. This stretch of the highway passes directly over the site of the popular gas stop of old Rancho Catavina and exactly follows the old road. The gas was siphoned into 5 gallon cans to measure it and then set on the truck to be strained through a chamois or a felt hat into the gas tank.

174 This is El Pariador trailer park and hotel La Pinta de Catavina. *Extra* gas is usually available, but a long wait is sometimes inevitable.
This area is considered by many travelers to be one of the most scenic in Baja because of its bouldery rugged beauty, the arid starkness of Desierto El Vizcaino, and its unique vegetation.

174.5 Shortly after leaving El Pariador the highway crosses the Arroyo Santa Ines with its perennially-running, spring-fed stream and another grove of native fan and blue palms. The picturesque view upstream of the rocks and another native palm oasis is spectacular.

175.8 The paved turnoff to the left leads 2 kilometers to Rancho Santa Ines. Services at the rancho include camping, good tacos and enchiladas, some spartan rooms, and a paved airstrip.

It is possible to travel up nearby Arroyo La Bocana about twenty-three 4-wheel drive kilometers to Mision Santa Maria. It was founded in 1767 by the Jesuit Priest, Father Victoriano Arnes, only a year before the expulsion of the Jesuits from Baja California. The mission is not badly deteriorated and is scheduled for restoration sometime in the future, probably "manana". If you do not have a 4-wheel drive vehicle it is worth spending some time in Santa Ines and having someone take you up the arroyo to Mision Santa Maria to explore the inhospitable terrain of this area.

South of Arroyo Santa Ines the highway leaves behind the picturesque granitics of the Las Virgenes region and follows the old road (to the left -- east) up the arroyo. The hills are still covered by extensive dark (prieta) lava flows. The landscape has become less spectacular and more rugged.

177 A view of the unconformity with basalt overlying tonalite is visible to the left rear (*See* Km 164.).

179 This grade climbs through Miocene fluvial sediments which cross the highway in a wide band (like an ancient river channel). The fluvial sediments are overlain by basalts similar to those on Llanos de San Agustin.

As the highway passes through the valley between volcanic hills, you will get an idea of just how rugged the old road, located in the wash about 100 yards west, used to be along this stretch of volcanic terrain.

Elephant Trees, Agave, Cardon, Cirio, Ocotillo, *Mimosa sp.* (the bright green, thorny trees) also grow abundantly in this area.

182 At approximately 2 o'clock (south) on the lava-capped mesa, a small conical hill can be seen. It represents the remnants of a small, pyramid shaped, eroded, basalt cinder cone.

183 This section of the highway passes through granitics overlain by volcanics. Several other conical-shaped hills, which also represents cinder cones, are in view on the horizon ahead.

184 A series of white dikes cut across the mixed granitics and metamorphic rocks between here and Km 191.

186 A number of native fan and blue palms are growing to the right in the nearby Arroyo Jaraguay. The vegetation of this area is denser than that of other parts of Desierto Vizcaino because of better more moist soil. The vegetational dominants are typical of the Vizcaino Desert flora as represented by bright green *Mimosa sp.* trees, Tamarisk, tall Cardon and Cirio, and a thick undergrowth of Garambullo, Pitaya Agria, Pitaya Dulce, Brittle-Bush, Creosote Bush, Ocotillo, *Atriplex*, Jumping Cholla, scattered Palo Estribo, and several species of annual composites.

187 Rancho San Martin is located at this kilometer mark. The "golden spike" was planted here and commemorates the completion of the Transpeninsular Highway in 1973. The highway was started in the north and in the south and met here in 1973.

191.5 This turnoff leads southwest (to the right) to Rancho Jaraguay and the old road. Just before the ranch on the left are the ruins of a number of adobe buildings destroyed by weathering. In the old days it was a bath house where earlier Baja travelers could actually get a shower. This was unusual because there were not many places where earlier travelers could even find drinking water.

Several endemic palms occur near the ranch.

Outcrops of gneisses and tonalite with andesite dikes are exposed along the highway at this kilometer mark. This region is one of impressive mixtures of metamorphic and granitic rocks, dikes, bouldery outcrops, and beautiful basalt-capped mesas such as Mesa Jaraguay, Mesa El Gato, and Mesa Prieta.

193   The highway climbs a steep grade and crosses over the path of the old road. Imagine making the same climb on the old rocky dirt road.

The compass plant of Baja (Barrel Cactus) is especially obvious on the slopes along the left side of the highway.

194.5 As the highway crests the top of Jaraguay grade (elevation 823 meters), a good view opens to the north. This viewpoint provides an overview of the volcanic table-land the highway has been passing through, the unconformity between the granitics and the basalts, and the relatively flat erosion surface that is underneath the volcanic strata.

A few Cirios are growing on the drier south side of the grade, and many more larger Cirios can be seen on the moister north side.

> **NORTH AND SOUTH FACING SLOPES**: Local variations of humidity and temperature exercise considerable control upon natural slope cover. In non-tropical regions, slope face (or aspect) is of great importance. Because Baja is north of the Equator, its southward-facing slopes receive more direct sunlight, and they are hotter and drier. As a result of the decreased humidity and increased temperatures, slope cover is sparse, low, and composed of grayish-colored species which are adapted to living in xeric (dry) environments. The soils are more weathered and have less organic matter.
>
> North facing slopes receive less direct sunlight and are more humid and cooler than south facing slopes. They support denser, lusher, taller, moisture-needing vegetation including trees characteristic of mesic (moist) environments. Wind is slowed, and soil temperatures and evaporation are decreased by the dense vegetation. The soils are less weathered and are humus-rich.
>
> The highway passes a number of good examples of north/south facing slopes on the way to "land's end" at Cabo San Lucas. They will be pointed out at the appropriate kilometer with a reference to this discussion of the significance of slope face.

195.5 At this kilometer a good view of Laguna Seca, which is normally a dry lake, is visible to the left. The old road used to bear to the left and crosses part of the lake bottom. At the present time the highway circles around to the right side of the lake on the high ground near the base of the hills.

> **HEAT WAVES OR ARE YOU O.K.?** On his first trip down the peninsula, John Minch (one of the authors of this guide) and his wife, Carol, were slowly approaching Laguna Seca while driving on the old dirt road on a very hot afternoon. That day the heat waves made the dry lake look like it was filled with water. As John looked at the Lake, he was amazed to see an 18 foot sail boat. He exclaimed to Carol, "There's a sail boat on that lake!" Carol felt his forehead and asked cautiously, "Do you feel all right?" However, John was right; there was a boat on the dry lake. Someone had tried to trailer a sailboat up the peninsula and had gotten as far as this dry lake before all the springs on the trailer broke. Arturo, a rancher at Rancho Chapala to the south, talked about the incident for years.

199 As the highway crests a low pass (elevation 671 meters), a good view opens to the south. Several volcanic peaks of the San Jose volcanic fields can be seen in the distance to the right. The rolling landscape in this region is covered with volcanic debris.

202.5 The highway crests over a rise and reveals the first view of Cerro Pedregoso.

206.2 The highway passes close to Cerro Pedregoso (which means stony or rocky) pluton. This granitic hill has been largely covered by volcanic and other debris so that only the top of it stands out like an iceberg above the volcanic plain (Pliocene-Holocene basalts and basaltic andesites). The granitic rocks have been spheroidally weathered which left large boulders of granite which look like they were piled on the surrounding hill.
A dark andesite dike cuts through the middle of Cerro Pedregoso. Cerro Pedregoso, a very prominent feature on the otherwise fairly barren, gently rolling landscape, acted as a beacon that earlier Baja travelers could see for many kilometers as they slowly approached the cerro over the old rugged dirt road.
The highway continues to move across a barely-undulating volcanic plain with views of other smaller granitic outcrops.

215 As the highway crests another small rise, the dirt road which approaches diagonally from the right rear and crosses the highway in the wash, is the old road. It is easy to imagine how miserable it was to bounce along for hours and hours through this rocky, dusty stretch of the "old road".
The dirt road to the left is a highway "maintenance" road, not the "old road".

215.9 This roadcut exposes several andesitic dikes in tonalite.
In the late spring the tall "weeds" with yellow-centered white flowers which grow along the roadside are called California Prickly Poppies.

217 The red and black pyroclastic cinders and basalt exposed in this roadcut indicates that an ancient eruptive center is located nearby.

218 A prominent white quartz dike is exposed approximately 100 meters to the left of the highway. An old road passed just below that dike.

221 The hill straight ahead is cut diagonally by a series of prominent, gray-white, granitic dikes.

222.7 One of the dikes noted at Km 221 forms the ridge approximately 100 meters to the left of the highway. This dike is approximately 7 meters thick and is very light in color.

223 The highway begins a gentle descent just north of Laguna Chapala as the dry playa lake of Laguna Chapala comes into view.
Outcrops of volcanic rocks and overlying granitic rocks are exposed along this section of the highway.

224 The mountains to the southeast are part of the Sierra la Asamblea. The valley in front of them is Valle Calamajue.

225.5 Several more prominent diagonal white granitic dikes cut the hills to the right front of the highway.

228 At this kilometer sign there is an excellent view of Laguna Chapala. In the distance to the left is the main part of the dry lake bed playa.

The old road went to the left across the lake to a small group of buildings (non-existant now) and trees. The dying trees, which are barely visible on the far side of the lake, are all that is left of the old Rancho Chapala.

> **Pulvo = Dust:** This was one of the dustiest parts of the old road on the entire peninsula. Laguna Chapala is a dry lake bed most of the time. The heavy traffic across the lake on the old road pulverized the dry lake bed sediments into a choking dust (Pulvo is Spanish for dust). Two former students of John Minch once crossed this area in an open jeep. One of them stood on the seat and held onto the windshield while he almost directed the driver through the ruts! The driver high centered the jeep, and they had to jack the jeep up in 10 inches of dust.
> There was no "best route" across Laguna Chapala.
> At the flatter south end of the dry lake, it was possible for a vehicle to achieve speeds of 60 mph!
> Now, the highway skirts the west side of the lake and passes between the upper and lower lake at the New Rancho Chapala.

At Laguna Chapala an obvious vegetation change can be seen. The Cirio almost disappears; Cardons become very small and are only seen against the foothills of Sierra De Calamajue. The vegetation adjacent to the highway is dominated primarily by the halophytes, low gray mounded Bursage, and Creosote Bush. An occasional Datilillo, Cholla Cactus, Pitaya Agria, Desert Mallow, and Teddy Bear Cholla are scattered among the halophytes. The vegetational change is primarily a result of the highly alkaline soil of the dry lake.

229.5 The roughly graded unpaved dusty road to the left leads to the northeast to Bahia de San Luis Gonzaga, Puertocitos, and San Felipe. Preparations are being made to pave the portion of the road between Laguna Chapala and Puertocitos. It is not recommended that passenger cars attempt this road at this time. The road to Bahia de San Luis Gonzaga winds to the northeast to the foothills of Sierra Calamajue, past Rancho Las Arrastras, and Loma (hill) San Francisquito, and on to Bahia de San Luis Gonzaga. Then it winds northward along the coast and ends at San Felipe (*See* the road log for Laguna Chapala to San Felipe). The road has recently been paved from Puertocitos to San Felipe, but unfortunately it is also badly weathered.

230.8 This is the location of the new Rancho of Laguna Chapala.

> **TILTING OF THE PENINSULA?** The old shorelines of Laguna Chapala are tilted relative to the Recent shorelines of the lake. This indicates that there has been Pleistocene to Recent tilting of this area.

232 The sand dunes on the south side of the lake indicate the prevailing wind direction which blows the sand and silt from the lake and forms the dunes. The stabilized dunes on the south end of Laguna Chapala are blown from the lake during normal dry spells. Dunes are often found where there is an abundance of sand such as in a dry lake or on a beach. A climb to the top of the dunes will provide an excellent view of Laguna Chapala.
The hills to the right are part of the extensive basaltic volcanic field which is located in this area.

234 The hills ahead of this kilometer mark are composed of tonalite which is cut by dark andesitic and basaltic dikes which fed the volcanic field mentioned at Kilometer 232.

235.7 In this roadcut excellent examples of black dikes which cut granitics are well exposed. The taller vegetation along both sides of the highway is composed of *Mimosa sp.* and Indian Tree Tobacco.

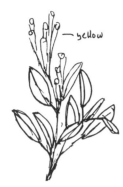

INDIAN TREE TOBACCO is the common name of the tall (1-3 meter) herb which grows in the disturbed soils along the roadsides throughout the peninsula. This plant is easily recognized by its yellow tubular flowers and disagreeably strongly-scented narcotic poisonous leaves. Baja's Indians used the plant to cure ailments of the chest and lungs and as a headache and toothache remedy. Its juice was used to promote wound healing, and the dried crumbled leaves were smoked for their narcotic effect. This plant is reported to be poisonous to stock. Some of the Indians died from its use.

238 The old road joins the highway from the left just before passing through Cuesta El Portezuelo.
Good stands of vegetation typical of Desierto el Vizcaino return. The soil of Laguna Chapala is too saline for them. The flora is dominated by Cirio, Cardon, Ocotillo, Elephant Tree, Barrel Cactus, Old Man Cactus, *Mammalaria*, and Cholla.

239.5 At this point the highway passes Cuesta El Portezuelo. A small shrine is located to the left on the old road below. This is the main peninsular divide where the highway passes east of a ridge for a short distance between the Pacific Coast drainage and the Gulf drainage.
Stop and look to the south at one of the finest views on the peninsula (*see* cover photo). To the rear of this ridge, the last view of the the lake bed of Laguna Chapala is seen in the distance.
The highly mineralized granitic and mixed metamorphic rocks of Sierra la Asamblea form the high mountains to the left front. The high light-gray part of the Sierra is a granitic pluton which is surrounded by metamorphic rocks. Several light-colored dikes cut the darker metamorphic rocks.

242 The highway passes through another picturesque granitic outcrop area.
The vegetation of this area is similar to the granitic boulder gardens which surround Catavina (*See* Km 153.5) and is dominated by specimens of Cardon and Cirio with scattered Elephant Trees, Old Man Cactus, Teddy Bear Cholla, Yucca, Agave, Jumping Cholla, Pitaya Agria, Palo Adan, and Ocotillo.

248.5 There is a view of Cerrito Blanco directly ahead to the left of the highway. It is a low light-gray granitic hill, which is highly jointed. The jointing makes the hill look like it is composed of bedded sedimentary rocks.
The highway passes through some light-colored, fluvatile-lacustrine sedimentary rocks.

250 Mixed granitic and metamorphic rocks form the low hills to the east of the highway.

251 The light-colored flat material along both sides of the highway for the next several kilometers is part of late Pleistocene lake-bed sediments.

253 The low white hill to the left is Cerrito Blanco. This jointed granodiorite hill sits on an alluvial plain which is unconformably overlain by white cross-bedded Paleocene sandstones.
To the north there is a view of a volcanic table-land and the steep cinder cone peak of Cerro el Volcacito.

256   Datilillo, Cardon, and Cirio have become the dominant tall plants of Desierto Vizcaino flora.

257   The highway crests a very low divide and moves into the Pacific slope drainage.

258.5 The old road turns off to Bahia de San Luis Gonzaga, Puertocitos, and San Felipe. This road can be used as a poor shortcut to reach the newer previously mentioned graded dirt road from Laguna Chapala at Km 229.5. This road passes by Mision Calamajue, Cerro el Volcacito, through Valle Calamajue between Sierra la Josefina and Sierra Calamajue, and connects with the graded road to Bahia de San Luis Gonzaga.
Several more raptor nests can be seen in Cirios along both sides of the highway.

262.1 This small grade represents a prominent fault scarp that cuts diagonally across the highway. The fault uplifts Miocene fluvatile sediments on the south side against the Quaternary alluvium and lakebed sediments on the north side. This is the north edge of the stable San Borja block (Gastil *et al.*, 1972). It consists of a pre-Miocene, west-sloping bedrock surface, which is discontinuously overlain by Cenozoic sedimentary and volcanic strata.
South of here the surrounding uninterrupted mesas extend from the main Gulf escarpment to the Pacific coastal plain.

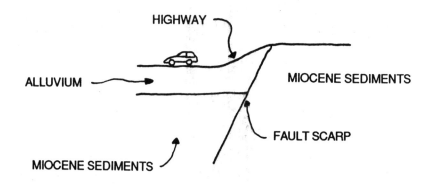

265   The highway begins a gradual descent into the drainage system of Arroyo el Crucero and follows it for several kilometers to the south. This drainage is developed on and weathered into Paleocene marine and non-marine sediments.
Just north of Punta Prieta, the plant species remain relatively the same as those seen since leaving Laguna Chapala. However, the dominant species alternate between Cirio and Datilillo (little palm) and the sagraro-like Cardon. The low sparse gray dead-looking "understory" is Bursage (*Franseria dumosa*).

HOW DO THE LOW SPARSE GRAY FLORA OF BAJA'S EXTREMELY ARID DESERTS SURVIVE? Most of Baja's desert landscape is dominated by low-growing vegetation (shrubs, cacti, and grasses) although some plants do grow to the size of small trees. All of these plants are remarkable in the many and varied ways in which they have adapted to a desert existence. Some are leafless (obligate drought-deciduous species) most of the year. In the absence of leaves, the green trunks (cladodes) act as photosynthetic leaves and produce carbohydrates to meet the plants required energy resource. Others have silvery or velvety foliage that helps reflect heat and retain moisture under the hot desert sun. Many are armed with spikes or thorns, perhaps to discourage animals from grazing on their slow-growing branches. The spiked leaves of many plants provide points from which dew can collect, fall to the ground, and water the plant.

A closer look at the "understory" also reveals specimens of Agave, Garambullo, Jumping Cholla, and *Acacia*. This Datilillo-Cardon/Datilillo-Cirio community continues for many kilometers.

266   Exposures of granitic and metamorphic rocks are seen along the highway.
The new highway almost follows the old road.

280.5 = 0
At the junction of Highway 1 south and Highway 1 to Bahia De Los Angeles, the roadside kilometer signs change to 0 (*See* the Los Angeles Junction to Bahia de Los Angeles road log).

Log 4 - L.A. Bay Turnoff to Guerrero Negro

Log 4 - Bahia de Los Angeles Turnoff to Guerrero Negro
[129 kms= 80 miles]

L. A. Bay Turnoff to Rosarito - *The Baja Highway continues south in the Miocene fluvial sediments with basalt mesas to the left and high rugged metamorphic and granitic hills to the right. It then drops into the main alluvial channel of Arroyo Leon, past Punta Prieta, with Paleocene fluvial sediments on both sides of the arroyo and metamorphic and granitic hills in the distance.*

At La Bachada the Baja Highway climbs up a grade through rolling hills onto the rolling Paleocene mesas with steep isolated hills of metavolcanic rock and high volcanic mesas in the distance. After passing a rugged metavolcanic hill to the left the two conical shaped Occidental Buttes composed of Paleocene fluvial sediments are seen to the right. The Baja Highway then enters a hilly area of mixed granitic rocks and drops into El Rosarito.

Rosarito to Guerrero Negro - *The Baja Highway follows the south bank of the arroyo with metamorphic rocks on the left, then passes through a canyon in the steep gabbro hills before turning south to again climb onto and through rolling hills in the undulating dissected mesas of marine Paleocene sediments. The Baja Highway drops into a steep narrow gorge in gabbro then alternately climbs onto the Paleocene marine mesas and drops into the alluviated valleys with the basalt capped Paleocene mesas to the east.*

The Baja Highway then drops onto the alluvial fans of the Llano del Berrendo. During the long crossing of this plain the low hills of metasedimentary rocks to the left become more distant. A low basalt cone is closely passed to the right and the distant basalt cone of Punta Santa Domingo looms ever closer. The coastal dune field and occasionally the Pacific Ocean are in almost constant view to the right. After passing Jesus Maria the Baja Highway begins to cross the limestone surface of the Pleistocene lagoon. The ever present dune field encroaches on the Baja Highway as the Eagle Monument is approached at the state line.

0   The highway to the left (east) leads to Bahia de Los Angeles (*See* Bahia de Los Angeles log) while the highway ahead continues 129 kilometers to the southwest to Guerrero Negro.

4   The flat mesa to the left is composed of Miocene fluvial sediments capped by basalt.

6.5   The Cardons which are seen along this stretch of the highway are reputed to be among the tallest in Baja -- even taller then some specimens in the large cardonal located at the south end of Bahia de Concepcion on Baja's southern gulf coast.

9   The dominant trees along the highway are two unrelated genera of Elephant Trees, *Pachycormus* and *Bursera*.

THE NAME ELEPHANT TREES or Torote Blanco is unfortunately applied to several unrelated desert trees in Baja. The two kinds of Elephant Trees in this region are not closely related at all. *Pachycormus discolor* is a member of the Cashew family (F. *Anacardiaceae*), while *Bursera microphylla* belongs to the Torchwood family (F. *Burseraceae*). These two Elephant Trees are easily differentiated because of the distinctive incense-like aroma which is given off by the crushed leaves or fruits of the *Bursera*. *Bursera microphylla* ranges to the south from Anza-Borrego Desert in the U.S.A. through the entire peninsula to the Cape region. A second species of *Bursera, B. hindsiana,* has almost the same distribution. Oil from the fruit of *Bursera* has been used as a dye and for tanning hides. From Bahia de la Concepcion south to the Cape Region in the Central Gulf Coast Desert, a fourth species of Elephant Tree, *Bursera odorata (fagoides)* may also be seen.

The confusion created by giving different organisms the same common names points out the importance of assigning a unique genus and species name for each different kind of plant, animal, fungus, protistan, and moneran of the vivicum (Aristotle's term for all living organisms).

13.2 This turnoff leads to Punta Prieta (Dark Point -- named for the dark basalts seen in this region). The main highway follows Arroyo Leon which is developed along a fault that is responsible for the arroyo's north-south trend. The Paleocene Sepultura Formation is exposed on both sides of the arroyo for the next 10 kilometers.

13.5 More "living" Datilillo fences are seen to the right.

14 The airstrip at Punta Prieta is located to the left of the highway. As the highway turns to the south, the hills to the right are composed of metavolcanics of the Alisitos Formation. The Paleocene sediments lapped against the irregular topography of the Cretaceous hills. The high hill to the east is composed of tonalite (quartz diorite).

16.5 The denser vegetation in this region continues to be representative of the flora of Desierto El Vizcaino. The plants along the highway are predominantly Cardon with occasional Palo Verde, tall lichen, draped Cirios, Agave, shorter infrequent Barrel Cactus, Datilillo, Pitaya Agria, Pitaya Dulce, two species of Elephant Trees in the washes, Jumping Cholla, Teddy Bear Cholla, Creosote Bush, Broom Baccharis, Cheesebush and the last scattered occurrences of Ocotillo. From this point to the south an Ocotillo look-alike, Palo Adan, will replace Ocotillo.

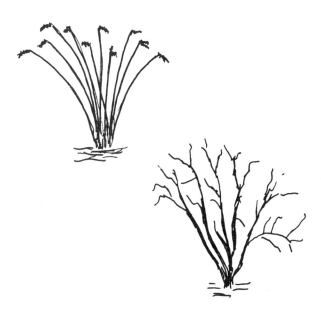

OCOTILLO OR PALO ADAN? These two plants along with the weird Cirio belong to the Ocotillo family (*F. Fouquieriaceae*), a group of spiny shrubs with long erect thorny whip-like branches. At first glance it may seem like Ocotillo (*Fouquieria splendens*) and Palo Adan (*F. diguetii*) are the same plant. Upon closer inspection they are very different. The characteristics that help separate these two close relatives are general trunk, branch, and flower morphology (external appearance); geographical distribution; and habitat preference. Climate, precipitation, and soil chemistry affect the habitats in which all plants, including these two spiny shrubs, grow. The chart below will help to distinguish between these two look-alike relatives.

	Palo Adan (Adam's Tree)	Ocotillo
Trunk	short and thick	none
Branch diameter	Thick; branches off a short trunk	Thin, slender, whip-like, spreads upward, fan-like from ground
Flowers	Panicles are smaller	Panicles larger
Geographical distribution	Abundant from Alta Calif., Baja Norte to 28th parallel (at Km 128 just north of Guerrero Negro) and rare south to the Cape	Abundant from the central part of the peninsula south to the Cape
Habitat preference*	Clay and granitic soils of alluvial plains	Desert slopes and plains

*The chemistry of soil and rock is an important factor which affects plant distribution. Localities which have distinctive soils generally have distinctive vegetation. Vegetation changes such as plant vigor or plant species may reflect soil changes across lithologic contacts. This can be useful information, as geologists seek to define formational boundaries.

24.5 The highway turns and crosses Arroyo Leon whose wash woodland is dominated by Mimosa and scattered Datilillo.

25.5 This is Rancho La Bachada whose well was once one of the better sources of water in this part of the peninsula.
In 1965 the San Diego State University geologic mapping crews were based at Punta Prieta. Once a week someone was sent to La Bachada to get 100 gallons of drinking water from the well. One week a crew member was sent to fill eighteen 5-gallon jugs. As he was filling the eighteenth jug, he lifted a bucket of well water which contained a dead decaying hairless rat. Not wanting to go elsewhere to refill the jugs, he pitched the rat, drew another bucket of water to fill the last jug, and returned to camp without saying a word (he used the other two 5-gallon jugs that week). No one found out what had happened until years later. Water is too valuable to waste in Baja!

26 The highway begins a steep ascent through Paleocene conglomerates.

29 At the top of the grade, the vista opens to the south and presents a spectacular view of the Pacific coast and the flat Paleocene Sepultura Formation which forms all of the flat-topped mesas in the immediate foreground (to the left) and into the distance. The rugged high peaks to the far right and the high sharp peak directly ahead are composed of metasedimentary rocks of the Alisitos Formation.
This area was once a Paleocene marine embayment. Shallow water non-marine to marine sediments from this embayment have yielded fossils of hackberry seeds, marine invertebrates, one tooth of the proto-horse *Hyracatherium*, and several non-marine vertebrate fossils (found by Occidental College).

THE PALEOCENE ENVIRONMENT: Fife (1968) reconstructed the probable Paleocene environment and stated, "The coast north of Punta Santa Rosalia... was rocky as it is today. The location of fossiliferous deposits indicates that heavy-shelled gryphoid oysters were deposited with conglomerates near shore; while turritellas and echinoids were preserved with finer clastic sediment in the shallow embayments..."
"South of Punta Santa Rosalia at least three major embayments existed..."

"The southern embayment is well exposed and contains shallow to brackish water faunas. These were areas of mud to sand bottoms. The position of fossil mollusca, corals, ostracodes, and foraminifers suggests that alternate shallow marine and estuarine or brackish water conditions existed. Seeds of the Family Chenopodieaceae and the remains of the proto-horse *Hyracatherium* are found in beds interfingering with typical estuarine strata. Ostracodes and charophytes indicate a lacustrine environment in the continental beds east of Rancho La Bachada."

The location at Kilometer 28 is in the northernmost portion of the Paleocene embayment.

THE ORIGIN OF THE HORSE AND ITS PLACE IN BAJA TODAY: It is hard to believe, but horses evolved in North America.

Modern domestic horses (*Equus caballus*) belong to a small order of mammals known as the Perissodactyla or odd-toed ungulates which first appeared in the late Paleocene (58 million years ago) in North America. The earliest of the horse-like ancestors *Hyracatherium* appeared in the Eocene about 54 million years ago. *Hyracatherium* was a small dog-sized mammal that browsed on low shrubs of the forest floors. It had already lost two hind toes on its hind feet and one on its forefeet, but the feet were still covered with soft pads. Its the tooth of this horse ancestor that was collected from the Paleocene Sepultura Formation.

When grasses first appeared in the early Miocene, hypsodont grazing equids appeared, and by the late Miocene equids had reached their peak of diversity. The need to run from predators and to travel long distances in search of food and water led to many changes in equid body shape including increased body size. By the early Pleistocene, two million years ago, the one-toed equids (*Pliohippus*) had spawned the genus *Equus* which spread rapidly over the world. The modern domestic horse is thought to have descended from some mutant of Prezewalski's horses. The center of equid evolution was North America. True equids did not migrate to the Old World from North America until the early Pleistocene about two million years ago. The Old World equids evolved from the three-toed North American immigrant equid *Hipparion*, and by the end of the Pleistocene modern equids had become widely distributed on all continents except Australia. For some unknown reason all North American ungulates, except the pronghorn antelope, became extinct about 10,000 years ago. In the Old World the modern horse, *Equus caballus*, was first domesticated in Asia about 5,000 years ago. They were initially used by inhabitants of the Old World as a means of transport, warfare, and agricultural labor and were later used for recreation and sport.

The domestic horse was reintroduced into North America (mainland Mexico) by the Spanish Conquerors of Mexico in the early 16th century. Exploration of the Baja peninsula began in 1535 when Hernan Cortez established a small colony on the present Bahia de La Paz which was abandoned in 1537 due to supply shortages. Exploration of Baja was continued by Hernando de Alarcon (1540), Juan Rodriguez Cabrillo (1542), Sebastian Vizcaino (1596), Nicholas de Cardona and Juan de Iturbe (1615), Francisco de Ortega (1664 and 1666), and Francisco de Lucenilla (1688). In 1697 Padre Juan Maria Salvatierra with six soldiers landed on Baja's east coast and established Mision Nuestra Senora De Loreto. Loreto became the first permanent Spanish settlement in Baja. Along with the soldiers, horses again arrived in Baja. The Mexican name for horse is caballo (a derivative of the species name *caballus*), and Mexican horseman are known as caballeros. Horses in Baja are used primarily for agricultural labor and transport. The leather craftsmen of Miraflores once made much of the tack for many of the Caballeros of Baja and mainland Mexico.

Today, populations of domestic and feral horses flourish in the open and mountainous temperate grasslands and semi-deserts of western North America, which includes Baja, South America, Europe, and Australia.

The domestic horse is a medium-sized herbivore that forages primarily on high-fiber, low-level browse and supplements its protein intake with buds, berries, fruit, bark, leaves, and roots. The horses of Baja are often extremely lean because of the scarcity of browse and overwork.

32.5   This hogback ridge is composed of complexly folded and overturned metavolcanic rock of the Alisitos Formation which is exposed in the roadcuts to the left for the next 4 kilometers.

34   The very sparse low grey vegetation of this region is predominated by Bursage, Maguay, Purple Bush, small Elephant Trees, occasional Barrel cacti, Cirio, and Datilillo.

38.7   Just before and after crossing Arroyo Santo Domingo, a turnoff leads 15 kilometers to the coastal fishing village of Santa Rosalilita located on the northern shore of Bahia Santa Rosalilita.
The view to the south is of Occidental Buttes.

39   The small palm oasis to the right is known as Agua de Refugio. The waters of the small stream originate from springs located to the left of the highway.

39.5   The highway crosses a small heavily vegetated wash with a perennial stream which originates in the metavolcanic hills to the left.

41.5   Ahead there are two small buttes which some American geologists have named Occidental Buttes. The local name is Tettes de Cabra. (Because of their diminutive size, they are not named on any maps of Baja.). Mother nature is taking a sun bath.

42   The highway ascends a small grade and passes through more Paleocene exposures.

44   Occidental Buttes, seen immediately to the right, morphologically resemble two small mamillariform buttes in the Paleocene Sepultura Formation. This is the site of numerous vertebrate fossil discoveries by an expedition from Occidental College in the mid-1960's.

PALEOCENE SEPULTURA FORMATION: "The most extensive outcrop of fossiliferous Paleocene marine rocks occurs in the southern part of the area, in the vicinity of and to the north of Rancho San Xavier. In this region at least one hundred feet of dusky yellow to reddish brown sandstone is interbedded with conglomeratic sandstones, concretionary lenses, siltstone, and mudstone. Several horizons, forming resistant strata, contain *Turritella pachecoensis* almost exclusively. Locality B5D-30 yielded *Cerithidea sp.*, *Ostrea sp.*, *Venericardia sp.*, *Glycymeris sp.*, and *Turritella pachecoensis*, plus several specimens of gryphoid oyster and unidentified horn corals, ostrocodes, and foraminiferas. This assemblage represents a sublittoral facies. Farther north, about six miles [ten kilometers] up the arroyo from El Muertito, the fossil assemblage suggests a lagoonal or littoral environment. At this location the remains of a small proto-horse, *Hyracatherium sp. nov.*, were interbedded with seeds from the family Chenopodiaceae (D. A. Preston, 1966, personal communication) *Cerithidea sp.*, *Calyptraea sp. nov.*, and *Ostrea sp....*"
"About six miles [ten kilometers] due north of the above locality, at Occidental buttes, Morris (1966) reported the discovery of ungulates of the Orders

Tillondontia, Perissodactyla and Pantodonta. Pantodonts of the family Barylambdidae were found stratigraphically above specimens assigned to Tillodontia and Perissodactyla..." (Fife, 1968).

4 5   The vegetation of this region continues to be dominated by species characteristic of the flora of the Desierto El Vizcaino area, and Cirio is the predominant tall plant. Plants associated with these Cirio are Barrel Cactus, Elephant Trees, Purple Bush, Agave, Pitaya Agria, and an occasional Cardon, Palo Adan, and Jumping Cholla. The common epiphytic lichen, *Ramalina reticulata*, can be seen growing on the Cirio and Elephant Trees.

4 6   The highway climbs through conglomeratic beds and begins a descent through marine redbeds of the Paleocene Sepultura Formation.

4 7   The high blunt mesa to the left (east) of the highway is the lagoonal section of the Paleocene Sepultura Formation which is overlain by basalts.

4 9   In addition to the lichen the Ball Moss (*Tillandsia recurva*) is growing epiphytically on the Cirio and Elephant Trees.

> **EPIPHYTES AND PARASITES:** From south of El Rosario along the Pacific coast to the Cape Region, trees, shrubs, and cacti such as Palo Adan, Cirio, Ciruelo, Lomboy, Broom Baccharis, Cardon, and Pitaya Dulce are abundantly covered with the moisture-loving epiphytic Ball Moss, a member of the pineapple family. Epiphytic Ball Moss is not harmful to the host plant, since it lives in a commensalistic relationship which depends only on the host plant for support. However, a close look at the same trees, shrubs, and cacti listed above will reveal several harmful parasites which live in a destructive symbiosis with them. The two most common parasitic organisms of this area are the evergreen mistletoe (*Phoradendron californicum*) and "witches hair" (*Cuscata veatchii*).
> "Witches hair", a flowering plant lacking chlorophyll, attaches its yellow or orange hair-like stems to its host by a modified stem called a haustoria. Using the haustorial stem, the "Witches Hair" steals sugar produced photosynthetically by its host.
> The second parasite, the evergreen mistletoe, hangs in trailing shaggy strands from many plants in Baja. Mistletoe also utilizes haustorial stems to drain sugar from its host. The moisture that sustains both the epiphytes and parasites of this desert comes from ocean fogs (Neblina) that roll in at night and lie during the early morning hours in misty layers among the hills until the sun "bakes" it off. Along the Pacific coast from the Cape north to San Francisquito, areas similar to this are known as coastal fog deserts. Mistletoe is less common on the drier Gulf side of the peninsula where fogs do not occur.

52.5   The main part of the small village of El Rosarito is located to the left of the highway. A very rough road from the center of town leads east approximately 32 kilometers through very dense vegetation to Mision San Borja and eventually ends at Kilometer 41.3 on the paved road to Bahia de Los Angeles. The mission was completed in 1762 with money supplied by Maria, the Spanish Grand Duchess of Borja. It was abandoned in 1818, but it has been restored. It is a beautiful place to visit with an off-road vehicle. The wash which roughly parallels the highway is vegetated by green grasses, rushes (*Juncus sp.*), and scattered native palms.

5 5   Datilillo, Cardon, Cirio (Boojum) and Elephant Trees are abundant; however, most of these Cirio specimens are rather short when compared with some of the "giants" of the

Log 4 - L.A. Bay Turnoff to Guerrero Negro

moister habitats to the north.
After you cross the arroyo the low hills to the right of the highway are gabbro.
The hills directly ahead and a bit to the left are prebatholithic slates.

56.8 As the highway turns south out of the arroyo of El Rosarito, a patch of granodiorite is exposed to the right in the lower end of the arroyo.
The road to the right leads 6 kilometers to Punta Rosarito on the Pacific coast.

5 9 Along this stretch thin beds of the Sepultura Formation are exposed on both sides of the highway, while the low hills to the east are schist and gabbro.

6 0 This is the first view of the ocean since El Consuelo (9 kilometers north of El Rosario).

6 1 The low pass to the left at 10 o'clock is composed of gabbro and diabase.

62.7 This turnoff leads to Playa Alta Mira on the Pacific coast.

6 4 To the east in the arroyos are good exposures of the marine red beds of the Sepultura Formation.

6 6 The highway descends a grade into a gabbro pluton exposed in the narrow neck of a canyon and climbs through the reddish beds of the Paleocene Sepultura Formation.
The southernmost Cirios (Boojum) are growing here along with Elephant Trees, Indian Tree Tobacco, Candelabra Cactus, Pitaya Agria, Palo Adan, and Creosote Bush. These species are all characteristic of Desierto el Vizcaino flora.

68.5 As the highway descends into the broad arroyo, the prominent red flat-topped hill directly to the left is a gabbro-serpentine pod.
The graded road to the right leads 5 kilometers to El Tomatal Beach and Miller's Landing. Onyx from the abandoned mines at Marmalito was once shipped from the white-water beaches of El Tomatal.
After it climbs out of the arroyo, the highway passes through more outcrops of the Sepultura Formation.

7 0 For the next 60 kilometers the highway travels south along a flat plain north of Guerrero Negro and provides panoramic views of flat-topped mesas to the east and the blue waters of the Pacific to the west.
The prominent dark-topped mesas to the left (east) are basalt overlying lacustrine lagoonal sediments to shallow water marine beds of the Paleocene Sepultura Formation.
To the right in the distance, a volcanic hill forms the north end of Laguna Manuela.
The highway continues to traverse a relatively flat gently undulating plain for several kilometers and occasionally drops into and through numerous small arroyos. Then it crosses the 150 Kilometer expanse of Llanos de Berenda which is often referred to as Antelope Plain because of the once abundant herds of antelope. At the present time there are about 15 antelope left. If you spot a deer in this region, it is really an antelope.

NOT REALLY A DEER AT ALL? The nutritious grasslands of the world are the homes of most of the great herds of herbivores. In Baja the Pronghorn Antelope (*Antilocapra americana*) is the only large feral native grazing ruminant which inhabits the "Antelope Plain" section of the vast Llanos de Berenda. The once numerous herds of pronghorn antelope have decreased to near extinction due to hunting pressures (now illegal in Baja) and the destruction of the grasses the antelope feed on as this region was changed by agriculture and cattle-grazing practices. Today they have retreated to rougher higher country unsuitable for agriculture or cattle-grazing. Natural enemies of the pronghorn are numerous. Any large carnivore will snap at the chance to take one, and even golden eagles have been known to kill them. Although they look like deer, the smaller pronghorn antelope are not members of the deer group at all, nor do they even have much connection with the Old World antelopes. The horns of the pronghorn antelope have a permanent bony core which is not discarded, although the outer horny modified hair-like covering (keratinized skin) is shed once a year. Old World antelope never lose any part of their entirely bony horns, and they lack the outer horn sheaths.

80   The low dark hill to the right is a very small basalt cone (*See* Km 98). The point of Guerrero Negro comes into view in the far distance.
The dune fields to the right parallel the Pacific coast and extend from the edge of Estero Laguna Manuela to the north end of "Scammon's Lagoon" (Laguna Ojo de Liebre). Near the old salt loading docks west of Guerrero Negro, these dunes are very well developed and are very active. There were many problems with dunes migrating into the old salt loading area at Puerto Viejo on Laguna Guerrero Negro, so they moved the barge loading docks to the interior of Laguna Guerrero Negro. The vegetation of these migrating dunes is quite sparse and consists of a few salt tolerant species (halophytes) such as Pickleweed and Sand Verbena. The tops of the well drained less saline soils of the dunes support greener less salt to errant specimens of Mesquite, *Atriplex*, and Ice Plant. They are found on the few stabilized dunes of the area.

Sand dune building along this stretch has resulted from the southward transportation of sand along the coast by long shore currents. The currents have caused a sand bar to build south of Punta Manuela. The strong winds in this area pick up the sand and carry it into the lagoon and landward away from the coast. This builds an extensive set of migrating coastal dunes both on the bar and on the landward side of the lagoon. An excellent place to see this relationship is at the old barge loading area west of town. (Go into town, cross a "river", and turn right at the main cross street after the bend.) The barge loading area, originally located here at Puerto Viejo, was moved farther south into Laguna Guerrero Negro, because navigation was hindered by the drifting sand that built sand bars in the lagoon. As the dunes progress inland, they move farther from the supply of coastal sand and soon become stabilized by plants which utilize the moisture trapped in the desalinized sand.

In this region most of Llanos de Berenda is underlain by Pleistocene limestones deposited when this part of the peninsula was covered by a warm shallow sea. Limestone is very alkaline and makes it harder for plants to establish themselves. As a result, the Llanos de Berenda is quite sparsely vegetated by the Palmer's Frankenia/Datilillo plant community with scattered Jumping Cholla (Refer back to Km 16.5 for a brief discussion of how soil chemistry affects plant distribution).

A plant community is a regional assemblage of interacting plant species characterized by the presence of one or more dominant species. Some plant communities are named for the tree or shrub species which are dominant in them. The term "dominant" refers to one or more plant species which may be the largest or most abundant species in a community. Because of the foliage cover or the extent of their root systems, dominants have a strong influence on the local ecology of the community of which they are members.

82.5   The highway passes between Rancho San Angel on the left and a low hill of basalt to the right.

Log 4 - L.A. Bay Turnoff to Guerrero Negro

The low canyons adjacent to the highway are seasonally brightened by abundant flowering Agave (Maguey), Broom Baccharis, Tamarisk, and Barrel Cactus. There are more of the living Datilillo fences here.

83   A view to the left rear shows a reddish cinder cone on top of the prominent dark mesa.

90   The highway passes between Esperanza Restaurant to the left and many stabilized dunes.

95.7   The paved road to the right by the old Pemex station goes to the governmental agricultural cooperative of Ejido Moralles y Pavan.
To go to Puerto Santo Domingo (8 Kilometers), travel 1.6 kilometers west on the road to Ejido Morelos and turn left.

98   At 3 o'clock Punta Santo Domingo basalt cone forms a dark peak by the north end of Laguna Manuela. It has an overall shield-like shape with a prominent, steep, dark, eruptive cinder cone in the center. The gentle slopes are lava flows, while the steep central slope is a cinder cone.

99   The road metal quarries on the left side of the highway expose the marine deposited Pleistocene limestone which covers large parts of the Vizcaino Peninsula south of Guerrero Negro and Llanos de Magdalena Plain.

100   On the stabilized well drained dunes along the highway, the vegetation is lush and dense, while between the dunes only the more salt-tolerant plants (hallophytes) survive. The limestone soils of Llanos de Berenda are very alkaline, but the salts are leached from the high spots (dunes) by precipitation which leaves a desalinated soil in which less halophytic plant species can grow.

108   The low white sandy hills to the right are a continuation of the coastal dune fields which stretch for many kilometers south of here.

114   On a clear day Sierra El Placer on the Vizcaino Peninsula is in view at approximately 2 o'clock.

117   Almost nothing grows over 0.3 meters tall from here to Guerrero. The low gray (1-3 dm) tufted mound-sloped plant which covers the Llanos de Berenda is a bursage, Palmer's Frankenia (*Frankenia palmeri*).

PALMER'S FRANKENIA is a stiff woody shrub which grows on sandy areas, salt marshes, beaches, and alkali flats throughout the peninsula. The white flowers, which bloom in November brighten the entire region around Guerrero Negro.

A walk through this seemingly monotonous ground cover of Palmer's Frankenia reveals a few epiphytic foliose lichens and extive algae mats that nearly cover all of the bare ground between the Bursage. Algae mats such as these are nitrogen fixers which add valuable nitrogen compounds to the nutrient-poor desert soils.
Near the highway shoulders or on the sand dunes, grows a taller gray-green leafed introduced Australian weed commonly known as Australian Saltbush (*Atriplex sp.*). This weed, now a naturalized "native", was originally cultivated for cattle forage but escaped and now grows extensively in saline soils and along the shoulders of the *Baja Highway* throughout the peninsula.

Log 4 - L.A. Bay Turnoff to Guerrero Negro

118   As the highway continues south toward Guerrero Negro, a 40 meter high metal eagle monument, "Monumento Aguila", dominates the middle of the highway. This monument was built on the 28th parallel to commemorate the completion of Highway 1 which joins the two states of Baja California Norte and Baja California Sur. On December 1, 1973, President Echeverria officially opened Mexico 1.

120   The highway approaches and then crosses a semi-stabilized dune field.

121   There are several beautiful active coastal dune fields to the right.

123   The estuary, Estero Laguna Manuela, will be in view to the right of the highway for the next half kilometer.

125.1 The paved road to the right leads to a little-used paved airstrip.

128 = 220.5
    This is the State Line eagle monument, the 28th parallel, and Hotel La Pinta de Guerrero Negro. The kilometer markings will now descend as they approach each zero point.

    The 28th parallel marks the boundary of the Pacific Time Zone (to the north of the 28th parallel) and Mountain Time Zone (to the south of the 28th parallel).
    For a number of years there was a museum in the building under the monument, then a school, but now both are gone and the building is abandoned.
    The huge nest of sticks to the left belongs to a pair of Ospreys (one of the predatory birds discussed at Km 147 of the San Quintin log) that have nested on top of the sign on the east (left) side of the monument for years.

OSPREYS or "Fish Hawks" breed along both coasts of Baja and the western coast of mainland Mexico (Sinaloa and Sonora). They are easily recognized by their clear white underparts and black "wrist" marks in flight. From their large nests the Ospreys fly to the Pacific and circles overhead while watching for the gleam of a fish near the surface or hovering with tail spread and feet dangling. From a height which may reach a hundred feet, the "Fish Hawk" dives into the water and quickly emerges with it talons impaled in the back of a fish. It takes the prey back to its nest and feeds it to its young, a piece at a time.

216.5 The highway forks here.
    The fork to the left (east) leads to San Ignacio; the one to the right (west) leads 2 kilometers into the town of Guerrero Negro where there are several gas stations, hotels and motels, restaurants and shops.
    The highway into town passes through supertidal flats which are intermittently flooded by very high tides.
    The Guerrero Negro economy is supported by exporting locally-produced salt.

Log 4 - L.A. Bay Turnoff to Guerrero Negro

THE WORLD'S LARGEST SALT PRODUCING REGION: Over 5,000 people live in the town of Guerrero Negro. The town's name "Black Warrior", is a reference to a whaling bark (ship) wrecked in the lagoon in 1858. According to Exportadora de Sal, the salt company which owned the town, the economy of Guerrero Negro is supported by the "world's largest" salt-producing operation.

Salt is a general term for naturally occurring sodium chloride (NaCl), a substance essential to life. Fortunately for mankind, it is one of the most abundant substances in the world. Salt is produced commercially from brine, salt beds, salt pans, and salt domes world wide. To the south of the highway on the vast tidal flats of Laguna Ojo de Liebre (Scammon's Lagoon), are thousands of man-made salt pans which cover over 300 square miles. Using bulldozing equipment, employees of Exportadora de Sal S.A. have diked some of the more shallow parts of the tidal flats of Scammon's Lagoon. This forms large shallow evaporating ponds (salt pans) which are approximately 100 meters square and one meter deep when flooded with sea water. As the intense sun of Desierto El Vizcaino evaporates the sea water, the sulfates and carbonates quickly precipitate out which leaves a salty brine solution that is moved to adjacent salt pans to precipitate the halides (table salt (NaCl) is the most common). When the brine has completely evaporated, the hard white salt precipitate is collected, loaded into large triple trailer bottom-dumping trucks (150 feet long), and transported to the loading docks southwest of town. At the loading docks salt is loaded on barges and lightered to Isla Cedros where it is trans-shipped to the United States, Japan, Canada, and mainland Mexico. It has been estimated that over 5,000,000 tons of salt are shipped throughout the world. Guerrero Negro is not the only salt-producing site in Baja. Another 50,000 tons are produced annually at the solar salt works located on one of the largest Gulf islands, Isla del Carmen.

Salt, limestone, coal, oil, and sulfur are the five basic raw materials of the world's chemical industries. In addition to its use as a seasoning, salt is used as a food preservative and in various commercial chemical processes. Baja is rich in several of the five basic raw materials. Potential oil-bearing layers exist in the Vizcaino and central Gulf coast deserts. Limestone is mined at Punta China near Ensenada, clays are mined in the Cape Region, and gypsum is mined on the Gulf island of Isla San Marcos. These three substances are combined to make cement in La Paz by Cementos California.

As an interesting footnote, people on Isla Cedros often drink water which falls as rain or snow on Mount Fujiama, Japan, because water is used as ballast on the Japanese ocean-going salt ships which arrive at Guerrero Negro and is off-loaded on this desert island to make room for their cargo of salt. The water is drunk by the islands inhabitants and visitors.

HOW SALT CAME TO MEAN SALARY: The word "salt" comes from the Latin word "sal". During the time of the Roman Empire, soldiers were paid partly with the coin of the empire and partly with salt. If a soldier failed to fully perform his duties, his ration of salt would be cut or withheld because he was "not worth his salt". The English term "salary" was derived from the custom of partially paying workers with salt. Today salary refers to a fixed payment received at regular intervals for services rendered. For the Roman soldier salt was used for seasoning his food and, more importantly, used to preserve food. Salt is still an important seasoning and preservative, and thus a vast and lucrative market exists for the salt derived from the solar evaporative salt works near Guerrero Negro and Isla Carmen.

Log 5 - Guerrero Negro to Santa Rosalia [217 kms = 141 miles]

Guerrero Negro -- Abreojos road. The Baja Highway crosses the extremely flat Vizcaino Plain, paralleling the Cretaceous syncline, past dune fields and cultivated fields as it approaches tilted Miocene volcanic mesas. Cretaceous metamorphic and sedimentary hills form the distant skyline to the west. As the highway approaches the Abreojos road a series of steep-sided volcanic plugs can be seen to the right.

Abreojos Road -- Tres Virgenes. The highway turns east to cross the peninsula on the tilted surfaces of volcanic flows passing near numerous volcanic centers and dune fields. East of San Ignacio a strato volcano is approached and closely passed.

Tres Virgenes -- Santa Rosalia. The highway drops down a series of fault controlled grades through volcanic rocks and then marine Pliocene rocks to the copper mining area of Santa Rosalia.

217 To go straight to Santa Rosalia take the left fork at the triangle. If you have gone into town and are heading east from Guerrero Negro take the right fork at the triangle. Mexico 1 turns to the left to head northeast toward Punta Prieta.

215 For many kilometers the highway will pass through fields of stabilized dunes which consist of sand blown to the northeast from Scammon's Lagoon.

The vegetation which grows on top of the dunes consists primarily of Mesquite (*Prosopis sp.*) and a few Saltbush (*Atriplex sp.*) plants.

MESQUITE is a large shrub or low tree which is found below 1500 meters in washes and on stabilized sand dunes throughout Baja. The pinnately compound leaves look like fern leaves. The small yellow flowers grow in slender spikes, the branches have pairs of nodal spines, and seeds are borne in tough pods that are eaten when they are ripe by rabbits, quail, deer, native rodents, cattle, and early Indians. Since Mesquite is one of the few trees which grows in the desert around Guerrero Negro, its sparse shade is welcome to a wide variety of terrestrial wildlife species and birds that frequently nest in its branches.

The **SALT BUSH**, which is associated with the mesquite, is also an important food source and provider of shade. This plant has a high forage value due to its nutritive quality evergreen habit, and seeds which are rich in sodium and other salts.

208.1 The large sign, "Parque Natural de la Ballena Gris", to the right side of the highway, marks the turnoff to Laguna Ojo de Liebre (Scammon's Lagoon) and a gray whale viewpoint 27 kilometers (17 miles) down a graded dirt road (the one perpendicular to the *Baja Highway*). The conditions of this road vary with the weather.
Atriplex, Palmer's Sprankinia, Cardon, Desert Thorn, and Mesquite are the most common plants seen along the road to the whale view point.

Log 5 - Guerrero Negro to Santa Rosalia

THAR SHE BLOWS! The best known of the great whales and the one most often seen along the Pacific Coast of Alta and Baja California is the California Gray Whale (*Eschrichtius gibbosus*). Gray whales feed in summer (mid-May to mid-October) in the plankton-rich western Bering Sea near Saint Lawrence Island and to the north into the Chukchi and Beaufort Seas. In winter (mid-October to early December) they migrate to the south along the more shallow Pacific coastal waters of North America to the various bays and lagoons of Baja California, especially Laguna Ojo de Liebre (Scammon's Lagoon), where they breed and give birth to their calves (early December through February). In the spring (March and April) they travel north along the coast and arrive at their arctic summer feeding grounds about the middle of May. Because they travel fairly close to shore it is relatively easy to see migrating Gray Whales from high points of land or from boats within a few hundred meters offshore or even in the surf along the shore. The whales have become a great public attraction, and many people visit "high spots" along the Pacific coast or take short "whale watch" cruises to see the migrating whales. It is estimated that the whales migrate about 10,200 kilometers (6,250 miles) each way every year by traveling 60 to 80 nautical miles (69 to 92 miles) per day at a speed of 4 to 4.8 knots per hour for 15-20 hours a day. As they travel, the frequently raise their heads out of the water "spy-hopping" to look around to get their bearings. It is believed that they find their way on the long trip by memory and vision.

THE REPRODUCTIVE CYCLE OF A FEMALE CALIFORNIA GRAY WHALE

June - July August - September October	24 hours of daylight allow continuous summer feeding in Bering, Chukchi, and Beaufort Seas - mid-May to mid-October
November December	Migration south, conception in route mid-October to Early December
January February	Wintering in Baja's lagoons
March April May	Migration north - March to mid-May
June - July August - September October	Summer feeding in northern seas - mid-May to mid-October
November December	Southward migration
January February	Birth of calves and nursing (7 months)
March April May	Northward migration, nursing continues
June - July August - September October	Summer feeding in northern seas Nursing ends in August

The California Gray Whale was once more numerous than it is today. In the 1800's Charles M. Scammon, a famous whaling captain and writer, estimated the gray whale population to be 30,000. However, Scammon and other whalers slaughtered the gray whales by the hundreds for their valuable oil. By 1937 it was estimated that their numbers had dropped to approximately 100. In 1938 they were given complete protection by an international treaty. Recently, counts of migrating whales from the shore and counts made in the lagoons of Baja from the air have shown that the gray whale population has increased to 15,000 to 17,000 and is still increasing yearly. Gray whales are mysticeti or baleen whales which feed mainly on small crustaceans (primarily a red shrimp-like organism known as lobster krill) (*See* Km 197 of the Santa Rosalia log) and plankton which are filtered from the water by sieve-like plates of "hair" in their mouths which is called baleen. The captured organisms are "licked" off the baleen by the whale's tongue and swallowed. Most feeding occurs during the Arctic summer months (mid-May to mid-October) but some does occur during migration and during the time they spend in Baja's lagoons.

Baleen whales are thought to have evolved in the warm temperate waters of the western South Pacific during the Oligocene. During the late Cenozoic they moved into the rest of the Pacific which included the northern seas presently inhabited by the California gray whale.

206.5 In early 1979 Pemex drilled an oil well approximately one kilometer east of the highway. In the future oil and natural gas may be another important source of income for residents of this region. There are a few scattered Datilillo, Cardon, Ice Plant, and Creosote Bush.

The highway passes through a rather large stabilized sand dune. A climb to the top of the dune affords a view of parts of Scammon's Lagoon, the town of Guerrero Negro in the distance, and the eagle monument on the state line.

OIL AND GAS: The geosynclinal structure of the Viszaino region is nearly identical to the great Valley of California. Large Geosynclines such as these produce much of the oil and gas in the world. Mapping in the Vizcaino and on the Magdalena Plain has indicated the presence of rocks and sedimentary environments favorable to oil and gas formation. After the traps where the petroleum accumulates have been deliniated, and this region may become a major oil producer.

202 This road metal quarry is being dug in the Pleistocene limestones which mantle this area.

194 In this region of Desierto el Vizcaino, the soil has become so dry and saline that the dunes are only sparsely vegetated. The few plants present along the the highway are predominantly the following xerophytes: Bursage, Australian Salt Bush, and Mesquite.

A xerophyte is a plant that is adapted to living where water is scant. No matter how dry the soil, there will be some plants that have adapted to the low level of water. Plants will not adapt to dry soil which has more than 6% salt concentrations. At salt concentrations greater than 6%, a "physiological drought" exists, and plants can't grow even if there is standing water.

189.5 This turnoff onto Mexico 18 leads to El Arco, a former gold mining town. The old road went inland at Rosarito north of Guerrero Negro and skirted the hills to El Arco. The old road headed south closer to Sierra San Francisco where it now joins the highway near Abreojos Junction. Early travelers avoided the sandy stretches closer to the coast near Guerrero Negro.

El Arco is the site of a porphyry copper deposit in the metavolcanic rocks.

> **YOU ARE SAFE, CLIMAX!** Porphyry copper deposits are usually mined in bulk, on a large scale, and in open pits, for copper and molybdenite (MoS_2). At the present time the world's largest copper/molybdenite mine, which produces 90% of the world's copper supply, is at Climax, Colorado.
>
> At one time the El Arco area promised to be one of the largest copper/molybdenite deposits in the world. They estimate 600 million tons of .7% copper ore. However, due to the spotty nature of the ore and low yields, El Arco may never become a major copper producer.
>
> Copper is a reddish or salmon-pink isometric mineral. It is ductile and malleable and a good conductor of heat and electricity.
>
> Molybdenum, a lustrous brittle silver-white metallic element derived from molybdenite, is used in alloys, windings for electrical resistance furnaces, and points for spark plugs.

187 The highly eroded volcanic mesas of the Sierra San Francisco lie ahead. To the right front are the volcanic plug domes of Sierra Santa Clara. To the right rear are the metamorphic and igneous rocks of Sierra El Placer. To the left and left rear are the metavolcanic hills near El Arco which are part of the southern end of the Peninsular Range Batholith.
Note: These mesas, domes, and ranges may not be visible at all on hazy days.

177 The low gray-leafed plants which grow in the disturbed soils edge of the pavement are Brittle-Bush (*Encelia farinosa*).

172 The sand dunes are vegetated with plants characteristically found growing on stabilized dunes Datilillo, Mesquite, Jumping Cholla, Cardon, Palo Adan, Purple Bush, and *Atriplex*. The alkali flats between the dunes are only sparsely dotted with stunted annuals.
Vegetation grows better on the dunes, since they hold moisture and have had the alkaline salts leached from them as rain water drains through the dune sands. Since the alkali flats are highly saline, only halophytic species can grow on them.

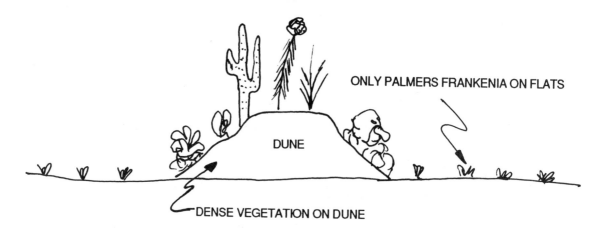

ONLY PALMERS FRANKENIA ON FLATS

DUNE

DENSE VEGETATION ON DUNE

Log 5 - Guerrero Negro to Santa Rosalia

165 Due to the extreme aridity and high salinity of the soil, little vegetation grows here except for stunted salt-tolerant annuals and sparse Creosote Bush which grows in the moister less saline soils of the low hummocks. Jumping Cholla, an indicator of disturbed soils, is growing with naturally occurring species of the desert. On the less saline well-drained drier hillsides in the distance, the Australian Salt Bush is smaller; in the lower wetter alkali flats, the halophytic Australian Salt Bush is larger and more densely covers the ground.

162 Jumping Cholla dominates the vegetation in this area. Disturbed areas or places that have been changed by man or domestic animals often result in the invasion and flourishing of opportunistic plants such as the Cholla Plants commonly seen adjacent to the pavements edge along this stretch of the highway include several opportunistic species such as the tall yellow-flowered large-leafed road-side Indian Tree Tobacco, Cholla Cactus, and several species of grass.

160 The farming area on the left is one of the more recent developments in this area.

A major **transpeninsular fault** roughly parallels the road in this area and provides a groundwater barrier which the farming enterprises are mining for irrigation. This fault is easily seen in the seismic and magnetic geophysical data that has been collected for this part of Baja.

To the east is the southern end of the Peninsular Ranges basement; it is largely covered by Tertiary volcanic rocks of Sierra San Francisco. There is very little Peninsular Ranges basement along the gulf coast south of this area.

The highway was built nearly parallel to the axis of a **Cretaceous syncline**, located a few miles to the west, with approximately 10,000+ meters of Jurassic to Paleocene sedimentary rocks. This geosyncline cuts across the peninsula and heads southeast toward Loreto. The southern part of the peninsula is entirely underlain by the Cretaceous syncline and overlain by Tertiary sedimentary and volcanic rock. The Sierra San Andreas (similar to the Coast Ranges of California) with the Franciscan assemblages and extensive exposures of sedimentary rocks is to the right in the distance.

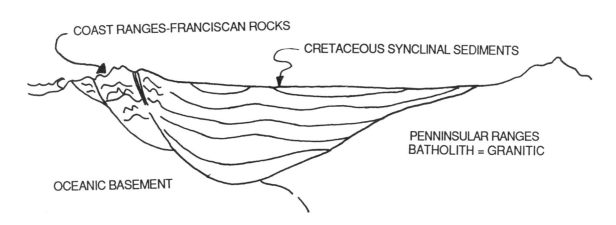

COAST RANGES-FRANCISCAN ROCKS

CRETACEOUS SYNCLINAL SEDIMENTS

PENNINSULAR RANGES BATHOLITH = GRANITIC

OCEANIC BASEMENT

CROSS SECTION OF THE VIZCAINO PENNINSULA

154.5 The buildings to the right are the government agricultural cooperative of Ejido Francisco J. Mujica.
The massif of Sierra San Francisco to the left is a series of lava flows which have been folded into a broad arch and tilted to the west. Some of the peaks rise above the main arch. This relationship again becomes very clear at the south end of Ejido Vizcaino (*See* Kilometer 144).

151 Just before this kilometer mark notice that Creosote Bush, Palo Verde, Copal, Garambullo, Pitaya Dulce, and Pitaya Agria are once again more abundant. After the kilometer Palo Adan and Datilillo along with many species of cactus become dominant.

144 The government agricultural cooperative and experiment station of Ejido Vizcaino is located at this junction. There are small restaurants, and a gas station that normally sells Nova (regular) and occasionally Extra (unleaded).

132 This turnoff leads to another government agricultural cooperative, Ramal Emilio Zapata.

124.3 Estacion Microondes de Los Angeles is located in front of a low volcanic hill to the right (southwest).

WHERE ARE ALL OF THE ANIMALS? Besides birds have you seen any other animals along the *Baja Highway*? The most likely answer to this question is, "No". However, despite the harsh conditions of deserts (intense heat during the day, cold at night, and scarcity of water, vegetation, and cover) many kinds of animals do live successfully in this and other deserts of the world. Most of the larger desert animals are shy, and many are nocturnal and are unseen by daytime travelers. Those that are out during the day tend to be small in size and light in color for camouflage and protection against the heat and dehydration (water loss). Smaller desert mammals are mainly fossorial (fitted for digging and living in burrows). The lower temperatures and higher humidity of burrows help to reduce water loss by evaporation. The large desert ungulates (hoofed animals) such as pronghorn antelope cannot escape the desert heat by living in burrows. But the glossy pallid color of their fur reflects direct sunlight, and the fur itself is an excellent insulation which helps to keep heat out. Additionally, heat is lost by convection and conduction from the underside of the antelope where the pelage (fur) is very thin. Ungulates conserve water by eliminating concentrated urine and dry feces.

If you want to see animals in the desert, the best time to look is at night. However, if you walk into the desert during the day, you may see many birds and small desert inhabitants such as colorful furry velvet ants (actually wingless wasps), lizards, black and red ants, and snakes. At the very least, you will see signs of many desert inhabitants such as the **tail drags** and **burrows** of rodents; **tracks** of birds, rodents, stink bugs, lizards, rabbits, coyote; and **scat** (feces) of numerous animals. Several good field guides are available for identifying the tracks and scats of animals which live in North America and Baja. So take a walk, stretch your legs, rest your mind, use your powers of observation, and you will see that, despite its barren appearance, Desierto el Vizcaino is teeming with life, especially birds. The birds you might expect to see in Desierto El Vizcaino are briefly listed below:

Bird	General Location
American White Pelican	Flying over water
Cactus Wren	Among cacti
California Brown Pelican	Flying over water
California Quail	Searching ground litter for food
California Thrasher	Searching ground litter for food
Gilded Woodpecker	Among cacti
Greater Roadrunner	Running on the ground
Ladder-back Woodpecker	Flitting through the air
Red-Tailed Hawk	Soaring in Baja's skies
Turkey Vultures	Feeding on carrion or soaring
Western Meadowlark	On fence posts or wires

118   This recently graded dirt road leads into the San Francisco Mountains.

THE SIERRA SAN FRANCISCO to the northeast is a mountain wilderness eroded out of large volcanic outpourings. These rugged mountains rise from the surrounding desert plains to heights of more than 1,500 meters and stretch northward for 50 kilometers. The Sierra San Francisco range was once a rather simple basalt plateau roughly circular in outline. It is now folded into a broad westward-tilted arch crowned by Pico Santa Monica (2.144 m.). During the last few million years, erosion has produced the rugged landscape seen today. Some hikers have composed valleys of the Sierra San Francisco to the topography of the Grand Canyon in Arizona.

Looking westward from their heights, sweeping views of Scammon's Lagoon and Vizcaino Plain can be seen, while the peaks of the volcanic Volcan las Tres Virgenes dominates the eastern horizon. Deep in the San Francisco mountains, a few ranchos are located near the rare groves of palm trees and pools of water. Some of Baja's mysterious painted caves are found hidden in the inaccessible canyons of these rugged mountains and in the Sierra San Pedro to the southeast. Mule trips to the caves are available from San Ignacio.

PREHISTORIC CAVE PAINTINGS: The mountains of central and southern Baja California from the Sierra San Borja south into the Sierras San Francisco, San Pedro, and Sierra la Giganta are riddled with isolated caves painted by unknown prehistoric people. These caves, located in some of the most inhospitable remote mountainous terrains of the peninsula, contain paintings of people, plants, unknown symbols, and animals. The figures are larger and more numerous than those of the famous prehistoric panels of Lascaux and Altamira.

Jesuit missionaries were probably the first "white men" to see Baja's painted caves. Leon Diguet, a French naturalist, was the first to publish an account of the caves after he visited them (1894). The caves were largely forgotten until the author, Erle Stanley Gardner, visited them in 1962 by helicopter. Since that time, many have visited the caves. Hopefully, these panels will survive the increased number of visitations.

An excellent book with beautiful photographs entitled *The Cave Paintings of Baja California* has been prepared by Harry Crosby.

117   The only plants that seem to be growing here are Datilillo, cactus, Jumping Cholla, and Cardon. Upon closer examination there are *Acacia,* many low herbaceous annuals, Mallows, Brittle-Bushes, and Sand Verbena.

112   The two isolated flat-topped buttes ahead are composed of Miocene sediments capped by dark basalt. They are erosional remnants of the extensive volcanic mesas of the Sierra San Francisco.

108   The highway leaves the very flat old lagoon surface and begins to climb the gently-sloping alluvial fans which are locally cut by small washes.

106   Elephant Trees again dot the landscape.
       Common Ravens, birds of the desert, are often seen in this area.

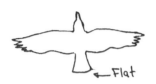

IS IT A COMMON RAVEN OR AN AMERICAN CROW?
There are three easy ways to distinguish between these two black birds: tail shape, habitat preference, and flight patterns. Both birds are black and may be a variety of sizes depending on their age. Color and body size are not good criteria to use. The following chart will help you identify these birds:

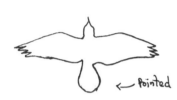

	Raven	Crow
Tail shape	Diamond	Fan
Habitat Preference	Deserts & cities throughout the peninsula	Not usually seen south of San Quintin
Flight patterns:	Can glide for more than 3 seconds	Have a very short gliding time - less than 3 seconds

102   Some of the Elephant Trees, Palo Adan, and Datilillo which grow here support the harmless epiphytic ball moss, *Tillandsia*.

98.5   The Pleistocene limestone, which covers parts of the middle of the Desierto el Vizcaino Plain, is exposed along the highway. This limestone was deposited in a shallow warm sea which covered this area within the last million years.
       The lagoons of San Ignacio and Scammon are small remnants of this embayment which probably isolated the Sierra San Andreas and the Santa Clara Buttes as islands.

       A SHALLOW SEA: During parts of the Pleistocene, this area from the foothills of the Sierra San Francisco was a warm shallow sea which connected the area of Scammon's and San Ignacio Lagoons. The Sierra San Andreas and the Santa Clara Buttes were islands some distance from shore. The limestone which mantles this area was deposited in this shallow sea.

98   At this point you will find the turnoff to Punta Abreojos.
       The gray Miocene marine sediments of the San Ignacio Formation are exposed under the basalt on the high hill to the right. Just beyond the turnoff to Punta Abreojos are more exposures of the Miocene sediments previously discussed at Kilometer 115.

       The isolation of the Vizcaino: The road to the right leads approximately 90 kilometers to the west to an isolated section of the Pacific coast and the small cannery and fishing settlement of Abreojos. It is a fairly good graded road which most two-wheel drive vehicles can make. The area around Punta Abreojos is one of the favorite surfing spots on the peninsula. The break of the waves off the point enables some surfers to have runs up to a kilometer long. The small isolated lagoon at Rene's Fish Camp offers excellent dry camping and fishing.

Boats can be rented in the area to explore San Ignacio Lagoon where the whale-watching is good.

The road continues approximately another 100 kilometers to the north to Bahia Asuncion and passed several small villages along the way. There is a small hotel and restaurant in Bahia Asuncion. This is an isolated part of the peninsula with very few people, beautiful beaches and lagoons, and small settlements. The road north from Bahia Asuncion to Bahia Tortugas is not frequently used. The best route to Bahia Tortugas is from Guerrero Negro.

97   Southeast of this point the vegetation is dense with Datilillo, Cardon, Jumping Cholla, Pitaya Dulce, Cardon, Palo Blanco, Elephant Trees, occasional Lomboy, Leatherplant, Palo Verde, *Acacia*, and occasional Ball Moss.

91   There is a large dip and bend in the highway.

The flat-topped mesas ahead on the right (south) are the mesas of Quarenta and Sierra San Pedro.

The lagoon of San Ignacio with the two white Salitrales (salt pans) on either side is in view to the right. The Santa Clara Buttes are Miocene (10-15 million year old) andesite plugs which have intruded into and domed on the overlying Cretaceous and Paleocene sediments. Their temporal relationships and geology are identical to the Marysville Buttes area of the Sacramento Valley in California.

88.2   This road leads to Microondes Albun microwave tower. The view from this tower is sweeping. On a clear day you can see south to Sierra San Pedro and the mesas of Cuarenta, San Ignacio Lagoon, the Sierra Santa Clara plugs, and the mesas of Santa Clara and Vizcaino to the west. To the northeast is the mountain mass of Sierra de la San Francisco.

The road metal quarry at the foot of the road to the microwave tower is in the San Ignacio Formation and has yielded some spectacular agatized (a translucent crypto-crystalline variety of white quartz) Turritella (*Turritella sp.*) fossils which are just below a light-colored volcanic tuff (ash) bed.

AGATIZED Turritellas: Approximately 11 million years ago this area was covered by a shallow sea, and numerous molluscs including *Turritella ocoyana* flourished in that sea. A volcanic eruption spewed ash over the area; this resulted in a mass mortality of these molluscs. Over the years groundwater leached the calcite from the fossil shells and replaced it with silica from the volcanic ash and produced agatized Turritellas.

86   The highway climbs and eventually skirts to the south of the foothills of San Francisco de La Sierra.

The road follows what amounts to a stripped-dip slope developed on a resistant bedding surface with basalt hills along both sides of the highway.

84   To the rear (southwest) is a good view of San Ignacio Lagoon (Salitrales). On a clear day you can see across Desierto el Vizcaino to the peaks and mesas of Sierra Santa Clara.

82   The highway dips into an arroyo cut into the lava surface.

81   The small red-brown conical hill to the left (northeast) is an extrusive volcanic plug.

78.5   As the highway crests a small rise, the view to the south is of the massif of Sierra San Pedro and the flat Llano El Angel.

Several dark conical-shaped cinder cones dot the landscape. The very large dark conical mountain in the far distance ahead is Volcan las Tres Virgenes.

78.25 This is the turnoff to a paved jet airport (Areopista) which serves San Ignacio.

77.5 The building on the left is the agricultural inspection station. On a trip north they are very likely to confiscate any Mexican citrus that travelers from the southern part of the peninsula may have with them. The government is trying to prevent the transportation of southern agricultural diseases and pests to the northern state of Baja (Baja California del Norte).

76 For several miles the road passes along the edge of several dark basalt mesas with views of the date palm oases of San Ignacio and San Lino. These mesas are capped by dark basalts and underlain by the white and greenish San Ignacio Formation.

Mina (1957) defined the **San Ignacio Formation** for the light-gray sandstones, tuffaceous sandstones, and tuff outcroppings near the town of San Ignacio. The San Ignacio Formation is a marine facies of the Comondu Formation which overlies and interfingers with the Isidro Formation. The San Ignacio Formation is Middle Miocene in age in the San Ignacio area; a volcanic tuff bed was K/Ar dated at 11 m.y., and some beds contain more of the agatized Turritellas (*Turritella ocoyana* and *T. inezana*). Further south part of the unit has been K/Ar dated at 22 m.y.

74.5 Excellent exposures of the San Ignacio Formation are seen here.
The conspicuous building in the middle of the palm oasis ahead is the mission church (white).

74 This is the turnoff to San Lino. This small community is a "suburb" of San Ignacio and contains a gas station which sells only regular gasoline (Nova).

73.5 This side road leads 3 kilometers to San Ignacio. Ground water surfaces in the arroyo above town; a river with an oasis of imported European date palms flows here.
The town has two hotels, campsites, cafes, stores and a gas station. It's well worth a turnoff into the town to see the square which is shaded by large Indian Laurel Fig trees and the impressive stone Mision San Ignacio de Kadakaman built by the Dominicans in 1786. Hotel La Pinta de San Ignacio is located on the road halfway into town.

HUERTAS DE SAN IGNACIO - Huertas is the Spanish name for garden or orchard, and it might be aptly applied to the desert oasis which surround the two small communities of San Ignacio and San Lino. It has been reported that over 80,000 date palms grow here. Date Palms (*Phoenix dactylifera*) were introduced for cultivation into mainland Mexico by Jesuit priests and have subsequently been cultivated in San Ignacio (since 1728), Mulege, Loreto, and San Jose del Cabo. Oranges, figs, grapes, limes, and flowers are also grown in this desert garden-orchard.
A summer swim in the cool waters of Rio San Ignacio is wonderful! Bring fishing tackle and try your fishing skills here.
San Ignacio is truly a fertile green spot in an otherwise very barren desert.

73 The date of 11 m.y. was obtained on the San Ignacio Formation in this roadcut.

ANOTHER VEGETATIONAL CHANGE?

Between El Rosario and San Ignacio the highway passes through the Desierto El Vizcaino area of the Sonoran Central Desert Phytogeographic Region of Baja. The vegetation of the dry Desierto El Vizcaino is dominated by Cardon, Cirio, *Yucca*, Ball Moss, Datilillo, Agave, and Burbush.

The region east of San Ignacio is even more arid than Desierto el Vizcaino because it is in the rain shadow of the peninsula mountains. Upon leaving San Ignacio the highway briefly passes through the northeastern tip of another part of the Sonoran Central Desert Region, the Llanos de Magdalena area. The northern part of the Llanos de Magdalena area is less arid than its Pacific southwestern end. The flora of the Llanos de Magdalena area east of San Ignacio is dominated by Lomboy, Cardon, Elephant Trees, Palo Verde, Palo Adan, and many varieties of cactus. An epiphytic lichen, *Ramalina*, grows profusely on many plants of this area. The Llanos de Magdalena area flora is discussed in detail in the log between Cabo San Lucas and La Paz via Todos Santos. A good place to stop to view the representative flora of the northeastern section of Llanos de Magdalena is at Km. 40.6.

71   Just east of San Ignacio near the school, the dark conical-shaped peak at 2 o'clock on the horizon is a cinder cone.
      The tuffaceous sandstones of the Comondu Formation form the brown outcrops along the edges of the arroyo.

69   The basalt at this location was dated at 9.7 my.

68   Many small-leaved *Agave deserti* cover the hill slope to the right.

68.5 The highway begins an ascent of a grade bordered by a dense cardonal. The predominant group of plants in this area are columnar and spreading cacti-- principally Cardon, Cholla and Pitaya Agria. This area has been heavily overgrazed by domestic animals which allow the cacti to dominate the vegetation.

      The old road is visible in the canyon bottom to the left. This was a short, very rough grade for earlier Baja travelers.

67   This is the first good view of the composite strato volcano, Volcan las Tres Virgenes.

      Volcanoes are classified on the basis of the type of cone which they produce, and the type of cone depends on the composition and viscosity of their lavas. Basaltic lavas with a lower content of silica (50%) flow more easily, while rhyolitic lavas which have a higher content of silica (70%) resist flowing(are more highly viscus) are more explosive basaltic lavas from cinder cones have a higher content of gas and are also more explosive.

      As the gases are released from lavas the basalt becomes more fluid and forms shield cones and lava plateaus. The world's well known volcanoes are **Strato Cones**; examples are Mount Vesuvius and Krakatoa. They are usually 2-3 miles high, tend to dominate the landscape, and are the most destructive types of volcanoes.
      The following table relates the types of cones with activity rock types formed, and material ejected.

TYPES	ROCK TYPE	CONE	MATERIAL
EXPLOSIVE	BASALT/RHYOLITE	CINDER	CINDERS+FEW FLOWS
INTERMEDIATE	ANDESITE	STRATO	TUFF & LAVA
QUIET	BASALT	SHIELD	LAVA FLOWS+FEW CINDERS
FISSURE	BASALT	PLATEAU	THIN LAVA FLOWS

65   The small brownish hill ahead with several sharp peaks is Cerro Colorado, a sub-recent basaltic eruptive center.

62   Between here and Kilometer 60.75 fossil dune deposits which exhibit cross-bedding are exposed in the roadcuts.

59.5   This is the road into Santa Marta and the southern Sierra San Francisco.

58   This long straight stretch of road presents views of the volcanic mesas and plains of the middle part of the peninsula.
The massif (French for massive) of Sierra San Pedro is on the right, and the relatively unexplored rugged volcanics of Sierra San Francisco is on the left.
The plants which grow along the pavement edge are Cheesebush, Indian Tree Tobacco, Prickly Poppy, and Brittle-Bush.
The large dark mountain straight ahead which dominates the horizon is Volcan las Tres Virgenes.

VOLCAN LAS TRES VIRGENES: This composite volcano is thought to have erupted as recently as the early half of the 18th century. There is a report from one of the early Spanish missionaries of an eruption in this area in 1746 which may well have been a description of the most recent eruption of Volcan las Tres Virgenes. The early Baja traveler would leave San Ignacio in the morning drive all day, and arrive in Santa Rosalia in the evening. A lot of time would have been spent studying this volcano at the 10 mph or less pace which vehicles were forced to travel on the "old road".

Is Volcan las Tres Virgenes an Active Volcano?
The activity of volcanoes is not readily apparent to us in our short life spans.

An **ACTIVE** volcano has a record of historic activity such as Mount St. Helens in the state of Washington. The lack of active volcanoes in Baja may be due to the isolation and the short recorded history of Baja or due to the fact that the sliding action of plates in Baja does not tend to produce much volcanic action.

An **INACTIVE** volcano shows no sign of activity and shows significant cone erosion such as Crater Lake in the state of Oregon.

A **DORMANT** volcano does not have a record of historic activity. It does have good relatively uneroded shape and shows signs of sub-Recent activity. Most of the Cascade Volcanoes such as Mount Rainier are considered dormant. Las Tres Virgenes appears to be a dormant volcano.

Log 5 - Guerrero Negro to Santa Rosalia

WHERE DID LAS TRES VIRGENES MAGMA COME FROM?

Magmas are molten or liquid rocks that originate at the base of the earth's crust and in the upper mantle. The majority of the active volcanoes today are in the Subduction Zones around the Pacific Ring of Fire and in the Alpine-Himalaya Belt. The **friction** generated in the Subduction Zones causes the melting. Another belt of active volcanoes is on the Mid-Ocean Ridges where the **release of pressure** causes the melting. The underlying source of the latent heat is the **radioactive decay** of elements. Volcan las Tres Virgenes is in the Pacific Ring of Fire. However it may relate to the formation of the Gulf of California.

5 2   Through this region the tall dominant plant is Datilillo, a member of the lilly family.

5 1   There is an abundant supply of loose sand in this valley. The heavy wind in this area and the supply of sand have combined to form the dunes which cover the faces of many of the hills.

4 4   Some of the tallest and most beautiful Elephant Trees (*Pachycormus discolor and Bursera microphylla*) of the peninsula grow on the lava flow to the southeast.

The vegetation which grows on the flat plain (Llano) between and around the lava flows consists of Brittle-Bush, Mallow, Palo Verde, Creosote Bush, Leatherplant, Pitaya Dulce, Cardon, Teddy Bear Cholla, Hedgehog Cholla, Garambullo, Jumping Cholla, Palo Blanco, Palo Adan, and Lomboy.

40.6   Just before the first lava flow is one of the few places on the peninsula where two types of Elephant Trees (*Pachycormus discolor* and *Bursera microphylla*) occur together so close to the road. A walk onto the flow leads you into a stark and jagged landscape where beautiful photo spots of the Elephant Trees are numerous. This is also a good place for a close-up view of the floral dominants of Llanos de Magdalena area introduced at Km 73.

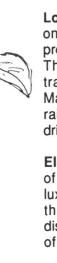

Lomboy - is a member of the spurge family commonly seen on the flats, bajadas, and mesas of this region. This plant produces an acrid sap and remains leafless most of the year. This is an adaptation which reduces water loss by transpiration in the extremely arid environment of the Magdalena Plain desert. Leaves appear after each infrequent rain and turn a distinctive red before falling off as the soil dries out again.

Elephant Trees - are represented by the unrelated species of the two genera *Pachycormus* and *Bursera*. They grow luxuriously as trees which store water in the cortical cells of their elephantine trunks. The *Bursera* are easily distinguished from the *Pachycormus* by the incense-like odor of crushed leaves or fruits.

Palo Verde - is a green barked tree which produces legume-like "bean" pods. However, Palo Verde is a member of the Senna family, not the legume family. Like Lomboy, this tree is normally leafless. The green trunk is a cladode, a stem that acts like a leaf which performs photosynthesis in the absence of leaves.

107

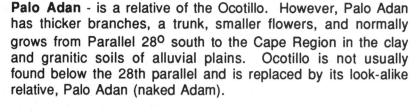

Palo Adan - is a relative of the Ocotillo. However, Palo Adan has thicker branches, a trunk, smaller flowers, and normally grows from Parallel 28⁰ south to the Cape Region in the clay and granitic soils of alluvial plains. Ocotillo is not usually found below the 28th parallel and is replaced by its look-alike relative, Palo Adan (naked Adam).

Creosote Bush is a very common resinous desert shrub of the southwestern U.S.A. and Baja. Unlike many other desert plants, it is green the year round. The waxy coating on its leaves reduces water loss by transpiration which allows the shrub to withstand long periods of extreme drought. The strong-smelling resinous leaves resemble the odor of the coal tar distillate-creosote. Notice that very few plants grow under Creosote Bush. The roots of this shrub produce a toxic substance that inhibits the growth of other plants except after heavy or frequent rains when it's leached from the soil which permits the growth of desert annuals. As the soil dries, the inhibitor accumulates and poisons the outsiders. This phenomenon is known as allelopathy and helps eliminate competition for water in a dry desert environment. Creosote Bush was considered a cure-all by Baja's early Indians, and early Spaniards used a decoction of this shrub to treat sick cattle and saddle gallon horses. In more recent times a leaf extract has been used to delay or prevent butter, oils, and fats from turning rancid. Creosote Bush leaf extract is not largely used, because the extract is now synthetically manufactured.

Ramalina - is an epiphytic foliose lichen formed by the combination of algal cells which live inside the cells of a fungus in a mutualistic symbiosis. The algal cells provide sugar to the fungus as its source of energy; the fungus provides protection, water, and carbon dioxide utilized by the algae during photosynthesis. There may be other species of crustose lichen on rocks. Each different species of lichen looks like a different "splash" of paint. They are environmentally important because they degrade rocks into soils by the corrosive action of the organic acids they produce.

Other plants associated with the plants listed above are Jumping Cholla, Creosote Bush, Cardon, and pavement edge opportunists such as Brittle-Bush and Indian Tree Tobacco.

40   The highway passes close to the west side of Volcan las Tres Virgenes and its multiple lava flows. The ground for several miles around is covered with pumice of an unknown origin which has been shown to be unrelated to the activities of Volcan las Tres Virgenes.

39.2   The buildings on the right are Rancho El Mesquetal.

38.7   The highway parallels the edge of a blocky clinkery basalt lava flow from Volcan las Tres Virgenes. The deep clefts (cracks) on the flow were caused by the pressure of the molten interior which pushed on the solid crust.
       Quite a number of unusually large Elephant Trees are growing on this lava flow.

Log 5 - Guerrero Negro to Santa Rosalia

3 8   The highway begins to climb through a small canyon on the western slope to the crest of the range and the Virgenes grade.

35.1   This is the top of the Virgenes' grade where the highway begins a long descent into the Gulf coast drainage southeast of Volcan las Tres Virgenes. Descending this grade used to be extremely difficult and dangerous. There was a shrine at the top of the grade and another at the bottom along the old dirt road. Travelers would stop at the top to pray that they would make it down and again at the bottom to give thanks that they had.

> **CHANGING VEGETATION REGIONS AGAIN?** From San Ignacio to the top of the grade (Kilometer 35.1) the highway briefly passes through the northeastern tip of the Llanos de Magdalena area of the Sonoran Central Desert Region. At this point the highway begins descending into the eastern drainage of Sierra San Pedro and enters into the Central Gulf Coast Desert area of the Sonoran Central Desert region. The Central Gulf Coast Desert area extends south from Bahia de Los Angeles along the eastern Gulf coast of the peninsula to just south of La Paz; it includes most of the southern Gulf islands. The predominant plants of the Central Gulf Coast Desert are Cirio, Ironwood, Palo Adan, Creosote Bush, Brittle-Bush and three species of Elephant Trees (*Pachycormus discolor*, *Bursera microphylla*, and *B. hindsiana*).

3 5   The very difficult switchbacks of the old road are visible over the scarp just beyond the crest of the grade.
This is a good spot to view the volcanic breccias of the Comondu Formation and the abundant pumice fragments.

33.8   There is a fault in this roadcut.

32.3   The highway crosses an eroded fault scarp on the "Highway Fault" which forms the base of the grade. This fault has a major lateral motion component. This fault and one to the north of Tres Virgenes may be causing a small rift area which is responsible for Tres Virgenes and two other volcanoes on the area. The hill to the left, Punta Arena, is a volcanic eruptive center which has domed the strata of Mesa El Yaqui into a hill along part of the Gulf Fault Zone.

3 2   The road to the right leads to a large geothermal project (Proyecto Geothermico Las 3 Virgenes) located a few kilometers northward. This project is under the control of the Commision Federal de Electricidad and will produce electricity by harnessing geothermal heat, heating water to steam which in turn drives a steam turbine generator that produces electricity for parts of Baja. They estimate an ultimate production of 15 MW.

3 1   The buildings on the left belong to Rancho Las Virgenes.
A dirt road heads north from here along the eastern side of the Volcan las Tres Virgenes.

3 0   The highway follows a relatively narrow flat surface developed on the flat-lying volcanic and fluvatile sedimentary rocks of the Comondu Formation.

18.5   This is the first view of the Sea of Cortez (on a clear day). The volcanic cinder cone visible offshore is the gulf island of Isla Tortugas.

> **THE ISLANDS OF THE GULF OF CALIFORNIA (SEA OF CORTEZ):** Two major groups of Gulf islands have been differentiated on the basis of their geographic location, physical geology, and environment: the Midriff Island group and the Southern Island group.

Log 5 - Guerrero Negro to Santa Rosalia

The Midriff Island group extends from near the head of the Gulf to the Loreto region and consists largely of late Mesozoic granitic plutons overlain by Tertiary and Quaternary basalts and andesites. Repeated volcanism and faulting have created topographies of high angle fault planes bound irregular horsts and grabens. These steeply-tilted fault planes are dissected by the drainage of countless ephemeral streams and arroyos, while the lower depositional slopes consist of coalescing alluvial fans which form bajadas and broad valley fills.

Precipitation patterns in the Midriff Islands resemble these of the Mediterranean climate zone of the southern portion of Alta California to the northwest where the heaviest rainfalls occur from August to October. There may be a slight additional amount of winter precipitation from December to March and brief but concentrated amounts of summer precipitation as a result of infrequent thunderstorms. The annual precipitation averages 100 to 150 millimeters.

The annual temperature pattern of the Midriff Islands is one of hot dry summers and cool moist winters with large diurnal temperature changes. Maximum daytime temperatures in late summer regularly exceed 38° C and may occasionally rise above 43° C on the eastern side of this island group. Minimum temperatures may fall near or below freezing in January and February. Unfortunately, almost no climatic records exist for any of the Gulf islands, so the precipitation and temperature patterns are just "best estimates".

Climatically, the Midriff islands of the northern part of the Gulf appear similar to the Mexican mainland to the east and the eastern coast of the Baja peninsula to the west. The climate of the Gulf islands is essentially the same as the nearby mainland. It seems reasonable to make this inference, since the physical environment of the Midriff Islands is basically the same as the adjacent Mexican mainland and Baja peninsula.

Since every island is close to the Mexican mainland, the floras of the islands are merely isolated samples of the Gulf region flora and are not by themselves a natural floristic unit. The identification of certain island groups by their dominance of particular vegetation types is strictly for convenience. Floristically, the Midriff islands all support vegetation typical of the Central Gulf Coast Desert area of Shreve's Sonoran Central Desert phytogeographic region. The plant communities of the Midriff Islands are characterized by their dominant plant species and their growth forms and follow variations in the physical environment. Plant communities change geographically as the climate changes and change locally with physical and environmental factors such as substrate (soil) depth, soil particle size, water-holding capacity (edaphic factors), and moisture availability. The dominant vegetation type of the Midriff Islands is Sonoran Desert scrub. Among the dominant plants species of the Sonoran Desert scrub are **trees** of the genera *Cercidium* (Palo Verde), *Rhizophora* (Mangrove), *Bursera hindsiana* (Copal of the Torchwood family), *B. microphylla* (Torote), *Olneya* (Ironwood), *Prosopis* (Mesquite), *Acacia*, and *Jatropha* (Lomboys and Leather plants of the Spurge family); numerous **cacti** which are the most conspicuous of the island plants and are represented by species of the genera *Ferocactus* (Barrel Cacti), *Opuntia* (Chollas), *Lophocereus*, and the tree-like columnar cactus *Pachycereus pringlei* (Cardons); **shrubs** such as Creosote Bush (*Larrea divaricata*), and many species of **annual composites** of the family Asteraceae. In general, the degree of endemism is low on both the Midriff and Southern Islands. Floristically, there are only 18 endemic plant species which, represent only 3% of the 570 plant species found on all the Gulf islands. Faunistically there are no endemic birds. The only endemic mammal is the fishing bat (*Pyzonyx vivesi*). Reptiles enjoy the highest level of endemism of any island vertebrate group.

It is possible that man has inhabited the Midriff Islands for about 10,000 years. At the present time, the islands are uninhabited. Spanish and Mexican settlement of the Midriffs has been impeded by the extreme aridity of the islands, the general lack of permanent potable (drinkable) water, the lack of precious metals, and the past hostility of the Seri Indians. The Seri were able to survive, because they survived on water obtained from a few tinajas (springs).

The Southern Islands group extends from Isla del Carmen near Loreto to Isla Cerralvo in the Cape Region. Like the more northern Midriff Island group, the Southern Island group is hot and dry. However, the seasonal patterns of precipitation are different. The Southern Island Group experiences a higher incidence of summer rains. Precipitation is primarily derived from summer tropical clockwise anticyclones. Less than 20% of the precipitation falls in the summer months on the northern part of the Gulf, while 40% of the precipitation falls in the summer months on the Southern Island Group. Floristically, the southern islands are primarily vegetated with thorn scrub. The dominant species of the thorn scrub include several **cacti**: *Pachycereus pringlei* (Cardon), *Ferocactus* (Barrel cacti), *Echinocereus* (Hedgehog cacti), *Mammallaria* (nipple cacti), *Opuntia* (Chollas), *Agave*; the following **nonleguminous trees**: *Rhizophora mangle* and *Avicennia germinans* (Mangroves), *Forchammeria* (Palo San Juan), *Pachycormus discolor* (Elephant Tree), *Olneya* (Ironwood), *Prosopis* (Mesquite), *Cercidium* (Palo Verde), *Bursera microphylla* (Torote), *Bursera hindsiana* (Copal), and *Bursera fagaroides*; **desert annuals** of the aster family.

*Note: boats can by rented for day or overnight trips to several of the gulf islands. Good places to check are the coastal hotels and resorts. A day on an uninhabited island is peaceful, exciting, and romantic! The shell hunting is terrific, and several islands have good fossil localities on their beaches.

17.5   The highway begins a twisting descent of the infamous Cuesta (grade) del Infierno in the Barranca Palmas (Palm Canyon) through yellow Pliocene marine sediments. It is easy to imagine this descent on the old narrow rutted dirt road, and it is easy to understand why it is infamous to those who made that descent before the road was widened, leveled, and paved. This section of the highway is very steep and narrow and has no turnouts or shoulders.

THE THREE FORMATIONS OF THE SANTA ROSALIA PLIOCENE: The Pliocene sediments of the Santa Rosalia area were deposited near a shoreline in a shallow marine environment interrupted by the deposition of conglomerates and tuffaceous material derived from explosive volcanic eruptions. It is part marine and part nonmarine and contains extensive gypsum deposits.

During the Pliocene the fault along the Gulf was active and periodically uplifted the area west of Santa Rosalia. This uplift resulted in erosion which initiated the deposition of conglomerates into the finer-grained marine sandstones and siltstones. Mineralizing solutions which rose along the faults flowed through the more porous and permeable conglomerates and mineralized the clays into the Boleo copper deposits.

The Pliocene strata of the Santa Rosalia area has been divided into three formations separated by unconformities and characterized by faunas which are believed to be Early, Middle and Late Pliocene in age (Wilson, 1948):

The Lower Pliocene **Boleo Formation** is a succession of tuffs and conglomerates which contain copper and manganese deposits. The Middle Pliocene **Gloria Formation**, later renamed the Tirabuzon Formation, is a sequence of fossiliferous marine sandstone, siltstone, and conglomerate. It can be seen between Km 4-8 on Mex. 1 north of Santa Rosalia. The Upper Pliocene **Infierno Formation** is a succession of fossiliferous marine sandstones and conglomerates.

Boleos in the Desert: Jose Villavivencio set out on horseback in 1868 to find a route across the barren mesas to the village of Santa Maria. On the way his horse dislodged a rounded bright blue and green ball of mineralized copper carbonate rock known as a boleo. This discovery led to the formation of the Santa Rosalia copper district under the operation of the French Compagnie Boleo. It was ranked as the second largest copper producing district in Mexico with over 500 kilometers of underground workings. Villavivencio was reportedly paid 16 pesos for his boleo discovery.

In 1885 Compagnie Boleo obtained from the Mexican government all the claims for the 200 square kilometer Boleo district. It developed the ore bodies and built the town of Santa Rosalia, satellite mining camps, the harbor, and a smelter which utilized blast furnaces. Copper matte was shipped across the Gulf to Guaymas, then by rail to New Orleans, and finally as ballast in steamers to France.

In 1922 the blast furnaces were replaced by a more efficient reverb-converter combination. This produced a blister copper product which was shipped to Tacoma, WA, in company steamers which returned to Santa Rosalia with fuel, petroleum coke, lumber, and mine timbers.

The area declined after 1930 as the highgrade ore was mined out. However, World War II and some government assistance kept Compagnie Boleo in operation until its final demise in 1950.

Atypical Ore Deposits: The Boleo district deposits are thin gently-dipping tabular bodies of relatively impervious clayey tuffs which overlie sandstone conglomerates. The main gangue mineral is a montmorillinite or bentonite clay, which is not typical of copper deposits. Low temperature hydrothermal solutions appear to have ascended through cracks and faults in the volcanics. They were blocked by the impermeable tuffs and permeated the tuffs by diffusion. This left the copper minerals finely dispersed in the clay matrix.

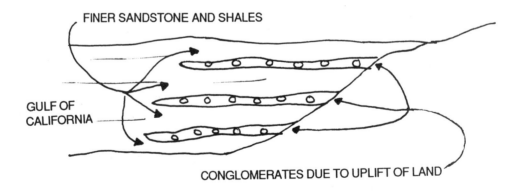

Underground mining developed by Compagnie Boleo consisted of driving entries to intersect the beds from the deep arroyos. Irregular drifts and room-and-pillar stopes and later more systematic methods featuring conveyor belts at the faces and double-tracked, mule-powered entries were used to mine the thin ore beds. The soft friable sedimentary deposits did not need explosives, but extensive timbering was required. An overhead tram was used in one mine, and a network of narrow-gauge rail lines with miniature Baldwin locomotives connected the mines with the smelter.

Smelting: Boleo ores are sulfide deficient for the purpose of making matte in a reverb. Local gypsum is used as a source of sulfur, and coal or petroleum coke is added to reduce gypsum sulfate to sulfide for matte production. The calcium in gypsum serves as a flux for the predominantly siliceous Boleo ores. The 25-30% moisture content of the bentonite gangue requires pre-reverb drying in a rotary kiln. The reverb is choke fed by a charging system which employs drag conveyors on top at the side walls. Reverb slag is stacked or disposed of at sea, and 99.5% pure blister is produced from an eight hour blow of the matte. Siliceous material from the Mulege area south of Santa Rosalia is also added as flux.

Present operations at Santa Rosalia are admittedly uneconomic but are sustained to support the local community while attempting to devise a viable and economic metallurgical future. Ore of the required minimum smelter feed grade is supplied by small-scale hand mining operations in two underground mines and in several small surface pits known as "descapotes".

15.9   Numerous faults are visible in exposures of light yellow-brown fossiliferous Pliocene sediments.

13.5   The highway crosses a major arroyo where Palo Blanco trees are seen along the highway for the first time. Elephant Trees, Cardon, Creosote Bush and abundant large stands of Palo Verde are also visible.

13   Nothing grows on this badland's topography. Due to the high percentage of gypsum and clay in the soil, this region is considered to be a saline physiological desert (*See* Kilometer 35.5 of the L.a. Bay to L.A. Bay log for a explanation).

11.75   This roadcut exposes massive well-bedded gypsum layers of the Pliocene.

10.5   To the south Isla San Marcos and its gypsum beds is now visible.

ISLA SAN MARCOS:
is a Miocene volcanic island covered with Pliocene marine sediments which are primarily composed of gypsum precipitates. The climate of this island is extremely harsh and receives less than 15 centimeters of precipitation a year, mostly during the winter months. Floristically, the island is in Shreve's sarcocaulescent desert area of the Sonoran Central Desert phytogeographic region. The dominant vegetation is Palo Verde, Elephant Tree, Cacti (especially Cardon and Cholla), Jatropha (Leatherplant and Lomboy), and many desert annuals. Extensive gypsum mining is done on the island. Gypsum is used mainly as a retarder in Portland cement, a flux in copper smelting at Santa Rosalia, and in making Plaster of Paris.

7.3   The highway descends to the south along the Gulf shore toward Santa Rosalia (a.k.a. Cachanla). A quick glance to the left reveals a dirt road which heads north to an airstrip and a camping beach called Playa Santa Maria. The shiny road metal base of this section of the highway is from the smelter tailings of the mining operation. The playa on the east side of the highway is composed of small cobbles and shingles of rock.

5   It is possible to drive along Arroyo Boleo on the right to view various parts of the Pliocene beds and gypsum crystals of this area.

> **Giant gypsum crystals:** Approximately three miles up the arroyo, the canyon becomes quite narrow just past a small road which turns to the right up a side canyon. Located in the right bank are a series of large gypsum crystals which are about two meters long. If the road begins to wind a little bit up a narrow canyon, you've gone too far.
>
> The commercial gypsum deposits on Isla San Marcos and in the Santa Rosalia area were deposited during the Pliocene in shallow marine basins with restricted circulation in the Gulf of California.

4   Between here and Kilometer 3.5 yellow Pliocene beds of the Tirabuzon Formation are well exposed in the cliffs and roadcuts next to the highway.

3   The building on the Gulf side of the highway is a fish cannery.

A last view of Volcan las Tres Virgenes is seen to the rear in the distance. The dark hills to the right between here and town are parts of the tailings dump for the Boleo Copper District.

The very black material is part of the smelter tailings from the Lucifer Manganese district.

> **MANGANESE** is a gray-white or silvery brittle metallic element which occurs in several alltropic forms and is found worldwide, especially in pyrolusite. Manganese is valuable, because it can by alloyed with steel to increase strength, hardness, wear resistance, and other properties, and with other metals to form highly ferromagnetic materials.

.25   There's a smelting operation on the right side as the highway passes underneath an ore ramp.

It is possible to drive onto the molle (mole) to the left which is made of slag which was poured in place to make a breakwater.

The highway parallels the quay (the stone wharf with facilities for loading and unloading ships) for a short distance.

0   To enter Santa Rosalia turn right. Directly to the front is a steam engine monument which is a reminder that this town grew to house a population in excess of 12,000 inhabitants in its hey day. The French-owned mining company, Compagnie Boleo, began mining operations in the 1880's and ended in the mid 1950's as the quantity and quality of ore decreased. The rustic French architecture and Eiffel's metal church are worth seeing.

> **AN EIFFEL THAT IS NOT IN PARIS**
> The sheet metal church in Santa Rosalia designed by A. Gustav Eiffel, the architect of the Eiffel tower in Paris, was brought to Santa Rosalia from France by mistake. The prefabricated metal church was originally destined for the 1898 World's Fair in Paris, France. It was loaded on the wrong boat and came to Santa Rosalia. Look inside for a view of Eiffel's structural genius.

CAUTION! Most of the streets in Santa Rosalia are one-way. There is good shopping, and most of the stores, supermarkets, panaderia (bakery), and pharmacy are on the main road into town. The tortilleria is one block west of the main square. The meat market is one block south of the supermarket. The merchants cater to the town's population, not to tourists, so it may be difficult to purchase certain goods.

Log 6 - Santa Rosalia to Loreto [196 kms = 122 miles]

Santa Rosalia -- Mulege. The Baja Highway travels on alluvial fans along the narrow fault controlled gulf coastal plains fringed by the Miocene volcanic mesas. Near Mulege it climbs through the Miocene volcanic hills to descend into Mulege and its Pleistocene terraces.

Mulege -- Loreto. The Baja Highway continues south along a major fault zone on the same coastal plains to Conception Bay with the Miocene volcanic mesas close on the right. The opposite side of the bay consists of faulted Miocene volcanic rocks.

South of Conception Bay the road climbs through a pass in the volcanics and follows a major alluviated graben along the Gulf fault zone with the same volcanic mesas to the west and faulted volcanic rocks to the east. Near Loreto it passes through a series of faulted marine Pliocene sediments.

197   The ferry terminal at Santa Rosalia has regularly scheduled service to Guaymas.
For the next two kilometers the road passes through numerous exposures of the Pliocene Tirabuzon and Boleo Formations and occasional pink tuffs of the Comondu Formation.
After you leave town, notice the beach. On several occasions the authors of this guide have seen innumerable beached pelagic red crabs covering the beach in a layer almost a half meter thick.

> **Krill:** Scientifically, biologists place these beautiful diminutive crustaceans in the Order Euphausiacea.
> Euphausiids are small pelagic marine shrimp like forms which differ from decapods in having biramous thoracic appendages and in other characters; most are luminescent, and all have well-developed pleopods for swimming. Euphausiids or "krill", important as food of whales, penguins, and several species of fish, are generally deep-living, but many perform diurunal vertical migrations and rise to the surface at night. Locally, schools may be encountered swimming near shore (as in Monterey Bay), and occasionally species of *Thysanoessa* and *Euphausia* may be washed ashore.

> "Just beyond the first screen of shrubs, my feet crunch through hundreds of translucent little husks, carapaces and claws of crustacea a couple inches long, now translucent and fragile but when alive, bright red and a favored food of whales." They were observed by early travelers. The Dominican, Louis de Sales wrote in the late 1760's that "while the ship Venus was thus following the coast to enter the Gulf of Cortez, the lookouts noticed red patches of whales blood. The presence of the whale-shops within sight might justify this guesswork supposition which however, was soon contradicted by the reality for soon, as we advanced, we crossed over these patches and recognized that their red color was caused by a multitude of small, vermilion colored crustaceans. These crustacea were big shrimps, but they had what shrimps lack, pincers like those of lobsters. We took some with a bag-net and preserved them in alcohol."

194.5 Hotel El Morro is located on the left side of the highway. To the rear (north) is the harbor and the Pliocene beds north of Santa Rosalia.

194   The large tree which grows on the right is a Palo Verde.

193.8 The beds directly ahead are gypsum and tuffaceous sandstones of the marine Pliocene Boleo Formation.

192 The highway crosses Arroyo de Santa Agueda and the Santa Agueda Fault and passes by exposures of both the Boleo Formation and the Infierno Formation.
The highway climbs a grade through sandstones of the Pliocene Infierno Formation. The head frame of the abandoned San Luciano copper mine can be seen below in the canyon to the right. The remnants of the town site of San Luciano (streets, foundations, etc.) are still visible on the gentle slopes behind the mining equipment. The hills around the mining region of Santa Rosalia are riddled with mines, exploratory shafts, and the remains of mining structures and equipment.
Many Palo Verde, Cardon, and Cheese Bush carpet the wash bottom.

189.5 The bleak unpainted gray cement fort-like structure on the Gulf side of the highway is a new federal prison. The gray, nondescript vegetation surrounding the gloomy prison is dismal looking and consists primarily of Palo Blanco, Cardon, *Bursera*, and several species of Cacti, and low yellow-flowered annual composites.

189 Notice twisted tree trunk utility service poles are still in use along the highway. New cement power lines have been erected on opposite sides of the highway. The occasional larger pole structures support longer spans of wire.

188.5 This Ramal (secondary side road) leads to Santa Agueda which supplies water for Santa Rosalia.

188 For the next several miles there are good views of Isla San Marcos.

> On **ISLA SAN MARCOS** the barren whitish slopes near the south end of the island are part of a gypsum deposit in the Pliocene Marquer Formation. The gypsum is mined for plaster and cement additives through the joint efforts of a Mexican corporation and the Kaiser Gypsum Company. At the tip of the south end of the island is the village of San Marcos where miners and fishermen live. One of the best views of Isla San Marcos is at Kilometer 176.

185 For the next few kilometers the local residents have planted small groves of date palms. The native flora which grows in and around the palms consists of *Acacia* and *Mimosa.*

184 There is a good view of Santa Agueda and the palm shaded cove of San Lucas.

> **SANDY SPITS AND BEACHES:** Most of the features along Baja's shoreline are produced by erosion or deposition. Depositional features along the Gulf shore in this area are built of eroded and weathered materials brought down to the shore by streams from the eastern escarpment of the Sierra la Giganta or material eroded from headlands by waves. At Santa Agueda sand/mud has been transported south by the waves (which form a finger-like extension of the beach). This depositional feature forms the sand/mud spit of Santa Agueda. Other materials have been moved by currents and deposited to form the sandy beach of San Lucas cove.

179.8 This side road leads up through the Comondu Volcanics to the Microondas San Lucas. There are many picturesque specimens of Elephant Trees near the top. There is a tremendous view of Volcan Tres Virgenes, and the Santa Rosalia area to the northwest, and Bahia de la Concepcion in the southeast. The road to this microwave tower is paved to the top with cobblestones.

Log 6 - Santa Rosalia to Loreto

174 A stop at this point will provide another good view of Isla San Marcos. Some people think they see the cartoon dog "Snoopy" lying in wait in the water when they look at the outline of Isla San Marcos.

173 The small settlement of San Bruno and it's date palms are seen on the Gulf side of the highway.

172 Here you will find a bus stop and Pemex station with an antique gravity feed gas pump. Once common, not many of these pumps are left in Baja. Buy gas just for the experience!

169 This side road leads to the old colonial village of San Jose de Magdalena. The village, located in a palm oasis, originated as a Jesuit visiting station of Mision Santa Rosalia de Mulege. Today it is a small agricultural community which grows table vegetables, citrus, and dates. The road to the village is rough but scenic. Ugarte built a ship for exploring the Gulf from timber cut in this area.

165 The hill to the right is a fault block composed of volcanic rocks of the Comondu Group.

163 The view to the southwest is of the high Gulf escarpment which is not very steep in this area. Between Santa Rosalia and Mulege the Gulf Fault Zone is a broad series of faults which cause the rugged foothills to the west of the highway.

161.5 Some of the densest stands of Elephant Trees (*Bursera sp.*) which grow on the peninsula are seen along this part of the *Baja Highway*. This years reddish growth lends a misty quality to the tops of the trees. Crushed leaves of *Bursera* produce an incense-like odor that immediately identifies them in the torchwood family.
The Mulege airport is located on the left.

159 The flora along this section of the highway is characteristic of the central Gulf coast Desert and is dominated by Cardon, Palo Blanco, Desert Mallow (apricot flowered), and several species of cacti and yellow-flowered annual composites. The annual composites and Desert Mallow are primarily growing opportunistically along the pavement edge or in the disturbed soils which border the highway.

156 The graded road to the left leads to a resort about 20 kilometers from the highway at Punta Chivato. Numerous exposures of fossiliferous marine Pliocene beds can be seen in the sea cliffs on Punta Chivato.

145 The highway follows an alluviated plain before it climbs a grade at Km 143 through the volcanic rocks of the Comondu Formation. The alluviated plain drains southwest into a gap in the hills and joins Rio Santa Rosalia in Mulege.

139.5 Ahead and to the left of the highway is a multicolored hypabyssal plug which is one of several 20 million year old intrusive plugs exposed in this area.

138.3 This is the first view of the desert palm oasis village of Mulege. The highway begins a descent through the volcanic strata.
Notice that there are a number of shears exposed in the volcanic rocks near the top of the grade. The yellow sediments at the top of the grade are probably marine Pliocene.

ANOTHER OASIS? Mulege is a refreshingly beautiful spot in a seemingly endless desert Mulege residents have built a small village which caters now to tourists, along the banks of the Rio Santa Rosalia de Mulege (locally known as

"Rio Mulege"). Mulege is located in a valley bottom whose sides resemble an extremely dry desert cactus garden. Like San Ignacio, Mulege began as a Jesuit Mission and was called Santa Rosalia de Mulege in 1705. Because of the presence of the river, another lush oasis of transplanted European date palms, citrus, olives, grapes, and oranges has developed here. Slightly upstream from Mulege (inland), the waters of the Rio Santa Rosalia have been dammed and partly diverted to irrigate palms, mangos, papayas, bananas, and citrus.

135 Purple andesite breccias are located at the north end of the Puente Mulege. The road to the left leads into Mulege along the north side of the Rio Santa Rosalia. The village of Mulege was originally named Santa Rosalia de Mulege. The name was later shortened to Mulege, as the northern French operated mining town of Santa Rosalia, it took the name "Santa Rosalia" due to its larger size and notoriety. Mulege has a varied and interesting history.

A CALL TO ARMS! One of the many battles of the Mexican war was fought in Mulege in 1864. Go through town and down the north side of the estuary to the end at El Sombrerito. Climb on the 20 million year old intrusive mass of El Sombrerito and imagine that you are commanding the American forces which have just landed from the sloop, U.S.S. Dale. The Mexicans hold the hill to the north across the sand spit. Needless to say, the Americans soon withdrew from their indefensible position and Mulege was "saved".

On the bridge there is a view of the Rio Santa Rosalia de Mulege, the estuary, and the now closed federal prison on the hill to the north (large white mission-like structure). In the past the prisoners (except rapists) were let out of the jail to work during the day. At the end of the day, the prison bell would ring, and the prisoners would return to their cells. Few of them tried to escape, since recapture meant a trip to Islas Tres Marias and its escape-proof "devil's island-like" prison.

The conical hill behind the prison is the same Miocene intrusive volcanic plug, which can be seen as the highway enters from the north of town.

133.6 The roadcuts here contain altered gypsiferous Pliocene strata cut by basalt dikes. Most of the yellow sandstone and siltstone layers in this part of Baja are probably Pliocene.

133.5 Notice the lighthouse to the left where the battle of Mulege was fought.

130.9 Just before the entrance to La Serenidad Lodge, the roadcut exposes yellow-brown sedimentary rocks of Pliocene age which contain oyster fossils. Overlying them are fossiliferous Pleistocene deposits of the Mulege Terrace. The Mulege Terrace is a 10 meter marine terrace of Late Pleistocene age which is extensively exposed in and near the town of Mulege.

A STABLE SHORELINE: In this area the Gulf shoreline has remained relatively stable since the Pliocene. There are nearshore Pliocene rocks exposed in several areas along the Mulege Estuary and nearby coastal areas. These Pliocene rocks are overlain by the Pleistocene Mulege Terrace with its diverse shoreline fauna. The present shoreline is only a few meters lower and nearby.

THE MULEGE TERRACE has been dated at 125,000 - 145,000 years and probably represents the Sagamonian 5e high stand of sea level. The fauna contained in the terrace deposits indicate a variety of environments including: open rocky shoreline, protected sandy shoreline, and estuarine.

126   To the left is a good view of Punto Gallito with its Pleistocene marine terrace and dune field. The north end of Punta Concepcion comes into view at this point.

BAHIA DE LA CONCEPCION: nearly landlocked and twenty five miles long, it is one of the most beautiful bays on the Gulf coast north of La Paz. Turquoise and ultramarine waters wash its steep rugged shores with the same milky blueness of tropical seas the world over. The color of the waters, produced by colloidal limes derived from the shells and skeletons of a myriad of marine animals, is the same as the color produced by colloidal suspensions in glacial streams and travertine springs, such as Havasupai in Arizona, U.S.A.. Miles of biological, "shell-sand" beaches are found in sheltered coves, such as Santispac, Coyote, and El Requeson. Many of the coves are bordered by small mangrove swamps.

Mountains covered with desert vegetation almost surround Bahia de la Concepcion and make it a land of extreme contrasts between mountain, desert, beaches, and tropical blue water. At the south end of the bay, is one of the largest densest cardonals in Baja.

Strewn over the landscape are scattered Ocotillo, Palo Blanco, and numerous other thorn shrub species.

124.5 A cinder blanket is visible in this roadcut.

The road to Microondas Tiburones circles around an ancient cinder cone. From the top of the cinder cone is a view of nearby Punto Gallito and the palm oasis of Mulege to the north. The alignment of three nearby hills, Punto Gallito and two unnamed hills to the south, corresponds to the trace of a known mapped fault. Farther to the south, the length of Bahia de la Concepcion and the entire Concepcion Peninsula including the Gulf Fault Zone are visible. For the next several kilometers there are many excellent, scenic views of Bahia de la Concepcion and Concepcion Peninsula. Patches of cinders are exposed in the hills for the next several kilometers. These cinders are often utilized locally for road material.

123   As the highway approaches Bahia de la Concepcion the spare flora consists of Palo Verde, Candellabra Cactus, Cardon, Garambullo, Mesquite, Busera, and Creosote Bush.

119   This is an excellent place to view Bahia de la Concepcion.

The numerous cinder cones in the area erupted along the Gulf Fault Zone.

118   The highway climbs a fault-line canyon and bypasses the old road alignment that followed the bay around Punta Arena.

116.2 As the highway crests over a low pass, the parking area to the left provides an excellent view of Bahia Santispac, one of the most beautiful little bays along this coast. The light, milky green patch in the middle of the bay is due to shallow waters that barely cover a sandy shoal. The white sands in this area are not lithic sand but materials derived from the abundant calcareous fragments of marine shells.

WHERE ARE THE SANDY BEACHES? Granitic rocks are coarse-grained and as they weather yield the sand-sized grains that compose sandy beaches. Because there are very few granitic rocks or granitic-derived sediments in Baja California Sur, there are very few quartz sand beaches in the southern part of the peninsula. As a result, there are few sand beaches along the Gulf between Santa Rosalia and La Paz.

The volcanic sediments derived from the Comondu formation which are prevalent in the southern part of the peninsula are initially fine-grained. When they weather, they yield even smaller mud or silt-sized grains. In areas of volcanic sediments there are no real sand beaches. Hawaii is another good example of this phenomena. Most of the "sandy" beaches in Baja are composed of bits and pieces of weathered shells and coralline material instead of granitic sand. This type of beach is called a biological beach.

WHAT IS A BIOLOGICAL BEACH? A beach is any sloping shore washed by waves or tides, especially the parts usually covered by sand or pebbles. Along Baja's Gulf shore these sloping shores are not commonly covered by the sand which normally covers shores along the Pacific coast. Sand is defined as any detrital particle smaller than a granule and larger than a silt grain which has a diameter between 1/16 mm to 2 mm. Quartz and feldspar form the major portion of most sands. However, the "sandy" beaches of Baja are not composed of lithic particles; instead, they are composed of weathered mollusc shells and coral skeletons. The "sandy" beaches of Baja originated from biologically derived calcium carbonate and calcium phosphate particles that have been weathered to the same detrital particle size as quartz sand particles. Since the "sand" of these beaches were derived from the shells of once living molluscs and corals, they are said to be "biological sands". However, there are a few beaches in Baja that are formed of quartz sand particles and they will be identified as the *Baja Highway* passes near them. A look at beach "sand" with a hand lens will readily reveal its nature.

114.6 Just before the turnoff to Bahia Santispac, a fault is exposed in the roadcut. This fault roughly parallels the axis of the bay and may have been involved in the origin of the bay.

114.3 This side road leads to Bahia Santispac. This is one of Baja's most scenic beaches with its white sands and azure waters.
The small red mangrove swamp, to the left, is the northernmost one which is directly visible along the Baja Highway. The inlet around the swamp used to have numerous clams before it were "clammed out". Bird watching can be rewarding in this swamp; pelicans, comorants, and frigate birds are among those birds commonly seen here.
The vegetation "growing" on the slopes to the inland side of the highway, appears to be sparse and dead because it matches the color of the metavolcanic soils. However, a closer look will reveal that they are growing quite well. It consists primarily of Cardon, Palo Verde, and *Bursera*.

A SWAMP IN THE DESERT? The *Baja Highway* passes numerous red mangrove swamps developed in the tidal creeks and estuaries which dot the Gulf coast from Mulege to the tip of the peninsula. The predominant plant of the swamp is the Red Mangrove (*Rhizophora mangle*), an evergreen shrub which form dense thickets in or near salt water or on alkaline soils. Soil and debris carried by the tides and stream run-off from the adjacent coastal environs, are washed among the network of stilt-like prop roots of the red mangrove and become caught. Over many years this process slowly extends the shore line of the peninsula to the east into the Gulf. When fertilized, the white or cream colored flowers of the red mangrove produce a brown fruit which matures and germinates into a plantlet before falling off the parent. The plantlet has a long tap root, and when it drops off the parent plant, it falls like an arrow into the mud and plants itself.
Several other plants commonly found in or near these swamps are Black Mangrove, White Mangrove, Pickleweed, Sand Verbena, and several species of native palms.

113.2 This very scenic view can be photographed if you park ahead and walk back to this spot. There are often one or two shrimp trawlers at anchor which adds to the aesthetics of the bay.

112 This view is of the beautiful Posada (hotel) Concepcion on Bahia Tordillo. It has a general store, air and diving gear for rent, and a small airstrip.

110.8 This spot provides another good view of a small sandy playa and a red mangrove swamp.

109.2 The beach below and the beach of El Coyote are both biological beaches. The highway continues to pass a number of these beaches which are signed as "Playas Publicas" (public beaches), where anyone can camp. A nightly fee per car per night may be collected as a maintenance fee.

107 The seacliffs on the south side of the cove exhibit a weathering phenomenon called a wave cut notch. A look into the water will reveal crystal clear waters with many changing hues on a bright day.

> **DRIVE IN THE GULF!** Just south of El Coyote you can drive down to a small beach that was once located along the old road. When earlier travelers first drove down this part of the peninsula they found that the old road took the route of least resistance which skirted the shoreline in most places and climbing into the hills only when absolutely necessary. Below the new highway the old road was forced to skirt a steep sea cliff. There were a number of large boulders on the outside edge of the road about 4 meters from the base of the cliff. At low tide the highway, which passed between the large boulders and the cliff, was awash, and vehicles had to drive through 15 to 25 cm of water. At high tide the entire road and the large boulders were often covered by seawater. If you wanted to pass, you waited until the next low tide.

106.5 The highway turns inland at this point to bypass a difficult section of the coastline. The cover photo of an early Auto Club Guidebook was taken here.

105 This beautiful fault line valley provides nice exposures of dark brown basalt and andesite breccias. One can really begin to appreciate the environmental extremes of Baja. The moisture dark-brown soils of the northern slopes along the right side of this valley support more vegetation--predominantly green barked Palo Verde, Cardon, and *Bursera,* while the drier reddish soils of southern hillsides (left side) of this region are more sparsely covered with the desert species of Mesquite and *Acacia.* A few kilometers down the highway a cardonal of tall columnar Cardon cacti dominates the landscape.

102 The highway passes through a dense Cardon forest for the next several kilometers. Cardon associates are *Bursera,* Palo Verde, and several other species of cactus.

100 The road cuts for the next few kilometers show the varied nature of the volcaniclastic rocks of the Comondu Formation.

99 Basalts form numerous barren talus slopes on the hills ahead. Talus slopes form rocks which fall a few at a time due to gravity and form a slope of debris which accumulates over a long period of time.

95.6 Be careful of the mud at this beach. It's easy to get a vehicle mired!

93.2   This view here is of the tombolo of El Requeson, Isla El Requeson, and a red mangrove swamp. Herons and egrets are often seen along the edge of this swamp. Good clamming on, the tombolo (sand bar) and snorkeling from the island have been reported. Its worth a visit.

> **TOMBOLO** = Italian for sand dune connecting two land areas.
> A tombolo is a sand bar that has been deposited by wind or currents and wave action between a mainland and an island or between two islands and connect the two features. At El Requeson a sand bar links the peninsula with a small island known locally as Isla El Requeson.

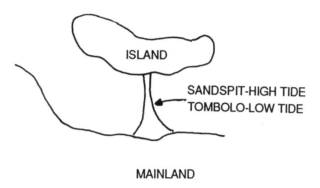

MAINLAND

9 2   This is the last view of the beach and tombolo of El Requeson.

9 0   The view ahead is of Playa Armenta, the last of the nice biological sand beaches which have dotted the shoreline since the highway left Mulege.

89.7   To the left a stretch of the old road is visible immediately below the new highway. This is another reminder of the challenges that traveling the old road once presented. In the "old days" (pre 1972) when Baja travelers made their way along this rough road, one group smelled something similar to pickles and mustard. It wasn't their imagination; one of the jar lids from their provisions had come loose. The knowledgeable travelers immediately stopped to check and cleaned up the mess before all was lost or ruined. Occasionally, due to the constant jostelling back and forth, labels would wear off of the cans and it was "*Pot luck anyone?*"

89   The view to the left (east) is Bahia de la Concepcion. Notice the numerous, long sloping alluvial fans on the far side of the bay on the Concepcion peninsula. The presence of these long fans is significant when compared to the relatively few short, steep fans on the highway side of the bay. The large eastern alluvial fans were formed by streams which carved material from the hills of the Concepcion Peninsula. There are no long fans on this side of the bay. This combination of numerous long fans on one side and a few shot fans on the other is good evidence for the recency of movement on the Gulf Fault Zone which parallels the western side of Bahia de la Concepcion. The movement resulted in a down-drop of the western side, while the eastern shore lifted. The long sloping fans developed from the east and headed west down the tilted down-dropped plain of the bay floor.

88   Watch for a series of Miocene cinder cones for the next five kilometers.

86.3   Notice the cinders in the roadcut.

Log 6 - Santa Rosalia to Loreto

83.5   This is Rancho Aguajito (not much water).

83   The cinders in this roadcut are part of a Miocene cinder cone which is one of several exposed along the highway over the preceding five kilometers. These cinder cones are probably distributed along a branch of the Gulf Fault Zone.
The lush growths of vegetation consist primarily of Palo Blanco, Palo Verde, Cardon, and *Acacia*.

76.6   Numerous very large Cardons can be seen growing in a dense stand known as a cardonal on the well-drained inland slopes. A quick look to the left shows that they rapidly become smaller and sparser toward the shoreline of the bay; this is due to the more saline soils and poor drainage. Cardons grow best on well-drained slopes. Dense stands of *Bursera*, Cochall, and Jumping Cholla are associated with the Cardon.

73.5   The bedded rock to the left in the far distance through a gap in the hills is flat-lying whitish to pinkish Pliocene strata.

73   As the highway ascends the grade, Bahia de la Concepcion is left behind, but its beauty will be remembered on the long drive through the desert as the highway proceeds to the south to the Cape Region. The beautiful view to the rear is the last one of Bahia de la Concepcion and the Concepcion Peninsula.

71   The highway descends through roadcuts which expose andesite mega-breccias.

68.1   A large dark basalt dike cuts the light pinkish mega-breccia here.
The vista opens to the south onto Loreto Graben. The alluviated valley which the road follows is a graben bounded on the west (right) by the high eastern escarpment of Sierra de Giganta and a horst composed of volcanic rocks to the left. The highway will continue to follow the axes of this graben all the way to Loreto.

68   This cobbled side road leads to the Microondas Rosarito and provides an excellent vista to the southeast.
The escarpment and the highway converge south of Loreto.

62.4   The highway passes through the small date palm oasis of Rosarito, the third Rosarito along the highway.

59.9   The graded road to the right leads to the towns of San Isidro, La Purisima, and Comondu.

56.8   The low hill 0.5 kilometers to the right is cut by two prominent nearly vertical dikes which are offset in a right lateral sense by one of the numerous traces of the Gulf Fault Zone.

55.1   The rancho on the left is Ascencion.
Another road to the right leads to the Pacific side of the peninsula via Canipole (8 kms.), Comondu (76 kms.), and La Purisima (74 kms.). This is as far south as most people drove before the road was paved because the old road continuing on to Loreto was a dead end and used only by people going there.
A side trip 2 kilometers to the north on this road, reaches the spot where the dike referred to at Kilometer 56.8 is offset by a major fault.

54   The prominent white hill approximately one kilometer west of the highway is a hypabyssal intrusive plug along the Gulf Fault Zone.

53.5 El Bombedor, another small palm oasis, is a small road side Rancho typical of this region.

44 The high peak to the right at about 2 o'clock is the outline of Gigantis, the peak which the range, Sierra de Giganta, is named. If one uses a little imagination the reclining figure of the Gigantis can easily be seen. She is facing to the north. The top of the high hill is the top of the headdress with her hair coming down; the bridge of her nose is the first saddle; the round peak is her nose; the two little hills are her lips; her chin comes into the second lower saddle.

> **A MYSTICAL LAND CALLED CALAFIA:** As the Spanish explored Mexico they brought with them legends of **a mystical land called Calafia**, an island somewhere to the west of Spain. Throughout their explorations of the seas the Spanish looked for the land of Calafia which supposedly was occupied by large "Amazon" women, known as Gigantis. They were said to have lots of gold and jewels, and thus, the real motivation of the search of the Spanish! When the Spanish traveled from Mainland Mexico across the Gulf of California to Baja California, they thought they had found the island of Calafia. It was not until much later that it was proven to be a peninsula. It is quite possible that California was named for the mystical island of Calafia, not for the Mexican word, Californax (which means "hot furnace"). The Gigantis were a mysterious group of large, amazonian-sized women. When the Spanish first settled in this area, they imagined they could see one of them reclining in the Sierra de la Giganta. Even though they found the Gigantis, they never did discover her gold and jewels.

36 There are numerous ranchos on the coastal alluvial plain. Aerial reconnaissance and photographs show that most of these ranchos are located close to linear fault features clearly marked by lines of water-loving, more mesic vegetation. The faults in this region create a zone of "crushed" rock which allows ground water to come near the surface in sag ponds. Ranchos are located where water is accessible.
Between Kilometers 36 and 32, the hills to the left contain numerous linear north-south fault traces. Several fault scarps and small horsts and grabens are readily apparent. These faults are part of the Gulf Fault Zone which passes through the Loreto embayment and Bahia de la Conception.
The pond at Kilometer 36.3 is a sag pond located on a fault and is easily recognized by the line of dense green tall, mesic vegetation.

35 Directly west, the high peak of the range is Cerro la Giganta elevation 1796 meters.
On the fan below the peak is a fault scarp which offsets the fan. The fault parallels the highway halfway down the fan with approximately 10 m. of offset and is marked by a low line of hills which run through the fan. Further to the left is a series of small, sharp-crested hills. These are granodiorites, dated at 145 and 87 m.y., which outcrop west of Loreto.
To the right large stand of Palo Blanco growing along the side of the highway. New growth on Elephant Trees is responsible for the red-colored tops of the trees.

30.5 This turnoff leads to the small date palm community of San Juan Bautista.
To the southeast is the Boca San Bruno.
Early Jesuits attempted to establish two visiting stations for the Loreto Mission in this area: Mision Guadalupe de San Bruno, 1683, and Mision San Juan Bautista Londo, 1687. Both attempts were unsuccessful.

29.5 The first of the marine Miocene-Pliocene beds is visible at this kilometer mark. The highway climbs through Pliocene sandstones and conglomerates.

A MARINE TECTONIC BASIN: Major movement of the Gulf Fault Zone appears to have initiated the formation of the Loreto embayment of Miocene(?)-Pliocene age; it is a thick sequence of conglomerate, sandstone, mudstone and limestone with pecten and oyster reefs, tuff, andesite and basalt. Tuff beds and a lahar indicate volcanic action during the filling of this basin. At least one major angular unconformity and the lensing of conglomerate beds suggests intermittent deformation. Basalt (6.7 million years) intrudes and overlies part of the section which may be older than the rest of the basin. Other dates of 1.9, 2.1 and 3.3 m.y. have been obtained from tuffs interlayered in the marine sequence (Hugh Mclean, 1986). The syncline of the Loreto embayment is folded into a N-S anticlinal structure with numerous N-S and NW-SE trending faults which may have one to two thousand meters of cumulative displacement. The conglomerates contain small amounts of granitic and metavolcanic clasts from outcrops to the west.

The Loreto embayment is one of the few tectonic basins in the southern part of the peninsula. The darker brown flat-lying Miocene rocks which cap the mesas to the west are as young as 10 million years old. This embayment was formed after faulting warped and uplifted the mesas. One dike, dated at 6.7 million years, cuts the sediments. At this time the northern part of the Gulf of California had already formed, and the more southerly parts of the gulf were being formed had moved to the south. The Loreto embayment was warped downward and received sediments from the surrounding highlands. The conglomerates indicate intermittent uplift of the same areas and more powerful streams. The yellow beds indicate wearing down of the source areas with less powerful streams and the coarse material is not carried as far into the basin. The area was continuously faulted. Several tuff beds are exposed in the section which indicate continuing volcanism. These rocks are highly fossiliferous.

28.9 Evaluation of the stratigraphy seems to indicate that the strata on this roadcut exposes andesite dikes which intrude into Pliocene beds. The prominent dike in the middle yielded a 6.7 m.y. K/Ar (potassium/argon) date. However, tuffs in the arroyo nearby yielded a 1.9 m.y. K/Ar date.

27.3 As the highway crosses a large arroyo, an autobrecciated, andesite lahar is exposed on both sides of the highway.

26.5 In the roadcut at this kilometer mark in a white tuffaceous sandstone outcrop in the hill above the highway blocks of tuff from the Loreto sediments are being quarried on the left side of the road for use as building material.

26 An oyster shell reef is exposed . The reef continues for nearly a kilometer to the south along the highway.
Mesquite, Cardon, and mistletoe are growing along both sides of the highway.

25.3 The oyster-shell reef and white tuffaceous sandstone parallel the highway for a short distance before crossing under the highway to the right to interrupt the yellow sedimentary beds exposed there.
The surface of the hill on the right is veneered by oysters of the genus *Ostrea*. The tuff yielded a 2.1 m.y. K/Ar (potassium/argon) date.

22.9 A small rancho is located along the highway. The yellow beds are well exposed in the hills near this rancho. They represent a time of low sedimentation. Benthonic foraminifera from these beds indicate that they were deposited at shelf-slope break depths.

The conglomerates exposed here represent periods of uplift of the adjacent highlands along the faults in the Sierra la Giganta.

20.1   The dirt road at this point leads to the small village of San Juan Londo. The vista to the rear provides a good view of the Gulf. Just south of the water is a small, rounded volcanic hill. This was the site of a small visiting station of the Loreto mission. There are approximately 300 meters of conglomerates and sandstones between the yellow beds in this area.

22   The road up the arroyo, to the west, leads to outcrops of granitic rocks, a rarity in this part of Baja.

19   To the southeast is the southern part of the Loreto embayment. The volcanic hills to the left side of the highway are overlain by the white tuffaceous sandstones and gray conglomerates of the lower part of the Carmen-Marquer Formation undifferentiated. These beds are thousands of meters thick and contain abundant fossils. Common fossils include: whale bones, *Argopecten sp., Ostrea titan, Turritella sp., Chama sp., Chione sp.*, and numerous other species of Mollusca (clams and snails). The southern part of the Loreto embayment was warped considerably before the deposition of the upper beds, which are also folded.

18.5   A pecten reef is located to the right above the highway.

18.3   There is a view to the left into a distant amphitheater of yellow beds overlain by conglomerates with an interesting isolated thumb of conglomerate in the center. The yellow beds have yielded very large oysters and whale remains.

17   Another conglomerate amphitheater is noticeable. Closer inspection reveal occasional pecten beds.

16.5   The high red hill to the east is composed of the volcaniclastic rocks.

15.8   A road metal quarry used to be here where the yellow beds on both sides of the highway are known to be highly fossiliferous.
Cliffs of gray conglomerates and light gray sandstones are seen to the east. Studies of maps of the beds from aerial photos and field mapping reveals that the cliffs do not follow the strike of the beds.

13.8   The highway descends into a small arroyo.
The limestone on the ridge to the left is much younger than and unconformably rests on the tilted edges of the Loreto sediments. There is an exposure of a pecten reef in the roadcut opposite the guard rail.

12.8   The highway crests a small grade and begins to follow Arroyo de Arce.
The white volcanic tuff bed seen in the roadcut is repeated five times for a cumulative separation of 200 meters on this bed alone. An abundance of sand dollars and pectens have been collected from the layer above the tuff bed.

12   Blocks of white tuff are mined at Rancho Las Piedras Rodadas to the left. This tuff is 3.3 million years old.

11.8   The same tuff bed can be seen in the wash below the left side of the highway.

10.7   The highway crosses the crest of an anticline. The conglomerates now dip to the south.

9.6   Note the prominent fault which dips 45 degrees north. Faults in this section appear to have a cumulative displacement of one to two thousand meters.

9.3   This side road leads up to Microondas Loreto. The tower is built on volcanic rocks which yielded a 14.9 m.y. K/Ar (potassium/argon) date.

9   These roadcuts reveal numerous small faults and scattered fossils of pectens. The highway crosses the deep Arroyo de Gua. This arroyo passes through a thick faulted section of the Loreto sediments.

7.5   The highway leaves the sandstones of the Loreto embayment behind. The beds are still dipping to the south on the south limb of the anticline.

6.5   This is the first good distant view of Loreto and Isla del Carmen.

6   The vegetational cover consists of Cardon, Pitaya Agria, Pitaya Dulce, Palo Blanco, Palo Verde, Acacia, Elephant Tree, and Leatherplant.
This is an excellent area for a bird walk. One of the most commonly seen birds is the large spotted-breasted Cactus Wren (*Campylorhynchus brunneicapillus*).

The **Cactus wren** is the largest wren of the deserts and arid hillsides throughout the entire Baja peninsula. They are commonly seen feeding and nesting below 1200 meters among thickets of thorny scrub, large cacti, clumps of yucca, or mesquite. Most members of the Family Troglodytidae are small, restless brownish birds with finely-barred narrow rounded tails that are held erect. The Cactus Wren is easily identified in the field by its wide eye stripe and heavily spotted breast. When it feeds, the Cactus Wren furtively searches through the ground litter for small invertebrates, usually insects.

3   The 30 kilometer long island which is visible immediately offshore is Isla del Carmen.

ISLA DEL CARMEN is surrounded by water with depths of less than 200 meters and exhibits greater water clarity than found along the peninsular shores. Increased clarity is due to lower plankton densities and smaller quantities of suspended sediments. Biologically, the flora and fauna of this island are similar to and were probably derived from mainland forms that are either widespread in North America in a variety of habitats or are restricted primarily to North American deserts. The variety of habitats suitable for mammals on the Gulf islands is limited because of the severe desert climate, the predominance of relatively unproductive rocky habitats, and the absence of fresh water.
There are no endemic birds on any of the Gulf islands. Generally, the islands support avian species whose populations are indistinct from those on the closest adjacent peninsula or mainland. The diversity, density, and productivity of plant species vary considerably on the Gulf islands, since seasonal patterns of precipitation in the Gulf strongly determine the availability of fresh water.

Log 6 - Santa Rosalia to Loreto

There are 18 species of plants endemic to the Gulf islands. *Ferocactus diguetii* var. *carmenensis* is the only endemic of Isla del Carmen. Botanically, the predominant plants of Isla del Carmen are *Agave*, Cholla, Elephant Tree, (*Pachycormus discolor*), Barrel Cactus (*Ferocactus diguetii*), Hedgehog Cactus (*Echinocereus brandegeei*), and nipple cacti (*Mammillaria sp.*). Generally, the southern Gulf island floras are composed of deciduous plants in dense and often thorny growths. Beginning with the shoreline and moving inland to the highest point on the island, botanists have identified the following plant communities on the larger islands of the Gulf, including Isla del Carmen: Littoral Scrub, Mangrove; halophytic scrub, desert scrub; and thorn scrub.

Geologically, Isla del Carmen is composed of Miocene volcanics of the Comondu Formation and marine Pliocene rocks of the Salada Formation.

Isla del Carmen is inhabited by employees of a solar salt works which has operated since the Spanish first settled Baja California. Numerous coves, anchorages, grottos, and reefs lure visitors who seek seclusion, skin diving, and great fishing in the clear shallow waters which surround Isla del Carmen.

2.0   This turnoff is a shortcut into Loreto down one of its many unpaved side streets.

0   The tower of Mision Nuestra Senora de Loreto can be seen; it is surrounded by palm trees in the main part of Loreto. The El Presidente Hotel is also visible just north of town.

Also to the north, is the crest of the anticline which forms the east side of the Loreto embayment. The dark-colored hills on the crest are volcanic rocks, circled by a lighter limestone with the sandstones and conglomerates of the Loreto Formation in the lower hills. Isla Coronado is now visible on the northern skyline.

ISLA CORONADO is a very recent volcano with some flows still devoid of vegetation. This island contains a Pliocene marine terrace and a large cobble beach bar at 10+ meters elevation. Many flows appear to have moved down canyons and are truncated by the ocean at their base. There are no terraces on the sides of the island with the fresh flows. The marine terrace indicates that the island is at least 125,000 years old. The truncation of the more recent flows by the sea suggests that the most recent volcanism is at least a few thousand years old. Biologically Isla Coronado is similar to Isla del Carmen.

LORETO is Baja's first city, and was founded at the delta of a large perennial stream, Arroyo de Las Parras, in 1697 by Jesuit missionaries. For the next 132 years Loreto was the capital of Baja California. In 1829 a hurricane destroyed Loreto and the capital was moved to its present location in La Paz.

Flood waters raging down Arroyo Las Parras have destroyed the town on eleven occasions since 1697. Recently, some efforts have been made to control the flooding with channels. The town has also been damaged by earthquakes. A particularly large one occurred in 1877.

A canopy of European Date Palms covers part of the town and extends down to the beach. At the beach the palms lean over the sand very much as coconut palms do on South Pacific Islands. The lean is the result of the perennial eastward blowing winds which move down the escarpment of the Sierra la Giganta toward the Gulf.

The mission in Loreto is the first and thus the oldest in Baja California and it was from here that Father Junipero Serra began in 1769 to establish the missions in Alta California. The church was completed in 1752 and later destroyed and rebuilt. Notice the clock in the tower. The Loreto mission museum is worth a visit. Today Loreto is the seat of the municipal (county) government and a resort and sport fishing center. Several good hotels are located in Loreto and all services are available.

128

Log 7 - Loreto to Constitucion [145 kms = 90 miles]

The Baja Highway continues south on the narrow Gulf coastal plain between the rugged Miocene volcanic mesas and the Gulf of California with its many faulted volcanic islands. South of Ligui the Highway climbs a grade through the Miocene volcanics to the mesa tops. It then follows a gentle canyon in the mesas to the flat Magdalena Plain with the metamorphic islands offshore.

120 LORETO TURNOFF: The uplifted fault scarp cliffs of flat-layered volcanic tuffs and sediments to the west are the main massif of the Sierra la Giganta. From this point it is hard to realize that there is a relatively flat tableland on top of the massif which extends west to the Pacific Ocean. The prominent peak to the right of the large pass in the Sierras is Cerro Pelon de Las Parras, a shallow intrusive andesite plug which yielded a 19.4 m.y. K/Ar (potassium/argon) date.

The graded unpaved road to San Javier goes through the pass to the left of Cerro Pelon.

The low hills to the northwest are composed of 94 m.y. old metavolcanic rock and 143 to 87 m.y. old tonalite with a moderate to complex structure intruded by a dike system which outcrops north and west of Loreto. The presence of older granitic and metavolcanic rocks at this point in the Gulf of California plus the lack of Peninsular Range basement in south-central Baja confirms geophysical evidence for the continuation of the Cretaceous syncline under a major part of the peninsula.

South of Loreto the Gulf Fault Zone and the highway converge until the highway is forced to follow along a narrow hilly coastal plain between the Gulf and the steep fault scarp cliffs of the Sierra la Giganta.

117.6 The graded road to the right leads 48 kilometers up Arroyo Las Parras into the ruggedly scenic Sierra la Giganta and past several picturesque ranchos to Mision San Francisco Javier de Vigge. This mission, which was founded in 1699, was the second Jesuit mission established on the peninsula. Some who have visited Mision Javier consider it the finest example of mission architecture in Baja. It has the distinction of being the only original mission church that has remained intact. All of the others have been destroyed and rebuilt at least once. The road is supposed to be improved as part of the mission's restoration program which began in early 1979. They say it will be finished "manana".

Several small agricultural ranchos are located along the road to San Javier. The primary crops of these ranchos are citrus and olives. Many beautiful growths of several species of native palms grow luxuriously along the perennial stream of San Javier. You may want to inquire in Loreto before you attempt the road to San Javier in a passenger car. The graded road crosses a Comondu section which is different from the other two sections crossed by the main highway at San Ignacio and south of Loreto.

116.6 This is the turnoff to the Loreto International Airport.

The highway continues south along the narrow coastal plain between the abrupt escarpment of the Sierra la Giganta and the warm beautiful waters of the Gulf. The escarpment was a formidable barrier to the early missionaries. They finally breached it at San Javier.

Isla del Carmen dominates the Gulf and the northern portion of the uninhabited Isla Danzante is just visible to the southeast.

111.1 This turnoff leads to Nopolo Beach and the small Rancho Nopolo. A beautiful small cove and small mangrove swamp are located near a tombolo that connects the peninsula to a small rocky island. A tombolo is a sand spit which connects an island to a mainland. At some high tides this tombolo may be awash. The scenic beach in this cove is a rarity in this area. Lithic sand, instead of crushed shells, forms this beach.

129

Log 7 - Loreto to Constitucion

A new El Presidente hotel has been built here by FONATUR, a government-managed development group. Along with Loreto this area has been targeted for major tourist development which will be patterned after similar projects at Cancun and Ixtapa on mainland Mexico. More extensive tourist facilities may eventually be built at Nopolo.

At Nopolo winter visitors may be treated to a strange spectacle -wildly-diving Brown Pelicans (*Pelicanus occidentalis*)! During the winter months currents and winds combine to pile up schools of small fish along the coast of this area. The pelicans take advantage of the conditions and become embroiled in feeding frenzies, a bizarre spectacle indeed!

The **California Brown Pelican** is one of the large aquatic fish-eating birds seen along both of Baja's coasts and on many of the Gulf islands in Baja where they nest in large colonies. They are commonly seen flying in long straight lines only centimeters above the surface of the water. Feeding is accomplished by diving into the sea from as high as 50 meters. The slow deliberate flight of the brown pelican, which is low over the water with sudden plunges for fish, makes its identity unmistakable. The Brown Pelican is the same semi-tame pelican commonly seen begging for food on fishing piers around the docks at Guerrero Negro and Puerto Escondido. Mexicans know these large birds as Pelacano Gris.

Many species of birds inhabit the seemingly barren Central Gulf Coast Desert. Some of the more common birds of this area are listed below:

Bird	Common Location
American White Pelican	Gliding along the shore
American Kestrel	Telephone wires and fence posts
Cactus Wren	On cacti
California Brown Pelican	Gliding along the shore
California Quail	On the ground
Costa's Hummingbird	Feeding on red tubular flowers
Gila Woodpecker	In the scrub
Gray Thrasher	On the ground looking for food in the litter
Greater Roadrunner	Crossing the highway
Ladder-back Woodpecker	Flitting in the air
Pyrrhuloxia	In chaparral and oak woodlands
Red-Tailed Hawk	Tops of telephone poles and fence posts
Turkey Vultures	Soaring in the sky looking for carrion
Western Meadowlark	Fence posts and fence wires
Xantu's Hummingbird	Feeding at tubular flowers

107.5 Loreto and its white church tower are seen in the distance to the rear.
The highway ascends a small grade through dark basalts with a lagoon, inlet, and the small mangrove swamp of Nopolo on the left.

A number of formerly inhabited caves have been found in the Sierra la Giganta to the east of Nopolo. They were occupied by Indians who subsisted on the clams and other marine life of the cove.

Log 7 - Loreto to Constitucion

106   In this region the highway was constructed in the Gulf Fault Zone. The disjointed and irregular hills in the foreground are in the fault zone. The crushed rocks adjacent to the highway do not exhibit bedding, while impressive flat bedding is well exposed in the high eastern escarpment beyond the fault zone to the west.

103   The ranch house of Rancho Notri is on the right (west).
To the left is Playa Notri, another lithic sand beach where many species of game fish, which include Marlin, Sailfish, Sierra, Dolphin Fish, Yellowtail, and Grouper, often come close to shore.

99.5   **STOP here to enjoy the view!** A roadside rest area is located on the left side of the highway where there is an excellent view of the little cove of Juncalito and a "Playa Publica", a public beach. Juncalito is Spanish for little tilted rock.
The water in the low pass to the southeast is part of Bahia Escondido which is located between the peninsular coast and Isla del Carmen. The high peaks near Punta Candaleros to the south of Puerto Escondido are andesite breccias and lahars.

        ISLAS DANZANTE, MONSERATTE, SANTA CATALINA, CARMEN, AND CORONADO: To the right (south) in the distance is Isla Danzante composed of faulted Miocene andesite breccias and volcaniclastic sediments.
        The north end of Isla Monseratte, composed of Miocene volcanic rocks and Pliocene marine sediments, and Isla Santa Catalina to the left, composed of Mesozoic granitic rocks, can be seen in the distance.
        The largest island, Isla del Carmen, composed of the Miocene volcaniclastic and Pliocene marine rocks, is directly offshore to the east.
        To the north is the Pliocene to Recent basalt cone of Isla Coronado (*See* Anderson, 1950, for a more complete description of the geology of the islands).

99   The roadcut exposes a well-jointed basalt.
The highway follows the Gulf Fault Zone in the narrow coastal plain with the main escarpment of the Sierra la Giganta rising to the right (west). The highway follows this fault zone for several kilometers. The low benches on the hillslopes to the right mark the traces of the fault.

99.3   The large solitary Wild Fig Tree (*Ficus palmeri*) which grows on the beach at the end of the gravel bar to the left (east), is the one that is pictured in Coyle and Robert's Field Guide to the Plants of Baja California (1975). A second edition (1989) of this excellent plant guide is now available (Natural History Publishing Co., P.O. Box 962, La Jolla, Ca. 92037).

WILD FIGS are members of the Mulberry family. They range from the palm oasis of San Ignacio south to the Cape region where they are usually seen growing alone on rocky cliffs, in canyons, and occasionally on gravel beaches such as this one. Don't run down the beach and look for a snack, because Wild Figs produce a barely edible dry fig in the late spring and early summer.
In Baja California Wild Figs are not cultivated, but they do provide food for local birds such as the Western Mockingbird, common Crow, and several species of Finch, Oriole, and Warbler.

97.5   This is the entrance to Juncalito Cove (Refer to Km 99.5). Boats may be rented here for trips to the nearby gulf islands.

131

Log 7 - Loreto to Constitucion

94.3   **PUERTO ESCONDIDO:**   This paved side road leads 2.4 kilometers to the deep water port of Puerto Escondido. Steinbeck in his "Log of the Sea of Cortez" claimed this as his favorite place in the Gulf. The authors of this guide have spent many weeks here and agree.

FONATUR is also developing Puerto Escondido as a tourist resort area. The port may eventually be the terminus for ferry service to Topolobampo on the Mexican mainland.

A fault is exposed in the saddle directly in front of the pier with darker-colored basalts on the near side and fluvatile andesite breccias on the far side. This area is worth a visit. It exhibits many excellent tide pools and the coastal waters abound with fish and other sea life. Twenty-five pound Yellowtail have been caught by the authors off the pier.

At night during the right season, many people have made spectacular sightings of sea lions which swim in a sea which abounds with a microscopic phosphorescent bioluminescent protozoan of the genus *Noctaluca.* The eerie bluish-green light of Noctaluca is strong enough to read by.

Boats for fishing or visiting nearby islands and secluded beaches may also be rented here.

93   The view offshore is dominated by Isla Danzante. Isla Carmen is to the left and Monseratte is to the right.

The three small isolated "rocks" in the bay to the right are Los Candaleros ("the Candles"). Los Candaleros are isolated pinnacles which are known as stacks to geologists. They were formed either by the collapse of sea arches or by the erosion of vertically fractured headlands (*See* the Friars, Km 6 in La Paz to Cabo San Lucas log).

89   The striking view to the right rear is of the uplifted steep eastern escarpment of the Sierra la Giganta. The flat to little-deformed and well-bedded strata extend from the Pacific eastward across the peninsula to the edge of the scarp. As they enter the fault zone the beds become chaotic, crushed, and deformed in the the narrow Gulf coastal plain and adjacent islands.

86   The highway continues south along cliffs of fluvial volcanic breccia which exhibit large clasts and numerous caves. Isla Danzante consists of this same material cut by a number of dikes and faults.

From this area south to the Cape Region, numerous White-winged Doves (*Zenaida asiatica*) are commonly seen on the ground along the highway or flying across the highway

WHITE-WINGED DOVES are the only doves with large white wing patches which contrast with general olive-brown colors of the body. Although they are wide-spread throughout the peninsula, they are most commonly seen in thorn scrub, Mesquite groves, Riparian Woodlands, and the open dry desert areas south of Loreto.

84.2   This turnoff leads to Ligui and a beautiful cove.

The flora of this area is dominated by *Acacia*, Garambullo, Pitaya Agria, Pitaya Dulce, Cardon, Mistletoe, Palo Blanco, Palo Adan, and the Vining Bougainvilla-like San Miguel. The overgrazed disturbed soils around the rancho support numerous Jumping Cholla.

83.5 A shear which is part of the Gulf fault zone is visible in this roadcut.
The highway turns through a wash, reaches the bottom of the grade, and begins the ascent of a steep grade south of Ligui.

78.8 There is a view to the left of the Gulf and the small village of Ligui. A beautiful little bay with a rare "real" sand bottom can be reached by road.
Islas Monseratte and Carmen lie directly offshore, and the low volcanic cinder cone of Isla Coronado is just visible to the north.
Between here and the top of the steep grade, the highway passes over a major fault zone. Most of the major motion along this fault was pre-Miocene. There is some evidence of lesser Miocene to Recent motion. The zone is difficult to identify because it is wide and diffuse. The complexly faulted areas, offset, and deformed bedding of this region is generally marked by a foothill belt rather than the undeformed well-defined bedding of the mesas of the western Pacific slope.

75.7 This turnout provides a good view to the north of the majestic massif of the Sierra la Giganta. The high crest of the range with the undeformed sedimentary rocks which extend from the western Pacific slopes drops rapidly to the east into the undulating fault-deformed foothills adjacent to the highway on the right.

73.7 The large orange-red splotches on the low hill to the left are crustose lichens. The primary role of lichens is in the first stage of plant succession.

71.1 In this roadcut two small faults are exposed, and the sedimentary beds are obviously sheared by traces of the Gulf Fault Zone.

69.8 As the highway crests the top of the Ligui grade, there is a road to the east which leads to Microondas Ligui. The highway descends through a canyon down the gentle western slope of the Sierra la Giganta for tens of kilometers.

69 The undeformed well-bedded strata of the Pacific drainage of the Sierras are now very obvious along the canyon walls.

68.2 This side road leads 41 Km to a small fishing village on the gulf at Bahia Agua Verde and Punta San Marcial.

64 The cliffs on the left are covered with two obvoius kinds of lichen (Fungus with an intracellular mutualistic single celled algae of the genus *Chorella*). The most abundant kind is green, the less obvious ones are orange-red (rust) colored. Lichens are "pioneer" plants living on bare rock. There presence here is related to edaphic (soil) and slope aspect. A closer inspection would reveal other kinds of lichens. Lichens are important to plants since they chemically weather rock into soils in which higher plant develop.

59.8 The highway proceeds through an east-west trending canyon.
The Cardon cardonals are extensive and are primarily located on the cooler moister north-facing slopes, while desert Mesquite grows abundantly in the well-drained canyon bottom. The two sides of the canyon show notable differences in vegetation typical of north and south-facing slopes. The edaphic factors, the moisture, and the directional differences of the slope faces combine to significantly affect local plant distribution.

56 The vegetation of this region represents an ecotonal zone (*See* Km 118.5 of the Ensenada to San Quintin log) of a mixture of plants of the Magdalena Plain desert area and the Central Gulf Coast desert area. It is dominated by a Cardon-Palo Verde forest mixed with scattered Pitaya Dulce, *Acacia*, Cholla, Beaver-tail, vining San Miguel, Palo Blanco, Palo Adan, Purplebush, Lomboy, and Elephant Tree.

54.5   On the hill to the south, chocolate brown basalt caps the lighter gray-brown andesite breccias, lahars, and fluvial sedimentary rocks of the Comondu Formation. They dip gently to the west. The highway descends at approximately the same gradient as the arroyo itself. The gradient of the arroyo is controlled largely by the slight dip of the Comondu Formation toward the Pacific Ocean. The arroyo descends for some distance along a single bed, drops down through a few beds, and then flows along another bed. Marine Miocene sections are not exposed along the highway as it crosses the peninsula in this region.

54   Andesite breccias, typical of the Comondu in this area, are exposed in this roadcut and on the opposite wall of the arroyo.

49   More andesite breccias are exposed in the opposite wall of the canyon. These monolithologic andesite breccias take the form of lahars which occur as andesite flows, flow conglomerates, and fluvatile conglomerates. They grade into finer sandstones and well-bedded sedimentary rocks. This is a facies of the Comondu Formation. Below the highway the present stream bed is following the bedding surface of one of the breccia layers.

44   The outcrops at the lower edge of the arroyo are fluvatile sandstones and conglomerates of the Comondu Formation capped by basalt.
The highway leaves the canyon and passes onto the Magdalena Plain. It is largely composed of Miocene and Pliocene rocks overlain by the same type of Pliocene-Pleistocene limestone which caps the Vizcaino Plain to the northwest. These sediments are only occasionally exposed in the arroyos or road metal quarries of the Magdalena Plain. Bahia Magdalena is a deeper remnant of this shallow embayment.

> **ISLAS MARGARITA AND MAGDALENA:** On a clear day the Pacific islands of Isla Margarita and Isla Magdalena, which are composed of Franciscan metamorphics, are visible ahead to the left. These islands are the remnants of the sea floor of the Pacific Plate which was subducted under the North American Plate. Radiometric ages obtained from these rocks seem to cluster around 135 m.y. They are very similar to the Coast Range Province of California.

43   The Central Gulf Coast Desert flora is represented by large cardonals with associated Pitaya Dulce, Palo Verde, *Acacia*, Wax Plant, Pitaya Agria, Garambullo, Candelabra Cactus, Greasewood, Mistletoe, Jumping Cholla, and Leather plant. Epiphytic Ball Moss (*Ramalina*) is occasionally seen scattered on the tops of the Palo Verde.

28   The sign on the right marks the entry of the highway into the Zcna de Neblina. This translates into zone of the fog. The moisture of the fogs in this zone enable an abundance of epiphytic gray-green Foliose Lichens and dark Ball Moss to grow on the shrubs and cacti.

20   This area is much drier than that near Kilometer 43 and supports significantly fewer shorter scattered Cardons, Pitaya Dulce, Candelabra Cactus, Ball Moss, Creosote Bush, Lomboy, Palo Verde, and Palo Adan.

10   The highway crests a low rise and drops quickly into one of the distributary channels of Arroyo Santa Cruz. It passes through the prosperous-looking farming area of Bueno Aires.

17   At the village of Ley Federal de Aguas Numero Uno, a government-sponsored project provides fossil ground water from wells drilled for agricultural use in the nearby foothills.
A gas station with Extra is located on the right side of the highway.

15.5   The size of the Que Reparrio bridge attests to the fact that on some occasions a large quantity of water flows over this plain.

7.5   The soils have become very dry and desert-like; The flora has become even more sparse and stunted than previously observed.

0   The kilometer markings change to 236 at this junction and descend as the highway approaches La Paz.
At Ciudad (city) Insurgentes the highway turns sharply to the southeast across the Magdalena Plain toward La Paz.
The highway will first traverse a flat, then a gently undulating desert terrain as it heads south toward La Paz.

236   Sorghum, an old world grass (*Sorghum vulgare var. saccharatum*) is cultivated as grain and forage or as a source of a dark heavy syrup popular in the southeastern and midwestern United States is grown in the agricultural fields throughout this area.

231   The Centro Receptor De Granos is a central grain storage location for the local ejido.

227   As the highway approaches Ciudad Constitucion, the land alternates between native desert flora, cultivated fields, and residential areas.

225   The area is heavily vegetated by native Pitaya Agria, Lomboy, Mesquite, Creeping Devil Cactus, Cheese Bush, several species of Cholla, Lichen, Torote, Cardon, Palo Adan, and Old Man Cactus. The vegetation of this region is characteristic of the very dry Magdalena Plain area of the Central Desert phytogeographic region of Baja California. This extremely dry region of Baja receives only 2 to 5 centemeters of precipitation annually.

212   **Ciudad Constitucion** is a thriving agricultural community and is the gateway to Bahia Magdalena. Constitucion, adjacent to La Paz, is the second largest population center of Baja California Sur. The important crops of this region are cotton, alfalfa, vegetables and wheat; they are shipped to mainland Mexico via the Cape from Puerto San Carlos on the mangrove-edged Pacific shore of Bahia Magdalena.
The road to the right leads to Puerto San Carlos; the highway ahead proceeds into the main part of Ciudad Constitucion.
Almost anything a traveler needs can be purchased in Constitucion. John Minch, one of the authors of this guide, had a blown out tire re-vulcanized here. It withstood 8,000 more kilometers of rough offroad travel in Baja.

Log 8 - Constitucion to La Paz [212 kms = 132 miles]

The Baja Highway crosses the flat Magdalena Plain with views of the offshore islands to Santa Rita. From this point the highway begins to traverse a series of gentle washes and dissected mesas in marine sedimentary rocks at San Agustin where it climbs onto a dissected surface of fluvial volcanic sediments and crosses the peninsula. Near La Paz the highway descends the Gulf Scarp through the fluvial volcanics to the alluviated La Paz Plain.

212 **CONSTITUCION** was a small inland village which is now a large agricultural community which produces wheat, cotton, citrus, peppers, sorghum, tomatoes, and alfalfa for export to other parts of Mexico. This is one place where the biblical prophecy "and the desert shall bloom as a rose" has come to pass. Farming has been made possible by deep artesian wells drilled by the Mexican Government which bring "fossil water" to the surface from ancient aquifers. The amount of water withdrawn from these aquifers through wells is carefully monitored to prevent the over usage and eventual depletion of this limited resource. Some water is naturally available from infrequent summer rainstorms or late summer-early fall chabascos or hurricanes. These produce sudden downpours which may overflow the arroyos in a matter of minutes. However, this water is not available to the flora of the Magdalena since it runs off quickly before much of it has a chance to soak to the roots of the plants.

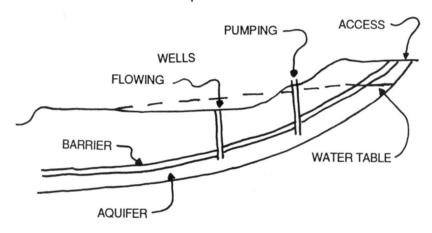

ARTESIAN SYSTEM

198 The village of Via Morelos is located in the middle of a farming area. Most of the non-agricultural regions of Llanos de Magdalena or Magdalena Plain support disturbed vegetation because the land has either been cleared or over-grazed.

190 Mision San Luis Gonzaga is located in the low foothills east of the Magdalena Plain. This mission is situated along a stream that follows a transpeninsular fault which offsets the Cretaceous geosyncline by a total of 50 kilometers in a right lateral sense. The fault has deformed lower Miocene sediments and is overlain by flat-lying 20 million year old volcanic tuffs. A good high clearance vehicle can reach the mission.

173.8 The road metal quarry on the right exposes limestones of the fossiliferous Miocene-Pliocene Salada Formation. This limestone can be seen extensively over the Magdalena Plain. The mission was formerly the site of a garrison of troops used to reinforce the sailors on the Manilla galleon when it came through the Bahia Magdalena area. There is a graded road just south of the quarry which leads 32 km to Cancun on Bahia Magdalena.

This flat plain is reminiscent of the Great Valley of California. Structurally, the two regions are nearly identical. The Magdalena Plain is underlain by up to 20,000 meters of Cretaceous and Tertiary sedimentary rocks.

The highway roughly follows the axis of the Cretaceous geosyncline as defined by geophysical surveys.

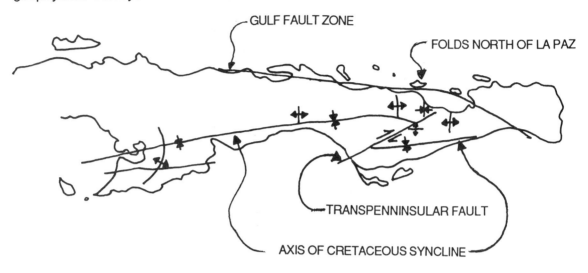

STRUCTURAL ELEMENTS IN SOUTHERN BAJA

190   The vegetational cover between this km and Santa Rita is usually very sparse; it reveals much bare ground. The flora of this area is predominated by Cardon, Cholla, Elephant Tree, Palo Verde, Palo Adan, Cheese Bush, and Creeping Devil Cactus, annual composites, Leatherplant, Greasewood, Garambullo, and Pitaya Dulce.
On clear days the Pacific islands of Isla Santa Margarita and Isla Magdalena can be seen to the west across Bahia Magdalena. These islands are composed of Franciscan-type rocks similar to the Coast Ranges of Alta California. They contain numerous thrust sheets, pillow basalts, serpentinite, and garnet hornblendites. These rocks have been K/Ar dated at 134 m.y. (Minch, 1971; Yeats, *et al.*, 1971).

185   This is Rancho El Coyote.

157   The small village of Santa Rita has only a few services available.
From this point the highway begins to traverse the gentle Pacific slope drainages through a series of washes and dissected mesas.
For the next several kilometers the highway passes through the poorly exposed dark reddish-brown and brownish-yellow beds of the Tepetate Formation.
The washes are populated by dense Palo Verde, while the hillslopes support very sparse Leatherplant and Palo Adan with occasional stands of Jumping Cholla and Pitaya Dulce.

144.3 This roadcut exposes a limestone which has been mapped as part of the Miocene-Pliocene Salada Formation. The Salada Formation (Heim, 1922) is named for exposures of marine Pliocene and Pleistocene sediments in Arroyo Salada in Baja California Sur. Juan Smith now feels that the type section of the Salada Formation is Miocene in age.

143   The floral species which cover the Pacific slopes of the Sierra de la Giganta are typical desert dominants of the Magdalena Plain area of the Sonoran Central Desert Phytogeographic Region and continue to be represented by epiphytic Ball Moss and

Ramalina lichen which grow on the elephant trees *Bursera microphylla* and *B. hindsiana*, Palo Adan, Leatherplant, Cardon, Jumping Cholla, Pitaya Dulce, and Garambullo.

135   The highway makes a long crossing through the bottom of an arroyo. Abundant sharks teeth have been found in the Miocene exposures located below the El Rifle microwave tower to the left of the highway.

130   The Datilillo and Cardons are a prominent part of the flora of the area.

127.1   This is the turnoff to Rancho San Pedro de la Presa. It heads east to Mision La Presa, north to the short-lived Mision San Luis Gonzaga (1737-1768), and back to Ciudad Constitucion. The dirt road traverses a cross-section of Miocene exposures in this part of the peninsula.

126.2   The bridge at Puente Ventura was washed out in a flash flood in 1978. Future washouts may occur since the highway crosses a wash that periodically and briefly conducts enormous amounts of water from the infrequent sudden seasonal downpours which occur during rainstorms, chabascos, and hurricanes that are common in this region.

122.5   The prominent peak to the east is Cerro Colorado (1500 feet elevation). A similar view of Cerro Colorado can be seen from the flats near Penjamo.
        As the highway climbs out of the arroyo, it passes through the yellow brown beds of the Eocene Tepetate Formation.

112   Mesas capped by dark brown and gray-green volcanic rocks can be seen to the left. Immediately below, sandy yellow sediments are visible in the middle of the section, and shaly yellow beds are at the base of the section. These rocks were originally referred to the Isidro, San Gregorio and Moterey Formations by earlier workers. They are now regarded as members of the El Cien Formation of Applegate.

110.3   The restaurant at Rancho Penjamo has been a favorite stopover of seasoned Baja travelers for many years.
        The hillside flora continues to be represented by desert species of the Magdalena Plain Desert flora. The prominent species of the flora are: Cardon, Pitaya Agria, Jumping Cholla, Palo Adan, Elephant Tree, Creosote Bush, Leatherplant, and Wax Plant.
        On the arroyo bottoms is the Wash Woodland sparse which includes vegetation with scattered specimens of Tamarisk, *Acacia*, Garambullo, and Pitaya Dulce.
        The Miocene and Paleocene formations described at Km 112 are well exposed in various cuts in arroyos over large parts of the Magdalena Plain. The plain is so flat that few rocks are exposed outside of the arroyos.
        The ground for miles around Penjamo is littered with small shale chip-fragments of the Monterey Formation.

108   For the next several kilometers the highway passes through the yellow beds that have been mapped as the Isidro Formation. These are near-shore facies, but not quite as near-shore, nor as tuffaceous, as the San Ignacio Formation seen to the north near San Ignacio. Locally within the unit are very shaly beds which interfinger with the Isidro. They are not actually mappable as separate units.

100   The highway passes through the small settlement of El Cien and climbs through the beds of the El Cien Formation.

On the left side is the 300 m section at Cerro Colorado which is at the core of a major anticline. Most of the exposures on Cerro Colorado are the Oligo-Miocene marine El Cien Formation with a nonmarine tuffaceous redbed near the top. The tuffaceous redbeds and a conglomerate bed on Cerro Colorado can be traced across the peninsula into the "Comondu" Formation on the Gulf. Redbeds and fluvial sedimentary rocks become thicker to the east; whereas, the marine Miocene rocks at the base of the hills becomes thinner. This indicates an eastern source for the volcanics. In the far distance to the right the "Comondu" Formation can be seen on the south limb of the anticline; it is also exposed on the Gulf north of La Paz. The view east follows the strike of the south limb of the anticline. Progressively younger beds of the "Comondu" Formation are exposed to the right.

> **FORMATIONS OF THE MAGDALENA COASTAL FOOTHILLS:** The name "Comondu Formation" (Heim, 1922) has been applied to all volcanic and volcaniclastic rocks of Miocene to recent age in Baja California. Radiometric dating has provided a basis for determining the relative positioning of the strata from widely separated areas.
>
> The **Isidro Formation** was defined by Heim (1922) as exposures of greenish, whitish, and yellowish sandstones with interbedded greenish shales in the La Purisima area. The Isidro Formation is Early Miocene in age and overlain by a 22 million year old tuff from the Cerro Colorado area. The widespread **Monterey Formation**, now renamed the El Cien and San Gregorio Formations, was also defined by Heim (1922) as exposures of hard, clear, siliceous, diatomaceous yellowish shales in the La Purisima area west of Loreto.

97   The highway passes through good road-cut exposures of the El Cien Formation for the next three kilometers. Abundant splintered pieces of siliceous shale scattered over the surface indicate the presence of this Formation.

95   Excellent exposures of well-bedded siliceous shales are visible on both sides of the highway near this kilometer marking.

92   The Magdalena Plain desert vegetation continues to be dominated by slope inhabiting species of Jumping Cholla, Teddy Bear Cholla, Cardon, Elephant Trees, Creosote Bush, Pitaya Dulce, and Pitaya Agria. The Wash Woodland vegetation continues to be predominated by scattered specimens of the leguminous Acacia trees and Palo Verde. Another interesting and vicious looking plant of this region is the Creeping Devil *(Machaeroocereus eruca)*.

THE CREEPING DEVIL is a prostrately growing cactus because of the weight of the heavy stems. This sharp spined, tire menacing cactus sends out a dense network of branches which often produce adventitious roots where they touch the ground. As the prostrate branches slowly grow forward, the older hind parts die; this plant spreads and multiplies itself by asexual, vegetative reproduction. This mechanism of reproduction is often used by species which inhabit arid environments as a way to avoid the "water expensive" process of sexual reproduction which involves the production of moist flowers and seeds which require water for germination. Creeping devil grows in alluvial soils all over Llanos de Magdalena.

89   The chevron folds exposed in this roadcut belong to the El Cien Formation.

88.6   The high cliffs to the left offer a cross-section of the geology of this part of the peninsula.   The upper thick pink tuffs and gray-green fluvial sandstones are the Comondu Formation; the middle yellow-gray sandy San Ignacio Formation is visible on the east side.   It grades downward into the thick-bedded, yellow, marine sedimentary rocks of the Monterey and Isidro Formations on the west side.

87.5   The highway passes through typical beds of the El Cien Formation.

85.5   The contact between the brownish marine Paleocene Tepetate Formation and the overlying yellowish marine Oligocene El Cien Formation is exposed on the hill to the left of the highway.   The flat-lying contact between the formations is a slight angular unconformity.   The rocks of the Eocene part of the Tepetate Formation were removed during a period of uplift and erosion producing the unconformity.

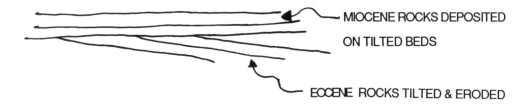

The Wash Woodland is vegetated by numerous *Acacias*.

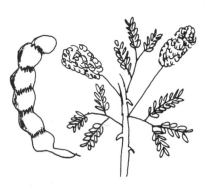

THE LEGUMINOUS ACACIA: There are more than 900 species of *Acacia* trees and shrubs in the world with 64 species found in Mexico. However, only about 20 species of *Acacia* occur in Baja from the northeastern Sonoran Central Desert region to the Cape Region. The fruit of the *Acacia* is a pod (a specialized folded leaf) with several seeds that are used by both man and beast. Indians and Mexicans are known to have ground the seeds into a meal for food. Cattle also relish the pods. In regions of North America where cattle are moved in "drives", *Acacia* is often found growing in straight lines along the path that the cattle followed. The straight line distribution of the *Acacia* puzzled early plant geographers until they realized cattle were "driven" in "straight lines" from grazing lands to market and had "planted" the seeds as they defecated along the drive.

84   The highway passes through exposures of redbeds and yellow-brown sandstones of the Tepetate Formation.   The roadcut above the highway has yielded the abundant discocyclinid *Coquina sp.* Discocyclinids are very large marine foraminifera that grew to one centimeter in size.

83   The Pacific Ocean can be seen to the right. Some of the distant small mesas are composed of Pliocene Salada Formation which overlie the yellow-brown Tepetate Formation.

82.2   The highway passes by Microondas El Coyote to the left.

81.9   Good exposures of the redbeds of the generally yellow-brown Tepetate Formation are seen just after the microwave tower.

81   The chocolate brown beds in the arroyo to the left are also part of the Tepetate Formation, while the overlying lighter-yellow mesas are part of the Pliocene Salada Formation.

80   This side road leads to the windblown Pacific "surf beach" of El Conejo (the rabbit).
      The vegetation of this area of Llanos de Magdalena consists of typical desert species with Pitaya Agria, Pitaya Dulce, Jumping Cholla, Cardon, Elephant Tree, Palo Adan, Leatherplant, and Creosote Bush predominating.

79   The hills to the left contain excellent exposures of the Tepetate Formation. The highway descends into an amphitheater-like area with exposures of the flat well-bedded strata of the Tepetate Formation. The vista to the north reveals the chocolate brown Paleocene marine Tepetate Formation and the overlying yellowish El Cien Formation.

78.5 Along the highway the surface of the hills appears to be littered with small flat shale fragments called "tepetates" (slabs); this accounts for the name of the this formation.

77   The highway enters Arroyo Conejo. There are excellent exposures of the Tepetate Formation on both sides of the highway. It is worth a walk both up and down the east bank of the arroyo to view this formation.

           Knappe (1974) stated that in Arroyo Conejo, "the **Tepetate Formation** consists of a series of Paleocene sandstones and shales exposed along the Pacific coast of Baja California Sur, Mexico. Foraminifera collected from a section of this formation in the vicinity of Arroyo Conejo are Eocene in age and correlate with benthonic and planktonic assemblages found in California, Oregon, Washington, and elsewhere. The oldest and youngest benthonic fauna examined correspond to the Penutian and Ulatisian stages of Mallory (1959). Planktonic species from the Tepetate section correspond to the *Morozovella aragonensis*, *Subbotina senni*, and *Truncorotaloides densus* zones of Schmidt (1970) which are approximately equivalent to the *Globorotalia formosa*, *Globorotalia aragonensis*, *Globorotalia palmerae*, and *Hantkenina aragonensis* zones of Bolli (1957,1966).
           Planktonic foraminiferal correlations suggest that the Ulatisian stage is lower and basal middle Eocene, and the Penutian stage is middle lower Eocene rather than middle Eocene and lower Eocene as suggested by Mallory (1959).
           The foraminiferal assemblage identified from the section is characteristic of upper to middle slope deposits and includes (after Sliter and Baker, 1972; Bird, 1967) : *Anomalinids*, *Bulimina* - costate forms, *Bathysiphon*, *Cibicidoides* - compressed forms, *Gyroidina* - rounded margin, *Siphogenerina* - costate forms, *Trifarina* - costate-spinose forms, and *Osangularia*."

76.2 Rancho San Agustin is located on a river terrace next to the arroyo.

76   At the turnout near this kilometer, a walk through the wash along the right side of the highway allows you to see Fairy Duster trees, especially large specimens of Elephant Trees, Jumping Cholla, Desert Hollyhock, and Creosote Bush.

75.4 The highway begins the ascent of a grade through the sandstones and shales of the Tepetate Formation. The Tepetate Formation referred to here as Paleocene although it may be largely Eocene.

74.5 To the right of the highway, a road-metal quarry exposes Tepetate sandstones and shales with more discocyclinid forams.

70.5   The El Cien Formation is exposed in this roadcut. The bedded strata along the highway are near the contact between the tuffaceous fluvial Miocene Comondu sedimentary rocks and marine rocks. In the canyon to the left are abundant exposures of the light-yellow to gray marine Miocene. In the near distance are the overlying red tuffs and gray fluvial sedimentary rocks of the Comondu Formation. The El Cien Formation is represented by well-bedded siliceous and tuffaceous sedimentary rocks which include shales, siltstones and cherts. The marine Miocene rocks on the west side of the peninsula are stratigraphically correlatable with nonmarine fluvatile and tuffaceous beds of the "Comondu" along the Gulf of California.

69   The vista is to the southwest of the Pacific Ocean and the low mesas underlain by the Salada Formation.
        The canyons along the highway contain abundant exposures of light greenish to yellowish gray rocks of the marine El Cien Formation.
        Between here and where the highway drops down into La Paz, all of the roadcuts are in the fluvatile sediments of the Comondu Formation which was nicknamed the "gray-green grunge" by a geologist who worked in this region

67.5   There is a small fault in the roadcut at Rancho Aguajito.
        The highway begins to travel along the tilted erosion surface of the gentle Pacific slope and passes through the Miocene fluvatile volcaniclastic sandstones of the Comondu. The Highway follows along this surface to Km 34 on the Gulf escarpment.

62   The dense dark evergreen trees with gray trunks scattered in this area are Palo San Juan (*Forchammeria watsonii*). It is a member of the Caper family (Capparidaeae) which produces an edible deep-purple fruit. Occasional Datilillo are seen scattered over the landscape.

RED

Turkey Vultures (buzzards) or **Zopilote de Cabeza Roja** are ubiquitous throughout Baja and are protected by law for their value as "cleaner-uppers" of dead bodies. Turkey Vultures are naked headed, diurnal carrion eaters which are commonly seen scavenging on the ground in open country and along roadsides. Along the "*Baja Highway*" one may see a small group of them devouring a dead animal which they had detected by sight or smell while soaring high in Baja's clear clean skies. They are also often seen in larger congregations, perching on the tips of Cardon branches "sunning" themselves.

"Sunning" is a phenomenon not well understood by biologists. At one time it was thought that "sunning" was performed to warm the birds, but Turkey Vultures have been sighted "sunning" themselves in the coldest rains, winds, and on the hottest days of the year.

The most identifiable field characteristic of the buzzards is the way they soar in wide circles while holding their two-toned black and white wings in a broad "V" while rocking quickly from side to side.

In the southern part of the peninsula, Vultures and the black and white crested Caracaca, another carrion feeder, are occasionally seen feeding together on the same carcass.

Log 8 - Constitucion to La Paz

4 2   The modified badlands topography along this section of the highway is well developed on the rather soft fluvial volcaniclastic sediments.
The vegetation consists of Lomboy, Elephant Trees, Datilillo, Greasewood, Pitaya Agria, Pitaya Dulce, Cardon, Hedgehog Cactus, Palo Adan, Palo Blanco, *Acacias*, Jumping Cholla, Teddy Bear Cholla, and occasional Mistletoe.

36.1   The highway passes Microondas Matape to the left.
It is not unusual along this stretch of the *Baja Highway* to see a number of Turkey Vultures (*Cathartes aura*) roosting in the columnar Cardon Cactus and other trees.

3 4   At the top of the grade there is a whitewashed shrine.
The view is spectacular on a clear day. The viewpoint is located on the south limb of a major anticline in the Miocene rocks which dips to the south under Llanos de Todos Santos. To the northeast are Islas Partida and Espirito Santo; they are composed of highly faulted-tilted volcanic rocks of the Comondu Formation. To the east the rugged granitic spine of the Sierra de la Victoria (65-75 million years) begins on the peninsula east of La Paz and stretches south to the Cape Region. This range is separated from Llanos de Todos Santos by a major fault zone (Normark and Curray, 1968).

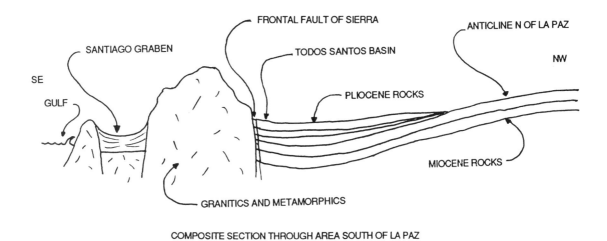

COMPOSITE SECTION THROUGH AREA SOUTH OF LA PAZ

ISLAS PARTIDA AND ESPIRITU SANTO are high angle tilted and faulted islands composed of the volcanic and volcaniclastic rocks of the Comondu Formation. The eastern escarpment shows many brightly colored tuffaceous beds of red, pink, green, ochre, and white.

33.5   The highway begins a steep descent through the volcaniclastic fluvial sandstones of the Comondu Formation.

2 8   Due to overgrazing, Cholla Cactus has become the dominant understory vegetation in this area. Scattered specimens of Pitaya Agria, Pitaya Dulce, Cardon, *Acacia*, Elephant Tree, Lomboy, Palo Adan, and Mistletoe are growing on the hillsides. The dark green shrubby Creosote Bush is the dominant plant of the Wash Woodland flora.

2 5   The view to the left rear from some of the low rises reveals the pink tuffs and gray-green fluvatile sediments in the south limb of the San Juan anticline which rises to the north and dips out of sight to the south. The highway crosses the anticline in fluvial volcaniclastic sandstones above the highest pink tuff. These rocks were deposited just

143

prior to the tectonic opening of the Gulf in this area.

The vegetation in this area consists of Lomboy, Palo Blanco, Palo Adan, Mesquite, Elephant Tree, Cardon, Pitaya Agria, Pitaya Dulce, Cholla, and Agave. This area is an ecotone (*See* Km 118.5 of the Ensenada to San Quintin log) between the flora of the desert vegetation of the Magdalena Plain subdivision of the Sonoran Central Desert phytogeographic region and the Cape phytogeographic region.

THE CAPE PHYTOGEOGRAPHIC REGION: In Baja California only the Cape Region in the south and the Mediterranean-climate California Region in the northwest are outside of the Sonoran Central Desert Region which covers most of Baja's peninsula. The Cape Region is a zone that includes the Cape block southeast of the low-lying land from La Paz south and west to the Pacific coast, extends north through Sierra de la Giganta and along the Gulf close to Loreto, and farther north in an attenuated form close to Santa Rosalia. This region has the highest rainfall on the peninsula; being below the Tropic of Capricorn below the 28th parallel. Most precipitation that the Cape receives occurs during the summer months. The Cape mountains receive more precipitation than the rest of the peninsula because tropical summer anticyclone storms dump most of their moisture on them.

The vegetation of the Cape Region is subdivided into two areas, the **Oak-Pinon Woodland** and the "impoverished" **Arid Tropical Forest**. The vegetation at lower elevations is thorn scrub with elements of tropical deciduous woodland. At higher elevations in Sierra de la Laguna and Sierra la Victoria the vegetation passes first into a chaparral-like vegetation and then into evergreen oak and pine forests. Pines do not occur in the northern part of Sierra de la Giganta and oaks are uncommon. Floristically, the Cape Region resembles the Pacific coast of southern Mexico. The low Gulf islands of the Cape Region are not high enough to support anything but the low elevation thorn scrub.

The **Oak-Pinon Woodland** community occurs in the granitic soils of Sierra la Victoria to an elevation over 6,000 feet (the transition life zone). The dominant species are Encino Negro (*Quercus devia*) and *Q. tuberculata*, *Pinus cembroides* (listed as a synonym for *P. edulis*, *P. monophylla*, and *P. parrana* by Munz, 1974), the Yucca-like Palmita (*Nolina beldingii*), Laurel Sumac, and the Medrona (*Arbutus peninsularis*) which resembles the Medrone tree (*Arbutus menziesii*) of northern California.

Since the Cape tropical region does not receive as much precipitation as other tropical areas of the world, **the Arid Tropical Forest** has been called an "impoverished tropical jungle". The trees of this forest are represented by the leguminous trees of the genus *Lysiloma* (Palo Blanco and Palo Mauto), Mesquite, and *Acacia*, the Coral tree (*Erythrina flabelliformis*), a shrub-like pea tree; the edible plum tree (*Cyrtocarpa edulis*); Palo Verde (*Cercidium praecox*); and Plumeria (*Plumeria acutifolia*).

The understory of the impoverished forest is predominated by shrub-like Palo de Arco (*Tecoma stans*) and several other thorn scrub species such as Cardon, Pitaya Dulce, Lomboy, and Palo Adan.

The highway continues to pass through the Cape Phytogeographic Region, to Cabo San Lucas and Todos Santos, until it reaches La Paz.

Mexican Chickadees, White-winged Doves, Cactus Wrens, Gilla Woodpeckers and Falcons are commonly seen flitting among the vegetation of this area. Bird-watching is surprisingly good!

Log 8 - Constitucion to La Paz

18.2   There is an excellent view of La Paz, the gulf coast capital of Baja California Sur. La Paz is considered to be one of the best sport fishing locales in the world. The sport fish of the area include Marlin, Roosterfish, Mahi-Mahi, Cabrilla, Yellowtail, Sierra, and many others.

17   The side road leads to the phosphate mining settlement of San Juan de la Costa. Phosphates are mined and shipped elsewhere in Mexico for use as a fertilizer. This mine supplies about 40% of Mexico's phosphate needs.

> **PHOSPHORUS** is a highly reactive, poisonous, nonmetallic element that occurs naturally in phosphates, especially apatite, and exists in three allotropic forms- white, black and red. It is an essential constituent of the protoplasm of all living cells and, depending on the allotropic form, is used in safety matches, pyrotechnics (fire-works), incendiary shells, fertilizers, glass, and steel. About 90% of the world's production of phosphorous is from sedimentary phosphate rock (phosphorite) of marine origin such as that found and mined in this area of Baja.

15   The highway passes through the small bayshore area of El Centenario.

13   The highway follows the bay across a supertidal flat with numerous mangroves along the shoreline. The vegetation seen inland from the supertidal flat consists of numerous *Acacias* and Palo Verde.

12   Bahia La Paz, the largest bay on the peninsula's east coast, and the muddy sand spit of El Magote are visible on the left. El Magote is a narrow sand spit formed by the southward transport of sand by currents along the eastern coast of the peninsula. It separates the main body of the bay from Ensenada de Los Aripes, the shallow inlet to the west.

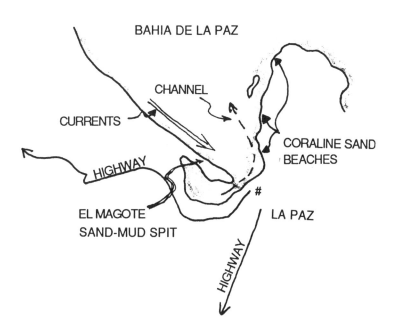

8.9   This turnoff leads to the right to the new La Paz International Airport, south of town.

6.8   The road to the right is the most direct route to the cape. Proceed toward the Gulf (east) to Padre Kino, right to Forjadores which becomes the main highway to the cape, or go past Padre Kino about 5 blocks to a major shopping area. There are at least two signed streets in town which direct traffic toward Cabo San Lucas.

           To reach Pichilingue and the Ferry docks, continue on Abasolo to the Malacon (the cement walkway along the beachfront).

5.5   The highway crosses Arroyo La Palma.

0   **LA PAZ**: The Malecon at La Paz is a coconut palm-lined, cement sea wall and pedestrian walkway combination which meanders along the bay in the main part of La Paz. At the intersection of 5 de Febrero, Highway 1 becomes Mexico 11, a coconut palm-lined water front drive, that quickly turns to the north along the bay toward Pichilingue, the terminus for ferries from Topolobampo, Guaymas, and Mazatlan. A ferry to Puerto Vallarta is based at Cabo San Lucas.

           Stop at Museo Antropologico de Baja California Sur at the corner of Ignacio Altamirano and 5 de Mayo. The museum features good geological, historical, and anthropological exhibits.

           SIDE TRIP TO PICHILINGUE AND THE FERRY DOCK VIA MEXICO 11: Mexico 11 to Pichilingue and the ferry dock goes around Ensenada de Los Aripes and leaves by way of Paseo Alvaro Obregon. There are a number of groins built along the beach to slow the drifting of sand due to currents which flow into the bay.

1.5   This road travels primarily through the pink tuffs and the gray-green volcaniclastic sediments and mega-breccias of the Comondu Formation which is clearly visible in roadcuts. There are a number of massive fluvatile bouldery conglomerates in the Comondu.

2   This is Hotel Palmira. The salt marsh estuary next to this hotel used to be a national park. It is now largely filled by sediment. As you travel in the cape region, watch for herons, egrets, storks and other marsh birds which are common here.

           If time permits, take a bird walk into any particularly dense-looking area of vegetation, and you will see many interesting birds common to the Cape Region.

           The **Cape phytogeographic region** is vegetated by a dense thorny and *Acacia* - dominated flora known as thorn scrub. Thorn scrub grows where summer precipitation exceeds 300 mm per year. The avifauna of this region is not very diverse, but the following species are commonly seen:

Log 8 - Constitucion to La Paz

Bird	Common Location
American Kestrel	Telephone wires and fence posts
Blue-Gray Gnat Catcher	Perched on desert vegetation
California Quail	On the ground
Common Ground Dove	On the ground
Costa's HummingBird	Feeding on red or yellow tubular flowers
Crested Caracara	Feeding on carrion
Gila Woodpecker	In the scrub
Gray Thrasher	Looking in ground litter for food
Ladder-Back Woodpecker	Flitting in the air
Loggerhead Shrike	Perched on wires and fences
Turkey Vultures	Soaring in sky looking for carrion
Varied Bunting	Perching on desert vegetation
Western Meadowlark	Fence posts and fence wires
Xantu's Hummingbird	Feeding at tubular flowers
Yellow-Billed Cuckoo	Flying through vegetation

2.5   The highway becomes a divided road.

2.8   The highway climbs a small grade through faulted pink tuffs and fluvial volcaniclastic sandstones of the Miocene Comondu Formation. This is the best place to observe exposures of these rocks which are exposed for over a hundred miles in the cliffs along the Gulf northwest of La Paz.
Mexico 11 will cross several steeply dipping north-south normal faults related to the frontal faulting of the Sierra Victoria.

4.1   On the inbound lanes the highway passes by the coralline biological "sand" swimming beaches of Coromuel. These beaches have been developed into a public plaza and bathing pavilion. A native wild fig tree (*Ficus palmeri*) can by seen to the right across from Coromuel beach (*See* Km 98 of the Loreto to Constitucion log).
Rainfall, scarce in La Paz, arrives infrequently in the form of violent tropical storms called Chabascos. As a result, summers are hot and dry, but the name "Coromuel" refers to the cooling wind which comes from the cooler Pacific Ocean to the south across the peninsula and refreshes the city every summer afternoon.

4.5   The channel markings delineate a narrow channel located very close to the near shoreline.

5.1   The Las Conchas Resort is located at El Caimancito.
The highway passes through more volcaniclastic rocks and tuffs of the Miocene Comondu Formation which is exposed around the resort. The small offshore rock, Islita Caimancito, received its name because it resembles a lurking alligator (Caiman).
On a clear day the major San Juan anticline in the Comondu Formation can be seen on the west side of Bahia de la Paz. This anticline and one to the north stretch for over 120 miles north of La Paz. The same bed can be traced for nearly the entire distance. These anticlines are strong petroleum prospects, since the oil-bearing Cretaceous geosyncline underlies the volcanics to the eastern edge of the peninsula.

5.3 The divided highway ends and returns to a single lane in each direction. There are exposures of pink tuffs for the next several kilometers.
Because of unfavorable edaphic (soil) features, the vegetation is very sparse on the surrounding volcaniclastic tuffs and consists of sparse Cardon, Lomboy, Palo Adan, Mission Cactus, *Acacia*, and Candelabra.

7.7 The Cementos Guaycura dock and concrete plant were located here. Raw materials such as limestone from Ensenada, gypsum ($CaSO_4$) from Isla San Marcos, and clays from the Cape Region are processed into Portland concrete mix at this plant. The cement mix is shipped all over southern Baja and to mainland Mexico for use in construction work.

8.2 Punta Prieta (dark point) is the location of the government owned and operated Pemex oil refinery docks and storage tanks. Oil is transhipped from mainland Mexico across the Gulf to Baja for storage and distribution. Even though oil bearing strata are known to exist here, there is no developed source of oil in Baja California.

9 A good exposure of the coarse fluvial conglomerates of the Comondu Formation can be seen here.

9.4 The view into a small bay with a Mangrove swamp and a small estuary reveals the first of a series of spectacular shallow coralline biological "sand" coves with azure blue water formed by recent submergence of this area.
The hills to the right are composed of tuffs and fluvatile sediments of the Comondu Formation.

10 A small restaurant is located on the shore of this beautiful playa. The beach is formed by a light-colored coralline biological "sand" and backed locally by a mangrove swamp.

10.5 The pond on the right is a shrimp farm.

11.8 As the highway skirts another picturesque cove, there are excellent exposures of very large mega-breccia fluvatile sediments of the Comondu Formation.

14 The highway cuts through the large mega-breccia fluvatile sediments of the Comondu Formation.
The water in this beautiful cove is very blue-green in stark contrast to the light-colored coralline biological "sand" beach. Great Blue Herons are often seen in the Mangrove swamp located along the shore of the cove.

Log 8 - Constitucion to La Paz

This is a good place to view a solution-cut terrace. A solution cut terrace is produced in arid areas where there is not much moisture and weathering of the hillsides is very slow. The rocks along the shoreline are moistened by salt spray. The increased moisture promotes increased weathering and the notch. Another effect which aids in the development is the salt in the water which crystallizes in the pore spaces and cracks and pries the rock apart just above the water line.

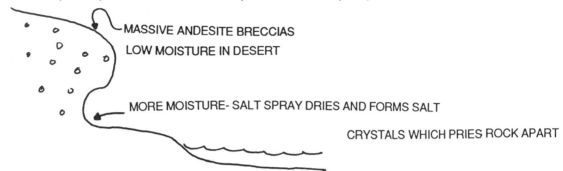

MASSIVE ANDESITE BRECCIAS

LOW MOISTURE IN DESERT

MORE MOISTURE- SALT SPRAY DRIES AND FORMS SALT

CRYSTALS WHICH PRIES ROCK APART

THE GREAT BLUE HERON is often seen in the marshes, on the beaches, or even in the dry fields of Baja. The tall lean solitary figure of the Great Blue Heron (*Ardea herodias*) can be seen standing motionless in a pool of water or advancing slowly one step at a time lifting each foot stealthily from the shallows without a ripple. Herons may stand still as a statue for over half an hour while waiting for prey to come. With a lightning-quick forward lunge of their long neck and bill, the heron captures its prey. It prefers fish but will also eat birds, small mammals, insects, snakes, frogs, and crustaceans.

Whether on land or in the air, a Great Blue is easily recognized by the long snake-like neck held in an "S" shaped curve, the slow wing strokes, long legs, and nearly two meter wing span.

In Baja look for the stately solitary Great Blue Heron on piers, docks, boats in harbors, rocks along the coast, sandbars, tombolos, or in estuaries, coves, marshes, cultivated fields, and the riparian woodland in the bottoms of desert river canyons.

14.5   The highway skirts a cove through a Mangrove swamp and traverses the super-tidal flat inland from it.

The vegetation on the supertidal flats is sparse and impoverished due to the highly saline soil (*See* Km 35.5 of the Bahia de Los Angeles log). A few Cardons are seen on the hillsides along with scattered specimens of Lomboy, Organ-pipe and Mission Cacti, and scattered *Acacia* trees. A small cardonal covers the high flat behind the lagoon.

15.4   The highway passes through a nearly vertical roadcut composed of massive resistant fluvial mega-breccias.

15.7   Isla Pichilingue can be seen across the lagoon.

16   Universidad Autonoma de Baja California Sur. The Lab is in area Interdisciplinaria de Ciencias Del Mar, Departamento de Geologia Marina. This is the Labs and Research facilities branch of the Universidad de Baja California Sur located on the nearby flats, while the main University is located in town

16.5 As Mexico 11 rounds a bend, the ferry dock with two loading areas is easily recognizable. Many pleasure yachts are docked here.

At the ferry docks the rocks in the roadcut are andesite mega-breccias. Beyond the ferry dock the gravelly road to the right leads to the water and a beautiful public beach, Playa Publica Pichilingue, situated in a beautiful cove. This is a good place to explore the coast. The highway crosses a causeway built to reach Isla Pichilingue. It is now referred to as Peninsula San Juan Nepomuceno on some maps of La Paz.

21.8 Bahia Pichilingue is a deep-water bay used as the main shipping point for La Paz Harbor; it avoids the narrow and difficult passage into the main harbor of La Paz.

> **BAJA'S FIRST SETTLEMENT**: Isla Pichilingue is the site of the first attempt to settle by Hernan Cortez the conqueror of Mexico, in 1535 in Baja California. However, supply problems resulted in the failure of that first settlement. Jesuits in 1720 established a mission here, but it also failed. La Paz finally became a permanent settlement in 1811 and became the state capital in 1829 after a hurricane destroyed the first capital, Loreto. Isla Pichilingue now supports a salt mining operation.
>
> Several dirt roads which lead northeast toward sandy bays and coves depart from this area.

Where To Now? Return to La Paz and continue to the south on Highway 1 using the La Paz to Cabo San Lucas log for your guide.

Log 9 - La Paz to Cabo San Lucas [211 kms = 131 miles]

The Baja Highway follows the Gulf fault zone in an alluviated graben-syncline. It then turns to climb over uplifted granitic and metamorphic horsts, first at El Triunfo, then San Antonio and San Bartolo to descend to the Gulf at Buena Vista. The highway then travels south on marine and non-marine sediments, along the relatively flat Santiago Trough between two high granitic horsts, to San Jose de Cabo. Finally the highway skirts the southern edge of the Sea of Cortez on alluvial fans to Cabo San Lucas and its granitic headland.

221   As the highway leads to the south toward the Cape region, the beautiful city of La Paz, with its warm beaches, good sportfishing, recreation, and shopping areas are left behind, but not soon forgotten. The best route out of La Paz toward the Cape is to go south on Padre Kino, then right on Forjadores.

210.5   The divided highway ends. The campus of the Universidad de Autonoma de Baja California Sur is on the right. During several particularly violent storms the Baja Highway south of this point was severely damaged in 1982 and 1984.

210   Andesite and Andesite breccias of the Comondu Formation are exposed for the next several kilometers as they dip toward the highway from the left. The white bouldery granitic outcrops of the cape region form the high hills to the far left.
        The route to Cabo San Lucas follows alluviated grabens to the south and crosses elevated horsts into the next graben at convenient passes or, in the case of El Triunfo and San Antonio, where mineralization has occurred in the older granitics.
        South of La Paz the edge of the Sierra la Victoria range is remarkably straight which is a result of the recency faulting in this area. The highway follows the Todos Santos graben-syncline which is situated in a basin between the well-defined Sierra la Victoria Fault and the south limb of the anticline in the tertiary sediments. This graben is filled with faulted Pliocene to Recent sediments.
        Along the highway there are several good views to the rear of the Cretaceous anticline, syncline, graben, and Sierra la Victoria.

        The Mesozoic granitic and metamorphic rocks of the Sierra la Victoria are similar in age, relationships and rock type to the Peninsular Range and Sierra Nevada Batholiths. They were all part of the same granitic belt prior to the Cenozoic extension which separated Baja from the mainland. Age relationships in the Gulf indicate that this separation took place at the mouth of the Gulf of California about 4-5 million years ago and still continues today.

186   The highway passes through the Desert Coastal Shrub vegetative area of the Central Gulf Coast Desert phytogeographic region of Baja. The predominate plants of the Cape Region flora in this area consist of specimens of the columnar Cardon cactus and a mixed "forest" of leguminous trees such as Palo Mauto, Minosa (*Lysiloma sp.*), *Acacia*, Screwbean Mesquite, and the senna, Palo Verde. Along the highway the dominant plant of the Cape Region appears to be the Cardon cactus. Next in order of decreasing dominance are Elephant Trees, Lomboy, and Palo Adan.
        Other less dominant plants seen growing in the Cape Region are Jumping Cholla (primarily in disturbed soils), *Plumeria*, Organ Pipe Cactus, Creosote Bush, and the yellow-flowered Vine-Yucca. Yucca is a morning glory relative which cover many plants like a large net.

THE BEAN TREES OF THE CAPE REGION: Trees are a conspicuous and important part of the desert flora of Baja. Many of Baja's conspicuous desert trees are legumes which produce a "bean" pod which contains numerous "beans" (seeds). Leguminous trees, members of the family Mimosaceae, occur most often at low elevations in the desert, arroyos, and foothills below 1,000 meters. They are common and conspicuous in the Cape Region. The most commonly seen leguminous trees in the Cape Region are Vinorama (*Acacia brandegeei*), Palo Mauto (*Lysiloma*), and Mesquite (*Prosopis sp.*). The following table will help identify these three common roadside legumes of the Cape Region:

	Vinorama *Acacia brandegeei*	Minosa *Lysiloma candida*	Palo Mauto *Lysiloma divaricata*	Mesquite *Prosopis pubescens*
Bark		Silvery-white,	Grayish-brown smooth	Thin, flaky
Spines	Slender, straight occurring singly	One of the few Baja legumes without thorns	None	Short, awl-shaped spines in pairs at Nodes
Flower	Yellow spikes	Creamy white ball-like clusters	- - - -	Yellow spikes
Pods	Long and slender	Long, thin-walled turn coppery red at maturity	Similar to Minosa (*Lysiloma* sp.)	Tightly spirally coiled pod - a "screwbean Mesquite"
Uses	Beans ground into meal by man	Missionaries used bark to tan hides	- - - - -	Beans eaten by man cattle; wood used in Tools and for fuel.

The most diverse of the leguminous trees of Baja is the *Acacia*. In the Cape Region *Acacias* occur on open flood plains, lower arroyos, and mesas. The *Lysilomas* and Palo Mauto are most abundant above 600 meters. It has been reported that the coastal plains south of La Paz were covered with Minosa (*Lysiloma* sp.), but they were cut down for use by a tannery. However, in the mountains along the highway to the south, they are still plentiful. Some people mistake them for birch trees of Northeastern U.S.A. The screwbean mesquite is easily recognized by its distinctive, tightly spirally, coiled, highly edible pod.

Another non-leguminous tree commonly seen growing with the four leguminous tree species of the Cape Region is Palo Verde. Species of the Palo Verde, a conspicuous and characteristic tree of the Sonoran Desert north of the U.S./Baja border, grows all the way to the Cape region. *Cercidium praecox* is the Palo Verde of the Cape Region. It is easily distinguished from the leguminous trees because of its bright green photosynthetic trunk and branches (cladophylls) and its leafless appearance. Palo Verde may be mistaken for a leguminous tree since it, too, produces a pod-like fruit which contains seeds about the shape and size of pod beans. The Palo Verde is not a legume and is in a completely different family, the Senna family.

185   This is the turnoff to Todos Santos. Just south of the turnoff toward Cabo San Lucas are large areas which have been cleared of native vegetation for grazing cattle.

MORE OPPORTUNISTS LIVING ON THE EDGE: Plants commonly seen along this stretch of the highway include several opportunistic species such as the tall, yellow-flowered, large-leafed Indian Tree Tobacco (*Nicotiana glauca*) and several species of grass.

The tropical Plumeria is also a common plant in this area.

THE PLUMERIA OF BAJA: Plumerias grow as a shrub or tree up to 9 meters tall in Baja's Cape Region from just south of La Paz to Cabo San Lucas along arroyos, canyons, and foothill slopes. For most of the year Plumeria is leafless but is easily recognized by the showy long, white, tubular flowers clustered at the ends of branches. The white blooms are abundant after summer rains. Plumeria are frequently seen in the gardens of ranchos where they are planted as ornamentals.

179.9   This side road leads to Rancho Los Algodones.

178   Over a small rise is a view in the distance of the high massif of the Sierra la Victoria. The roadcuts are in pinkish alluvial material derived from the decomposed granitic basement.

176.8 Large Crested Caracara are also occasionally seen on the ground. Several other types of birds, including the red-tailed hawk, white-winged dove and aplomado falcon, are often seen sitting on the ground and on telephone wires along this stretch of the "*Baja Highway*".

THE CRESTED CARACARA of open desert scrub is a long-legged scavenger which spends much of its time on the ground. In flight the larger head and beak, longer neck, white throat and black and white-banded tail set it apart from the vultures (buzzards).
Because of its long legs, the Crested Caracara walks along the ground gathering food which consists of small creatures, carrion, and sometimes plant matter. They have also been seen stealing food from other birds.

175   As the highway crosses a series of undulating shallow ravines, it passes over the Sierra la Victoria Fault and into the main mass of the Sierra la Victoria which have been uplifted along this fault. Along the highway south of La Paz, the frontal fault of the Sierra la Victoria cuts off the metamorphic screen on the edge of the batholith. The highway crosses directly from the alluviated plain across the frontal fault into granitic rocks with very few metamorphic rocks.

174   The highway passes through roadcuts which expose pinkish granitics.

171.5 The highway descends along a rather large arroyo and passes through alluvial fan gravels derived from the Sierra la Victoria.
The trees visible along this section of the highway resemble the Palo Verde but are really an *Acacia* known locally as Vinorama (*Acacia brandegeei*).

168.4 Low-grade phyllitic schists are exposed along either side of the highway.

168   After leaving La Paz, the highway ascends through the foothills of Sierra la Victoria. There is a small mining area with a mine shaft and mine workings on the right side of the highway. These foothills are pocked with prospectors' holes and covered with Palo de Arco (*Tecoma stans*).

 **PALO DE ARCO** is a small shrub or tree which produces large golden-yellow flowers after rains. The stems of this shrub are used to make shipping crates for raw sugar (panocha) produced at the sugar cane mills of Todos Santos on the Cape's south Pacific coast.

167.7 High-grade ptygmitic gneisses are exposed in this roadcut.

167   Altered and brecciated rocks are visible in this roadcut. A fault zone separates the gneisses from the weathered granitic rocks.

166.7 Slightly past the power station there is a wall of rock up the side of the hill on the left at about 3 o'clock. Since wood suitable for fence-building is scarce, rock wall building is fairly common where there is an abundant supply of rocks. The granitic rocks of this region make stout durable walls.

165.2 There is a spectacular view of the old mining region of El Triunfo.

164   The small mountain village of El Triunfo (562 meters elevation) was established in 1862 with the discovery of silver and gold. This town was the center of a major silver mining operation after 1862. Two yellow church towers rise between the smoke stack and mine buildings on the hill where $50,000 worth of silver and gold were produced monthly. These ores are concentrated in dikes in the metamorphic rocks near the contact with the granitics. A side trip to the main mines can be taken on the first road to the right after you enter town and you cross the bridge. Follow it for two blocks, go left at the wash, and cross an old brick bridge. The road wanders to the smelter and the old tower. It is possible to climb inside the tower and look up the old brick smoke stack at a small patch of sky. The view is dizzying!

160   The highway passes through outcrops of mixed gneissic and granitic rocks.
The hillside vegetation is primarily an impoverished rain forest of several species of leguminous trees. The area is so dry that it looks like it's been burned. Other plants commonly seen are Pitaya Dulce (it looks almost like a Cardon in this environment), Elephant Tree, and Palo Adan. At this southern more mesic latitude, the desert plant Palo Adan, a relative of Ocotillo, becomes less abundant and is largely restricted to the lower sandy Wash Woodlands.

159.5 The highway crests a grade.

159.4 There are prominent granitic dikes in the roadcut. The rocks at the crest of this pass are mixed metamorphics with gneiss and dark-colored granitics invaded by numerous granitic dikes.

158   The highway descends into the town of San Antonio, another "old time" mining community.
The Minosa (Lysiloma sp.) forest has become more dense as other types of vegetation become decreasingly sparse.

Log 9 - La Paz to Cabo San Lucas

157.5 A number of prominent dikes and sills cut the mixed metamorphic and granitic rocks in this roadcut.

This side road leads to San Juan de los Planes, an agricultural community which uses irrigation water drawn from deep wells to grow cotton, beans, chiles, and tomatoes.

156 The historical gold and silver mining town of San Antonio is located in the foothills of the Sierra la Victoria at approximately 410 meters elevation. This mining town was founded in 1756 when Gaspar Pison opened a silver mine over 100 years before the establishment El Triunfo. Now San Antonio is just a cattle ranching center. Many of the ornaments, hats, and baskets woven from palm leaves sold in La Paz come from San Antonio. These products may cost less if purchased here.

155.5 The highway which ascends a grade to the south reveals a view of Llanos San Juan de Los Planes, which extends to the north to Punta Colorado and to the Gulf. The volcanic Isla Cerralvo is visible offshore. The San Juan plains are part of the graben into which the highway will descend after cresting the grade.
The leguminous tree Minosa (Lysiloma sp.) along with *Acacia* and the bright-green barked Palo Verde compose the "forest" in this area.
Lomboy and Indian Tree Tobacco are commonly seen growing opportunistically along the edge of the highway.

155 High grade epidotized gneisses are exposed in the roadcut. The small turnoff provides another good view of the village of San Antonio.

154 This is the best view of the alluviated Llanos de San Juan region.

153.5 The highway proceeds through metamorphic rocks cut by prominent granitic dikes while crossing over the main horst and the high granitic spine of the Sierra la Victoria. The highway drop into a valley (graben) which contains the towns of Santiago and Miraflores before crossing another smaller horst and descending into the Gulf agricultural and tourist town of San Jose del Cabo.
Notice the vines entwined on many of the trees of this area. They are either San Miguel (Antigonon leptopus) or Yuca (Mersemia aurea).

SAN MIGUEL VINE: The vine-like plant which grows on some of the trees of this region is known as San Miguel or Coral vine. This member of the buckwheat family reminds one of the commonly cultivated bougainvillea of Southern California. San Miguel grows from central Baja to the Cape, and its seeds and potato-like tubers (modified underground stems) were eaten by Indians.

The **YUCA** vine is a member of the morning glory family which climbs upon and covers many of the desert plants of this area. When the Yuca die, they cause the host to appear as if they are covered by a blackened, burnt net. Yucca have bright yellow trumpet shaped flowers that bloom all year long, especially after a good rain.

As the highway drops lower along the grade, the vegetation becomes more dense; this indicates that moisture is increasing toward the cape (a phenomenon known as the tropical effect).

155

151   The Minosa (*Lysiloma sp.*) in this area seems to be primarily restricted to the well-drained higher slopes of the Sierra la Victoria. In the flat areas and in the bottom of the washes they occur only sparsely.
The dominant vegetation of the Wash Woodlands is Palo Adan, Elephant Tree, Jumping Cholla, Organ Pipe Cactus, Pitaya Agria, *Acacia*, and Pitaya Dulce. Lomboy is apparent in this region on the flat along with quite a number of Cholla. Abundant Cardons are growing in a narrow belt at the base of the hills.

149   The road to the left leads to Rancho Los Encinos.

NORTHERN MOCKINGBIRDS are commonly seen in this flat region. They are robin-sized birds with white breasts and black wings which show white patches in flight and a long narrow tail. Mockingbirds are expert mimics and repeat most of the songs of local birds while perched or in flight. These mimics sing more at night than do other members of the family Mimidae, an interesting but irritating fact if you are trying to sleep!

147.5 The highway splits in a wide "Y". The fork to the right leads to San Antonio de la Sierra. The fork to the left continues toward Cabo San Lucas.
Outcrops are in mixed granitic and metamorphic rocks with numerous light-colored dikes.

145.7 The granitic rocks at this kilometer mark have been dated at 73 million years. The flora is dominated by Minosa (*Lysiloma sp.*) and Pitaya Dulce. Palo Adan is seen as the highway climbs the slope.

145   The flora is dominated by the large umbrella-like *Acacia*, trees with the legume Palo Mauto.
The forests of the Cape region are "double-canopy" forests. Palo Mauto and *Acacia* form a higher canopy which shades the lower plants; this produces a moister more mesic environment and reduces evaporation.
The Organ Pipe cactus get shorter as they grow higher on the well-drained slopes, while the taller Organ Pipe cactus grow at the bottoms of the hills where water collects as it drains off the surrounding hills.

143   Palo Mauto and Plumeria are begins to occupy just the very high parts of the hills. *Acacia* begins to take over and becomes the dominant canopy tree.

139   Throughout this region, Loggerhead Shrike may occasionally be seen.

LOGGERHEAD SHRIKES are easily recognized by their heavy hooked beaks, black masks, and large white wing patches which contrast with their dark wings. They are also known as "butcher birds", since they habitually capture small lizards, insects, rodents, and small birds and impale them on cactus thorns, tree thorns, or barbed wire. This prevents their meal from escaping.

Log 9 - La Paz to Cabo San Lucas

138 At Rancho El Rodeo the Cochal or Candelabra Cactus is seen to the left of the highway. A few Cardon are mixed with the Organ Pipes along this stretch of the highway.

136 Weathered granitics are cut by dikes in this roadcut.

134 The highway begins to roughly parallel an arroyo on the right. The vegetation of the arroyo is primarily Cheese Bush.

131 There are good exposures of light-colored granitics with darker zenoliths along the road. A wild Fig tree is growing here and Yucca are becoming quite common.

130 A small rancho is located on the left. Broom Baccharis grow in the disturbed soils along the side of the highway with nearly leafless branches crowned by a green, stiff, broom-like mass. Often bundles of branches are tied together and used as a broom.

128.5 Growing in profusion around the tropical agricultural village of San Bartolo are avocados, sugar cane, lemons, limes, mangos, papayas, figs, date palms and fan palms. The vegetation of this arroyo is lush and tropical with *Acacia* as the predominating plant. Occasional Palo Adan, Elephant Tree, Palo Mauto, and Organ Pipes are scattered among the *Acacia*.
South of San Bartolo the highway follows the northeast bank of the arroyo. Numerous exposures of granitics occur in the arroyo and on the hills.
It is possible to drive 5 km up a cobbled road to the microwave tower on Cerro la Campana south of the town.

125 The stream terrace on the other side of the canyon was formed when sea level was higher; this caused the streams to grade the fans to a higher level.

124 Massive exposures of fresh granitic rocks are exposed in the roadcut just before Puente El Saldito.

123 The highway drops almost into the arroyo where roadcuts expose the stream terrace material and climbs out of the arroyo onto the terrace surface. The wash vegetation consists of Palo Verde and Cheese Bush.

121 This is the second view of the Gulf after leaving La Paz.

120 This area was a basin at one time which in-filled with very coarse granitic debris. Now this basin is being uplifted and dissected.
The hills on the opposite side of the arroyo to the south give the impression that they have been burned. They are covered with gray granitic gravels that underlie this uplifted area. These gray granitics coupled with the sparse impoverished vegetation give the impression of a burned over area. However, this impoverished forest is lush and green during the summer rainy season.

119.5 The highway crosses the main wash of San Bartolo with outcrops of the sub-Recent to Pleistocene sediments. These sediments are uplifted alluvial fan material composed essentially of granitic debris from the Sierra Victoria.
Minosa (*Lysiloma sp.*), Tamarisk, and Lomboy are growing abundantly along the edge of the wash. Frequent floods, indicated by the rarity of trees, occur in this wash. The high energy of the floods is indicated by the width and depth of the wash. Cheese Bush is the dominant shrub of the wash bottoms. It is able to re-establish itself more quickly than other plants; it can grow in the washes between the intermittent floods. Cheese Bush

grows everywhere on the peninsula in disturbed areas. From time to time a yellow-flowered *Acacia* can be seen in the wash.

118   There are four levels of terraces which indicate different periods of uplift. The main older fan surface is on the far side of the yellow cliffs. Just below is a secondary surface which has large Palo Verde, Palo Mauto, and *Acacia* growing on it. A third level is closer to the highway with some smaller trees growing on it. And the fourth is the level of the wash bottom next to the highway. The higher hills beyond the fourth surface are alluvial gravels from a still older fan level.

114   Very coarse alluvial fan material is exposed in this roadcut.

113.5 The highway crosses Arroyo Buenos Aires and reveals good exposures of alluvial fan material, large granitic blocks, and sandstone lenses. These blocks are nearly all granitic with only a few metamorphic clasts.

110   This turnoff leads to Rancho El Cardonal 23 and the small village of Los Barilles.
The view is of Bahia las Palmas and the Gulf coastal tourist villages of Buena Vista and Los Barriles.

108.8 A Pemex station marks this Km marking. A change in the vegetation is noticeable around Los Barriles. Everything seems to be much shorter than before; this indicates the reduction in moisture as compared to the cooler moister mountain elevations near La Paz. Abundant Elephant Trees, *Acacia*, Lomboy, Candelabra Cactus, Fan Palms, and a few scattered Cardon are seen scattered among the shorter thorn scrub of this region.

106.1 This side road leads to the Gulf resort of Rancho Buena Vista Lodge.
Some parts of the hills to the southeast of Los Barriles are metavolcanic. Moreno has dated the metamorphics on the west side of the Sierra at 73 million years. The granitics near El Triunfo have been dated at 73 million years and those nearer the Cape at 63 million years.

101   The highway passes between two blocks of granitic horsts in a relatively flat graben which has been filled with thousands of meters of sediments, has been uplifted, and is being dissected similar to the San Bartolo wash.
The two sides of the graben can be seen in the long line of granitic hills to the southeast and in the line of the granitic spine of the Sierra la Victoria to the left.
The Santiago Formation is a series of marine and non-marine basin-filling sediments. Abundant fossils are exposed in numerous arroyos in the basin.

98   Candelabra Cactus and Pitaya Agria are abundant at this kilometer mark forming the impenetrable, sprawling thickets along the side of the highway. The edible fruits of Pitaya Dulce were eaten by both natives and Spaniards.

THE FRUIT OF THE SECOND HARVEST is the large tasty red fruit of the Pitaya Dulce (*Lemaireocereus thurberi*) which ripen in the late summer and fall. Gulf coast native Indians would gorge themselves on these fruits when they were in season during the "first harvest". The fruits, like strawberries or raspberries, contain small black seeds (achenes) too numerous to remove. The Indians knew that the "first harvest" would only last a short time and then they would be hungry again. In an effort to utilize all of the resources available, the Indians defecated in one spot and would later sift through the dried feces and separate the small seeds of the Pitaya Dulce, the "fruit of the second harvest". The seeds were ground into meal and made into the "bread of the second harvest".

95   The highway descends into an arroyo; this arroyo bottom (Wash Woodland) is densely vegetated. Like Cheese Bush, Tamarisk grows densely in disturbed soils.

93   The roadcut before the arroyo contains finer-grained silty turbidite sediments.

92.5   Excellent exposures of the marine Santiago Formation with alternating fine and coarse-grained yellow sandstones can be seen.
       Just north of La Ribera the dominant plant species are Organpipe, Palo Mauto, *Acacia*, Palo Adan, and Lomboy.
       The road to the right leads to Las Cuevas (the caves) where there are supposed to be good Indian pictographs (paintings on rocks) [see Km 59.5 of the Guerrero Negro log].

       The highway to the left leads 12 kms to La Ribera on the coast: then it goes 30 kilometers south along the Gulf to Cabo Pulmo, the only true coral reef in the Gulf of California. Cabo Pulmo consists of a large bay with a small fishing village and a rustic campground. Fishing is excellent and skin diving is great along the reef with abundant tropical fish. There is also a small restaurant - Tito's Place This road is normally passable for most vehicles all the way to San Jose del Cabo. Just beyond Cabo Pulmo is Punta Frailes, the most eastern point in Baja California.

       CORAL REEFS are found where 1) the average water temperature is 78º and the coldest month is not below 60º, 2) there is average salinity, 3) there is a lack of turbidity and 4) sunlight (less than 150 m deep). Actually, corals can and do live in deep and cold water. These requirements are for the calcareous algae which bind the corals together to form the reef.

92   A Papaya grove can be seen on the left side of the highway. Along the highway the rounded shrub with purple bell-shaped flowers is Rama Parda.

90   The highway crests a small grade and passes through more excellent exposures of the Santiago Formation.

89   At the crest of the hill is a good view of the Santiago graben. The Santiago Formation stretches for several miles to the base of the hills to the west. The frontal fault at the base of the hills trends north-south, roughly parallel to the highway. The hills to the east are on the east side of the graben. Caliente Manantials hot spring is located to the west along the fault near Agua Caliente.
       Along the roadside large *Agave* and small milkweeds with yellow flowers and long 10 centimeter seed pods are often abundant during the wet season.

88   Excellent exposures of the turbidites of the Santiago Formation can be seen along the highway for the next kilometer. They are mostly massive sandstones with interbedded shales and siltstones.

84.7   This road leads to the agricultural community of Santiago. The Pericu Indians once inhabited this region and revolted against the Spaniards in 1734.

       JESUITS, MISSIONS, AND THE PERICU INDIANS: Spanish Jesuits first arrived in Baja at Loreto in 1697 where they established the first and oldest mission in the New World. The purpose of the mission was to convert the native Indians to Christianity. The Jesuits were the first farmers of the peninsula and worked very hard to develop an irrigation system that allowed them to grow date

unskilled labor provided by the native Pericu Indians. The conditions of the peninsula were so harsh that the Jesuits were never able to raise enough food for themselves and all of the Pericu, so only a few Indians lived at the mission. The rest continued to live as they had before the arrival of the Spanish and came into the mission only occasionally or for religious holidays. The Jesuits were evicted from Baja by decree of Charles III of Spain because they had exploited the Pericu by using them as slaves in order to accumulate great wealth (perhaps $12-60 million). Before the Jesuits were evicted, the Pericu rebelled against the priests in 1734 and killed priests, mission workers, and even the crew of a Spanish Galleon that had docked at Santiago for provisions and water. They rebelled because they did not want to accept Christianity; they were polygamists and looked to powerful witch doctors for guidance. The Jesuits tried to stop polygamy by reprimanding the Pericu in public for this un-Christian life style and tried to discredit the witch doctors. After the rebellion the Pericu returned to living as they always had. In 1768 the Jesuits were evicted and replaced by the Franciscans, then the Dominicans. The Indians died out as a result of syphilis spread by soldiers, and the missions failed since there was no purpose for their continued existence.

82.3 Crest over a small rise for a panoramic view of the graben. The straight nature of the fault of the Sierra la Victoria and the very flat nature of the sediments that in-filled the graben are quite obvious.

81.8 This is the Tropic of Cancer which is the boundary between the Temperate Zone and the Torrid Zone.

70.9 The highway passes the turnoff to Miraflores. The craftsmen of Miraflores produce fine leather work.
The road into Miraflores offers a spectacular view of the massif of the Sierra la Victoria. There are two very high peaks on either side of a large pass almost straight ahead. The peak to the left is Cerro Santo Genoveva, 1,892 meters high. The peak to the right Cerro is 1,824 meters high. The town has a leather shop where belts, shoes, holsters, etc. may be purchased.

67 The highway drops into a major arroyo with fine-grained fanglomerate sediments on both sides and coarse fanglomerates above.
The wash vegetation is dominated by *Acacia*, Cheese Bush, and Palo Verde.

61 *Acacia*, scattered Cardons, Lomboy, some Candelabra cactus, Palo Mauto, Palo Zorrillo, Elephant Trees, and Palo Verde are the predominant vegetation of this region of the Cape.

59 The highway descends into an arroyo with more exposures of the Santiago Formation.

53 On the flats the vegetation has thinned due to the lack of water. The vegetation is locally dominated by Elephant Tree, Jumping Cholla, Lomboy, and scattered *Acacias*, Pitaya Dulce, Cardon, Palo Verde, Fairy-duster Mimosa, and flowering Mistletoe.

49.5 To the east are exposures of the Santiago Formation on the edge of the Santiago basin. The beds are tilted up toward the edge of the horst.

43.5 This turnoff leads to the Los Cabos International Airport. Planes from Mexico and Alta California fly tourists in and out for vacations at Cabo San Lucas and surrounding resorts.

Log 9 - La Paz to Cabo San Lucas

39.2   This is the farming town of San Jose Viejo.

37.2   There are numerous escaped European date palms and *Acacia* in this arroyo; this indicates available underground water.

35   Near San Jose del Cabo the Lomboy, covered with a parasitic Mistletoe, becomes the dominant plant of the area (more than 2/3 of the vegetation). *Acacia* and Cholla comprise most of the rest of the vegetation.

33   The highway forks here. The right fork continues to Cabo San Lucas. The left fork goes into San Jose del Cabo.
        San Jose del Cabo is a farming and tourist center which is being developed by FONATUR. There are some interesting orthagonal joints in the granitics across the street from the Pemex Station.
        Since there are abundant granitic rocks in this area, the beautiful white beaches are all composed of quartz and feldspar.

27.8   A small cardonal of Cardons is growing in the arroyo along the beach. On the hill there are more Cardons, Pitaya Dulce, Palo Adan, Palo Mauto, Elephant Trees, Cholla, Pitaya Agria, and Lomboy.
        North of the village of Palmilia, Lomboy, Acacia, Elephant Trees, some small Pitaya Dulce, Pitaya Agria, and Minosa (Lysiloma sp.) dominate the flat areas. In the washes Palo Adan predominates. Most of the vegetation is no more than 2-3 meters tall which is characteristic of the short thorn scrub of the Cape Region.

27   The granitics are overlain by fluvial sediments (mostly decomposed granitics). These exposures continue for a number of kilometers down the coast.

25.4   The road metal quarry on the right is located in very dark granitics.

25   There are more trees in this area, and Palo Mauto becomes the dominant tree of the landscape. Scattered among the Palo Mauto are Elephant Trees, Lomboy, Pitaya Agria, and Palo Adan.

22   Sweeping views toward the cape are visible along the highway for the next several kilometers. The surf is much stronger here due to the proximity of the Pacific.
        Highly weathered, altered, and jointed pink granitics are well exposed in the roadcuts.

21.4   The granitics exposed in this roadcut have been dated at 63 million years.

19   The highway continues to traverse the dissected undulating alluviated fan surface.

16.2   There are a number of relatively unweathered and well-jointed dikes which cut the weathered granitics.

14.7   The palm oasis of Hotel Cabo San Lucas is nestled along the coast. Many of the small offshore rocks and points along this coastline support small coral colonies.

10.5   The two large trees on the low hill to the left are fig trees.

6   There is a spectacular view of the cape, the bay, the arches and stacks (called the "Friars" [Los Frailes]) at the point of the Cape. The arches are similar to those seen at Big Sur in northern Alta California, U.S.A. This area is commonly referred to as "Land's End".

THE FRIAR'S STACKS OR ARCHES: The arched rocks visible at the end of the cape of Cabo San Lucas are locally known as "The Friars". Geologically, the Friars are stacks--isolated arch-like rocky islands detached from the tip of the peninsula by wave erosion. At some time in the future "The Friars" will be completely destroyed by wave erosion along joints. Waves pounding against a wave-cut cliff produce various features as a result of the differential erosion of the weaker sections of rock. Wave action may hollow out cavities or sea caves in the cliff, and if this erosion should cut through a headland, a sea arch is formed. The collapse of a roof of a sea arch leaves a mass of rock called a stack, which is isolated in front of the cliff.

5   The fairly prominent terrace on the high hill is part of the main part of the point. There is a fairly large coastal dune field graded at about the 10 meter terrace level which extends up the coast for approximately five kilometers.

3   The highway drops down close to sea level. There are large amounts of Mesquite and some Lomboy.

2   The highway crosses a wash. Take the road to the right to Todos Santos.

1.5   A Pemex Station is located at this kilometer mark.
     In the flats which surround Cabo San Lucas, Screwbean Mesquite is the dominant plant accompanied by scattered Lomboy, Cardon, both Pitaya Dulce and Agria, Cholla, and Tamarisk.
     To continue all the way to the cape follow the divided highway around the harbor.
     The large rocks between Hotels Solomar and Finisterra contain tremendous **zenoliths** - as much as 2 meters across and 1 meter thick with predominantly vertical axes.

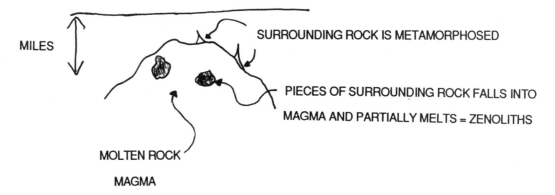

Log 10 - Cabo San Lucas to La Paz via Todos Santos [157 kms = 97 miles]

From Cabo San Lucas the Baja Highway heads northward traveling largely on the dissected surfaces of alluvial fans from the granitic Sierra Victoria. Extensive dune fields and supra tidal flats are near the road where it lies close to the ocean. Near Todos Santos the road climbs through several low passes in the mixed granitic and metamorphic rocks. At Todos Santos the road turns inland to travel on a dissected alluvial surface along a major fault close to the granitic hills of the Sierra Victoria.

123   There are two routes from Cabo San Lucas along Highway 19 to Todos Santos and La Paz. Retrace the route back to the Pemex station and turn left on Highway 19 north or take the business route from town which is Paseo Morelos. This is the route north through Todos Santos.

         From Cabo San Lucas the highway goes northwest on alluvial fans toward the granitic massif of Sierra la Laguna. In this area the highway passes through the Cape phytogeographic region. The vegetation on either side of the highway consists of a heavy thorn forest underbrush dominated by species of *Acacia*, Organ Pipe Cactus, Cardons, Elephant Tree, Yucca Vine, Lomboy, Palo Mauto, and several species of Cholla.

122   As the highway crests a pass, there is a beautiful view to the left of the Pacific Ocean and numerous active coastal sand dunes.

118   Although the Palo Mauto tree is most abundant above the 600 meter elevation in most of Baja, it grows in many of the lower elevation washes crossed by the highway.

115   The highway undulates through an area of mature topography cut into the alluvial slopes. The lack of outcrops in this area is the result of the deep tropical weathering of the granitic rocks and subsequent burial of the outcrops by alluvium.

113   Cardons have become the predominant taller vegetation with a sparse desert "understory" of leafless Leather Plant.

         The highway passes through several roadcuts in the highly weathered granitics. Somewhat fresher granitics are visible in the washes of this region.

112   The gracile Plumeria trees which grow here resemble Crepe Myrtle trees which are often grown as an ornamental tree in California. Numerous composites and Indian Tree Tobacco are growing densely along the pavement edge.

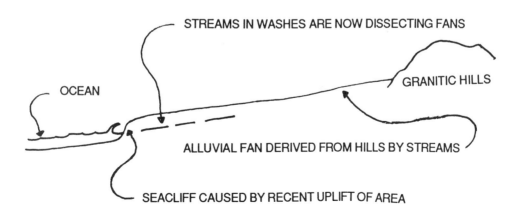

111 The highway crests another pass with sweeping views of the Pacific Ocean and descends a long grade on the alluvial fan surface toward the pacific coast.

107.1 As the highway crosses a wash, excellent exposures of granodiorite can be seen in the lower part of the wash.

107 The highway climbs a long grade over the surface of another dissected alluvial fan.

104.5 As the highway crests over a small pass, another view of the Pacific Ocean and many active coastal sand dunes is visible to the west.

103 The species composition of the vegetation is essentially the same as that listed at Kilometer 123, but the trees are noticeably shorter, rarely exceeding 3-4 meters in height. Lomboy and Leatherplant dominate the understory of a short "impoverished forest" of Elephant Trees, Cardon, and a few scattered *Acacias*.

DOMINANT REPRESENTATIVES OF THE MAGDALENA PLAIN FLORA: The flora of the Magdalena Plain was briefly introduced at Kilometer 73 on the way to Santa Rosalia. The five most commonly seen plants of the Magdalena Plain flora in this region are discussed below in more detail.

STANCH IT WITH LOMBOY OR NATURE'S "CHAP STICK": The low shrubby Lomboy (*Jatropha sp.*) frequently seen along the highway on flats, bajadas, and mesas in this part of the Magdalena Plain is a member of the spurge family (F. Euphorbiaceae). Members of the F. Euphorbiaceae usually produce a milky acrid sap. Over 8,000 species of euphorbs grow around the world. Some furnish food and valuable oils, while others are of ornamental or medicinal value. The two species of *Jatropha* commonly seen along Baja's highways on plains, hillsides, mesas, and sierras are *J. cinerea* and *J. vernicosa*. The sap of *J. cinerea* is highly astringent and is said to stanch bleeding wounds, prevent chapped lips, and, unfortunately, permanently stain clothing. Specimens of Lomboy grow from Punta Prieta on the Pacific side of the peninsula and Bahia de Los Angeles on the Gulf side south to the Cape. Like many of Baja's desert plants, Lomboy is leafless most of the year until the rains come. The three-lobed leaves turn a distinctive red color before falling off during dry periods. Lomboy is one of the most abundant, leafless low scrub plants which grow in this area.

Leatherplant Another euphorb, *Jatropha aurea*, a leafless low shrub, grows abundantly in this area.

Elephant Trees of this area are represented by the unrelated species of the two genera *Pachycormus* and *Bursera*. Because they store water in the cortical cells of their elephantine trunks, Elephant trees grow luxuriously despite the extreme aridity of this region. The *Bursera* are easily distinguished by the incense-like odor produced by crushed leaves or fruits. *Pachycormus* tissues are odorless.

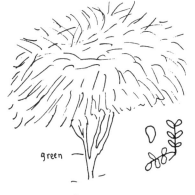

green

Palo Verde is a green trunked tree which produces legume-like "bean" pods. However, Palo Verde is in the Senna family, not the legume family. Like Lomboy, this tree is also normally leafless, an adaptation which reduces water loss by transpiration (a process of water evaporation through thousands of leaf pores) during dry periods. The green trunk of the Palo Verde is a cladode; that is, it's a photosynthetic stem which acts like a leaf and performs photosynthesis in the absence of leaves.

Palo Adan is a relative of the Ocotillo which is commonly seen in the northern deserts of Baja. However, Palo Adan has thicker branches, a trunk, smaller flowers, and normally grows from Parallel 28° south to the Cape Region on the clay and granitic soils of alluvial plains. Ocotillo is not usually found below the 28th Parallel.

Ramalina is an epiphytic foliose lichen formed by the combination of algal cells which live inside the tissues and cells of a fungus in a mutualistic symbiosis. The algal cells provide sugar to the host fungus which utilizes it as a source of energy. In return the fungus provides protection and the water and carbon dioxide utilized by the algal symbiont during photosynthesis. Other species of lichen form living crusts on rocks in this area. Crustose lichen look like variously colored "splashes" of paint. A lichen is a symbiotic relationship between an algae and non-photosynthetic fungus. Due to a very specialized life system, they can exist on bare rock and obtain food from the air, sunlight, rain water, and rocks. They are instrumental in the breakdown of rocks by their production of weak organic acids which result in the production of soils. The lichen also keep the rock moister and promote more local chemical weathering. Lichens are common desert dwellers and often represent the dominant vegetation in certain local desert ecosystems.

98 As the highway crosses a low wash vegetated with Broom Baccharis, it passes roadcuts of mixed granitic rocks with pods of metamorphic rock cut by dikes.

99 The mountains in view along the highway to the right (east) are the granitic Sierra la Victoria.

98 As the highway crests a low pass, there is another view of the Pacific Ocean. Numerous active and stabilized dunes near the coast are seen to the west.
The vegetation in this region has become sparse. The taller plants are Elephant Trees and Cardon, and shruby, leafless Lomboy and Leather Plant dominate the low brush of the "understory".

97 The bottom of this wash reveals mixed granitic and metamorphic rocks.
The vegetation in this wash is denser than that of the surrounding flats and forms a Wash Woodland dominated by *Acacia*, Cardon, Leather Plant, Lomboy, Indian Tree Tobacco, and

Broom Baccharis. The vegetation on the surrounding drier well-drained slopes remains "impoverished", shorter and sparser than other tropical forests at the same latitude due to the lower precipitation of Baja's Cape region.

96   For the next few kilometers the highway parallels the coastline which ranges from 1 to 2 kilometers to the west of the highway. Along this stretch there are almost continual views of the Pacific Ocean and its fringe of active, semi-stabilized, and stabilized sand dunes.

91   The highway drops into another wash where the dirt road to the west leads approximately one kilometer down the wash toward the Pacific and ends at a beautiful sandy beach with rocky points and headlands composed of granitic rocks.

89.5   As the highway passes a road metal quarry cut in mixed granitic rock, it begins a descent through exposures of granitics.

82.5   A beautiful beach is located on the sloping alluvial surface at the bottom of this gentle grade near Las Cabrillas. However, it is unsafe to swim here because the surf in this area is dangerously rough.

82   From this point an alluviated surface stretches to the beach. It is truncated by the 10 meter terrace level above abundant sandy beaches.
Granitics and mixed metamorphics are seen occasionally in the roadcuts. The highway in this area was built on a base of very coarse decomposed granitic soil that developed on the alluvial fans which stretch west to the Pacific. The granitics originated in the high Sierra la Victoria and were brought down by stream action and run-off.
The predominant vegetation of the washes in this area is Cheese Bush. On the well drained drier slopes the sparse vegetational cover is composed of the same species as those listed at Kilometer 97.

79   There is a view of the Pacific Ocean and a large rancho which is surrounded by numerous Fan Palms and fruit trees.

77.5   The highway travels over a well-developed alluvial surface for some distance.

75.5   A coastal storm beach berm has trapped water in the low land behind it and forms a supertidal flat.
An abundance of tall Cardon and a few scattered Mangrove Trees are growing behind the berm. A few Cardon are also growing on the surrounding well-drained drier hillside slopes. Due to the scarcity of water, the vegetation of the slopes has become shorter and is not much more than one meter high in the "best" spots.

74.5   A good short road approximately 100 meters long leads to the west to the beach. A short walk in this area makes possible a close inspection of the coastal storm beach berm, supertidal flats, and alluvial surface.
For the next kilometer there are excellent exposures of steeply dipping gneiss cut by several dikes in the roadcuts.

73.7   As the highway crests a low pass through gneisses, the view to the north reveals several kilometers of the quartz sand clad Pacific coastline.

Just after the pass a dirt road skirts the hills to the west and leads the curious explorer to a small Fan Palm oasis and cove nestled in the lee of two hills and a active coastal dune field.

71   Ball Moss grows profusely on the Cirio and Palo Adan of this region.
The vegetation of the coastal flats is dominated by Lomboy, Leather Plant, and Cardon with a few scattered Jumping Cholla, Lichen, Organ Pipe Cactus, Pitaya Dulce, and Elephant Tree. Broom Baccharis is still the dominant inhabitant of the washes. *Acacias* are conspicuously absent.

69.2   Another good view of a super-tidal flat (Salitrales) is visible. Salitrales are often dry a good part of the year, and farther north on the west coast of Baja they form hard surfaces that are excellent to travel upon. In some places the Salitrales are hard enough for small planes to land on. However, when they flood, which may be quite seldom during the summer rainy season, they become wet, slick and "soupy", and very unusable.

68   The highway continues to traverse the alluviated fan surface with numerous views of Punta Lobos. Gneisses and other metamorphic rocks form Punta Lobos.

63   The highway passes through a small agricultural community which produces mangos, papayas, and several types of table vegetables.

52.2   **Todos Santos** is a relatively small agricultural village developed in a lush green valley (Valle Todos Santos) near the Pacific and is located close to the Tropic of Cancer. The town began as a farming community and a mission visiting station in the early 1700's and finally gained mission status when the Mision Todos Santos de Santa Rosa was built in 1732. Today table vegetable farming and fishing provide the main economic support for Todos Santos' residents. The tall shiny-leafed trees which line the highway into Todos Santos are Mango Trees. The fertility of the land is obvious by the numerous Mangoes, Palms and sugar cane fields of the valley.
At the sugar cane mills of Todos Santos, cane is delivered and crushed which produces a sweet liquid. The liquid is cooked into a dark liquid which is poured into hollowed-out cone-shaped forms which produce a coarse grade of raw dark-brown sugar the Mexicans call "panocha". "Panocha" is eaten, sold locally, and exported.

51   The highway passes through the north end of Todos Santos.
There are usually many cattle grazing along the *Baja Highway*. They are attracted to the lush, green roadside vegetation and some are killed by car drivers as they feed at night. Watch for roadside cattle when driving after dark! It's best not to drive at night in Baja.

50.8   An anticline is visible in the metamorphic rocks in the roadcut on the right.
To the north away from Todos Santos, the highway roughly parallels the Sierra la Victoria Fault Zone that continues across Baja Penisula and passes just east of La Paz. To the left is the faulted graben of Llanos de Santo Tomas. The Todos Santos graben is underlain successively by Pliocene sediments, Miocene volcanics and marine sediments, and ultimately by a Cretaceous syncline which is truncated by the Sierra la Victoria Fault.

47   A particularly dense cardonal is seen along this stretch of the highway.

45   As the highway rounds a curve, the low foothills of the northern end of the Sierra la Victoria can be seen. The frontal fault of the Sierra la Victoria cuts diagonally toward the highway from right to left.
To the left are the flat Llanos de Todos Santos and the Cretaceous syncline.

42   A large dam, Presa Saint Inez, has recently been built near Todos Santos; it ensures a more reliable year-round water supply for the agricultural concerns of the region.

39   The highway descends into a large arroyo through exposes of granitic rocks.
A small terrace covers the granitic rocks while coarse blocks of granitic debris are visible downstream.
Locally the massif of the Sierra la Victoria has been planed off into a pedimented surface. The pediment is seen as a gently sloping erosion surface developed by running water at the base of the abrupt and receding front of the Sierra la Victoria. The pediment is underlain by a bedrock of granitics and metamorphics mantled with a thin discontinuous veneer of alluvium derived from the upland massif of the Sierra la Victoria. This thin veneer passes over the fault and becomes quite thick on the down-dropped side of the fault. There are a complex series of faults in this frontal fault zone.

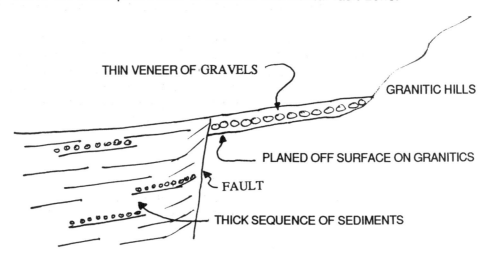

34   Watch carefully as you drive this section of the *Baja Highway,* and you may see a Cuckoo Bird (*Geococcyx californianus*) run across the road.

The **GREATER ROADRUNNER** is the large terrestrial Cuckoo Bird which may be seen running through the chaparral, desert scrub, and thorn scrub throughout the entire peninsula. The most identifiable field characteristics of the roadrunner are its black crest and long black, white-tipped trailing tail. A close look at the eye will reveal that it's flanked by beautiful red, white, and blue feathers. The food of this fleet-footed predator consists of anything that moves (primarily lizards, snakes, and insects). The Mexicans know this shy rapid ground runner as Correcamino norteno.

29   There is a good view to the right rear of the massif of the Sierra la Victoria. The highway continues to the northeast across the flat alluviated surface for a number of kilometers and then turns to the east toward La Paz. As the highway traverses this flat featureless plain, it approaches the smaller massif of the Sierra las Calabazas. This small range, which resembles bald heads, is visible to the right of the junction of Highway 19 and Highway 1.

0   Junction Highway 19 north leads to La Paz; Highway 1 south leads back to Cabo San Lucas. From the junction it is approximately 34 kilometers to La Paz.

Log 11 - Laguna Chapala to San Felipe via Gonzaga.
[215 kms = 133 miles]

NOTE: Until this road is paved we do not recommend that you take this extremely rough road in any type of vehicle. The kilometer markings will probably change. Use the main points as relative references.

0   The highway proceeds east on a roadbed which is elevated above the dusty lake bed, cutting across the north end of Laguna Seca Chapala.
The hills in the distance straight ahead are mostly undifferentiated granitic rock.

2.6   This is the Old Rancho Laguna Seca Chapalla which is now abandoned. The site was chosen because of the mines, which are low on the hill to the north, and because the old main road down the peninsula intersected another crude road going east to the mines at Las Arrastras and on to Bahia San Luis Gonzaga. The main highway now bypasses this Ranch completely. After passing the abandoned ranch, there are a series of mines in the granitic rock to the left. For the next 5 Kilometers the highway will travel through a mixed granitic and metamorphic terrain.

7.8   1st Cardon

7.7   After crossing a small fault, the highway climbs out of the arroyo over a hill in a belt of prebatholithic volcanic rocks which have been faulted between granite, slate, and schist.

8   Crest a small hill.- Orotillo, Agave

8.6   The highway is following the old road. It crosses first into granitic rocks then into metamorphic rocks then makes a bend and heads up a canyon within the metamorphic rocks.
The vegetation consists of Creosote, Brittle-Bush, Garambullo, Cardon (small and sparse), Cirio, Deadly Nightshade (opportunistic along the road), Ocotillo, and coastal shrubs such as Rabbit Brush and Purple Sage (as in Zane Grey's "Rider's of the Purple Sage").

9.7   Cross over a little divide in the metavolcanic rocks, and begin to descend a canyon in metavolcanic rocks. The metavolcanic rocks are dipping to the northeast at about a 70 degree angle.

10   The hill to the right is cut by several small quartz dikes. The quartz is weathering out and scattering down the sides of the hill.
Brittle Bush is the low, gray roadside plant.
There isn't any particular place in the San Felipe Desert that's particularly good for viewing birds so pick any place and see what's there. Surprisingly there are quite a few species in this seemingly empty land.

Log 11 - Laguna Chapala to San Felipe via Gonzaga

The following bird species are typical of the **Desierto San Felipe** area between the International Border and Bahia De Los Angeles:

BIRD COMMON NAME	MOST LIKELY LOCATION
American Kestrel	Telephone wires and fence posts
American White Pelican	Gliding along the shore
Anna's Hummingbird	In the chaparral-feeding on red or yellow tubular flowers
Bendire's Thrasher	Flies from bush to bush, feeds on ground
Black-chinned Hummingbird	In the chaparral-feeding on red or yellow tubular flowers
Cactus Wren	On cacti
California Brown Pelican	Gliding along the shore
California Quail	On the ground
California Thrasher	On the ground
Costa's Hummingbird	In the chapparral-feeding on red flowers
Gila Woodpecker	Nests in holes in giant saguaro cacti
Gilded Woodpecker	
Greater Roadrunner	Crossing the highway
Ladder-back Woodpecker	Within the desert and borders, sometimes nest among the agave stalk
LeConte's Thrasher	In sparse vegetation, flies when necessary
Loggerhead Shrike	Telephone wires and fence posts
Red-Tailed Hawk	Tops of telephone poles and fence posts
Scrub Jay	In chapparal and oak-woodlands
Turkey Vultures	Soaring in the skies or feeding, on carrion, on the highway
Western Meadowlark	Fence posts and fence wires

11   Crest of a grade.

13.6   Old Man Cactus, Buckwheat, Barrel Cactus, and T.B.C. The highway follows down a fairly broad and rather steep canyon. In the metavolcanic rocks, the highway is going up dip and is getting to progressively lower parts of the metavolcanic section.
There are bigger Ocotillo, Cardon, and Elephant Trees with Teddy Bear Cholla in the bottom of the canyon. On the sides of the canyon, the Elephant Trees become sparse, and the Cardons drop out leaving only Ocotillo and Agave. There is much more Agave in this area.

14.5   As the highway exits the canyon, it crosses a high angle normal fault onto uplifted alluvial fan material.

15   There is much more vegetation in the washes where there is more water. The vegetation gets sparser on the slopes due to sun exposure and lack of water. The dominant plant cover is *Yucca*, Brittle-Bush, *Agave*, Chemise, and Elephant Tree (*Pachycormus discolor*).

15.4   The highway follows along the faulted edge of a tonalite body with an alluviated valley to the right.

16.6   For the next 5 Km the highway passes through roadcuts and crests a small pass in tonalite and mixed metamorphic rocks.

17   Smoke Tree in washes. Wide ampitheater of Creosole Bush, Ocotillo, Old Man Cactus, and Palo Verde.

20.5 The vista to the north is similar to the view at 14.8. The tonalite ahead and to the left are capped by rhyolites. Most of the area is underlain by tonalite. The vista opens up to the north, and while the Gulf cannot be seen from here, the view is in the direction of Bahia San Luis Gonzaga and Ensenada de San Francisquito.
      Most of the terrain in the near distance is tonalite. In the far distance the hills are tonalite, slates, and metamorphic rocks interspersed with thin basins of alluvium.

21.3 Intersection: the left branch goes to Rancho Alposo while the main highway continues to the right.
      The tonalite exhibits some of the typical spheroidal weathering often characteristic of desert terrains .

0   This side road to the right leads to Puerto Calamuje while the main highway continues on, to the left, to Bahia San Luis Gonzaga.
      The kilometer markings start at "0" again at this junction.
      The main highway leads westward crossing an open alluviated plain with tonalite bodies visible on all sides. The low hills, about 0.5 Km, to the left are an eroded fault scarp formed by a fault paralleling the highway.

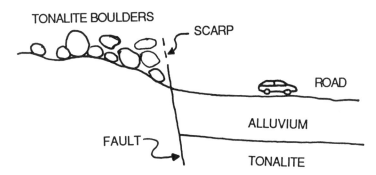

      The vegetation of the large amphitheater between Km 0 and Km 5 growing on the large boulder hillsides is Creosote Bush and occassional Cardon, Ocotillo, Dodder on Elephant trees, and Brittle Bush.

3   The low hills on the right is sparsely vegetated by Elephant Trees, Palo Verde, Cheese Bush, and Ocotillo.
4   Very picturesque, spheroidally weathered tonalite are visible on both sides along this stretch of the highway.
      To the north is a view of the rhyolitic rocks covering the Sierra's north of Bahia San Luis Gonzaga. There is an outcrop of rhyolite covering basalt on top of the hills, to the left.

6   The highway bends to the left to the Old Rancho Las Arrastras. Just past the ranch the highway drops into a rocky granitic arroyo.
      Directly ahead are basalts unconformably overlying tonalite.

7   The small reddish-brown mammi-form conical (complete with aerolea), to the right, is covered with rhyolite and surrounded by a talus slope.
      From Rancho Las Arrastras, the highway now follows down a branch of the Arroyo las Arrastras, cut in the tonalite, to join the main arroyo visible to the left at Km 12.5.

8   Some of the surrounding darkly banded hills to the left, with steeply dipping layers, are metavolcanic rocks.

10.5   Views to the left of the rhyolites of the volcanic field unconformably covering the tonalite.

11   The rocks of this area are predominated by sheet-like jointed tonalite. Xenoliths, the darker, partially melted remnants of the rocks which originally enclosed the tonalites, are visible embedded in the tonalite. The tonalite often weathers into almost hollow cavernous boulders. Good examples of cavernous weathering are exposed here and at Km 12.

> **CAVERNOUS WEATHERING**: For any one of a number of reasons part of the tonalite boulder is more protected and does not dry as fast. Chemical weathering proceeds at a faster rate and changes the feldspars to clays. This change pries the grains from the surface and produces an even more protected area. The wind blows the loose grains away gradually forming the caves.

12.5   Here the highway drops down into the main part of the Arroyo las Arrastras. A walk through this region at dusk or dawn will reveal many birds. One that is especially spectacular is the crimson *pyrrhuloxia*.

The spectacular, crested **Pyrrhuloxia** (*Cardinalis sinuatus*) is a beautiful crimson and gray colored cardinal relative with a yellow, straighter parrot-like bill. Pyrrhuloxias are commonly seen in the mesquite scrub along the road to the gulf's Bahia San Luis Gonzaga and surrounding Loreto where they usually feed on the ground, taking seeds and insects. This bird derives its name from the Greek, meaning crooked-billed red finch. Pyrrhuloxias inhabit the southern half of Baja where they are known as the Cardonal Gris [the gray bird of the cardon cactus].

This is an excellent spot for photographing an unconformity of tonalites covered by rhyolite. It is also a beautiful camp site.

13.5   There are interesting hollows (cavernously weathered boulders) in the rocks in the canyon to the left giving the impression that someone had mined here. Several light colored dikes in the darker tonalite are visible in the roadcut.

14   As the highway crosses and recrosses the Arroyo las Arrastras it begins climbing onto the surface of a gravelly Quaternary terrace. The Arroyo la Turquesa is visible to the left (southwest) of the highway.
Here the highway finishes making a double crossing of the wash.

15.5   Here the highway drops into another wash lushly vegetated with Cats Claw Acacia and Cheese Bush.
The Wash Woodland vegetation is similar to that of the Anza-Borrego Desert in southeastern Alta California. The predominant floral cover consists of Creosote Bush, *Atraplex*, Burroweed, Garambullo, Cardon, Ocotillo, and mistletoe laden Palo Verde (*See* Km 15.5 of the L.A. Bay log).

15.8   The highway again climbs up onto the high, gravelly Quaternary terrace vegetated with beautiful stands of Ocotillo and tall Elephant Trees with sand Verbena growing spottly along the roadside.

Log 11 - Laguna Chapala to San Felipe via Gonzaga

15.9 The area to the left is Miocene andesite that had been faulted into a series of benches resembling a series of giant steps leading down toward the Arroyo las Arrastras.

18 The hills visible in the view to the north are part of a coastal rhyolitic volcanic field stretching northward from Bahia San Luis Gonzaga to just south of Puertocitos.

The Quaternary fluvial terrace material that the road is following parallel the present-day San Francisquito Creek and probably represents part of the ancestral bed of the creek when sea level was higher. When sea level was lowered the area was subsequently abandoned by the creek leaving a relatively smooth terrace. The creek has moved over as it cut down the north side of the terrace.
The Arroyo las Arrastras is vegetated by a vast expanse of Ocotillo, Brittle-Bush, Burroweed, Creosote Bush, and scattered Teddy Bear Cholla. The Creosote Bush and Ocotillo are the largest plants of the wash woodland flora and seem to be dominant.

21.1 This side road is marked as the turn off to Punta Final.

23.5 This is the first view of Ensenada San Francisquito and Bahia San Luis Gonzaga. The far point directly ahead which looks like a low hill is Isla San Luis Gonzaga. The small point to the left is Punta Willard the north point of Bahia San Luis Gonzaga. The island and Punta Arena separate the main part of Bahia San Luis Gonzaga from the Ensenada San Francisquito.

26.9 The first good view of Punta Final with Isla San Luis Gonzaga (Isla locally known as Willard) (the light colored "hill" in the background).
The north point of Punta Willard is the reddish peak on the left.

27.1 The vista ahead reveals good views of Isla San Luis Gonzaga, Alfonsinas airstrip on Punta Arena, the main port area of Bahia San Luis Gonzaga, and Ensenada San Francisquito. In the far distance, to the northwest, the gray looking point is actually Isla San Luis.

27.5 The highway passes through a wide part of the Arroyo las Arrastras. This crossing provides evidence that the entire area was uplifted. The stream has incised about 10 meters below the level of the braided stream drainage of the old alluvial fan. The upper surface probably represents the surface graded to the Sagamonian 5E high stand of sea level about 125,000 years ago. This high stand has been documented with coral dates at Mulege to the south (Ashby and Minch, 1989).

The dominant vegetation of the arroyo is the Smoke Tree, a few scattered Mesquite, large *Atriplex*, and low herbaceous perennials.

Upon crossing the arroyo the highway heads almost directly toward Ensenada San Francisquito. Bahia San Luis Gonzaga is on the right.
Isla San Luis Gonzaga, an andesitic volcanic island, lies to the right ahead.
The village of San Luis Gonzaga comes into view. On the sand spit to the right is Hotel Alfonsina's and an airstrip. There are several airstrips in the Gonzaga area: one at Punta Final to the south, one here at Alfonsinas (Willard Airstrip), and one at San Luis Gonzaga proper to the north. Alfonsinas, the most centrally located airstrip, is the most popular because its administrators cater more to the tourist than either of the other two airstrips.

35 This turnoff leads to Alfonsina's (3 Kilometers). The road is on an old alluvial fan. Alfonsina's is on a sand spit between Isla San Luis Gonzaga and the mainland. The Estero

San Luis Gonzaga, to the northwest (left) of the sand spit was once a beautiful lagoon known for its great clamming.

35.5 The view to the right is of Bahia San Luis Gonzaga as the highway heads into and passes through a series of low andesite hills. The actual turnoff for San Luis Gonzaga is to the north since that is the direction from which most people approach.
This area is only sparsely vegetated with Creosote Bush and Ocotillo.

36.5 The highway passes through a roadcut blasted into andesite material. The ground here is littered with dark colored cinders.
From Bahia San Luis Gonzaga north to San Felipe the highway passes through the San Felipe Desert subdivision of the Sonoran Central Desert Phytogeographic Region (*See* Km 108 of the Mexicali to San Felipe log).

37.2 The kilometer markers change and descend from this point to San Felipe. Kilometer 37.2 is 154.3 Kilometers south of San Felipe.

154.3 This is the turnoff to the north part of San Luis Gonzaga.
The layered nature of the andesitic volcanics is very obvious on the north point of San Luis Gonzaga. The hills to the north are andesitic volcanics. Just around the edge of Punta Bufeo is the gray mass of Isla San Luis. Notice the ash-gray cinders littering the ground here.

147.5 The highway rounds a corner and drops slightly into a flat alluviated area.
The Pliocene marine sediments seen here form a "badlands-like" topography under the alluvium. The highway is flanked on both sides by the andesite hills.

146.7 The mainland range to the left are all rhyolites. This roadcut reveals the slightly altered sediments of the Salada Formation.
At the crest the vista opens with the gulf and a number of islands in the distance. The islands, in succession, are: the first small one; Chollito, which looks like a divided island; Isla Lobos, the pointed one; and, to the left, El Muerto, which almost looks connected to the mainland. Isla El Huerfanito ("the Little Orphan") is not yet in view.

On the alluviated plain the reddish and yellow beds of the Pliocene marine sediments of the Salada Formation are exposed to the left in the gully below. They are overlain by terrace material. The bouldery outcrops on the higher hills behind the Pliocene are spheroidally weathered tonalite. The andesite volcanics drape over the older formations. The highest hill is a small basalt shield cone called Cerro el Portrero.

Here the highway descends through the Pliocene sediments of the Salada Formation onto the flats, with a series of very low Pliocene hills in the near distance ahead.
The vegetation covering the Pliocene marine terrace consists of Ocotillo, Palo Adan, and Creosote. It is sparser here than it was at the vista point back at the crest of the hill (Km 146.7). Smaller Smoke Trees, Rabbitbrush, and Burroweed predominate in the washes along this stretch of the highway.

144.9 Pliocene beds are exposed in the roadcut at the edge of this wash.
Along this stretch, the highway alternately climbs up on the low fluvial terrace, drops down into a wash, and returns to the terrace again. The low hills to the left exhibit exposures of the Pliocene Salada Formation. Volcanics are visible to the right.

The vegetation has dramatically changed. Almost all of the plant mentioned at Km 146.7 have disappeared, except for the Creosote Bush and several species of annual grasses. A few very small Ocotillo can be seen growing on the rises between the washes.

141.7 The north end of Isla San Luis is directly east of the highway

> **ISLA SAN LUIS** consists of several low lying rings of pumice (the gray material) with a very obvious obsidian dome (the darker material). The same geological conditions exist at Mono Craters in Central California. The south end of Isla San Luis is a Maar, an explosion pit consisting of a large pumice ring with no dome. The southern point of the island is the west rim of the explosion pit. The islands cliffs were formed by the sea eroding the soft pumice. The obsidian on the larger dome was dated using obsidian hydration rates and found to be as young as 100 years. The darker material at the north end of the island is another obsidian dome.

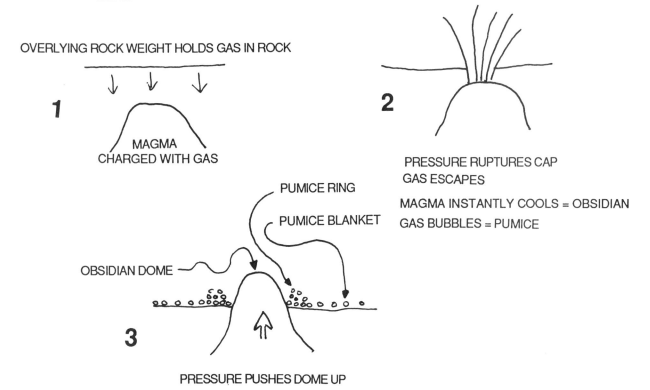

141.2 The highway descends from the alluvial terrace through a small roadcut to the turnoff at Punta Bufeo. At the north end of Punta Bufeo, the vegetation consists almost entirely Creosote Bush and a few Brittle-Bush, annual grasses, and Ocotillo which appear mostly on the edges of the washes or occasionally scattered about on the Fan surface.

The alluviated Pliocene plain, since leaving San Luis Gonzaga, has been littered with dark colored sand derived from the combination of the granitic and volcanic rocks moved gulfward from the tonalite hills to the west.
This turnoff leads to the beach at Punta Bufeo. A small, semi-stabilized coastal dune field lines the coast near this junction.

138.6 The excellent view northward across the alluviated fan is of Isla San Luis and most of the other small offshore islands located to the north of Punta Bufeo.

Log 11 - Laguna Chapala to San Felipe via Gonzaga

The diked tonalite hills ahead are covered with the brown mottling effects of desert varnish. The light colored material cutting across the hills in streaks are the dikes.
A thin cinder blanket is readily apparent in the road cuts of this area.

134   The highway crosses the Arroyo Mal de Orin. The prominent wash woodland vegetation of this arroyo consists of Smoke Tree, Elephant Tree, Hore-hound, Princess Plume Mustard, Spanish Bayonette Yucca, Pencil Cholla, and Palo Verde.

132.8 There is mistletoe laden Palo Verde (*See* Km 16.5 of the L.A. Bay log). Sporadic Garambullo and Cheesebush are the tall floral dominants. An interesting member of the squash family, a bush with a yellow-orange, trumpet-like flower called a Devil's Claw or Unicorn Plant can occasionally be sighted from the highway.

The vegetation along this stretch of the coast varies depending on whether you're in the wash or up on the flats. Some of the larger bushes are overgrown by a purple flowering vine called San Miguel, a beautiful climbing vine common in the southern parts of the peninsula.

133   The highway has been traversing an active alluvial fan for several kilometers. The low ridge ahead (15 to 20 meters high) parallels the surface of the fan. This ridge is an older terrace deposited when sea level was higher.

131.1 The vegetation has changed dramatically - the ground is almost entirely obscured by a thick cover of Brittle-Bush. In the springtime the area is illuminated by the bright yellow flowers of the Brittle-Bush. There are a few scattered Creosote whose numbers increase as you look toward the beach.
The highway approaches the end of the coastal alluviated Pliocene marine terrace. The low hills ahead are volcanic.
The tonalite on the left is cut by numerous nearly vertical, light-colored, ribbon-like dikes.
A foothill "screen" of dark metamorphic rocks is exposed close to the volcanic hills forming a low belt of darker colored, steeper hills than the volcanic hills straight ahead.

127.6 The volcanic hills of Isla el Muerto lie directly offshore. The white on El Muerto is bird guano.
The hills approaching the coast from the left are andesitic volcanic rocks.
The low, dark colored, jagged hills to the left of the volcanics are the metamorphics. The highway follows the alluviated terrace, then skirts the volcanic field along the seashore, and returns to another alluviated terrace.

126.4 The Brittle-Bush, seemingly the only plant growing here, looks like little gray "buttons" all over the hills. Because each plant has its own nutrient and water requirements, they space themselves naturally, appearing to have been planted in rows. At the lower elevations, between the highway and the gulf, Creosote and Ocotillo are occasionally seen growing among the Brittle-Bush.

124.8 The highway crosses a rather narrow but deep wash (Arroyo Miramar) cut into fanglomerate material. Hard, well cemented, fanglomerates are well exposed in the bottom of this arroyo.

124.5 The view to the south is of Isla el Muerto with sandy gulf coast beaches stretching southeastward to Punta Banda, and on a clear day one can see all the way to the south to Punta Bufeo. Punta Final is hidden from view by Punta Bufeo.

123.9 The highway descends steeply into a wash, in the fanglomerates, framing a view of Isla el Muerto to the east.

Magnificant Frigate birds are commonly seen soaring off shore here.

The Magnificent Frigate-birds (*Fregata magnificens*) are probably the most aerial of all sea birds and thus present a common but thrilling sight over the waters along the gulf coast of Baja. These birds possess the greatest wingspan (up to 2.5 meters), in proportion to their body, of any known species and are hardly equaled by any bird in their powers of sustained, soaring flight. Their most identifiable field characteristics are the prominent crook in the slender, streamlined wing, the long slender forked tail, the way they soar high in the sky, apparently hanging motionless, their steep, swift dives to snatch fish from the sea, and the naked red inflatable throat (gular sac) of breeding males. Immature birds have white on their heads and throats. They often act in an aggressive and piratical manner, chasing and colliding with blue and brown-footed boobies, terns, and gulls upsetting them so much that they regurgitate their last, fishy meal, which the Frigate then aerobatically snatches from mid-air. No doubt the name Frigate (a pirate ship) was derived from this behavior. Another method of obtaining food is to steal chicks from tern colonies or as a last resort to fish for themselves. Frigates nest on off-shore islands in large untidy stick structures placed in anything from a low bush to a large mangrove tree. Nesting is done on small uninhabited islands to avoid predation by the four footed predators that inhabit the nearby peninsula.

122.3 After passing a very small cove the highway rounds a corner to skirt a large cove with a beautiful curved cobble, shingle beach with a number of storm berms, and the ruins of a small settlement behind them.

The cove is a beautiful place to camp. Shingle beaches are in volcanic terrains near the shoreline usually covered by rounded pebbles and cobbles. These cobbles are often flattened and stacked like shingles on the beach face.

116.3 A sudden change has occurred in the vegetation. There has been an increase in the densities of Cardon, Palo Adan, Ocotillo, Garambullo, Palo Verde, Elephant Trees, Cheesebush, Ocotillo, large Acacias, and a variety of low annual grasses.

Smoke trees are generally found in washes, because their seeds have a very resistant seed coat which must be scarified by sand grains as water flows down the washes.

109.9 The view ahead is of the village of El Huerfanito and the white, bird guano covered Isla El Huerfanito.

Just to the left of El Huerfanito the view is of the highway climbing up the first of the steep grades of the Cuesta La Virgin.

The dark colored hill mid-way up the coast, behind the grade, is the basalt cone, Volcan Prieto.

107 The highway climbs up a dip-slope grade through volcanic rocks.

The Brittle-Bush again resembles little gray "buttons" on the dark volcanic material.

Atriplex and Wild Buckwheat are seen infrequently scattered among the Brittle-Bush.

105.8 The andesite flows of the extensive volcanic field between El Huerfanito and Puertocitos dip gently to the south-east.

106.2 The highway crests the first little grade then drops into the Arroyo El Huerfanito, for a kilometer or so, before climbing the main part of the first big grade.

106.6 Climbing the grade is a view of the series of stripped dip-slopes, dissected by little streams, reaching down to the ocean. Below the slopes the shoreline forms a number of embayments which look like beautiful steep sided fjords.

104 Near the crest of the first big grade. At the top of the roadcut is a pinkish rhyolite with a 15 to 30 cm. baked zone. Below that is a very muddy rhyolitic or andesitic lahar which looks like a mud flow and a bedded layer of basaltic cinders.
The highway eventually drops down into a major wash - the Arroyo Heme - the first north of the first grade. It should be possible to go down the wash to the beach.
There are beautiful, lush, mistletoe laden Palo Verde trees growing here. The highway climbs up out of the wash to a view of a nice rocky beach with a storm berm. There is a good flat spot for camping and there may be good diving in among the rocks.
As you drive along the ocean, watch for shrimpers out of mainland Mexico. The boats usually have a rusty, white hull and long seine net booms extending outward over both sides. The net booms and their seine nets look like huge grasshopper legs from the side and like wings from the front.

102.1 The small dark hill is a Quaternary basalt cone.

103.8 Near the top of the grade, where the highway crosses to the east side of the ridge the view to the north and west at the volcanic tableland looks deceptively flat, because you are looking at the dip-slope. Where this flat face is cut by canyons it is revealed as being a steep slope.

101 Halfway through the east side of the ridge is a road cut with a rhyolite flow overlying a very thin mudflow. There is a slight angular unconformity, where some deformation and erosion took place between deposition of the beds. Below that is a 0.7 meter thick cinder blanket of basaltic fragments.
After crossing over the edge there is a turnout at a wide spot with a panoramic view to the south. In the far distance is Isla San Luis Gonzaga, the edge of Punta Final, the south end of Bahia San Luis Gonzaga, the highway where it seems to disappear at the north point of Bahia San Luis Gonzaga, Isla San Luis, Ensenada San Francisquito, and the high parts of the Sierra La Asamblea south along the main peninsular divide. To the right of the view is the stepping-up of the dip-slopes of the rhyolitic rocks with a flat slope, a steep rise, flat slope, steep rise, etc., showing where each successive layer of the rhyolites has been stripped off.

The vegetation of this area is very sparse. Brittle-Bush dots the dip-slopes like gray buttons on a dark brown quilt.

100.5 About a kilometer and a half down the grade, a 1.5 meter thick black basalt cinder blanket is visible. This Quaternary basaltic cone may have been an eruptive center during the Pliocene when the rhyolites were being deposited.

97 The second grade descends until it nears sea level on the alluvial surface. After passing the rocky beach the highway begins to climb another hill.

95 A stop at the top of this hill will provide another spectacular panoramic view to the south. All of the near coast gulf islands are clearly discernable. Along the right hand side of the highway, at the very southern end of the large basaltic cone, a large sandy

tidal flat, often below sea level, is easily seen. Fresh water from one of the arroyos or sea water, during high tide and storms, can fill this entire area.

94.7   The highway crests here at about 130 or 140 meters above sea level then descends and begins undulating again following a terrace level. The little point in the distance is the north point of Puertocitos.

89   The hills nearer the highway are covered with white *Eriaganum* - another species of wild Buckwheat. The other hills are covered with Brittle-Bush, Ocotillo, and mistletoe laden, wash woodland trees.
       There is a road going down to a small settlement on a fine gravelly beach. A tombolo extends to a small, near shore, rocky island at low tide.
       The highway passes numerous sandy beaches providing excellent camping and swimming. Extensive tide pool areas exist below the highway. A dip-slope dam has created many excellent, beautiful tide pools.
       Keep an eye out for Frigate birds and Pelicans in the area of Puertocitos.

87   There is a sign here advertising lots for rent in a camping area at Playa Christina. As this area becomes more and more popular, lots for rent will undoubtedly become scarce and rates will climb.

85   The grade just south of Puertocitos provides a nice view of the harbor. Look for shrimp boats, Magnificent Frigates, Brown Pelicans, and Gulls in the bay.

80   **PUERTOCITOS** is an elongated, northwest-southeast oriented, linear bay formed by faults along both sides of the bay. The rocky shores (horsts=height) on the west and east are formed by uplift along two faults with the down-dropped (graben=ravine) block forming the sandy beach in the middle. Because of a 8 meter tidal range in this area, the high tide on this beach will come up to the foundations of the buildings. At low tide the bay is almost devoid of water.

       Toward the edge of the point, about 3/4 of the way down the east side of the bay, there is a hot spring. At low tide the steam can sometimes be seen rising from the area. The hot spring is located along the fault.

       Fossiliferous Pliocene marine beds are exposed along the highway in the graben north of Puertocitos. At the north end of the graben there is another cove which is less protected from the winds.
       The main highway closely follows the fault line on the west side of the graben. The cliff on the left side is a fault scarp. More of the fossiliferous Pliocene beds are exposed near the airport in the graben.
       The highway climbs out of the graben through a low pass in the hills. Most of the dark rock on the beach side of the highway is rhyolite.

79.5   Beautiful rocky points and pocket coves are present along the highway where the resistant rhyolite beds dip into the ocean.

75   Here the highway crests a low pass in the hills and drops down through volcanic rocks..
       Fairly wide sandy beaches with rocky points and a number of residential and vacation homes are visible.
       Several levels of alluvial fans are now visible which were graded to sea level at their toes at one time and which now, due to the uplifting of the land surface, end in sea cliffs. The relative ages of some of these have been estimated by calculating the rate of the drop in sea level.

71   The mustard yellow colored hills on the left are Pliocene marine beds capped by an alluvial fan.

68.4   The highway climbs up through more yellow beds and turns through a low roadcut.
         The vegetational cover here consists of Ocotillo, Elephant Trees, Creosote Bush, Mesquite with Mistletoe, and Cheese Bush.

68   North of Puertocitos the highway drops into the large Arroyo Matomi.
         Most of the hills in the distance are volcanic capped. The tonalite plutons of this area are covered by some fluvial and marine Miocene and Pliocene volcanics and sediments. The large hill on the horizon at about 10 o'clock is the high point of the Sierra San Fermin, a volcanic eruptive center composed of rhyolite. Here the highway runs "as straight as an arrow" across alluvial fan material.
         This stretch of the highway can be monotonous, especially when it is hot. The high granitic crest of the San Pedro Martir and Picacho Del Diablo can be seen in the far distance at about 11 o'clock.

61   The low hill on the horizon to the south-west (left rear) is Picacho Canelo, a rhyolitic volcanic eruptive center.

58   Toward the end of the flat plain, the highway climbs up on the terrace in the low foothills of the Sierra San Fermin, makes a deviation to the left, and crosses more washes and terraces.

54.2   The side road to the left leads down to Playa Cristina where a small lagoon and a coastal dune field have developed. Dry camping is available here at Campo Christina.

53   The highway drops from the elevated terrace back onto the alluvial fan.
         Here the highway crosses Arroyo de Chale.

48.8   Campo Coloradito ("little red" camp)
         The mountain range to the left is the Sierra San Felipe. This range will continue northward to San Felipe.
         In this stretch of the highway there are many signs for developments. We will mention only the ones which appear to be large and well maintained.

37   The vegetation changed drastically here to a Creosote Bush/Ocotillo community typical of the Desierto San Felipe flora (*See* Km 0 and 108 of the Mexicali to San Felipe log).

35   Campo el Virgel. This one has a minaret-like lighthouse and an airstrip.

33   La Roca - small airstrip.

32   Campo Nuevo Mazatlan.
         The new highway bypasses the Agua De Chale sulphur mines. The sulphur was brought to the surface by vapor and hot water along a fault line. The hot spring or fumarole activity has altered the rhyolite beds.

30.6   Bahia Santa Maria. The road to the left goes to Agua de Chale and the sulphur mines.

         SULFUR is a non-metal, native element which combines in many forms. Elemental sulfur is a bright yellow solid with a resinous lustre. Hot vapors rising along a fault zone alter the volcanic and sedimentary rocks in the area.

The sulfur is deposited as small yellow crystals and crusts in the cracks and lines cavities in the rocks.

30   The vegetation stabilizing the coastal dunes is primarily Creosote Bush, Mesquite, Atriplex, Smoke Trees (in the washes), Garambullo, Palo Adan, Brittle Bush, and *Acacia*. The high hill to the north, between Punta Estrella and Punta Digs, is Cerro Punta Estrella, a largely tonalite hill with some prebatholithic metamorphics along its flanks.

27   Numerous stabilized dunes have formed along the coast. The coastline here is a wide mud-flat in back of the beach behind the storm berm. A lot of Smoke Trees and Garambullo is growing between the dune fields. The vegetation on the dunes is primarily Mesquite and a few Creosote Bush, Cardon, and Palo Verde.

20.5   This road leads to the super-tidal flat of Laguna Percubu.

18   The tonalite pluton of Cerro Punta Estrella straight ahead is becoming very impressive. It looks as though the highway is heading straight into the mountain range. In this area everything seems to be at a great distance. A semi-circle of hills surrounds the bowl-shaped depression on the alluvial fan.

17   There is a cove like indentation in the tonalite hills which contains dark metamorphic rocks cut by numerous light colored dikes.

A large dune field is on the north side of the large tonalite hill. The highway passes through the hummocky topography of stabilized dunes which have been blown from the coast by the prevailing wind.

6.8   Hotel Farro Beach - Parts of the Sierra San Pedro Martir and Picacho del Diablo are in view on the left front. The high peak there is Picacho del Diablo which is the highest peak in Baja California, (3,115 meters, 10,126 feet). The highway drops behind and follows along the edge of the stabilized dune (10 to 15 meters high) for about 16 Kilometers to the turnoff to the airport.
The dunes in this region are moving. Some of the vegetation growing on or near these dunes consists of *Ephedra*, Creosote Bush, Ocotillo, *Atriplex* and Cat's Claw *Acacia*. These two plants are deep-rooted and the dunes hold moisture so they can survive in this area. On hummocks the sand is held in place by the roots. As the sand builds up the tree grows higher.

0   Here the highway divides. The road to the left goes to the airport; the one to the right climbs up onto the dunes and goes about 5 Kilometers into San Felipe.
As the highway crests over a dune the beautiful expanse of Bahia de San Felipe and the town of San Felipe comes into view. The coastline here is muddy because of the Colorado River and the volcanic terrain which produces finer grained material. The highway travels along the crest of this stabilized dune for the next several kilometers. As you drive down the highway you can see the sand being blown across the highway because there is little brush to stop it.

The highway soon crosses an arroyo.
The right point of the harbor is Punta El Machorro consisting of tonalite. The slightly higher hill to the left is Cierro El Machorro, consisting of granodiorite. The low-lying hills in the foreground, behind the city, are prebatholithic carbonaceous rocks of undetermined age.

Log 12 - San Felipe to Ensenada via Valle Trinidad [245 kms = 152 miles]

San Felipe to Ensenada Junction - *The Baja Highway climbs onto uplifted alluvial fans and passes through a series of steep mixed granitic and metamorphic hills. For several kilometers north of the hills the Baja Highway undulates across the dissected uplifted fans. The granitic Sierra San Pedro Martir form the high mountains on the far left. The largely granitic Sierra San Felipe form the nearer desert varnished foothills. As the Baja Highway crosses the alluvial fans, the last views of the Gulf of California fade into the distance across the supertidal flats of the Salinas de Omotepec. The Baja Highway crosses several of these dune areas with sand blown from the Gulf and supertidal flats. The Baja Highway continues for many kilometers along the alluvial fans descending from the rugged Sierra de San Felipe with views ahead of the distant rugged volcanic Sierra Pintas.*

Baja Highway 3 to Valle Trinidad - *From the intersection of Baja Highway 3 the Baja Highway heads west across the uplifted dissected alluvial fans past the rugged hills of mixed granitic and metamorphic rocks of the Cerro El Borrego and the Sierra de San Felipe, towards the crest of the granitic and metamorphic Sierra San Pedro Martir. After skirting the north end of the alluviated Valle San Felipe graben the Baja Highway enters a rugged, steep area of mixed granitic and metamorphic rocks in San Matias Pass at the end of the Agua Blanca Fault Zone. The Baja Highway then follows the trace of the Agua Blanca Fault Zone at grade through the steep hills of mixed granitic and metamorphic rocks to the broad alluviated area of Valle Trinidad. Miocene volcanic rocks cap the mesas to the north of the pass.*

Valle Trinidad to San Salvador - *At Valle Trinidad the Baja Highway turns and climbs a steep grade on a scarp of the Agua Blanca Fault, through rugged hills in the mixed granitic and metamorphic rocks onto the flat El Rodeo surface. Miocene volcanic rocks form the steep mesas to the northeast. The Baja Highway travels through rolling hills in the mixed granitic and metamorphic rocks, then skirts a large flat alluviated area and approaches a low line of hills which mark the approximate trace of the San Miguel Fault Zone. The Highway then descends a gentle valley in the rugged tonalite hills along the trace of the San Miguel Fault Zone to San Salvador.*

San Salvador to Ensenada - *The Baja Highway continues to follow a gentle valley along the San Miguel Fault Zone in the rugged mixed granitic and metamorphic hills, then turns west and descends a relatively smooth rocky surface to the broad flat alluviated Ojos Negros Valley. It then passes one of the numerous isolated steep metamorphic hills which dot the valley and heads toward an escarpment of rugged metamorphic gneiss hills with isolated granodiorite bodies. The Baja Highway crosses the frontal fault and passes through rugged bouldery granodiorite hills to descend a steep narrow valley in the rugged hills of granitic and metamorphic rocks and climb a steep grade in rugged steep metasedimentary and metavolcanic hills. After going over a pass the Highway descends the narrow rugged Arroyo del Gallo in the metavolcanic, gabbroic and tonalitic hills. After climbing out of the arroyo at Piedras Gordas it follows a rolling ridge through tonalites, gabbros, and gneisses and finally descends a grade through rolling tonalite slopes to Ensenada.*

189   As the road leaves town, the point of Cerro El Machorro on the right is composed of tonalite and granodiorite. The rocks just to the right at the big monument circle are prebatholithic carbonate rocks. On the left in the distance are the Sierra San Felipe which are almost exclusively composed of tonalite of the Peninsular Range Batholith. The road approaches the low hills on the right then makes a large bend and passes through them. They are made of prebatholithic carbonate rocks which are faulted in several places. The road follows along a slightly elevated and dissected alluvial terrace.

187   Pass through the low range of prebatholithic hills. They are covered by a heavy desert-varnish which gives their surface a very dark appearance. There is a pot factory on the left, and there are several brick yards with small ovens which are used for firing the clay bricks.

182   To the right is a fence made from cut ocotillo. Some of the posts have rooted and started to grow again. This is similar to the detilillo fences in other parts of the peninsula.

      North of San Felipe for several kilometers are a whole series of roads which go to the beach to camps, trailer parks, etc.

180   The high part of the Sierra San Pedro Martir begins to come into view. Picacho del Diablo (3,115 m., 10,126') is the highest point in Baja California.

179   This is the road to Colonia Morero and El Saltio. This very sandy, barely passable road crosses the Santa Clara Valley and heads north along the Laguna Diablo to intersect Mexico Highway 3 east of Valle Trinidad.
      The road crosses a small longitudinal dune. For the next several kilometers the road passes semi-stabilized dune fields composed of sand blown to the east from the sandy beaches of the Gulf. There is a view of the Sea of Cortez. If the weather is clear the volcanic peak Consac Rock can be seen in the middle of the Gulf.

175   To the left are the high peaks of the San Pedro Martir and the Peninsular Range Batholith. The highest peak is Picacho del Diablo which is in the center at approximately 9 o'clock.

170   To the north and to the right of the road ahead is a small hill called Moreno which is composed of Miocene volcanic rock. The hills to the left in the near distance are also Tertiary volcanics. The lower darker gray hills to the right of these hills are composed of prebatholithic slates and schists. The high hills in the distance are all tonalite.

167   To the right after the road passes the hill, there is a small inlet on the coast which is in the southern part of the Salinas de Omotepec. These are super-tidal flats which continue along the coast to the head of the Gulf of California. They are related to the very high tidal range in the Gulf and the Colorado River and empty into the upper end of the Gulf of California.

165   The hills to the left are desert varnished tonalite. The vegetation is very much like that of the Anza-Borrego Desert. There are Ocotillo, Palo Adon, Garambullo, abundant Mistletoe, Wait-a-minute Bush, Mesquite, Acacia, and Burrobrush. This typical desert vegetation extends from here to Palm Springs, California,. Along the roadside the disturbed opportunistic vegetation such as Cheesebush can be found. It is almost the only thing green here. Red-tailed Hawks are often seen in this area.

161   The shoreline of the Gulf of California begins to diverge from the road as it heads toward the Colorado River Delta area and Isla Montague. The slope that the road is on descends to the flat area of the Salinas de Omotepec. The Salinas de Omotepec are laced with little sloughs which are often flooded during super-tides. To the north the Salinas are quite wide.

157   The Sierra Pinta ahead are largely composed of Pliocene rhyolites with a core of carbonate metavolcanic rocks. At the north end of the Pintas is the location of the first discovery of Paleozoic rocks with Permian crinoids within Baja California. Since this

discovery, Paleozoic rocks have been found in a number of places. At this point is a final view of the Gulf of California and the extremely wide Salinas.

150   At the base of the fan on the flats is a salt-flat area where the water which comes into the super-tidal area drains and evaporates and leaves a little salt pan.

148   The road descends with a good view of the Sierra Pintas to the north. The Sierra Pintas are highly mineralized. There are several gold mines including the Moctezuma Silver and Gold Mine. The main hills to the left are granodiorite. The hills behind are more tonalite. El Chinero is a small dark-colored volcanic hill at the right end of the Pintas in the near distance. Years ago some Chinese immigrants were dropped off at San Felipe by an unscrupulous sea captain and told that Los Estados Unidos were just to the north. They walked until they got to this hill. Reportedly this is as far as they got before most of them died -- still a long way from the United States.

140.5   There is an interesting Pemex station which has old-style pumps. You have to pump the gas into the glass container on top, measure the amount, then drain it into your car. These were fairly common in some parts of Baja.

140   This is the junction of Highway 3 to Ensenada (195 Kilometers) and Tijuana (300 Kilometers). Turn to the left (west) and begin to cross the peninsula. At this point the impressive scarp of the Sierra San Pedro Martir and the peak of Picacho del Diablo are directly ahead. The Sierra Borrego hills are to the right; the Sierra San Felipe are the hills to the left. The Sierra Pintas are to the far right.

     The kilometer markers now decrease to Ensenada.

195   The crest of the Sierra San Pedro Martir (except for the peak of Picacho del Diablo) is very flat. The face of the range is actually a 3000 meter high scarp. Valle San Felipe in front is very close to sea level. The valley has over 2000 meters of alluvial fill making the offset on the fault in excess of 5000 meters (3 miles).

194   The highway makes several bends and heads directly toward Cerro El Borrego, the high peak of the Sierra San Felipe (just slightly to the right of the highway) which is a little granodiorite pluton. The lower grayer rocks to the right around it are prebatholithic carbonate sediments. The slightly lower hill to the left of Cerro El Borrego is also granodiorite. Running off to the north, the hills are a mixture of granodiorite, tonalite, and prebatholithic carbonates until, at about 3 o'clock, they become the Miocene volcanic rocks of the Sierra Pinta. The vegetation is largely the same. As in other parts of Baja, sometimes it seems like it is all Ocotillo, other times all Smoke Brush or Mesquite in the washes. It basically depends on what part of the slope they are on, what the substrate is, and at what angle the sun hits. It seems like the vegetation is constantly changing, but it is just dominance that is changing. In the spring this section of desert is ablaze with the yellow flowers of the Brittlebush.

186   The highway again follows the elevated fan with washes on either side that are about 10-20 Meters below the fan. This whole area has been uplifted slightly and the washes are now re-grading the fans to the new base level. Here and there the road drops down into one of these washes where the Mesquite and Smoke Trees become dominant with lesser Ocotillo and other scattered species. Burrobrush and Brittle-Bush are much more plentiful in the washes than up on the terrace. The Burrobrush and Brittle-Bush look very similar - like little gray rounded balls. There is also some Desert Holly which is an Atraplex. The really bright green plant along the road is Cheesebush. These are roadside opportunists, where there is a lot more runoff. They are not out in the regular

climax vegetation communities because they cannot compete very well. If they were there, they would be very small and not very noticeable. The hills have some Mesquite.

184   Pass through a series of low Miocene basalt hills.

181.3 The Laguna Armaga, a dry lake bed

179   Pass abreast of the Sierra San Felipe. There is a granodiorite hill to the right with a low skirt of metamorphic rocks around it. Notice the difference between the weathering characteristics of the Sierra San Felipe, which is very light, and the darker granodiorite cut by a number of small dikes which forms the low hills at about 2 o'clock. The highway begins to pass by and through a series of hills to the left which are part of the old Pliocene alluvial fan which has been largely removed by the present drainage and is being dissected as hills. In the Pliocene the top of these hills would have been the surface of the alluvial fan. Now the surface has been elevated and forms hills which are being dissected by the new stream drainages. In this desert terrain, you typically get severe erosion of older sediments which are then re-mixed into the newer sediments and washed down into the washes.

175.5 The oblique dirt road to the left leads to Valle San Felipe and Laguna Diablo.

173   Roadcut in Pliocene conglomeratic sediments. Out of the valley into the higher elevation there is more Ocotillo, Spanish Bayonette, Teddy Bear Cholla, Creosote (replacing Cheesebush as a roadside opportunist), Barrel Cactus, and Brittle-Bush. Brittle-Bush are the little rounded plants with distinctive large gray-green leaves and a bright yellow flower on a little stalk. The slight change in vegetation is due to the higher elevation where it is cooler and moister.

171   View south of Laguna Diablo and Valle San Felipe. Very thick Teddy Bear Cholla and Creosote form a very thick underbrush. Taller plants are Ocotillo and some Acacia.

168   Lots of Cheesebush. Tall dominants are Ocotillo, Acacia, and Yucca.

169   Granodiorite hills next to the road. These rocks exhibit a prominent fracture pattern and are spheroidally weathered. They are cut by a light colored dike swarm.

165.5 The hill to the left, Cerro Coyote, is capped by a small patch of basalt. There is another view down into Laguna Diablo and Valle San Felipe with the Sierra San Pedro Martir as a backdrop. Rancho Santa Clara is at the south end of the lake.

165   This turnoff goes to the Sierra San Pedro Martir. The Sierra San Felipe come right to the highway.

164   Good view of the Valle Santa Clara which is crossed by several branches of the Arroyo Taraiso which dissect the fan material that the highway is traveling across. There are good cross-sectional exposures of the uplifted, dissected pediments. Notice how very small the alluvial fans are on the face of the range. Their small size for such an elevated range, indicates very recent, very active faulting. Some of the fans to the south bear slight benches which were produced by faults cutting across the fans. At about 10 o'clock there are a series of dissected fans which have very obvious fault scarps on them. There is a change in vegetation. Annual grasses are replacing the roadside opportunists. On the floor of the playa lake there is a forest of Smoke Trees. Cheesebush is growing under the Smoke Trees. Cholla, Ocotillo, Creosote, Acacia with Mistletoe, Agave, Desert Mallow, tufted yellow grasses, and "living fences". Coyotes have been seen in this area.

160   View down the axis of the impressive graben of Valle San Felipe. Ahead the road will be entering San Matias pass. The hills to the right are metamorphics cut by tonalites. Most of the material to the left is the massive tonalite of the Sierra San Pedro Martir. Picacho del Diablo is still in view as the high peak to the left.

154   As the highway enters the San Matias pass there is a gray granodioritic hill on the right. The small brown hill in front is gneiss cut by numerous dikes. The highway will pass through a roadcut in this gneiss, which shows the series of dikes. The highway then enters Canon San Matias pass, proper, which is a very interesting low level pass through the range considering the impressive scarps on both sides and the fact that this is an at-grade pass. There is very little climbing, except what is needed to get up to the level of Valle Trinidad on the other side of the pass. As the highway enters Canon San Matias pass there is a whole series of what almost appear to be sheet dikes. There seem to be, at times, more dikes than any other rock. The south side of the pass is largely gneiss cut by the dikes and the north side of the pass is largely granodiorite, which is probably doing most of the cutting. There is some gneiss on both sides of the pass. There is a series of K/Ar dates here in the pass - too many to list. This pass seems to be at the end of the Agua Blanca Fault Zone which was crossed near Ensenada. This fault zone is rather wide with quite a bit of movement on it and the pass is a logical place for it to go through. It just seems to end here though. The rocks on both sides have been dated and mapped extensively and it appears as though the fault ends here or continues through the pass as a sub-crustal feature. Yet it is a very strong feature with literally tens of kilometers of offset as it reaches Ensenada.

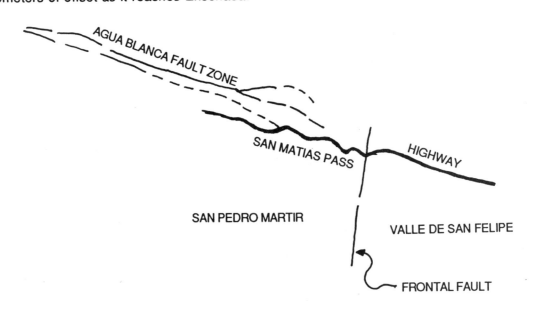

END OF AGUA BLANCA FAULT ZONE IN SAN MATIAS PASS

Cardons on hills, Mesquite, Palo Verde, Organpipe Cactus, Agave, Barrel Cactus, and low annuals.

155   View to the south down the Valle San Felipe.

153.5 Good stands of Cardons, Acacias on mountains, Ocotillo, Agave, Barrel Cactus, Cheesebush, Creosote. This area is similar to the area around Santa Rosalia.

Log 12 - San Felipe to Ensenada via Valle Trinidad

150.5 The roadcuts on the south side of the highway provide good exposures of the relationship between the metamorphic rocks, tonalites, and the dikes.

150 The vegetation is getting more dense. An elevation gain brings a cooler and moister habitat.

149 Dominant tall vegetation is Creosote with scattered Ocotillo. The north facing slopes have tall Ocotillo, Agave, Acacia, Creosote, Brittle-Bush, and Datilillo. The south facing slopes have Brittle-Bush, small Ocotillo, and other low species. There is Datilillo in the wash on the northern side of the highway.

148 Below the highway, in the wash on the right, is the old road through this pass. It actually was a high speed road in this area. There is a lot of Barrel Cactus in the pass.

146 The pass begins to open up and enter a wide flat alluviated area. One of the side valleys to the left is called Valle Picacho.

145 The Agua Blanca Fault Zone forms the north side of the pass. The impressively straight-faced tonalite hill that comes down in a very smooth slope is the fault scarp of the Agua Blanca Fault Zone which, here, shows a vertical component of normal movement.
The Valle San Matias. Datilillo, Yucca Valida, Creosote, Pencil Cholla, Acacia, some Mistletoe, Honey Mesquite (dominant - almost forest-like area).

143 A forest of Mesquite, loaded with beans. There is also a lot of Yucca. Flocks of pigeons.
A small patch of the basalt cap can be seen on the high hill at 3 o'clock.

141.5 The town of San Matias. Gasoline, restaurant. There are Marsh hawks in this area.

138.4 Road to Mike's Sky Ranch and the high Sierra San Pedro Martir. This road connects to the main highway Mexico 1D at San Telmo.

132 To the left there a swarm of dikes cutting the dark gray gneissic rocks. Ahead is the main area of Valle Trinidad. The hill to the right is basalt covering rhyolites and fluvial sediments. The lower parts of the hills are lahars and fluvial sediments. The upper part is basalt. Much of the geology is not obvious due to vegetational cover. In the far distance ahead beyond Valle Trinidad are the granitic and metamorphic rocks of the Peninsular Ranges Batholith.

127 The highway follows directly along what is mapped as one of the traces of the Agua Blanca Fault Zone. A second trace follows along the base of the hills to the right. As the road bends, it comes directly onto the line of the fault, then bends away again.

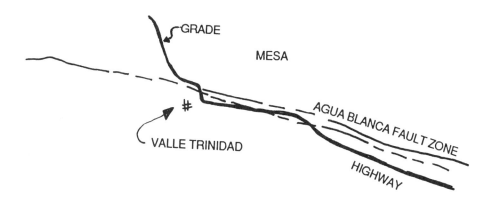

125 On the hillsides to the right are lots of Barrel Cactus up to a meter in height, all leaning to the southeast. The hills are covered with Beavertail Cactus and Opuncha which is a sign of overgrazed disturbed soils. There is also Jumping Cholla, Creosote, and Yucca growing among the Beavertail. Creosote grows very thickly in the washes.

123 Cross a big wash with Rabbit Brush.

122.5 Outskirts of Valle Trinidad.

121.3 Turnoff to Valle Trinidad on one of the traces of the Agua Blanca Fault Zone. The hills to the west are composed of gneisses and tonalite. The road cuts up a small valley to climb a grade from Valle Trinidad, and heads across the scarp onto the El Rodeo erosion surface. The road now travels through tonalite with a volcanic capping on the hill to the left.

119 The old road up this grade was extremely rough. Early Baja travelers who went down it were often unable to return, and had to go out through San Felipe. On the grade the layered nature of the tonalite is obvious. This is a mixed rock area with dikes cutting through tonalite. There are zenoliths in the tonalite and numerous faults and joints. There is a vegetation change here. Climbing the hill the Ocotillo drops out to be replaced by Manzanita, Toyon, Chemise, Oak trees, Rabbitbrush. It is a basic desert chapparal area. The bare areas have been burnt off.

118 The bare spots on the hills are the result of fires in the area.

114.5 Top of the grade. The view opens to the east of the high rhyolite capped mesas of this part of the ranges. Views of the flat erosion surface, with the mesas rising above them.

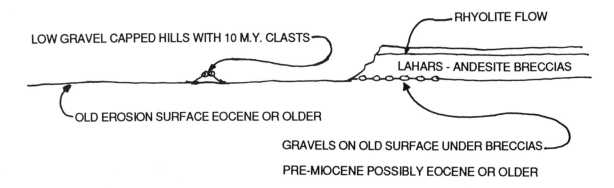

The pygmy coniferous forest is very short here. Most of the trees are under 3 Meters tall.

110 The road leaves a small hilly area and passes onto the El Rodeo erosion surface in an area of mixed gneisses with some tonalite. This impressive flat erosion surface was cut during the Eocene. To the west at about 1 o'clock the two low hills are capped by gravels. These were probably a stream course during the cutting of the erosion surface and now due to inverted relief, they exist as hills on the erosion surface. Since these gravels contain some of the 10 my old rhyolites, the streams must have been carrying the gravels sometime less than 10 million years ago. This gives a minimum rate of erosion of 100 ft./million years, or 1 mm/300 years, for this surface. On top of the erosion surface there is a change in the vegetation: Junipers and Purple Sage are now dominant. This area looks like a Pinyon/Juniper pygmy coniferous forest without the Pinyon Pines. There are also Acacia, narrow-leafed Yuccas (*Yucca angosteda*), Beavertail

Cactus on some of the disturbed soil along the road.

107   The gravel capped lava hill is part of an old rivel channel.
      On a clear day, there is a striking view to the north of the very flat El Rodeo erosion surface which climbs gradually into the high peaks of the Sierra Juarez. The mountains do not look very high from this vantage point yet they are quite steep and rugged in some places. The erosion surface was developed when this area was much closer to sea level. It has been elevated and tilted to the west.

106   View of the flat plain with the lava-capped mesas to the east, and the irregular tonalite and metamorphic hills to the west.

103   Ejido Reforma. There are Meadowlarks, Ravens, and House Finches in this area.

102   The highway is on the flat erosion surface. To the west the hills which seem to rise from the edge of this surface are the coastal range of metamorphic mountains. To the east is the ring of rhyolite and basalt capped lahars and mesas. The surface that the highway is built on is no longer covered by lahars.

99   Pinyon Pines now join the Junipers in the pygmy coniferous forest. This area used to be covered with Pinyon Pines and in some areas Ponderosa Pines. However, the gold mines of El Alamo consumed much of this forest for the charcoal to smelt the gold and timber to shore the mines.

97   The very low range of hills directly ahead represent a horst between a pair of faults that are at a right angle to the Agua Blanca Fault and seem to offset one of the branches of the Agua Blanca Fault Zone. The pond is developed as a result of the impounded drainage along the horst. There are Mockingbirds and scrub jays in this area. The two hills to the right are Cerro Cienega and Rancho Viejo.

96   The road crosses over this horst and into a little valley which is called Los Positos. The vista opens up to the east to the lava-capped mesas underlain by lahars These are impressive remnants of the basaltic field which covered most of this surface at one time.

93   Independencia - an urban zone with a number of buildings. The road east to Santa Catarina leaves from this town.

91   The low hills to the left are covered by Miocene volcanics, The road is running approximately along a normal fault scarp, with schist on the right and tonalite on the left.

89   Drop down into a broad, flat, alluviated valley of Llano Colorado. Below the main hill in the far distance to the left is the little (used to be huge) gold mining town of El Alamo. The main hill to the right of that hill (still to the left of the road) is gabbro.

86.4 This turnoff leads to El Alamo (the Cottonwood) (26 Km.)

83   After the turnoff to El Alamo the road climbs into an area of mixed granitic and metamorphic rocks. The rocks in the roadcuts are sheared, altered, and cut by numerous dikes. These dikes very typically contain sphene.
      The Llano Colorado has been disturbed by agricultural activities. As the highway leaves the Llano Colorado it rises up onto the terrace again which is vegetated with the pygmy coniferous forest. Rabbitbrush, Yucca, Agave, Pinyon Pines, Juniper, Laurel Sumac, Toyon, and Manzanita are typical species.

8 1   To the right is what appears to be a reasonably straight line of low hills. These hills mark the approximate trace of the San Miguel Fault Zone. In 1957 this fault zone was the location of a series of earthquakes. The road is still passing through schist. The boundary between the rocks which are predominantly schist and the tonalite rocks is in the near distance in the low hills ahead.

76.5   Locally the schistose nature of some of these rocks is very evident. The road leaves the flat surface and begins to descend into a valley.

7 6   Rabbitbrush covers this region with an occasional tall Pinyon Pine and small Junipers - some with Mistletoe.

74.5   Pino Solo area. This area was once covered by a pine forest. The need for timbers for shoring and for charcoal in the smelters at El Alamo caused the area to be almost entirely logged off. There was one lone large Ponderosa Pine left in this area (Pino Solo). It was a giant survivor of what was here before the extensive logging claimed most of the trees in the area. The road descends a valley through the tonalite.

7 4   The spring to the right along the road is at the end of a fault line. The Broom Baccharis once again becomes the predominant species.

72.3   The small conical peak Cerro Colorado comes into view to the left (1/2 Kilometer). It is a small red hill of tonalite which has weathered to a reddish color rather than the usual gray.

7 2   Cerro Colorado. The road to the left eventually reaches Santo Tomas, or makes a circuit through Escondido and and on to Ojos Negros. Numerous Quail, Mockingbirds and Scrub Jays are seen along the road from Pino Solo to here.

6 9   The highway crests a small rise and begins descending into a little valley. Straight ahead is the extremely flat crest of the Sierra Juarez. The fault which fronts the Sierra Juarez into Ojos Negros Valley forms the jagged slopes directly ahead. Descending from the level of that surface down into the Ojos Negros Valley. The vegetation consists of extensive stands of Broom Baccharis, Chemise, Purple Sage Brush, Willows, Manzanita, and low yellow flowered composites.

6 7   Descending through a small valley cut in the tonalite. Occasionally there is a glimpse, in the wash on the left of the old road. It is largely washed out, as it was developed in a wash. In the old days, this was a fine stretch of road because it was a long sandy and smooth wash which allowed traveling at a pretty good speed.
The road was lined with Broom Baccharis blocking any view of the road ahead. You would be traveling down the road at 30-40 mph, and meet someone who would be traveling up the road at a similar speed. At the last moment both of you would end up digging one wheel up out of the rut, touching a little brush, and passing each other with ease.

6 4   The darker hills without bouldery outcrops ahead and to the left are composed of gabbro.

6 2   San Salvador - a rancho dating back many years.

61.5   Along this stretch of highway there are several ranchos, and is a stretch of cottonwoods and sycamores planted for windbreaks and shade.

59   A running stream bordered by large willows crosses the road. This stream is from a spring which is along one of the faults in this area. It is a nice rest stop or camping area. There may be some superstition surrounding this area. Years ago when we tried to camp in this area some of the locals coming through spoke of spirits and ghosts and "bad blood". Sangre de Cristo is a little village near here and we weren't sure if they just didn't want us to camp there or whether they were really afraid. The topographic map indicates that there was a graveyard in this area which may be the reason they spoke of ghosts, etc.

55.3 The road to the right goes 35 Kilometers to Laguna Hansen.

55   The view opens to the coastal range called Cerro el Encino Solo (hill of the single oak), of metavolcanic and granitic foothills west of the fault and the very broad, flat, agricultural valley of Valle Ojos Negros. This valley is heavily alluviated and has extensive groundwater resources, but is not heavily irrigated or farmed.
      The valley is bounded on the west side by a series of steep fault scarps and on the east side by an obscure fault, which has little topographic expression. The low area of the valley itself is ahead.
      The low isolated hills ahead and to the right are metamorphics. To the right is the fault scarp and the high parts of the Sierra Juarez with its relatively concordant summits.

51   Riparian stream side community to the south of the road. There are many Cottonwoods with Mistletoe in them. The natural vegetation is mostly coastal scrub with Cat's Claw *Acacia*, Purple Sage Brush and lots of Mesquite. The vegetation is very sparse due to overgrazing.

49   The road passes out into Valle Ojos Negros.

48.6 A prominent granitic dike cuts across the road at the edge of a tonalite body. This flat area is Valle San Raphael which is extensively farmed on occasion depending on the season and the year. They grow a lot of barley which is destined to get into that familiar red can, Tecate Beer.
      Off to the right are the high parts of the Sierra Juarez, which are not quite as impressive here because they are a tilted fault range block with a very gentle western sloping erosion surface.
      The hills to the west of the valley are variously composed of tonalite and granitic schists and gneisses with some granodiorite forming very knobby outcrops.
      To the left ahead is the long linear scarp of one of the faults which forms the west side of the valley. The knobby appearing hill to the left ahead with all the boulders on it is a pod of granodiorite. Most of the rest of the hills are part of the prebatholithic gneiss (some schist) grading into what we call mixed plutonic rocks which are areas near the top of the batholith where the rocks are mixed together and it is difficult to discern or separate the boundaries.

40   The highway takes a little bend to the left and passes by some very low gneissic hills, the Cerro Eulalia, to the right front at about 2 o'clock. Cerro Eulalia is a series of truncated conical peaks.
      In the agricultural fields in this area the mesquite look more like trees than shrubs. This is because the cattle love to eat the green shoots, exposing the trunk more. There is also Mistletoe in the Mesquite. Olives are planted in this area.

39.5 The road to Ojos Negros is to the right. The road to Ensenada continues straight to cut across a corner of the old highway.
      The hill directly ahead in the little gap is granodiorite as are the other hills to the left of

the road. The hills, cut by white dikes, to the right of that are prebatholithic gneiss and mixed metamorphic and plutonic rocks.

Flocks of Starlings and House Finches are often seen here.

Black

The **European Starling** (*Sturus vulgaris*), like the Blackbird and Loggerhead Shrike, is a member of the Shrike family. The short-tailed Starlings are often confused with the unrelated, longer-tailed Blackbirds. Since their introduction into North America these gregarious, aggressive birds have become widespread and are commonly seen roosting in in Baja in a variety of habitats, including villages, agricultural fields, woodlands, telephone wires, fences, and open desert. Like the Gila Woodpecker, they nest in Cardons and other cacti. Because of their ubiquitous occurrence, Starlings are considered "weed birds" and can be real pests often damaging cultivated vegetables and fruit orchards. They even do damage around feedlots where they consume and foul the feed of domestic cattle. Two field characteristics making Starlings easily identifiable are their yellow bills and glossy purplish-greenish tinted black head.

37   The highway crosses the frontal fault of the range near where a diagonal fault offsets it. The erosion along the diagonal fault line probably accounts for the low pass that the road now goes through.

36   The large spheroidally weathered boulders indicate a general lack of or widely spaced jointing in the granodiorite, which yields big chunks of pinkish rock.

35.5   The hills to the right are gneisses extensively cut by light colored granitic dikes. The granodiorite is still on the left and comes up to the road at about Km 35.
       The hills are covered with typical overgrazed and burned off chaparral vegetation consisting of Buckwheat, Purple Sage Brush, and occasional Broom Baccharis and California Bays and Oaks in the stream bottoms.

34   Sharp curve. The roadcuts are on the contact between the granodiorite on one side and the gneisses on the other side.
       The road descends grade through a series of mixed rocks which appear to be mostly tonalite cut by prominent, light-colored, granitic dikes. Locally, there are outcrops of metamorphic rocks.

29   The road climbs through prebatholithic metavolcanic rocks. and then crosses a fault. Jimson Weed, the narcotic, poisonous, white bell shaped flowers, are commonly seen growing along the pavements edge from here to Ensenada.

26.2   Crest of the pass and a road to the left to Agua Caliente hot springs (7 Km) and the old San Carlos Hot Springs.
       The main road now descends various canyons and drainages to the coast at Ensenada.

25   To Km 24 there is a drastic change in the vegetation: An Oak woodland grows in the narrow valleys along the side of the road. Basically this is a riparian stream-side community with Willows, Toyon, large Scrub Oak, and lots of grasses. On the overgrazed hillsides the vegetation is characteristic of the desert coastal shrub community with Yuccas, Chemise, "Witches Hair", Yarrow, Purple Sage Brush, and Black Sage.

2 1   Climb out of Arroyo del Gallo and into a gabbro body with its typical subdued topography with very few outcrops.

2 0   Another pod of gabbro at a rancho.

1 9   The highway rejoins the old road.
        This area of tonalite is known as "Piedras Gordas" or "fat rocks", mainly because of the large, rounded tonalite, and locally granodiorite, boulders. For the next several kilometers the road will alternately pass through an area of mixed rocks consisting of gneisses and tonalites Generally the tonalites have the bouldery outcrops and the gneisses do not. Close to the coast the tonalites often weather to deep granitic soils because of the effects of moisture in the coastal weathering.

1 6   A grove of Olives with California Pepper Tree wind breaks grow on both sides of the road. This small community is growing the olives as a cash crop.

1 3   The road goes through a small pass for a view of the ocean, Bahia Todos Santos, Ensenada, and Islas de Todos Santos. As the road drops toward the coast, it passes through an area of tonalite which has been deeply weathered and is now covered by a rich soil.

1 1   The high hills to the right for the next kilometer are all prebatholithic volcanic rocks, as are the hills off to the left. The area near the road is a bowl in the less resistant tonalites.

9   Outcrops of tonalite.

6   The town ahead is the coastal port town of Ensenada.

3   Enter the main part of Ensenada.

0   Monument.

Log 13 - Tijuana to Mexicali [179 kms = 111 miles]

Tijuana to La Hechicera - The Baja Highway heads east from Tijuana on the elevated terraces of the Tijuana River with higher mesas of Tertiary marine sediments north of the river and faulted rolling hills of Eocene sediments to the south. The steep andesitic volcanic plug of Cerro Colorado dominates the north mesa. The Baja Highway climbs a metavolcanic hill to cross Presa Rodriguez at a narrows in the metavolcanic rocks. The Baja Highway then follows the marine and fluvial terraces on the south side of a gentle valley bounded by high rugged metavolcanic hills. The north side of the valley is a rolling terrace underlain by marine and fluvial sediments and dominated by steep, conical, Pliocene andesite plugs. The Baja Highway then crosses a belt of rugged, steep, metavolcanic hills and continues through steep bouldery granodiorite hills with numerous gabbro pods. It crosses over a railroad and through an area of steep tonalite hills, finally reaching Tecate.

East of Tecate the Baja Highway passes through steep hills of gabbro, follows a steep sided canyon between tonalite and granodiorite, and then through the granodiorite to emerge on a flat elevated erosion surface developed on tonalite. The Baja Highway travels for many kilometers across this surface with views to the north of the Laguna Mountains and to the south of flat gravel capped hills.

La Hechicera to Mexicali - The Baja Highway enters a relatively flat area of rolling gneiss and schist hills locally cut by pegmatites. Between El Condor and La Rumarosa, conglomerates capping hills are exposed on both sides of an alluviated valley. Isolated hills of marble in the rolling hills of granitic rocks are being mined on both sides of the Baja Highway near La Rumarosa.

The Baja Highway begins to descend the steep gulf escarpment and drop through bouldery outcrops of granodiorite and tonalite and then through gneiss and schist cut by dikes. At the base of the escarpment the Baja Highway crosses the frontal fault and descends the gentle alluvial fan to reach the rugged tonalite ridge of the Pinto Mountains. The Baja Highway then crosses a fault in a wash and climbs onto the uplifted older fan surface to continue its gentle descent on the fans toward Laguna Salada in view to the right. The Baja Highway crosses the active Laguna Salada Fault Zone and a low pass in the northern end of the Sierra de los Cucapas, a rugged complex area of granitics, metamorphics, and Tertiary sediments. Signal Mountain is the high rugged tonalite peak to the left. Then the Baja Highway descends more gentle fans to the fertile Colorado River Delta area of the Mexicali Valley.

179   Turn left (east) away from Mexico 1 which continues on to Ensenada. The highway leading eastward (Mexico 2) follows the Tijuana River drainage with Pleistocene terraces on either side. The terraces on the right (southwest) have been disrupted by faulting. Turn right at about the third or fourth monument, then left on Agua Caliente.

176   Greyhound dogs run daily at the Agua Caliente racetrack. This racetrack was built on the site of the Agua Caliente Hot Springs on the Agua Caliente Fault Zone.

        HOT SPRINGS: The highway proceeds southeastward for about 10 Kilometers paralleling the drainage of and traveling over the low river terraces of the Rio de las Palmas. The Rio de las Palmas roughly follows the path of the ancestral Las Palmas River that was Eocene in age. The high terraces on the left are part of the mesas which stretch from the San Diego area of Alta California into the eastern Tijuana region. They are made up of Pleistocene material underlain by Miocene and Pliocene sedimentary rock.

Log 13 - Tijuana to Mexicali

NOTE: Kilometer markings are few and far between along this stretch of the highway so watch for them carefully in order to keep up with this part of the log

175 The highway passes a monument in the center of the road which is a representation of the Aztec viaduct in Mexico City. There are a number of similar monuments in other places in Mexico.

At Tres Hermanas there is a 4-way pedestrian overpass - a rather unique site.

167 This is the first kilometer sign seen on Mexico 2 East since leaving Mexico 1.

166.5 The highway makes a bend and begins the climb up onto the metavolcanic hills. The red double-peaked mountain to the left is Cerro Colorado, a Pliocene andesite plug. This is one of a number of such plugs which stretch east toward Tecate. To the left of Cerro Colorado is the lower Cerro San Isidro, another Pliocene plug. The plug closest to the U.S. border is Cerro la Avena. Otay Mountain, part of the San Isidro Mountains, U.S., is the northernmost peak visible at this point.
The hills to the right, in the sediments of the La Mesa region, were deposited in the delta of a large Eocene river. The high hills to the left beyond the mesa are metavolcanic.

> **VOLCANIC PLUGS (OR NECKS)** are cylindrical masses of rock sealing the vents and conduits of volcanoes which become readily visible as the more erodible surrounding rock is eroded.

165.4 Here the highway crosses Presa (dam) Rodriguez, a concrete dam 1,935 feet long, that was built in a narrow gorge between metavolcanic hills. The metavolcanics are exposed along the road for the next several kilometers.
The turnout on the left, as you cross the dam, is a good place from which to view the chaparral vegetation and the dam. The vegetation in this area is very sparse and is typical chaparral species (*See* Tijuana log Km 14.8). The chaparral vegetation in this area consists of Black Sage, Chemise, low annuals, Cheesebush, Broom Baccharis, California Pepper Tree, and Buckwheat. After rain there may be lots of low green herbage growing on the normally bare metavolcanic soils of this area.

> **THE CALIFORNIA PHYTOGEOGRAPHIC REGION** dominates Baja Norte. In this area there are three vegetational areas which consist of the **Coniferous Forest** area, the **Pinon Juniper Woodland** area, and the **Chaparral** area. Each area is typically characterized and recognized by its association of dominant plant species known as indicator species. Each of these three areas and their dominant species will be discussed in detail as they are encountered along the highway.

164.6 The dry lake behind Presa Rodriguez is a reservoir supplying water for Tijuana. This reservoir is built along a possible fault line which probably is responsible for the alignment of the Tijuana River drainage. The low hills on the west bank of the reservoir are part of the Eocene sediments. The Eocene sediments are yellow on the bottom, sand-colored in the center, and darkest on the hill tops. Ahead to the right, the higher hills are metavolcanic. Nearly all of the rock in view ahead, as the highway makes the second bend on the dam, is metavolcanic.

164 Cerro las Abejas is the sharp triangular shaped volcanic plug on the left. The white flat region west of Cerro las Abejas is called Lomas Blancas.

163.5 The left fork in the highway returns to Tijuana on the north side of the Rio. Stay to the right to continue eastward to Mexicali.

162 There is a large olive orchard extending back onto the northeast side of the Cerro las Abejas, up the valley, and to the right toward Las Labuelas and Dos Palmas.

161.5 The two andesite plugs visible to the left (north) are Cerro Colorado and Cerro las Abejas. The highway is following a poorly defined valley in terrace material with metavolcanic rocks on the right and a terrace developed on Eocene? and Pliocene sediments to the left.

161 The highway passes through a small pod of granitic rocks.
There are extensive groves of introduced European olives on both sides of the highway which extend into the foothills.

160.2 This roadcut exposes Pliocene sediments.

160 Numerous dairy farms and extensive olive groves are seen along this stretch of the highway because dairy cattle and olives are the primary commercial products of this area.

OLIVES (*Olea europaea*) are Old World semi-tropical evergreen trees having an edible fruit, yellow flowers, and leathery leaves. They were introduced to Mexico because the small ovoid fruit of this tree has been an important food from the earliest historical times and as a source of olive oil. Olive oil is pressed from olives for use in salad dressings, for cooking, as an ingredient of soaps, and as an emollient. Olives are grown, consumed locally, sold throughout Baja, and exported.

157.9 The grand residence marked by two large wrought iron gates, on the left side of the highway belonged to Miguel Aleman, a former president of Mexico.
The high hills to the right are metavolcanic.

156 The low rolling hills to the left are middle Tertiary sediments.

153 The conical peak (Cerro La Posta) in front on the right is another andesite plug with Tertiary terraces developed on its sides. Prebatholithic metavolcanics are now exposed on both sides of the road. The high hills to the right are composed of prebatholithic metavolcanic and metasedimentary rocks.
The vegetation covering the hills in this region are typical, low chaparral species dominated by Sagebrush, Wild Buckwheat, Black Sage, White Sage, and various low annual herbage. Along the highway there are a number of rock planters planted with decorative California Pepper Trees. The fruit of this tree does produce a pepper that could be used as a seasoning but the pepper used as a seasoning food is most often derived from dried, ground berries of the wood vine *Piper nigrum*.

152 The level of the high terrace ahead to the left is the same as that of the andesite plug mentioned above (Km 153).

150 A marcadum ("asphalt") plant is located on the right side of the highway.

MARCADUM: Asphalt (or mineral pitch) is a brownish-black **solid** or semi-solid mixture of bitumens (hydrocarbons obtained by distillation from coal or petroleum) obtained from native deposits or as a petroleum byproduct, used in paving, roofing, and waterproofing. Asphalt is used in the U.S.A. for paving highways. In Baja, Marcadum is usually used as a paving material instead of asphalt. Marcadum is a naturally occurring **liquid** petroleum hydrocarbon used for paving, roofing, and waterproofing.

148   The vegetation growing in this wash are those typical of riparian stream side floral communities. The predominant large plants of the wash are Broom Baccharis, Mesquite, and Tamarisk. The Tamarisk is an introduced European species which has become naturalized in North America.

THE VEGETATION OF RIPARIAN HABITATS: In Baja the plant community (or floral association) of riparian habitats is composed of those mesic species (moisture loving) that occur along drainage ways and associated floodplains that differ from the species inhabiting the surrounding arid peninsular desert.

Two types of riparian habitats exist in Baja: "subtle" and "obvious".
The **subtle riparian habitat** is represented by small rills, perhaps no more than two inches deep, along which plants are arrayed in lines that follow these tiny drainages. For example in the San Felipe Desert, Creosote Bush and Purple Bush appear to grow in straight lines on alluvial fans. This is no illusion; they are because they are following the rills where water is more frequently found. However, most of Baja's riparian habitats are more obvious.

Obvious riparian habitats develop along major watercourses where a stream channel or wash and two well-developed terraces parallel the water channel of the stream, river, or wash. On the first terrace trees such as willows and cottonwoods grow close to the water. The second terrace is a zone most often occupied by Mesquite that form a dense thicket or thorn forest. The roots of the Mesquites stabilize the banks of the second terrace with their deep roots and accumulate silt and organic matter.

143   The highway enters an area of mixed granitic rocks and darker diorite cut by dikes with masses of bouldery tonalite on the hills.
The vegetation is once again typical of the chaparral.

Notice the **crosses** with flower offerings located frequently along the highway shoulders. They are monuments erected in places where people have been killed in car accidents. These commemorative markers occur throughout the peninsula, especially along dangerous (Peligroso!) stretches of the highway.

Be especially watchful for cattle and game on the highways. Also keep in mind that many Mexican people drive at dusk without headlights or possibly only with their parking lights on.

141.5 The curious nondescript walls and towers along the ridgeline to the left are part of a prison.

141   In addition to the olive orchards, notice the extensive grape vineyards growing at Huerfanito.

Log 13 - Tijuana to Mexicali

A BERRY: Some members of the grape family (*F. Vitaceae*) are edible and are good thirst quenchers. Numerous wild and cultivated species of the genus *Vitus* occur in both of the Californias. In Baja, some grape species have long been cultivated for their berry. The berry of the grape, a many seeded fleshy fruit, has been used to make wines, grape juice, jellies, preserves, and for eating whole, since the earliest mission days. Wild species of native grapes occur in riparian and oak woodland habitats throughout the peninsula.

140.6 The highway crosses over the railroad tracks of the Tijuana and Tecate Railroad (beltline) near Los Lauelas. It used to be called the San Diego and Arizona Eastern Railroad (S.D. & A.E.). A trestle was washed out in Carrizo Gorge near Jacumba in the late 1970's and has been out of service ever since. The San Diego part of the line is now the Tijuana Trolley.

139 The highway now passes through granodiorite into tonalite. The clay pits of the tile and brick operations of Tecate have been developed in the gabbro soils of this area. Around the town of Tecate numerous brick kilns produce piles of Tecate's famous bricks which are for sale. In Tecate ceramic tiles can be "made-to-order" for a very reasonable price.

136.5 Introduced California Peppers and native Oaks grow together in this area. California Pepper Trees which were planted ornamentally in this region have escaped and become naturalized. Notice that all of the oaks are "flat-bottomed".

> **WHY ARE THE BOTTOMS OF THE OAK TREES FLAT?** Cattle love to browse the oak foliage and so the trees are "pruned" as high as their necks can reach resulting in "flat-bottomed" trees. Trees growing where cattle do not browse are shaggy bottomed with foliage reaching nearly to the ground.

136 The Rancho La Puerta, on the left, is a famous resort and spa specializing in natural vegetarian foods, sports, exercise classes, massage, and much more.
The large boulders of this area are composed of tonalite.
The vista ahead is of the town of Tecate occupying the center of a bowl-shaped valley. The main features of the valley are the white tower with the red "Carta Blanca" sign and the red and white "Tecate Beer" sign. East of the town the small dark-colored nob with no outcrops (Cerro la Panocha - *See* Km 129) and the unnamed high hill on the right side of the valley (south of town) are gabbro bodies. The high hill to the left with roadcuts in it is Tecate Peak which is on the U.S. side of the border in the San Isidro Mountains.

133 **TECATE:** The small town of Tecate (elevation 1,690') is located in a bowl-shaped valley surrounded by tonalite boulder covered hills. Tecate was established in the 19th century as an agricultural center because of its abundant water and fertile soil. Although home to both the Carta Blanca and Tecate beer breweries, agriculture remains the mainstay of Tecate's economy. The primary crops produced here are grapes, grain, and olives.
The zocolo ("village square") in Tecate is shaded by beautiful old palm and Box Elder (*Acer negundo*) Trees. It is a nice place for a picnic lunch.

131.5 Just east of downtown Tecate is the intersection of Mexico 2 (Avenida Juarez) and Mexico 3 (Calle Ortiz Rubio). Mexico 3 heads southwestward 107 Kilometers and connects with Mexico 1D on the Pacific coast at El Sauzal, 1.5 Kilometers southeast of

Log 13 - Tijuana to Mexicali

San Miguel. Highway 2 continues eastward and crosses over the tracks of the old San Diego and Arizona Eastern Railroad east of Tecate. The highway then follows the railroad eastward up a canyon.

129   Cerro la Panocha is the small round, gabbro hill that looks like the raw brown sugar (panocha) cones produced as the syrup of sugar cane is poured into hollowed-out, cone-shaped forms. Cerro la Panocha straddles the International border - its north slope is in the U.S. and its south slope is in Baja.

128   The highway follows a gabbro body on the left. The bouldery hills to the right are granodiorite. Granodiorite has weathered into the bouldery hills in this part of the Peninsular Ranges. To the left of the highway is typical riparian vegetation.

123   The railroad tracks of the S.D. & A.E. can be seen, across the valley to the left, running along the hills. Occasionally they are hidden from view by the vegetation and by the roadcuts. The tracks turn left and head north across the U.S. border toward Arizona.

120   This is the small town of San Pablo. Directly ahead to the left of the highway is the Cerro la Rosa de Castilla.

119.5 The vegetation of this area is typical of the chaparral plant community and is predominated by sages and Buckwheat.

119   The Rancho Rosa de Castilla is located in a beautiful oak woodland area.
For the next 6 Kilometers the highway passes in and out of several oak woodland valleys.

OAK WOODLANDS The three most common oaks of Baja Norte are Coast Live Oak (*Quercus agrifolia*), Scrub Oak (*Q. dumosa*), and Canyon Oak (*Q. chrysolepis*). These three oaks can be identified by studying the following chart.

characteristics	Q. agrifolia	Q. dumosa	Q. chrysolepis
evergreen	yes	yes	yes
height	10-25 m	5 m	6-20 m
growth habit	large, broad-crowned trees	shrub often forming dense thickets	large tree forming oak woodlands below 2000 Meters
usual habitat	below 3,000 feet in coastal valleys and foothills bordering chaparral in open grasslands	in chaparral communities	in canyons, on moist north facing slopes, and in chaparral
leaf	shiny, dark green,	shiny, gray-green,	oblong or ovoid, bluish-
morphology	oval upper surface; hairy at vein on undersides of leaf; leaf margin toothed; up to 6cm long	curled leaves; under surface covered with brownish hairs; leaf margin toothed; 1-3cm long	green above; covered with a yellow or silver powder below; leaf margins toothed; 2-6cm long
acorn	slender; pointed; 2.5-3.5 cm long		oblong-ovoid with turban-shaped cups; 2-6cm long
bark	gray with broad checked ridges		smooth to scaly gray

199

Oak woodlands are in danger of extinction in both Californias wherever livestock are pastured because sheep and cattle eat young seedlings before they can grow to mature trees. Therefore, when the old, mature oaks die, oaks will disappear from grazing areas. Urban development also significantly reduces the acreages of oak woodlands.

118.5 The massive granodiorite cliff ahead is locally referred to as Cerro Rosa de Castilla. With a little imagination it looks something like Half Dome in Yosemite Valley.

118 Another beautiful oak woodland is growing in this low valley. Large poplars have been planted alongside the highway.

117.5 The hills are covered with bouldery outcrops and true chaparral vegetation.

117 The highway passes through a series of broad flat valleys in the granodiorite.

115 The mountain directly behind the small Rancho San Valentin is Cerro San Valentin.

114 In the grape vineyards of this region of Baja, the farmers do not have smudge pots. Instead they keep stacks of old tires around and when temperatures drop to dangerous lows the tires are burned to keep the grapes from freezing. This practice does wonders for the air quality.

113 The highway passes by stands of oaks which have been trimmed to make windbreaks for the vineyards. More smudging tires can be seen stacked around the vineyards.

111 The highway climbs a long grade through diorite outcrops cut by numerous light-colored granitic dikes. For the next several kilometers the highway passes through the metamorphic rocks of the Julian schist which are also cut by quartz dikes.

110 As the highway travels across a Cretaceous erosional surface, the dominant plant species is Broom Baccharis which is growing in almost pure stands. Broom Baccharis received its name because early residents of Baja often bound bunches of stems and foliage into disposable, make-shift, but highly effective, cheap brooms.

109 As the highway reaches the top of a long grade it begins to cross a broad flat erosion surface developed on the La Posta quartz diorite.

> **EROSION SURFACES**: This surface was developed during the late Cretaceous and Early Tertiary when this area was closer to base level. It is the effect of prolonged weathering in a more humid climate. The flat-even topped hills on the skyline to the southeast are capped with Eocene gravels. These gravels were deposited by a large river which flowed across this area during the Eocene. The source of this river was near Nogales in South-Central Arizona, U.S.A. It flowed across the area of the Gulf of California which did not exist at that time. The delta of this Eocene river is in the Tijuana area.
> When streams are near their base level they cannot erode downward. Instead they cut laterally and tend to form a flat plane near base level. If this surface is not uplifted it will remain a flat surface. This surface has been lowered as a unit by the low-powered streams. The gravels were not removed and, thus, become resistant ridges above the surface.

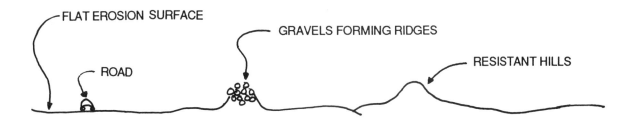

FLAT EROSION SURFACE

GRAVELS FORMING RIDGES

ROAD

RESISTANT HILLS

107   Bulls are being raised at Rancho las Juanitas for bullfights in Tijuana.

105.5 This turnoff leads southward to El Compadre and Valle Ojos Negros ("black eyes") and meets Mexico 3 at Km 55.3.

104.5 This side road leads to Rancho Jacomun. The highway has passed through another oak woodland. In this area it is possible to see the pipe which brings water for irrigation to this region of Baja Norte, via an aqueduct, from the Colorado River.

103   There are large boulders covered with lichen here. Lichens are lower plants made up of single-celled algae living inside the tissues of a fungus. These two plants live in a mutualistic symbiotic relationship in which both benefit. Organic acids secreted by lichens degrade rock into soil preparing the way for the establishment of higher plant forms - a process known as plant succession.
Red-stemmed buckwheats are growing in the disturbed soils along the highway shoulders. The seeds of buckwheats were ground into a meal and baked into cakes or made into a mush by native Baja Indians.

100   There is a large bend in the highway as it turns to the south and passes through the small village of Hechicera.

99.5   To the right of the highway is a road metal quarry. The term "road metal" comes from an abbreviation of "road material" (road mat'l).

98.5   The small village of Luis Echeverria Alvarez (El Hango) is located to the right of the highway.

97.5   The gray bank low on the hills to the left is a rock quarry in the La Posta quartz diorite.

97   The distant Laguna Mountains of San Diego County can be seen from here. Their flat concordant summits are part of the same erosion surface at about 1200 Meters higher elevation. By a round about route, the Laguna erosion surface descends gradually to the level of the surface near the road.

93   The stringers of white boulders exposed in the hills for the next 4 miles are weathered Pegmatite dikes.

89   This is a good turnout to view the vegetation of this region such as Broom Baccharis with Laurel Sumac, and Black and White Sage. Scrub Jays may also be seen in the area.

87   The flat-lying pegmatite dikes on the hill, under the power lines, have yielded gem Topaz, Beryl, Garnet, Tourmaline, and Smokey Quartz crystals. Pegmatite dikes such as this one are abundant in San Diego County. Here the highway passes through exposures of thinly-bedded prebatholithic gneisses and schists assigned to the Julian Schist. These metamorphic rocks are probably Paleozoic in age and represent the remnants of the

rocks into which the granitic rocks and pegmatite dikes were intruded.

83.5   Good examples of Julian schist are exposed in this roadcut.

82.8   This turnoff leads to the small settlement of El Condor located on the general level of the high erosion surface. The road south from El Condor connects up with the main La Rumarosa-Laguna Hansen road after about 15 Kilometers. This was used as a cut-off by early Baja travelers heading to Laguna Hansen in the Sierra Juarez.
        The hills ahead to the left and to the right in the middle distance are covered with Eocene river gravels discussed at Kilometer 109.

81   Just east of El Condor the highway enters a Pinyon-Juniper coniferous forest. Scrub Oak, Broom Baccharis, Chemise, Yucca, Black Sage, and White Sage also grow in association with this coniferous forest. Ravens may be seen in this area.

THE PYGMY-CONIFEROUS FOREST: In Northern Baja the California Juniper (*Juniperus californica*) is often associated with the desert mountain Pinyon Pine (*Pinus quadrifolia* and/or *P. monophylla*). This association forms the Pinyon-Juniper community, which because of the short trunks is commonly called the "pygmy" coniferous forest.

The leaves of Junipers have been reduced, by natural selection to reduce water loss, to bright green, imbricated (overlapping like tiles of a roof) scales that closely clothe the smaller branches. They are coated with a waxy cuticle that helps keep moisture in. Another adaptation reducing water loss are the small, dry, berry-like fruits with their protective waxy bloom. The shaggy ash-gray bark provides insulation from the desert heat, keeping tissue temperatures down, another water-conserving adaptation.

The Pinyon Pine grows taller than the Juniper. The leaf stoma of the Pinyon are found in the bottom of pits in the needles, reducing water loss. The pits appear as small white stripes on the needles. The Pinyon has a fungus growing on its host's roots (a mycorhizzal mutualistic association). The fungal symbiont provides water for the tree and protects the roots from disease; the host Pinyon provides sugar for the non-photosynthetic fungus which cannot produce its own.

A walk into this pygmy forest will quickly reveal the identity of Pinyon pine and the Juniper. Both Pinyon pines and junipers have been and are still useful to man and animals in Baja. People still collect the protein rich seeds, or Pinyon nuts for food. Many of Baja's birds, rodents, deer, and antelope also rely on the Pinyon nuts for food. The nuts are produced on the sporophylls (seed leaves) of the large female pine cones. Male cones are very small, producing only pollen.

Junipers provided useful products for early native Indians of Baja who chewed the sap like a gum, ate the berry-like fruits (really cones) drying or grinding them into a meal to make into a gruel (mush) or cake. They even made a soup from the nuts to give to babies.

Today, the wood of the Juniper is primarily used to make fence posts in Baja where they grow. In other countries the cones of *Juniperus communis* are soaked in alcohol to leach the oils from the seeds and cone tissues which are used to give gin its characteristic flavor.

Both the Juniper and Pinyon Pine are especially plentiful on the dry slopes of the Sierra Juarez and Sierra San Pedro Martir below 5,000 feet in the Upper Sonoran Life Zone. Overgrazing in northern Baja is allowing them to increase in abundance and extend their domain into places formerly occupied by grasses thus reducing the available range land and necessitating increased use of cultivated forage and fodder. While reducing range lands, their increase is helping native hoofed-browsers like Deer and Antelope which feed on the twigs and foliage of both conifers. In addition to their wildlife food value, they also provide important protective and nesting cover for numerous bird species in Baja Norte like Robins, Sparrows, Mockingbirds, and Warblers.

76.5   The hills on both sides of the road are composed of conglomeratic Eocene river gravels. 30 Meters east of the 76 Kilometer mark there is a dirt road to the left which can be followed for 200 Meters northward to exposures of the Eocene conglomerates. These conglomerates are poor in the usually present exotic meta-rhyolites due to the mixing with materials of another Eocene stream which contained no meta-rhyolite clasts. The highway is sitting on a metamorphic schist and gneiss basement at this point.

73   Marble quarried from the roadside road metal quarry on the hill to the left and others in the area is used as decorative rock and to make cement. Several small caves decorated with stalactites have been found in the marble. This is of some concern to the miners as empty caves reduce their estimated marble reserves.
        The microwave tower Microondes la Rumarosa is located to the left of the highway.
        The thick Pinyon-Juniper forest growing in this region is made quite scenic by granodiorite bouldery outcrops. This area is reminiscent of the Catavina boulder fields (*See* Km 153.5 of the San Quintin log) except the boulders here are smaller and more numerous.

72   The conglomerate exposures north of here can be reached by taking the dirt road opposite the Laguna Hansen road 1 1/2 miles to the north. As expected, the gravels there contain more exotic meta-rhyolite clasts since the junction of the Eocene streams is located west of here. These exotic meta-rhyolite clasts have their source area in the Canelo Hills east of Nogales, Arizona. The turnoff for Laguna Hansen and Parque Nacional Constitucion de 1857 is about 200 meters east of this kilometer mark.

67.5   La Rumarosa is a popular summer resort for residents of Mexicali. The fault scarp which is much steeper and more evident to the south is not as steep here due to exposures of the more easily eroded schists. A dirt road leads southeastward from La Rumarosa, into the Sierra Juarez, to the Parque Nacional Constitucion 1857 and the Laguna Hanson (Laguna Juarez).

        Upon leaving La Rumarosa, the highway begins its steep, winding drop down the Cuesta la Rumarosa into the desert along the eastern gulf drainage of the Sierra de Juarez. The rocks exposed at the top of the grade are granodiorite. Further down the grade tonalites and finally schists are exposed.

65   The highway crosses through a picturesque area of spheroidally weathering granodiorite. (*See* San Quintin log at Km 94.) This descent of the Cuesta La Rumarosa, often called Cantu Grade, is the steepest and most dangerous paved road in all of Baja. Notice that the flat westward sloping erosion surface stretches to the crest of the range. Here the steeper gradient Gulf streams are rapidly cutting eastward into the scarp.
        On the slopes of the eastern drainage of the Sierra Juarez, the granodiorite boulders are intermixed with beautiful Pinyon Pines, Junipers, Manzanita, White and Black Sage.

62   There is a beautiful view to the left into a bouldery valley with a small stream. The pipe with two green surge towers is part of the pipeline bringing water from the Colorado River to Tijuana.
        The desert to the northwest in the U.S.A. is called the Yuha Desert. In the far distance West Mesa is visible.
        Directly to the left, just barely beyond the edge of the hills is the U.S.A. town of Ocotillo. To the right of Ocotillo, in the far distance, the Salton Sea is visible. Further to the

right the white spot in the nearer distance is Plaster City. Gypsum mined from Split Mountain in the U.S. is hauled to Plaster City via the railroad where it is processed into wall board primarily used in residential construction. This railroad is part of the San Diego and Arizona Eastern Railroad. Although this railroad is still utilized in the Imperial Valley, U.S.A., it no longer goes up the grade.

Just barely in view to the right is Signal Mountain or Cerro la Centinela, a high peak in the Sierra Cucapa. The hills in the far distance, northeast of Split Mountain in the U.S.A., are the Chocolate Mountains.

The viewpoint just past La Rumarosa offers a beautiful view of the San Felipe Desert in the Valle los Alamos which extends to the northeast.

61.5   This turnout on the edge of the granodiorite pluton offers a good view of the San Felipe Desert. The viewpoint itself is in the northern part of the Sierra Juarez. There are several other turnouts all of which offer a good view.

60.5   The green towers are surge towers of a pumping station on the aqueduct transporting water to Tijuana from the Colorado River.

59.5   Laguna Salada has come into view for the first time.

58.5   A dark gray to black basalt dike cuts the granodiorite in this roadcut.

57   As the highway comes around a corner a bedrock landslide is visible at Km. 56.8.

56.7   The buildings on the ridge to the left are part of one of the pumping plants for the water pipeline that pumps water up and over the Sierra Juarez westward to Tijuana. The green surge towers release the air that gets trapped in the water preventing large air bubbles from building up and blocking the movement of the water as it descends along the western slopes of the Sierra Juarez.

55   As the highway nears the bottom of the Cuesta la Rumarosa grade, in view to the left are Laguna Salada (foreground), Cerro Colorado (the dark linear ridge in the middle-ground), and the Sierra Cucapas with Cerro la Centinela (background).

Cerro Colorado is composed of granitics that are covered with a dark-colored desert varnish.

The Sierra Cucapa are a lighter reddish-brown and lie in the background on the far side of Laguna Salada. They are also covered by a patina of desert varnish but not as darkly as the surface of Cerro Colorado.

DESERT VARNISH: A minor weathering feature of the desert is a thin, shiny, reddish-brown to blackish coating called desert varnish that occurs on some desert rocks. This shiny blackish-brown stain is only one or two micrometers thick and appears to be an amorphous gel, rich in silica and alumina that takes its color from unusually high concentrations of iron and manganese. The chemicals of the varnish originated from atmospheric dust, the stones themselves, and underlying soil and chemicals dissolved in films of moisture formed on rock surfaces by rain, fog, or morning dew.

As moisture evaporates from warming rock surfaces it leaves ions of the dissolved chemicals behind as a coating that gradually builds up over hundreds of years, increasing the thickness of the varnish. The rate of varnish formation is extremely slow. Desert varnish occurs on the upper surfaces of rocks on alluvial fans and the mosaic pebbles of desert pavement. Similar stains are widely found around seeps, especially as dripping, large, black streaks on canyon walls. The undersides of many varnished rocks are orange (iron rich) while only their sides and tops are blackish-brown (manganese rich). Since iron is less soluble than manganese it is left behind under the rocks as the more soluble manganese is drawn upward to concentrate on the exposed sides and upper exposed surfaces.

53   The highway passes through predominantly metamorphic gneiss and schist of the Julian Schist with granodiorites and tonalites mixed in here and there.

The hills of this area are vegetated with Yucca, Teddy Bear Cholla, very low and scraggly-looking, sparse Palo Verde and Ocotillo. This area is a good place to observe vegetational differences between north and south facing slopes.

> **NORTH AND SOUTH FACING SLOPES**: Slopes facing south receive more solar radiation throughout the year and are hotter and drier, and their soils have weathered more. South facing slopes consequently support only short, sparse desert types of vegetation in Baja.
> Baja's cooler and moister north facing slopes receive less solar radiation and support taller plants that grow more densely because of the more mesic conditions.

49.7   A prominent pegmatitic granitic dike cuts the metamorphic rocks in the roadcut on the left.

48   To the right the Rio Agua Grande runs through the Canon los Llanos. The bottom of the canyon is a broad stream meander. There is some running water as evidenced by the row of vegetation following the meander. The flora of this area is typical of a Wash Woodland vegetated by Willows, Stinging Nettle, *Acacia*, and Creosote Bush.

46   This is a good place to observe Cat's-Claw Acacia and Creosote Bush growing on the left side of the road.

45   The extreme aridity of this area gives the impression of passing through a barren, dry, lifeless desertscape. However, Brittle-Bush and the southward leaning barrel cactus grow densely in this area.
Specimens of *Pachycormus discolor*, the Elephant Tree, grow here and extend northward into the Anza-Borrego Desert in the U.S.

44   This is a good turnout for viewing the vegetation of the eastern drainage of the Sierra Juarez. Creosote Bush, Bursage, Palo Verde, Tamarisk, Cat's Claw *Acacia* and Ocotillo are all visible.

43.5   The highway crosses the Rio Agua Grande. It is possible to hike up the Rio Agua Grande to the Canon los Llanos to observe the flora of the wash woodland. The predominant trees growing along the Rio Agua Grande are Smoke Trees and *Acacia* parasitized by mistletoe. Both trees are characteristic and indicator species of Wash Woodlands.

> **WASH WOODLANDS**: Because of the limitations of water supply in the area occupied by Creosote Bush and Bursage, the water courses (washes or arroyos in Baja), which are dry most of the year, support a characteristic flora that takes advantage of the relatively abundant supply of water during rainy periods of the winter in Baja Norte. Some botanists recognize the region of a wash and its characteristic flora as a Wash Woodland, a separate plant community not belonging to the surrounding arid Creosote Bush Scrub plant community. In Baja's deserts the flora of the Wash Woodland is dominated by Palo Verde, Smoke

Log 13 - Tijuana to Mexicali

Tree, Cat's-Claw *Acacia*, and Mesquite.
The seeds of many Wash Woodland species are covered by a very hard (sclerophyllous) seed coat (integument) and will not germinate no matter how long the seed is soaked in water unless the seed coat is broken (scratched through) by a process called scarification. That is, it is necessary to scratch the seed coat, allowing water to enter the seed and initiate seed germination. Scarification (breaking the seed coat) is accomplished by the grinding action of sand and rocks in the flash floods occurring periodically in the washes in Baja Norte that also provides the germinating seedlings with abundant water which will supply their growth requirements during the first few weeks of germination. Flash floods also serve to dispense the seeds. Like many desert perennials, seedlings of Wash Woodland trees produce only two or three leaves immediately after germination and seemingly become dormant. However, these plants are far from dormant during this time but are devoting their chief energies to developing extensive, deep root system that will enable then to survive long after the moisture from the infrequent flash floods of this region have dissipated. Plants developing deep root systems enabling them to tap underground water sources are known as phreatophytes (phreato = well; phyte = plant).

43 Here the highway begins to cross numerous alluvial fans developed along the eastern escarpment of the Sierra Juarez.

42 The highway descends an alluvial fan surface developed from the base of the Sierra Juarez.
The vegetation growing on the alluvial fan surface consists mainly of Ocotillo, Brittle-Bush, Cholla, and Creosote Bush.

37 The highway crosses another of the meanders of Rio Agua Grande developed along a fault and climbs onto an elevated fan surface. This fault attests to the fault activity which continues today in the Imperial Valley and along the northern Gulf of California. The dark, desert varnished hills to the north along the fault are locally referred to as the Pinto Mountains. This area has long been a popular collecting area for the colorful "Pinto Mountain Rhyolite" and petrified wood which is often polished by the wind. Be careful not to stray across the border if you explore this area. The road to the south skirts the foot of the Sierra de Juarez and eventually reaches a beautiful palm oasis at Canon Virgin de Guadalupe (a better road to this area is located further east at Km 27.5). The *Acacia* in this vicinity are confined to the washes since their seeds must be scarified by sand carried in running water (*See* Km 43.5 above).

34 The prominent peak to the left ahead is Signal Mountain (Cerro la Centinela), a high granitic peak at the north end of the Sierra Cucapa. The low hills to the left consist mostly of Tertiary sediments uplifted along the active Laguna Salada Fault Zone.

30 The view to the rear is of the impressive eastern granitic scarp of the Sierra Juarez.

27.5 The road to the right goes down the Laguna Salada to Canada Cantu de las Palmas and Canon Virgin de Guadalupe. Laguna Salada has had considerable amounts of water in it in recent years. It is also supertidal at the south end and connects with the Gulf of California during very wet periods (*See* Km 73 of the Mexicali to San Felipe log). The Laguna Salada Fault Zone passes close to this junction.
As the highway leaves the Laguna Salada area the vegetation changes. The ground has become very rocky and the gray vegetation consists of *Acacia*, Bursage, an occasional Creosote Bush, and Cheesebush growing in the disturbed soils along the power line.

Log 13 - Tijuana to Mexicali

25.5 To the left a large dune has developed in the lee of one of the nearby hills. The stabilized dunes is called El Oasis. A Pemex station is located at the village of El Oasis. However, it may not always have fuel available for sale.

The dirt road to the right leads down to El Centinela campground located on the muddy beach of Laguna Salada. The trees on this beach were underwater at one time as evidenced by their barnacle encusted trunks. Barnacles can be seen as high as 3.5 Meters off the ground. Both the water and the soils of the laguna are very salty. Salt crystals "growing" on the surface of the shore soils are formed by efflorescence as the salt-laden water evaporates. This beach is very muddy and the laguna is shallow but despite this it is quite a scenic region.

The vegetation on the east side of the road to the beach is typical of the San Felipe Desert with Creosote Bush and Bursage dominating.

23 The highway makes a sharp bend and winds its way up through a small pass which marks a small fault and a horst of metamorphic rocks.

The hill in front is highly desert varnished.

As the road turns to the right, the vertical striations on a fault plane are visible ahead at road level.

Adjacent to the highway the vegetation consists of numerous tall *Acacia*, smaller Smoke Trees, Creosote Bush, Bursage, and scattered Tamarisk trees.

20 The highway now descends east-sloping alluvial fans into the fertile Mexicali Valley, one of Mexico's richest agricultural regions.

19 The *Acacia* in this region is heavily parasitized by Desert Mistletoe (*Phoradendron californium*).

MISTLETOE is a woody, perennial ever-green parasite that steals sugar from its host by way of a modified stem called a haustoria. The sticky seeds are disseminated on the feet and bills of birds that eat the pearly-pink mistletoe berries.

15 This area was built up by the Colorado River as it built a delta across the northern end of the Gulf of California. The Imperial Valley in Alta California is a segment of the gulf that was cut-off and isolated by the Colorado River Delta. Indio, California, is 11 feet below sea level. The Salton Sea is man-made. It is the result of an error in judgement in 1906 which allowed the full flow of the Colorado River into the valley for over a year. The low point of the delta between the Imperial Valley and the Gulf of California is only 35 feet above sea level. In the Imperial Valley this level is marked by the shorelines of the ancient fresh water Lake Cahuilla.

14 Extensive alfalfa fields are being cultivated on both sides of the highway. Alfalfa (*Medicago sativa*) is widely used as forage for domestic animals in Baja such as horses, cows, and sheep.

5 Cotton (*Gossypium sp.*) is being grown on the right side of the highway. Cotton is cultivated for the white, soft, downy epidermal hairs growing from the seeds. These hairs are used in making textiles (woven or knitted cloth, thread, or yarn). After the hairs are removed by ginning the seeds are added to cattle fodder which produces a higher butterfat milk. There may be egrets in the fields among the cotton eating the cotton seeds. The area is reminiscent of the southwestern end of the Salton Sea which is often referred to as the "Dixie of the West" because of its extensive cotton fields.

4   A bull ring is to the right of the highway. East of the bull ring Date Palms are being cultivated and Tamarisk trees have been planted for windbreaks.

0   The highway diverges at a "Y" fork. The right fork is the continuation of Mexico 2. Mexico 2 connects with Mexico 5 in another 8 Kilometers.
The left fork leads into Mexicali.

MEXICALI, the state capital of Baja California, is the largest city in Baja. Agriculture is the backbone of Mexicali's economy. Irrigation water for the Mexicali valley comes from the Morelos Dam, on the Colorado River just south of the Mexico/U.S.A. international border. Baja's first brewery, the Mexicali Brewery and tasting room, are also found here.
The Paleontology, Archaeology, and mission exhibits of the Museo Regional Universidad de Baja are well worth a visit.

0   Mexicali is to the left and San Felipe to the right on Mexico 5.

Log 14 - Mexicali - San Felipe [190 kms = 118 miles]

Mexicali to the Sierra Pinta - *This segment of the Baja Highway heads south across the flat delta sands of the Colorado River, crosses the Cerro Prieto Fault Zone, and climbs onto, and begins to follow, the undulating alluvial fans of the Sierra de los Cucapas.*

The high, rugged Cucapas to the west are uplifted fault blocks of granitic and metamorphic basement uplifted during the opening of the Gulf of California. The conical basalt cinder cone of Cerro Prieto and its geothermal area are in view to the east. South of El Tare junction the Baja Highway crosses a delta mudflat where a low pass in the metamorphic rocks denotes the start of the almost continuous rugged granitic and metamorphic Sierra Mayor. To the left is the delta region with the Rio Hardy and the Colorado River channels. South of El Mayor the Baja Highway follows the trace of the frontal fault of the Sierra Mayor. At the south end of the Sierra Mayor the Baja Highway crosses the supertidal flats of the upper Gulf of California. This area is the entrance for the gulf waters into Laguna Salada.

Sierra Pinta to Ensenada Junction - *At the south end of the supertidal flat the Baja Highway enters the highly faulted and very rugged Tertiary volcanic area of the Sierra Pinta. The low steep hills to the left of the Baja Highway at the north end of the Pinta are calcareous Paleozoic sediments. The dune field was blown from Laguna Salada. The Baja Highway will then travel through several low passes in the volcanic rocks passing remnants of uplifted and dissected alluvial fans.*

South of the Sierra Pinta the Baja Highway undulates along the lower edges of uplifted alluvial fans to the junction of the Ensenada Baja Highway. The supertidal salt flats of the Salinas de Omotepec dominate the view to the east. Nearer the junction the high rugged hills on the right are the granitic and metamorphic rocks of the south end of the Sierra Pinta. The rounded volcanic hill on the left is El Chinero.

0   This log of the Baja Highway starts at the Junction of Mexico 2 and 5 at Kilometer 0.
     Initially, the two lane relatively straight highway heads south through the lush irrigated agricultural fields of Valle de Mexicali that are developed in Colorado River delta sands, passes over alluvial fans with occasional relatively barren salt pans (salitraes), and through desolate desertscapes on the way to San Felipe.
     At first glance this region *appears* to be fairly simple and uniform geologically and floristically when compared to other regions along the *Baja Highway*.

     DESIERTO SAN FELIPE: Desierto San Felipe is one of four sub-deserts of the Sonoran Central Desert phytogeographic region. Generally, the sparsely vegetated extremely arid Desierto San Felipe of northeastern Baja extends south from the International Border along the eastern escarpment of the two major peninsular ranges, the Sierra de Juarez and the Sierra San Pedro Martir; to Bahia de los Angeles. This desert is extremely arid because it is in the rain shadow of the peninsular ranges. The two dominant plants of this region are Creosote Bush and Bursage which comprise the Creosote Bush Scrub plant community (*See* Km 108). Several places to view the dominant plant species which characterize Desierto San Felipe are identified later in this log.

2   As the highway crosses Rio Nuevo (the New River in the U.S.A.), notice the spillway gate and pond on the south side of the highway. Rio Nuevo flows north into the Salton Sea on the U.S.A. side of the International Border. It is a source of controversy between the U.S.A. and Mexico because the sewage dumped into Rio Nuevo in Baja eventually spills into the Salton Sea. On the other hand, the U.S.A. dumps salt into the Colorado River to the east which spills into the irrigated farmlands near Mexicali. Neither situation is acceptable, but no solution has been found to resolve either problem.

Log 14 - Mexicali to San Felipe

3   Cottonwoods, Bursage, and Palo Verde are taking advantage of the "Highway Edge Effect" along this stretch of the highway.

> **LIVING ON THE EDGE:** In a region as harsh as a desert, microclimates become particularly important. Any fortuitous and fortunate circumstance which provides more mesic (moisten) habitats where moisture remains longer than in other environments provides conditions more favorable to life. Highway pavement edges (shoulders) are classic examples of moisture microenvironments in arid deserts. Runoff collects along the edge of the highway and favors the growth of vegetation. Plants which grow along highway edges are taller, greener, and more lush than individuals of the same species which grow in the drier soils a few meters from the highway edge because of the additional moisture they receive from drainage from the highway.

5.8   The highway crosses the meandering Rio Nuevo for a second time.

10   The highway heads to the south through the fertile lush irrigated agricultural fields of Valle de Mexicali and passes packing plants and supply and distribution areas. Many of the crops grown here are shipped to other parts of Mexico and the U.S.A. for consumption. The irrigation water arrives in the valley from the Colorado River via an extensive canal system from Presa (dam) Morales located near the border town of Algodones.
The range of mountains to the right is the Sierra Cucapa. To the far right the higher ranges of the Sierra Juarez are visible. The low hill ahead to the left is called Volcan Cerro Prieto. It is a Quaternary volcanic cone described in more detail at Kilometer 16.6.
Nopal or Mission cactus (*Opuntia fincus - indica*) is grown in many of the yards of the houses on the right side of the highway.

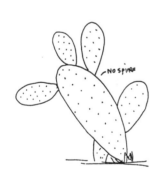

THE VERSATILE NOPAL CACTUS (*Opuntia*) belongs to the family Cactaceae and looks like beavertail cactus. Young Nopal leaves are larger and do not develop spines right away but instead have little knobs which are not sharp. Nopales leaves are harvested young, shredded, and used to add vegetable fiber and bulk to the Mexican diet. They are also cooked like green beans, fire roasted, or pickled with chilies. They are chopped and added to eggs (huevos). In the U.S.A. Nopales omelettes are often found on menus in southwestern states. Fresh cactus pads can be purchased in most Mexican markets.
The delicious fruit of the Nopal cactus is called "las tunas". Syrups, jams, and jellies are made from this fruit or it can be dried and used in soups or ground into flour.

16.6   This canal marks the trace of the Cerro Prieto Fault Zone. Areas along fault zones in Baja including this one are explored for geothermal energy (*See* Km 32 of the Guerrero Negro to Santa Rosalia log).
The prominent 250 meters high dark peak to the left front at about 10 o'clock is Volcan Cerro Prieto (Prieto means "dark"), a Quaternary volcanic cone with uplifted Tertiary sediments on its sides. The Mexican government generates thousands of kilowatts of power (620 MW at this time) from geothermal wells located southeast of Cerro Prieto. These geothermal power plant facilities are the second largest in North America exceeded only by the "Geysers" geothermal facilities located north of San Francisco, California.

Log 14 - Mexicali to San Felipe

There are hot mineral springs and mud volcanos in the area near a swampy area locally called Laguna Volcano.

21.2 A road metal quarry which utilizes materials from the area where the Sierra Cucapas are uplifted along the fault zone, is located to the right of the highway.
Streams from the Mexicali Valley area are eroding into the alluvial fan to the right which establishes a new gradient at the new base level about 3 to 5 meters below the former base level. This has created a series of sharp arroyos and abandoned fan terraces in the sediments. To the south these dissected fans are quite obvious as the highway crosses the numerous alluvial fans of the Sierra Cucapa (also Cucapa).

24 To the east the vegetation of Desierto San Felipe is uniformly low and sparse. The flora of this region is predominantly *Acacia* and Smoke Trees, low Bursage, and spindly Ocotillo. The *Acacia* and Smoke trees of this area are heavily parasitized by the evergreen mistletoe (*See* Km 15.5 of Bahia de los Angeles). On the right nearer to the Sierra Cucapa, the vegetation becomes taller.
The extensive road metal quarry of Villegas, which is located on the right, is developed in granitic alluvial sands. This uplifted area has been extensively eroded into a badlands type of topography.

25 The highway approaches and skirts the Sierra Cucapa (named for a local Indian tribe). The Sierra Cucapa were uplifted along several fault zones which bound and diagonally cut across the range. In the central part the range is largely tonalite and granodiorite.

26 The plumes of steam which rise from the ground in the distance to the left are produced by the geothermal power plants located near Volcan Cerro Prieto.

29 The range in the far distance is the Sierra el Mayor.

36 Granitics of the Sierra Cucapa outcrop along the highway.

36.6 Another large road metal quarry has been developed here in the granitics of the Sierra Cucapa.

37 El Tave junction marks the intersection of Mexico 5 south and BC 18 east. South of this junction, the massif of the Sierra Cucapa is largely composed of granodiorite, prebatholithic schists, and calcareous meta-sediments.

42 The Sierra Cucapa has declined into a low range of foothills. To the right front is a low pass which separates the Sierra Cucapa from the Sierra el Mayor which is the main mountain mass ahead to the right.

49 At El Medanito the highway curves southeast along the base of the Sierra el Mayor. A cemetary is located in a series of stabilized dunes at the base of the Sierra el Mayor on the right.

49.5 Behind and to the right the alluvial fan terraces of the Cucapas are visible.
The metamorphic rocks of the Sierra el Mayor come very close to the highway.
To the east there is a beautiful view of the Rio Hardy. The sloughs and banks of Rio Hardy provide excellent fishing and birdwatching.

50 The hills on the right have a series of smooth sloping small terraces developed on them. Each represents a different time of uplift of the Sierra el Mayor.

52   Campo Sonora is located to the southeast on Rio el Mayor, a stream tributary that flows into the larger Rio Hardy near Las Cabanas. The campos are a series of ramshackle temporary campsites developed along the stream and slough shores. A few of them offer facilities and hook-ups.

53   There is an excellent view ahead of the uplifted dissected terrace surfaces.

53.5   As the highway skirts the massif of the Sierra el Mayor, it passes an abandoned backwater slough on the left of Rio Hardy. The river has changed its course many times in the past and may even return to revive this abandoned slough at some future date.

55.5   The small settlement of Campo Rio Mayor Solano (La Carpa) is located on one of the major side channels of Rio Hardy.
The hills to the south are the Sierra el Mayor. Like the Sierra Cucapa, they are composed of granodiorite flanked by schists and calcareous meta-sediments.

56   The vegetation of this area is typical of a slough. The vegetation in the marshy slough soil along both sides of the highway is much shorter than those plants growing in the disturbed soils of the highway's shoulders. The slough vegetation is dominated by masses of flat narrow sword-shaped monocot culms (stems) that look like iris.
The roadside vegetation, predominantly *Acacia* and Cheesebush, is very tall and takes advantage of the "highway edge effect".
Tamarisk, Broom Baccharis, Acacia, and Palo Verde, and matted masses of monocot culms which look like cattails or bullrushes are growing on the slopes of the foothills of the Sierra Mayor.

66   Because of the high salinity of the soils in this area only a few halophyte (salt-loving) species are able to grow. Consequently, the vegetation to the left (east) is dominated by almost pure stands of halophytic Creosote Bush and Bursage sparsely interspersed with Tamarisk.

69   More granitic rocks of the Sierra el Mayor are exposed along the highway.
As the highway heads south, it travels across a broad flat salt pan.
The range directly ahead is the Sierra las Pintas. To the right of the highway across the salt pan, the Sierra las Tinajas, a lower range of mountains, are visible. Behind them the higher range farther to the west is the rather flat crest of the Sierra Juarez.

73   The highway crosses the supertidal flats of Gulfo de California on an artificial levee. During very wet periods this area is connected with Laguna Salada, a basin located to the northwest (*See* Km 27.5 of the Tijuana to Mexicali log). Actually this area is the southeastern end of Laguna Salada. Do not drive off of the highway here! You might sink out of sight!
The extensive barren salitraes (flat salt pan areas) begin, and the characteristic vegetation of Desierto San Felipe briefly disappears only to reappear a few kilometers down the highway. This region is very barren except along the highway shoulders where plants grow sparsely.

80   A series of active and partially stabilized sand dunes are located along both sides of the highway. Creosote Bush and very tall Bursage are growing abundantly on the dunes. In this area on hot days mirages are commonly seen on the salt pans around the Sierra las Pintas.

         MIRAGES are often seen on the dry barren salt pans, supertidal flats, and playas of Baja. Mirages are optical phenomena that create the illusion of water. They are often complete with inverted reflections of distant objects identical to real bodies of standing water. They result from the distortion of light by alternate layers of hot and cool air. Mirages are also known as "fata morgana" because they are attributed to the witchcraft of Morgan le Fay, the sorceress sister and enemy of the legendary sixth century British hero, King Arthur.

83   The hills to the left ahead are composed of upper Paleozoic meta-sediments which contain Crinoid fossils. These were the first Paleozoic sediments to be documented in Baja California.
The Sierra las Pintas are the higher mountains to the right ahead. They are composed of a thick sequence of Tertiary volcanics.

87   On the left an extensive dune field has developed on the foothills of the Sierra las Pintas. They originated as winds blowing southwest across Laguna Salada picked up sand and deposited it on the eastern slopes of the range.

97.3   The highway travels along the eastern edge of the Sierra las Pintas for many kilometers. The broad white flat area to the left is part of the Salinas de Omtepec, a supertidal flat located at the northern end of Gulfo de California (Mar de Cortez). Supertidal flats are coastlands that are inundated during very high tides.

105   The small settlement of La Ventana is located on the right side of the highway.

108   This is an excellent place to stop to take a walk and observe the flora of the Creosote Bush Scrub, the plant community characteristic of the **Desierto San Felipe area of the Sonoran Central Desert phytogeographic region.** The vegetation, which grows on the eastern foothills of the Sierra las Pintas consists of Creosote Bush, Bursage, Brittlebush, Candelabra Cactus, Honey Mesquite, Spurge, Cat's-Claw Acacia, Smoke Tree, Desert Thorn, and Palo Verde.

THE CREOSOTE BUSH SCRUB PLANT COMMUNITY OF DESIERTO SAN FELIPE: The highway from Mexicali to San Felipe passes through the Creosote Bush scrub plant community of the Desierto San Felipe area of Baja's Sonoran Central Desert phytogeographic region. This community is found below 900 meters on slopes, alluvial fans, and valleys in the desert. The precipitation is low, varies from 5 to 40 centimeters per annum, and mostly comes in the spring with a few summer showers. The pedocal soils which support this community are usually well drained, and the extremes of temperature are great (*See* the San Quintin log, Km 152.5). The community is so named because plant surveys have determined that Creosote Bush (*Larrea divaricata*) is the largest most abundant plant of Desierto San Felipe. Along with Bursage (*Franseria dumosa*) these two plants compose nearly 90% of the foliage cover of Desierto San Felipe. Vast acreages between Mexicali and San Felipe are covered by Bursage and Creosote Bush.

Creosote Bush is a shrub which is commonly 1 to 2 meters high with very small resin-covered evergreen leaves.

Bursage is a low rounded ashy-gray-green shrub which is 2 to 6 decimeters high with grayish-white bark and stiff intertwining branches.

WHY DO THE PLANTS OF THIS COMMUNITY LOOK LIKE THEY ARE GROWING IN STRAIGHT LINES?: The two dominant shrubs of this region, Cresote Bush and Bursage, look as though they have been hand planted in straight lines. However, they are naturally spaced as an adaptation for utilizing water more efficiently. Every plant requires a certain amount of water. In wet soils plants grow closer and more randomly; in dry environments plants are spaced almost territorially and grow evenly and widely spaced to ensure that each plant receives its required amount of water and minerals. The drier the environment, the wider and more regular the spacing. This is easily seen by noticing how widely spaced and short the Creosote Bush is on the tops of the hills. On the slopes Creosote Bushes become more numerous, more closely spaced, and taller. Taller and more closely spaced Creosote Bushes grow at the bottoms of the hills where runoff collects. The very tallest lushest Creosote Bushes grow along the shoulders of the highway where they receive the runoff from the highway and are able to grow their best.

Another factor responsible for the linear arrangement of Bursage and Creosote Bush in straight lines is the majority of these two dominant plants grow along tiny drainages, known as rills, that are less than five centimeters deep. Even small rills in desert landscapes may alter vegetational distribution patterns and community composition.

A third phenomenon that is responsible for the wide spacing of the Creosote Bush is **allelopathy**. If seeds of the Creosote Bush or other plant species were allowed to grow under or between the Creosote Bush, they would compete for the meager soil water and minerals available in the extremely arid nutrient-poor desert soils of the San Felipe Desert. To prevent competition resinous leachates from the Creosote Bush's leaves and stems "poison" the soil, which prevents the growth of other plants. This explains why the vast acreages of Creosote Bush look so barren. Despite the barren appearance, quite a variety of desert species grow here forming a regional assemblage of plant species known as the **Creosote Bush Scrub**. They are:

PLANT OF THE CREOSOTE BUSH SCRUB	COMMON LOCATION
Bursage or Burroweed(*Franseria dumosa*)	Widespread-usually with Creosote Bush
Creosote Bush (*Larrea divaricata*)	Slopes, washes, highway edges
Ocotillo (*Fouquieria splendens*)	Slopes, flats, washes
Cheesebush (*Hymenoclea salsola*)	Washes, highway edges
Cholla (*Opuntia sp.*)	Primarily on rocky slopes and disturbed soils
Desert Willow (*Chilopsis linearis*)	Infrequently along watercourses

110   On a clear day or evening Gulfo de California and the city of San Felipe (in the distant south) are visible.

123   La Fortuna and Moctezuma mines are located in the hills to the right. At one time silver

Log 14 - Mexicali to San Felipe

and gold ore was extracted from both mines, but they are not currently worked.

125   The flat region ahead to the right is Llano Cerro el Chinero.

134   The volcanic hill to the left is Cerro el Chinero where a group of Chinese trying to reach the United States from San Felipe and is said to have perished.

The amphitheater in the center of Cerro el Chinero contains volcanic cinders indicative of an eruptive center. At the base of Cerro el Chinero sand dunes that have blown against the hill have been dissected by streams which gives the impression of cone-shaped alluvial fans. However, the low part, not the narrow apex, of the fan is at the streams' head; the "fans" are upside down because they are really dunes. The dunes on the western flank of Cerro el Chinero are sparsely vegetated with small tufts of grass, scattered Brittlebush, and Skeleton Weed. Cerro el Chinero, itself, is covered by relatively dense stands of Ocotillo.

The surface of the dune slopes are covered with large coarse-grained quartz and granitic material blown from somewhere else. These coarse materials have weathered and formed desert pavement.

> DESERT PAVEMENT: Deflation (from the Latin meaning "to blow away") is an erosive process by wind that blows the unconsolidated sand and dust particles from a deposit and leaves the larger pebble or cobble-sized particles. Aided by alternating wetting and drying of the ground, the pebbles slowly rotate, settle, and concentrate into a flat armor-like mosaic called desert pavement. In some regions of Baja, the mosaic is made of several different kinds of rock, and patches occur where every stone is a different color. The pebbles which form the desert pavement on the slopes of Cerro el Chinero are a uniform brownish color. The even surface of the mosaic floor no longer offers any elevations that the wind can attack, further deflation ceases, and the weathering process ends.
>
> Do not be fooled by the hard look of desert pavement! It often superficially covers vast areas of soft deep sand, and a car driven onto desert pavement may sink up to its axles!

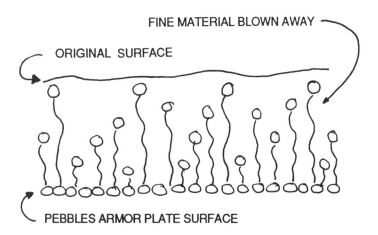

The broad flat area beyond Cerro el Chinero to the southeast is Salinas Gulfo de California, a supertidal flat.

135   As the highway passes Cerro el Chinero, the high ridge to the right in the distance is the crest of Sierra San Pedro Martir and its high peak, Picacho del Diablo (elev. 10,126') located in Baja's "Parque Nacional San Pedro Martir Constitucion, 1857".

136 Dense Cheesebush and large Brittlebush are growing advantageously along the highway. If you crush the leaves of Cheesebush between your fingers they produce a cheese-like odor.

141 At this junction the highway to the right is Mexico 3; it leads to the west 210 kilometers to Ensenada (*See* San Felipe to Ensenada log).

140.5 The Pemex station on the right is equipped with an old-style gravity flow gasoline pump that dispenses only Nova (regular). The gas is pumped into a glass container, the amount is measured, and the gas drains by gravity into the car. These pumps were once fairly common in Baja. Near the gas station the highway crosses Arroyo el Borrego (borrego = sheep).

150 At the base of the fan to the left a salt-pan area is visible. The Gulf waters and run-off from surrounding highlands arrive at this super-tidal area and evaporate which leaves a salt pan.

WHAT IS A SALT PAN?: Plain old table salt (sodium chloride, Halite, or NaCl) and mud compose most of this salt pan. However, several other salts are mixed with the Halite and mud in variable proportions. Originally, rainwater dissolved all of the various types of salts from the highland bedrock to the west. Run-off and groundwater seepage have slowly moved the salts toward the lower eastern elevations along the Gulf coast. Different salts move at different rates and they settle in different localities depending on their solubility in water. The salts in the soils of the alluvial fans on the eastern slopes of the Sierra San Felipe mountains are predominated by the least soluble carbonate salt known as *Calcite* ($CaCO_3$). Calcite crystallizes from groundwater as a natural cement and is commonly visible as white seams of caliche in pedocal soils (*See* Km 152.5 San Quintin to LA. Bay log) as they move away from the alluvial fans to the edge of the salt pan, the slightly more soluble sulfate *Gypsum* (hydrous $CaSO_4$) becomes abundant both as caliche-like veins and occasionally as gypsum crystals that have formed by efflorescence on the soils surface. Giant gypsum crystals can be seen around the Santa Rosalia region (*See* Guerrero Negro to Santa Rosalia log, Km 5). As mentioned earlier, the central lowest parts of the salt pan are mainly Halite (NaCl) since it is the most soluble salt. There appears to be a crudely concentric zonation around the salt pan, which reflects increasing solubility from carbonates to sulfates and to the highly soluble chlorides concentrated on the floor of the pan.

161 The shoreline of Gulfo de California approaches the highway from the Colorado River Delta area and the gulf island, Isla Montague. The slope that the highway is on goes down to the flat area of the salt pans of Salinas de Omtepec (first noted 64 kilometers ago). Salinas de Omtepec is laced with little sloughs that often flood during super high tides. They are super-tidal flats which continue along the coast to the head of Gulfo de California. They are related to the very high tidal range in the gulf and the emptying of the Rio Colorado into the upper end of Gulfo de California.

WHY IS THE VEGETATION SO SPARSE ON SALINAS DE OMTEPEC?: Plants are extremely sensitive to changes in water quantity and quality. A sudden decrease in plant height, species density, and a change in the species composition of an area can give clues to the quantity of water available and the quality of that water. Plants which need permanent water supplies (Riparian Willows, Maples,

Sycamores, and rushes), are called **phreatophytes** (well plants). Plants which need little water to survive, (Creosote, Bursage, and various cacti), are called **xerophytes** (dry plants). Plants are very useful in dry desert areas such as Desierto San Felipe to determine both the depth and the salinity of the available water. This enables botanists to map the water quantity and quality of salt pans and tidal flats such as Salinas de Omtepec.

No matter how dry the soil, there will be some plants that have adapted to the low level of water. However, few if any plants can tolerate more than 6% soil salinity. The high salinity of the salt pans and super tidal flats of this region is produced by run-off carrying dissolved salts from higher topography collecting and concentrating the salts at lower elevations. In the desert salt pans and super tidal flat areas are often devoid of vegetational cover. This probably indicates that the salinity of the soil is greater than 6%. There may be standing water in these areas, but a "physiological desert" exists. Plants simply cannot absorb water when surrounded by water saltier than their own tissue (the osmotic pressure is too great).

165   The brown hills to the right are composed of desert varnished tonalite.
The vegetation is similar to the flora or the Anza-Borrego Desert. The predominant plants are Ocotillo, Garambullo, abundant Mistletoe, Wait-a-minute Bush (Cat's-Claw Acacia), Mesquite, and Purple Bush. Opportunistic types of vegetation such as Cheesebush are growing along the side of the highway. It is almost the only green plant in this entire area. Red-tailed Hawks (*Buteo jamaicensis*) are often seen here.

PREDATORY HAWKS OF THE DESERT: The **Red-Tailed Hawk** is a well-known buteo (the largest subfamily of the *F. Accipitridae*) commonly seen perched on top of telephone poles or fence posts along the highway and wherever there are open hunting grounds in Baja. Usually hunting alone, this hawk may sit motionless for hours, then suddenly emit a high scream, and swoop down to prey on rabbits, rodents, and other ground dwelling prey. Two field characteristics which make red-tails easily identifiable are their uniformly colored red tail and their dark belly band. The Mexicans know these birds as Aguila Parda.

THE AVIFAUNA OF DESIERTO SAN FELIPE: As mentioned in the introductory chapter to the biology of the peninsula, the bird species of the Gulf coast of Northeastern Baja are the same as those found in the Californian Region of Alta California, the desert regions of mainland Mexico, and the Southwest U.S.A.. In Desierto San Felipe the Californian Region extends from the International Border to the latitude of Bahia De Los Angeles. The following sixteen species are typically seen along the northeastern peninsular Gulf shoreline and in the Creosote Bush plant community of Desierto San Felipe between the International Border and San Felipe:

BIRD SPECIES	COMMON LOCATION
American White Pelican	Fly low over coastal waters
American Kestrel	On telephone wires
Anna's Hummingbird	Near red or yellow flowers
Bendire's Thrasher	On the ground in the brush
Cactus Wren	Flying or perching on cacti
California Brown Pelican	Flying over coastal waters or on lakes
California quail	On the ground in coveys
Coasta's hummingbird	Near red or yellow flowers
Gila Woodpecker	On telephone poles or in large plants
Gilded Woodpecker	On telephone poles or in large plants
Greater Roadrunner	On the ground or crossing the highway
Ladder-back Woodpecker	On telephone poles or in large plants
LeConte's Thrasher	On the ground in the brush
Red-Tailed Hawk	perching on telephone poles or soaring
Turkey Vultures	ground feeding on carrion or soaring in circles overhead
Western Meadowlark	On fences bordering meadows

167   To the left the highway is Cerro el Moreno, a Miocene volcanic plug. Nearby to the east there is a small inlet on the coast, Estero Primero, which is in the southern region of Salinas de Omtepec.

170   The high hill to the right in the near distance is Cerro el Colorado which is composed of Tertiary volcanics. The lower hills in front of Cerro el Colorado are all tonalite. The low darker-gray hills to the southwest of Cerro el Colorado are composed of prebatholithic slates and schists.

175   In the distance to the right are the high peaks of the Sierra San Pedro Martir and the eastern escarpment of the Peninsular Range Batholith. The massif of the Sierra San Pedro Martir is the highest range on the peninsula of Baja. The highest peak of the range is Picacho del Diablo (Devil's Peak; 3115 m., 10,126'). It is located to the right at approximately 3 o'clock. The mountains in the foreground are the Sierra San Felipe. The vegetation in this region is still dominated by Creosote Bush and Bursage.

177   For the next several kilometers the highway passes semi-stabilized dune fields composed of sand blown from the sandy beaches of the Gulf.
There is a view of Mar de Cortez, and if the weather is clear, Isla Consag, a steep sided volcanic peak may be visible in the middle of the Gulf 30 kilometers offshore. This isolated volcanic peak, was named for Padre Fernando Consag, an early explorer of Mar de Cortez (1746).

179   The side road to the right leads northwest to Colonia Morero and El Saltio. This road crosses Valle Santa Clara and goes north along Laguna Diablo to intersect the main Mexico Highway 3 east of Valle Trinidad (*See* Km 175.5 of San Felipe to Ensenada log).
The highway crosses a small longitudinal dune.

182   To the left is a "living" fence made from Ocotillo cuttings. Some of the posts have rooted by adventitious roots, so the plant has started to grow again. This is similar to the living Datilillo fences seen in other parts of the peninsula (*See* Km 56 Ensenada to L.A. Bay junction log).

Log 14 - Mexicali to San Felipe

As the highway approaches San Felipe, the desert vegetation seems to meet the sea, and numerous side roads (mostly unpaved) lead to the east to beach campos, trailer parks, and resorts. A few have showers, cabanas, and banos (bathrooms) available for a small daily fee.

187   The highway passes through a low range of prebatholithic hills. They are covered by a heavy desert-varnish which gives their surface a very dark appearance (*See* Km 134) There is a pot factory, which includes several brick yards and small ovens, on the right.

187   The highway passes by Cerro la Turquesa on the left.

189   As the highway enters San Felipe, Cerro el Machorro and the point of Punta el Machorro which are composed of tonalite and granodiorite are to the left.
The rocks just to the left at the big monument circle are prebatholithic carbonate rocks.
On the right in the distance are the Sierra San Felipe which are almost exclusively composed of the tonalite of the Peninsular Range Batholith.

The town of San Felipe is located between the low foothills of Sierra San Felipe and the 610 meter high Punta San Felipe. The economy of San Felipe is supported by tourists and sportsfishing.
The headland of Punta el Machorro provides shelter for both commercial boats and pleasure craft.
Floristically, the area near San Felipe is relatively simple and is primarily composed of Creosote Bush and Bursage, the dominant members of the Creosote Bush Scrub community of Desierto San Felipe. They are both well adapted to survival in this very arid environment which receives less than 5 centimeters of rainfall per year.
San Felipe is especially interesting to sailors. Because of the constricted nature of the Gulf, the tidal range can vary more than 6 meters; this makes navigating very difficult.

WHERE NOW?   The highway does continue south to Puertecitos, Bahia de San Luis Gonzaga, and connects with the main highway at Laguna Chapala. Until this road is paved, it is not recommended for normal travel! (*See* the Laguna Chapala log).
You may return to the north on Mexico 5 to Mexico 3 and turn east 210 km to Ensenada.

Log 15 - Ensenada to Tecate [114 kms = 71 miles]

The Baja Highway travels up a gentle alluvial valley flanked by steep hills of the marine Rosario Formation, then climbs a steep grade into the rugged metavolcanic hills. After passing through the metavolcanic hills the Baja Highway travels through a rolling bouldery area of tonalite on the south side of the Valle Guadalupe eventually travelling on the alluviated floor of the valley with steep metavolcanic and granitic hills in the distance on both sides. The Baja Highway then travels through more granitic rocks and crosses a fault into an area of rugged hills in slatey metamorphic rocks with scattered granitic hills. The Baja Highway enters steep bouldery tonalite hills near El Testerazo and climbs a grade through the conglomerates of the Las Palmas Gravels. On top of the grade the Baja Highway crosses the flat surface of the gravels with views to the north and east of the flat to undulating erosion surface with granitic peaks, and views to the west and south of the rugged metavolcanic foothills.

The Baja Highway then descends a grade through the conglomerates to the alluviated Las Palmas Valley. North of the valley the Baja Highway climbs through steep tonalite hills and then through the bouldery granodiorite. The Baja Highway follows a spectacular contact between a dark, smooth, gabbro hill on the left and a light, bouldery, granodiorite hill on the right then travels through the rugged granodiorite hills past several gabbro hills to descend steeply through tonalite into Tecate.

This log begins at the junction of Mexico 1D (Km 101.3, TJ - Ensenada log) and Mexico 3 and ends at Tecate 114 kilometers to the north.

The highway immediately enters an agricultural area in which fast growing naturalized Eurasian Tamarisk (Athel or Salt Cedar) have been planted for windbreaks (*See* Km 10 of the San Quintin log for a detailed discussion of Tamarisk). Date palms and Nopal Cactus (*Opuntia Ficus-indica*) are cultivated around residences primarily for personal consumption (*See* Km 10 of Mexicali to San Felipe log).

104.5 The highway initially goes inland (northeast) in the alluviated valley of Rio San Antonio. It is bordered by Cretaceous hills on both sides.

103 The south-facing slopes are sparsely vegetated. The north-facing slopes are thickly covered with chaparral vegetation, dominated by Laurel Sumac, *Acacia*, Buckwheat, White and Black Sage.

> **NORTH AND SOUTH-FACING SLOPES**: Local variations of humidity and temperature exercise considerable control upon natural slope cover. In non-tropical regions slope face, or aspect, is of great importance. Because Baja is north of the Equator, its south-facing slopes receive more direct sunlight; they are hotter and drier. As a result of the decreased humidity and increased temperatures, slope cover is sparse, low, and composed of grayish-colored species adapted to living in xeric (dry) environments. The soils are more weathered and have less organic matter. North-facing slopes receive less direct sunlight and are more humid and cooler than south-facing slopes. They commonly support denser lusher taller moisture-needing vegetation characteristic of mesic (moist) environments. This includes trees. Wind is slowed, and soil temperatures and evaporation are decreased by the dense vegetation. The soils are less weathered and are humus-rich.

Groves of olives have been planted adjacent to the highway and extend into the foothills The California Sycamores which grow here are heavily parasitized by mistletoe

101   The highway begins to climb through prebatholithic metavolcanic rocks.

98.7   The roadcut at the top of the grade exposes a massive purple andesitic breccia, a common rock type in these prebatholithic metavolcanic rocks. The highway continues to pass through the metavolcanic rocks for the next 2 kilometers.
The plants which grow along the disturbed soils shoulders of the highway is Laurel Sumac. They are bigger and more lush than those which grow away from the highway because they receive more water in the form of runoff than the plants which grow away from the highway shoulders.

96   The highway enters the southwestern end of a valley in the Oak woodland. The highway passes through numerous Oak woodland areas intermixed with chaparral areas all the way to Tecate (*See* Km 119 of the Tijuana to Mexicali log).
For the next 30 kilometers the highway passes through an extensive area of tonalite. This valley was formed by Rio San Antonio in the more easily eroded tonalites.

92.8   The small rural village of San Antonio de Las Minas (Villa de Juarez) is to the right of the highway.
The highway begins to pass through irrigated cultivated fields. The boulder-covered slopes of this region are underlain by tonalite and the smoother slopes by metavolcanics and slates.

92   The road to the left to Alegre (El Tigre) connects with the Free Highway between Tijuana and Ensenada.

88   The flat hill to the left is a remnant of an old terrace level from one of the alluvial fans that was deposited when the valley was at a higher level.

86.5   Citrus and Olive groves are growing to the left, and a grove of Pistachio (*Pistacia vera*) trees can be seen to the right.

> **PISTACHIOS:** The Pistachio tree has been introduced into Baja. It is a native of the Mediterranean region and of western Asia. The small hard-shelled "Pistachio nuts" of this tree have an edible oily green kernel. Pistachio nuts, commercially grown in Valle Guadalupe, are consumed and sold locally and exported.

83   The main part of Valle Guadalupe can be seen to the left.
The hills on the far side are prebatholithic metavolcanics and bouldery tonalite.

82.5   Extensive grape vineyards are growing to the left of the highway.
The floor of Valle Guadalupe is almost completely under cultivation. Watering of the crops, orchards, vineyards, and groves is now commonly done by drip irrigation, a method used to conserve water, a scarce resourse in Baja, California.
The fast-growing introduced Tamarisk and California Pepper trees have been planted among the cultivated fields for windbreaks. The small stream which meanders through the center of Valle Guadalupe is bordered by a Riparian Woodland (*See* Km 148 of the Tijuana to Mexicali log)

78.6   Some old copper prospecting pits are visible to the right of the highway. These exploratory pits were dug because copper mineralization is relatively common in the prebatholithic metavolcanic rocks. However, economic deposits were not discovered.

77.4   The highway crosses Rio Guadalupe which originates in the Sierra Juarez near Laguna Hansen and meanders to the west through Ojos Negros, Valle Guadalupe, and to the sea at

Boca la Mision. Most of the waterflow occurs underground, as ground water and leaves the stream-bed surface dry.

The vegetation in the stream-bed the consists of Tamarisk, Broom Baccharis, and Willow.

76.8   This turnoff to the left leads to Colonia Guadalupe, the site of a Russian agricultural colony established in 1905. The Dominican Mision Nuestra Senora de Guadalupe was also established here in 1834. It was the last mission to be established in Baja California.
The highway follows the west side of Guadalupe Valley at the base of the tonolite and granodiorite hills.

72.5   The highway begins to follow a fault line valley in tonalite.

72   For the next several kilometers many small Riparian Woodland areas are seen along the right side of the highway. The dominant vegetation along the stream banks is Coastal Live Oaks, Scrub Oak, Sycamores, and Willows. *Acacia*, Broom Baccharis, Chamise, Toyon with Dodder, and Wild Buckwheat are the plants which grow on the low surrounding hills.

68   The highway passes through roadcuts in the mixed granitics.

66   Prebatholithic slates, phyllites, and argillites outcrop along the highway. These outcrops are probably Paleozoic in age.

63.5   The small buildings to the right of the highway belong to Ejido Ignacio Zaragoza, a small agricultural community which grows forage crops along both sides of the highway.
The Riparian vegetation has been temporarily left behind prior to entering the valley of Ejido Ignacio Zaragoza and the highway passes through a coastal chaparral scrub community which consists of Rabbitbrush, Scrub Oak, and several species of composites. Numerous granitic dikes to the east cut the metamorphic rocks. The well-known ring dike of El Pinal (Duffield, 1969) is a few miles to the east. The major northwest-southeast-trending Vallecitos Fault Zone crosses the highway near the south end of the valley. Some geologists have speculated that this fault zone may continue through Tijuana River Valley.

> **Ring Dike:** Dikes form as molten material fills a crack in the rocks. A small pluton of granitic rock was intruded into the El Pinal area. As this pluton cooled, it cracked parallel to its circular outline. The resultant crack was filled by the dike material and left a "ring dike" which is prominently seen on the Baja map.

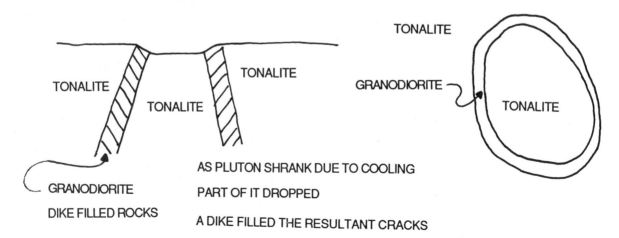

222

Log 15 - Ensenada to Tecate

63 The roadcuts for the next 5 kilometers expose dark-colored slatey to phyllitic prebatholithic rocks. Geologists have searched these roadcuts for evidence of fossils without success.

62 The Riparian woodland areas are now visible to the left side of the highway. A beautiful park-like oak woodland extends along the drier banks of the Riparian woodland. The large silver-barked trees are sycamores; the dark-green trees are Oaks.

62.5 The highway passes through roadcuts with good exposures of schist and gneiss cut by a dike.

60 The highway has entered the broad alluviated Vallecitos which is ringed by metavolcanic hills with a few scattered patches of tonalite. Dikes cut some of the hills.
The large green trees along both sides of the highway are Tamarisk, Cat's Claw Acacia, Cottonwoods, and Willows.

55.4 The lower part of the small valley ahead is vegetated with Riparian cottonwood trees that are heavily parasitized by mistletoe.
The bright green plants which grow along the pavement edge are Broom Baccharis and Palo Verde. In the spring the white flowers are Wild Buckwheats.

52 The conglomeratic hill ahead has been uplifted between two branches of the Falla de Calabasas. The highway has been built in a tonalite body. Numerous small shear zones cut the rocks for the next kilometer.
The valley at Kilometer 51.2 is a fault-line valley. The highway runs parallel to the fault zone at the Kilometer 51 mark.
The Riparian vegetation of this fault-line valley consists of oaks, Cottonwoods, and Cat's Claw Acacia ("Wait-a-minute bush").

50.5 The highway crosses Rio las Calabazas. To the right of the highway the wash woodland vegetation is Toyon; to the left the plants are Tamarisk.

50.2 This is another fault-line valley which parallels the one at Km 52.

49 This is the large village of El Testerazo.
The hills ahead are composed of Eocene conglomerates which were deposited in a major river 45 million years ago.

48 The high hills to the left are metavolcanics; to the right a tonalite body is visible.

47.2 The wash which runs southwest from Canon El Alamo is vegetated with the same Riparian vegetation as listed at 50.5 km.

47 As the highway begins to climb a grade, it passes several Eocene conglomerate outcrops. The bright green roadside plants are Broom Baccharis.

45 The conglomerates are more firmly cemented in this area. The red color of the upper cuts is due to slope wash; that is, the red iron oxides from upper sediments have been leached out and have run down over the face of the lower sediments which coats them with a reddish wash.

43 The vegetation of this area belongs to the Coastal Sage Scrub plant community (*See* Km 14.8 of the Tijuana to Ensenada log).

223

40.5 The viewpoint on the right is a good place to view the local geology (elevation 650 meters).

> **CONGLOMERATES AND EROSION SURFACES:** The conglomerates which comprise these intervening hills are part of a string of conglomerate exposures which stretch from here to the crest of the Peninsular Ranges to the east. They contain a small percentage of rhyolite clasts similar to those of the Poway Conglomerate of the San Diego area. (Minch, 1972) The conglomerates rest upon an Eocene or older erosion surface. The erosion surface can be seen to the east and southeast of this stop.
> Cerro La Libertad to the northeast was a monadnock on this surface. Monadnocks are scattered erosional remnants on a low-relief erosional surface (peneplain). West of this area the surface has been largely destroyed by erosion.
> The hills to the west and southwest are part of the metavolcanic coastal range which did not develop erosion surfaces.

39.5 The hills along the road have been heavily overgrazed and are almost barren.

38.9 Metavolcanic outcrops which formed part of the north bank of the Eocene channel are visible in this roadcut.

38.6 The broad valley to the right has been cut in tonalites.
Rancho Viejo, which is located in the valley on the right, is a modern winery and distillery which processes locally-grown grapes.

37 The vista opens below to the tonalite hills cut by several light-colored granitic dikes. The light-colored linear bouldery outcrops are erosional remnants of these granitic dikes.
Two granodiorite peaks form the skyline: Cerro los Bateques is the lower to the east; Cerro La Libertad is the higher peak to the right.

35.8 The highway passes through decomposed pebbly mudstones and sandstones which underlie the surface conglomerates of this region. These gravels represent a pre-Eocene channel similar to the Cretaceous Lusardi conglomerates in the San Diego, U.S.A., area. They were deposited by short streams as the batholith was uplifted and eroded during Mesozoic subduction. These older gravels are only exposed on this side of the Eocene valley.

PRESENT EROSION HAS REMOVED SIDE
OF VALLEY AND LEFT A
CONGLOMERATE RIDGE

CRETACEOUS VALLEY
FILLED WITH COARSE GRAVELS

EOCENE VALLEY CUT INTO SIDE OF OLD
VALLEY AND FILLED WITH EXOTIC GRAVELS

224

Log 15 - Ensenada to Tecate

32   The Falla de Calabasas that the road crossed near El Testerazo is seen again near the break in the slope ahead and passes through the notch between the two very high hills, one is Cerro Bolla, and across the valley to the right of the zig-zag in the highway.

31   For the next 3 kilometers the highway passes along the edge of the riparian valley of Valle de Las Palmas. A small stream is visible to the left of the highway.
The olive orchards in this valley are protected by windbreaks of Tamarisk, Eucalyptus, and California Pepper Trees (*Schinus molle*), introduced natives of Eurasia and South America.
The highway between here and Tecate leads to the north through various types of intermediate granitic rocks.

30.5 The road to the left climbs to the top of Cerro Bola where Microondes Cerro Bola is located. The lower part of the road crosses a smooth gently sloping surface which is part of the old alluvial fans that developed in this area before it was uplifted.

28.2 Nopales are grown on the right.

28   The highway crosses Arroyo Seco.

25   The highway passes through an area of extensive bouldery outcrops of granodiorite.

21   One cannot help but be impressed by the stark bouldery granodiorite outcrops and hills.

16   Notice the contact between a granodiorite hill on the right (east) and a gabbro hill on the left (west) along the highway. The gabbro weathers easily and has no outcrops, while the granodiorite hill weathers more slowly and has bouldery outcrops. As the gabbro weathers, it forms clay soils. Below the surface these clay soils protect the underlying gabbro from further weathering; this results in fresh gabbro relatively near the surface. However, the granodiorite weathers to a sandy soil which allows further deep weathering and leaves only a few surface boulders.

15.5 As the highway climbs the grade, there is a gabbro clay pot fabricating plant with a kiln for firing the pots to the right.

14.5 The highway crests over a hill with a view of the erosion surface.

14   The highway enters an area with an extensive brick-making operation scattered haphazardly over the hillside.

13.5 There is a place to buy tile, etc., from the local brick-making operations. The pots, bricks, and tiles are for sale locally or in Tecate, where higher prices are usually charged to cover the overhead involved in doing business in a city.

      TECATE CLAY PRODUCTS The clay pits which supply materials for the tile and brick operations of Tecate, are developed in the clayey gabbro soils of this area. Around the town of Tecate piles of Tecate's "famous bricks" and the kilns where they are fired are readily apparent. Also look for stacks of colorful ceramic tile in Tecate that can be made-to-order for a very reasonable price.

7.5   The high peak in the distance is Tecate Peak on the U.S.A. side of the border.

3   The descent into Tecate begins. The numerous brickyards in this area exploit the clay soils developed on isolated gabbro bodies.

0   The highway crosses railroad tracks at Tecate on Calle Ortiz Rubio.
Cerveceria Tecate, one of the largest breweries in Mexico, is two blocks left at the first stop sign (on Avenida Hidalgo).
The main Tijuana to Mexicali highway, Avenida Juarez, is at the second stop sign. Tecate is 30 miles east of Tijuana. Those who wish to continue directly to the United States should turn left for one block (to signal) then turn right on Calle Lazaro Cardenas to the Tecate border crossing. This log joins the Tijuana-Mexicalli log at Km 131.5.
It is worth noting that while this desert area seems to be very arid, the world's record for high intensity rainfall was set in the small town of Campo just north of the International Border east of Tecate. The record is 11" in 80 minutes. Campo was a camp when they were building the San Diego & Arizona Eastern Railroad.

Log 16 - L.A. Junction to Bahia de Los Angeles [66 kms = 40 miles]

The Highway gently climbs eastward on the flat surface of the Miocene fluvial sediments toward a low rolling series of metamorphic hills. It then drops into an alluvial wash and climbs out to pass south of rugged rhyolite hills then between a series of rugged metamorphic hills in a broad sloping alluvial valley. The high hills and mesas to the north are capped by rhyolite and basalt. The Baja Highway then steeply descends a pass in metamorphic rocks to skirt the south side of the dry lake of Laguna Amarga along a series of rugged metasedimentary hills.

The opposite sides of the playa are a steep, rugged series of faulted, mixed metamorphic and granitic rocks capped by mesas of basalt tuffs, and rhyolite. After crossing the southern part of the lake the Baja Highway again descends a steep canyon in rugged hills of metasedimentary rocks to the alluvial fans on the shore of Bahia de Los Angeles. Here the Baja Highway turns south on the fans and parallels a fault scarp in the granitic and metasedimentary rocks.

0	About 10 kilometers north of Punta Prieta is the junction of the highway and a paved road that heads east toward Bahia de Los Angeles.

0   About 10 kilometers north of Punta Prieta is the junction of the highway and a paved road that heads east toward Bahia de Los Angeles.

For the first ten kilometers the highway gently climbs on the surface of the Miocene fluvial sediments that mantle this relatively flat area.

The prominent mesa to the right consists of volcanic and fluvial sediments capped by dark basalt. As the highway continues eastward it approaches a granitic and metamorphic hill, Mesa La Pinta.

The vegetation along this highway consists of species typical of the Desierto el Vizcaino flora (*See* Km 69 of the San Quintin log).
Cirio, Ocotillo, Elephant Tree, and Cardon are the dominant taller plants. Datilillo, Yucca, Cholla, Garambullo, and numerous species of desert annuals form the low "understory". Here and there an occasional Palo Verde or Mesquite is visible. The Mesquite in this area is heavily parasitized by Mistletoe.

5.5   Hills of rounded granitic rock and mixed metamorphic rocks can be seen about one half kilometer to the left of the highway.

1 0   The highway enters an area of low hills with mixed metamorphic and granitic rocks exposed on both sides of the highway. Many of the granitics are spheroidally weathered.

14.5   Here the highway dips into an alluvial wash primarily vegetated by Datilillo and Cardon.

15.5   As the highway quickly climbs back onto the surface of the Miocene fluvial sediments notice the epiphytic, pineapple relative Ball Moss abundantly covering the Cirio, Desert Aster, Skeleton Weed, *Atriplex*, Mesquite, Desert Hollyhock, Coyote Melon, and Indigo Bush, two species of *Agave*, Elephant Tree, and Ocotillo in this area.

> **EPIPHYTES AND PARASITES:** From south of El Rosario along the Pacific coast to the Cape, trees, shrubs, and cacti like *Acacia*, Palo Adan, Cirio, Ciruelo, Ironwood, Lomboy, Mesquite, Broom Baccharis, Cardon, and Pitaya Dulce, are often covered with the moisture loving, epiphytic Ball Moss (*Tillandsia recurva*), a member of the pineapple family (*See* Km 74.5 San Quintin log). Epiphytic Ball Moss is not harmful to the host (primarily Cirio here) plant since it lives in a commensalistic relationship depending on the host plant for support only. However, a close look at some of the same trees and shrubs listed above will reveal several harmful parasites living in a destructive symbiosis

227

with them. The two most common parasitic organisms (symbionts) of this area are the evergreen Desert Mistletoe (*Phrygillanthus sonorae*) and "witch's hair" (*Cuscata veatchii*).

"Witch's hair", a flowering plant lacking chlorophyll, attaches its yellow or orange, spaghetti-like stems to its host (exclusively Elephant Trees here) by a modified stem called a haustoria. Since "Witch's Hair" cannot make its own food it uses its haustorial stem to "steal" sugar produced photosynthetically by its host.

The second parasite common to this region is the woody, evergreen mistletoe seen hanging in large, shapeless masses, in the branches of many plants in Baja (primarily Mesquite here). They look like clumps of vegetation that are the wrong shape and wrong color, not matching the foliage of the host plant. Like "Witches Hair", Mistletoe utilizes haustorial stems to siphon sugar from their host. If the mistletoe is thick enough it will kill its host and itself at the same time. However, strong, healthy host plants can withstand the parasite attacks.

Along the Pacific coast, the moisture that sustains both the epiphytes and parasites of this desert, comes from ocean fogs that roll in at night and lie during the early morning hours in misty layers among the hills until the sun "bakes" it off. Along the Pacific coast, from the Cape Region northward to San Francisquito, areas similar to this are known as coastal fog deserts. With only a few exceptions, these plants are unknown on the drier Gulf side of the peninsula where fog (Neblina) does not normally occur.

17 The pinkish colored flat-lying hills of the Mesa Tinajas Coloradas, off to the left of the highway, are Miocene extrusive rhyolites overlying the Miocene fluvial (river and stream) sediments.

For the next 7-8 kilometers, the highway passes through an area of mixed granitic, prebatholithic metasedimentary rocks and volcanic capped mesas.

18 For about one half kilometer the highway skirts a dark colored, gabbro hill to the left of the highway. Very few gabbro hills are accessibly exposed along Baja's highways. Gabbros are dark colored basic, intrusive igneous rocks composed principally of labradorite or bytownite and augite. It is the approximate intrusive equivalent of the extrusive basalts.

23 The vista opens up ahead, as the highway descends a broad alluvial plain on the Pacific coast drainage, into the Valle Agua Amarga.

Along the right side of the highway is an impressive Elephant Tree forest. Although the Elephant Trees look "dead" most of the year, during the rainy season they put out leaves and look lush and green. When they flower they look as though they are capped by a pinkish haze. All of the well-drained drier slopes in this area are covered with beautiful, thick stands of them. Cirios and Cardons vegetate the lower, flatter elevations.

30 As the highway crests a low pass it enters the Gulf drainage.

The hill to the left is composed of a mixture of several different types of rhyolite and andesite overlying the Miocene fluvial (produced by river action) sediments which the highway is passing through.

31 At the crest of the pass, the vegetation consists of Datilillo, Garambullo, Agave, Greasewood, Cirios and Cardon. The dominant tall plant here is the thick-trunked Elephant Tree.

As the highway descends from this low pass the vegetation is relatively abundant.

Ahead the highway skirts the Playa Agua Amarga salt pan.

32.5   The hills directly ahead are prebatholithic metasediments with numerous resistant light colored layers.
The fine-grained, white bedded layers along the highway are Quaternary lacustrine sediments which may represent dissected remnants of a tilted ancient lake bed.

33   Ahead the vista opens to Playa Agua Amarga, the dry lake bed at the bottom of the Valle Agua Amarga.
The Sierra el Toro, located on the far side of the Valle Agua Amarga, consists of a mixture of various rock types including granitic, metamorphic, sedimentary and volcanic rocks.
The low mountains to the southeast are the Sierra Salorlos.

WHAT IS A PLAYA LAKE?: Playas are classically defined as the flat, dry, barren area of an undrained desert basin underlain by clay, silt, or sand, and commonly soluble salts. It may be covered by a shallow, intermittent (ephemeral) lake during the wet season that dries up, by evaporation, during the hotter summer months. When the standing water of the ephemeral lake evaporates, it leaves behind a playa covered by salt-laden deposits of calcium and sodium.

Originally the Valle Agua Amarga was a deeper valley, but valleys get filled up over geologic time due to the actions of gravity, wind, and water. The deep valley fill is composed of the silt, salt, and windblown sand which was originally weathered, eroded, washed, blown, or dissolved from the bedrock of the surrounding highlands and deposited in the valley, a process that is still occurring.

Since water always spreads out to a common level, it also distributes its load of fine sediment thinly and evenly forming extremely flat areas known as playas. Playas and their silty-salty surfaces are the flattest, natural places found on land. After a brief desert rain storm, several centimeters of water may thinly, ephemerally cover hundreds of acres of the Playa Agua Amarga making it look like a lake.

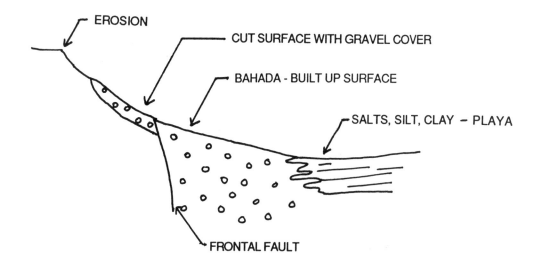

229

Ahead the highway skirts the Playa Agua Amarga salt pan. The barren, highly saline, white central portion of the playa is clearly visible and is totally devoid of life. However, the less saline soils along the edge of the playa are vegetated by a few hearty salt tolerant halophytes (salt lovers).

WHAT IS A SALT PAN?: Plain old table salt (Halite = NaCl) and mud make up most of the flat floor of the Valle Agua Amarga forming the Playa Agua Amarga. However, several other salts are mixed in with the Halite and mud in variable proportions. Originally rainwater dissolved all of the various types of salts from the bedrock of the surrounding mountains. Run-off and groundwater seepage have slowly moved the salts downward toward the lower parts of the valley floor resulting in the formation of the playa. Different salts move at different rates and so end up in different localities depending on their solubility in water (*See* the diagram below).

The salt in the soils of the alluvial fans is predominated by the least soluble carbonate salt known as *Calcite* ($CaCO_3$). Calcite crystallizes from groundwater as a natural cement and is commonly visible as white seams of caliche (*See* Km 152.5 San Quintin log).

Moving down the fan, to the edge of the playa, the slightly more soluble sulfate *Gypsum* (hydrous $CaSO_4$) becomes abundant both as caliche-like veins and occasionally as gypsum crystals that have formed by efflorescence. Efflorescence is the process by which crystals grow, on surfaces, due to the evaporation of salt-laden water. Gypsum crystals can also be seen around the Santa Rosalia region (*See* Guerrero Negro log, Km 5).

As first mentioned, the central, lowest parts of the Playa Agua Amarga are mostly Halite (NaCl) since it is the most soluble salt. Thus, there appears to be a crudely concentric zonation around the salt pan, reflecting increasing solubility, from carbonates at the top of the slopes to sulfates and finally to the highly soluble chlorides concentrated on the barren, lifeless floor of the salt pan.

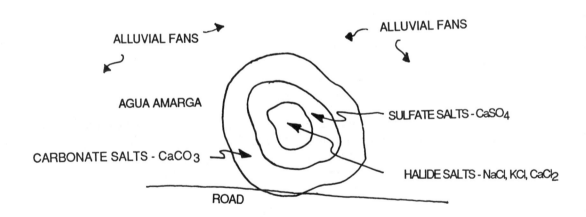

34.8   The buildings of the deserted Rancho Amarga are visible to the left.

35.5   As the highway begins to skirt the edge barren of Playa Agua Amarga the rocks along the right side of the highway are prebatholithic sediments and schists of the Sierra Cinta de la Cantera.

Log 16 - L.A. Junction to L.A. Bay

WHY IS PLAYA AGUA AMARGA NEARLY DEVOID OF VEGETATION?:
Plants are extremely sensitive to changes in water quantity and quality. A sudden decrease in plant height and/or a change in the species composition of an area can give clues as to the quantity of water available and the quality of that water. Plants needing permanent water supplies, such as willows, alders, ferns, and rushes, are called phreatophytes (well plants). Plants needing little water to survive, such as Baja's Mesquite, Greasewood, Palo Verde, and various cacti, are called xerophytes (dry plants). Plants are very useful in dry desert areas as indicators of both the depth and the salinity of the water and allow botanists to map the water quantity and quality of available water. No matter how dry the soil, there will be some plants that have adapted to the low level of water. However, few, if any, plants can tolerate more than 6% soil salinity. The high salinity of playa soils is the result of run-off, carrying dissolved salts from higher topography surrounding the playa, that collects and concentrates in the low, central portions of playas.

In the desert and on playas like Agua Amarga, areas of ground are often devoid of vegetational cover. This most likely indicates that the salinity of the soil is greater than 6%. There may even be standing water but with a salinity of greater than 6% a "physiological desert" exists to which no plant can adapt. Notice that a few plants are seen growing on low hummocks in the playa and along the margins of the playa. This indicates that the soil salinity there is less than 6%.

The Mexican name, Agua Amarga, means bitter water, a reference to the highly saline, unpotable waters found in the valley.

3 9   Notice the dramatic vegetation change that occurs as you look from the slopes down onto the playa salt pan. These changes reflect slope drainage and increasing soil salinity. The hills to the right are covered with Elephant Trees; the lower slopes are covered with Cardon, Jumping Cholla, and Ocotillo; the flats are densely vegetated with Creosote Bush, Teddy Bear Cholla, and Greasewood. The very Saline Salt flats are bare.

4 1   A dense stand of Smoke Trees are growing in the wash on both sides of the highway. Smoke Trees only grow in washes since their seeds must be scarified by the sands of the wash during wet periods and water is necessary to lead out germination inhibitors. Both assure their seedings have enough water to grow into mature plants.

41.3   The sign here indicates there is a rough, unpaved back way to Mision San Borja. Because of better road conditions, the road from El Rosarito (Km 52.5), south of the Bahia de Los Angeles Junction, is the preferred route. Agua Higuera ("tree") spring and cattle ranch are located about 1 kilometer up the wash to the right. The road then continues on to Mision San Borja (*See* Km 52.5 of the Bahia de Los Angeles Junction log for a discussion of this mission). This back way to San Borja is recommended for 4-wheel drive vehicles only.

43.8   This side road also leads to Mision San Borja. Both this road and the one at kilometer 41.3 meet at Agua Higuera spring.

4 5   The vegetation of this area is typical of that commonly found growing on similar flat areas along this section of the highway. Ocotillo, Cardon, Mesquite, Datilillo, two species of *Agave*, Jumping Cholla, Old Man Cactus, Cirio, and several species of annual composites are growing at the foot of the slopes. On the higher, drier parts of the slopes, Elephant Trees, Teddy Bear Cholla, Jumping Cholla, and Cirios grow in abundance. The

vegetation growing along the pavement edge are Cheese Bush, Brittle Bush, Nightshade, and Desert Hollyhock.

48   Here the highway briefly crosses the south end of Playa Agua Amarga.

48,5   The Elephant Tree on the left is nearly covered by parasitic "Witches Hair".

51   The vegetation along the right side of the highway is predominated by xerophytic Greasewood and a mixture of other drought tolerant, low, scrubby species.

52   The alluvial fan slope descending toward the highway from the right is densely covered with Elephant Trees and the smaller, more delicate, green-trunked Palo Verde.

53   Along with the first view of the gulf, the distant 75 kilometer long bulk of Isla Angel de la Guardia is visible to the northeast. It forms the distant line of hills in the gap in the peninsular hills to the left.
The highway descends along an alluviated stream course with prebatholithic meta-sedimentary rocks exposed along both sides.
There are a large number of Cirios and a few Cardons in this area. From this point the Cirio will gradually disappear leaving the other vegetation relatively unchanged.

55   A number of impoverished (smaller and sparser) Elephant Trees and Ocotillo are growing on the hills in this area.

56   The vegetation of this wash includes species characteristic of "Wash Woodlands". It is predominated by Smoke Trees, Palo Verde, Ocotillo, Greasewood, Wax Plant, *Ephedra*, Cholla, a few large scattered Cardon and Cirio, and assorted species of low annual scrub.

56.7   The highway enters a canyon cut in the prebatholithic metasedimentary rocks. These metasedimentary rocks are intruded by numerous light colored dikes.

58   To the right, below the highway, there is an incised gorge in the volcanics which was cut as an old stream meander was deepened by stream rejuvenation and uplift. The rejuvenated stream cut a terrace surface on the metasedimentary rocks and, as a result of uplift, the stream incised a gorge 3-5 meter deep leaving a bedrock terrace on each side of the gorge

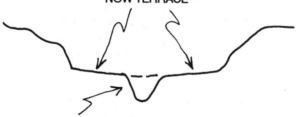

CHANNEL BEFORE LAST UPLIFT

NOW TERRACE

UPLIFT CAUSES STREAM TO CUT A NOTCH ("INCISED") TO NEW BASE LEVEL

58.5   The vista ahead is of many the small, closer islands in the Bahia de Los Angeles. Isla Angel de la Guardia dominates the center of the bay.

        ISLA ANGEL DE LA GUARDIA: Some evidence (shell middens, rock cairns, etc.) has been found indicating that this island was inhabited by prehistoric people. But, like most of the Gulf islands, little more can be said than this until intensive archaeological studies are performed and reported

Physically, the island is a large, rugged, arid desert nearly 80 kilometers long that ranges from 5 to 20 kilometers wide.

Geologically, the oldest rock types are metamorphics of unknown age, which are intruded by quartz diorite. These are unconformably overlain by a series of Miocene volcanic flows, tuffs, and sandstones up to 1,000 meters thick that make up the bulk of the exposed rock of the island. These in turn are unconformably overlain by a series of Pliocene volcanic flows and breccias and a younger succession of sandstones, conglomerates, and fanglomerates up to several hundred meters thick. Structure, rock association, and clast types in fanglomerates indicate that until about 1 million years ago the island was joined with the peninsula about 20 kilometers northwest of its current position.

Floristically the island belongs to the *Bursera-Jatropha* region of Shreve's sarcoaulescent desert. The known vascular flora consists of 199 species including 4 endemics. The flat regions of this island are dominated by desert scrub with cacti and century plants; the rock mesas and drier exposed south facing slopes are dotted by sparse, small perennials; the arroyos contain Ironwood and Palo Verde; deep canyons contain a few palms, suggesting permanent, underground water sources; the summits support dense stands of Cirio; the moister north facing slopes are covered by massive Elephant Trees.

Faunistically the island has many birds (none of which are endemic) and thirteen species of reptiles including 6 endemics. Animals are rarely seen on the island since most of them are nocturnal and/or crepuscular - adaptations enabling them to escape the heat and low humidity of the harsh desert days.

60.5   Here the highway drops down to an alluviated surface and turns to the south following the coastline southeastward to the main part of Bahia de Los Angeles.

62.3   The main town of Bahia de Los Angeles comes into view with the sandy point and lighthouse of Punta Arena visible to the left in the foreground and the south point of Punta La Herradura ("horseshoe"), which forms the outer point of the bay, in the background.
The dry slopes around this horseshoe shaped bay are sparsely vegetated by Ocotillo, Palo Verde, Creosote Bush, and occasional, small Elephant Trees.

66   **BAHIA DE LOS ANGELES** is protected by the "midriff" islands producing a relatively calm bay loaded with corbina, yellowtail, sea bass, and other popular game fish.
Floristically the area is relatively barren, seeming almost devoid of life. However, many visitors return again and again because they say they like the stark contrast of the nearly barren, lifeless mountains and the dark blue waters of the Sea of Cortez.

WHERE TO NOW?   To leave Bahia de Los Angeles either return the way you came or take the 4 wheel dirt road leading southward through Las Flores, San Pedro, El Progresso, and El Arco that eventually joins the main highway (Mexico 1) between Guerrero Negro and San Ignacio.

The BAJA HIGHWAY

a geology and biology field guide

A guide to the geology and biology of the *Baja Highway*
for the enjoyment
of the average person who has an
interest in the unique geology and
biology of the Baja California
Peninsula.

Copies of The BAJA HIGHWAY @19.95=$_____

California Sales Tax 7.75% =$_____

Shipping and Handling one book =$___2.00

(Two or more) =$__FREE

Total =$_____

Send payment to:
John Minch and Associates, Inc.
27126 Paseo Espada, Suite 1601
San Juan Capistrano, Ca. 92675
Phone (714)496-3080 Fax (714) 496-3650

Please Allow 2-4 weeks for delivery